The late **Hilary Sumner-Boyd** was professor of humanities at Robert College, Bosphorus University. His magisterial work, *The Seven Hills of Constantinople: A Study of the Byzantine and Turkish Monuments of the City*, was unpublished at the time of his death in 1977 and is now being prepared for publication by Bosphorus University Press.

John Freely was born in New York and joined the US Navy at the age of seventeen for the last two years of World War II. He has lived in New York, Boston, London, Athens and Istanbul and has written over forty travel books and guides, most of them about Greece and Turkey. He is author of *The Grand Turk*, *Storm on Horseback*, *The Cyclades*, *The Ionian Islands* (all I.B.Tauris), *Crete*, *The Western Shores of Turkey*, *Strolling through Athens* and *Strolling through Venice* (all Tauris Parke Paperbacks). He is currently professor of physics at Bosphorus University in Istanbul.

Praise for John Freely

Strolling through Athens

'A magnificent walking guide to the city . . . His knowledge is encyclopaedic . . . he brings the millenniums of history alive. If you want a cultural guide to the ancient city, this is the one for you.'   Anthony Sattin, 'Books of the Week', *Sunday Times*

The Western Shores of Turkey

'. . . Enchanting guide . . . a work of genuine scholarship, lightly worn and charmingly conveyed. I fell in love with the book and stayed enamoured until the final page.'

Paul Bailey, *Sunday Times*

Inside the Seraglio

'Freely provides a fascinating, easy-to-follow overview, beautifully researched and riveting in its detail.'

Christopher Fowler, *Independent on Sunday*

Tauris Parke Paperbacks is an imprint of I.B.Tauris. It is dedicated to publishing books in accessible paperback editions for the serious general reader within a wide range of categories, including biography, history, travel and the ancient world. The list includes select, critically acclaimed works of top quality writing by distinguished authors that continue to challenge, to inform and to inspire. These are books that possess those subtle but intrinsic elements that mark them out as something exceptional.

The Colophon of Tauris Parke Paperbacks is a representation of the ancient Egyptian ibis, sacred to the god Thoth, who was himself often depicted in the form of this most elegant of birds. Thoth was credited in antiquity as the scribe of the ancient Egyptian gods and as the inventor of writing and was associated with many aspects of wisdom and learning.

STROLLING THROUGH ISTANBUL

The Classic Guide to the City

Hilary Sumner-Boyd
and John Freely

TPP

TAURIS PARKE
PAPERBACKS

Published in 2010 by Tauris Parke Paperbacks
An imprint of I.B.Tauris and Co Ltd
6 Salem Road, London W2 4BU
175 Fifth Avenue, New York NY 10010
www.ibtauris.com

Distributed in the United States and Canada Exclusively by
Palgrave Macmillan
175 Fifth Avenue, New York NY 10010

First published by Redhouse Press in 1972

Cover image: Suleymaniye Camii (Suleiman the Magnificent mosque) on
the Golden Horn, Istanbul, Turkey © Robert Leon, Photographer's Direct

ISBN: 978 1 84885 154 2

A full CIP record for this book is available from the British Library
A full CIP record is available from the Library of Congress

Library of Congress Catalog Card Number: available

Printed and bound in India by Thomson Press India Ltd

Contents

Maps and Plans

Plates

Colour photographs by Anthony E. Baker

1. (above) Topkapı Sarayı on the skyline above the Golden Horn
   (below) Yeni Cami, with Haghia Sophia above and to the right
   on the skyline
2. Interior of Haghia Sophia from the north-west
3. (above) Dome and western semidome of Haghia Sophia
   (below) Topkapı Sarayı: Throne Room in the Third Court
4. (above) Mosque of Sultan Ahmet I
   (below) Interior of SS. Sergius and Bacchus (Küçük Aya Sofya
   Camii)
5. (above) The Süleymaniye on the skyline, Rüstem Paşa Camii
   below and to the right
   (left) Tiles in the mihrab of Rüstem Paşa Camii
6. (above) Kariye Camii (St. Saviour in Chora)
   (below) Kariye Camii: mosaic of the Virgin and Child in the
   dome; below are 16 kings of the House of David
7. (above) Ortaköy Mosque and the first Bosphorus bridge
   (below) Fortress of Rumeli Hisarı and Fatih Mehmet bridge
8. (above) Köprülü Yalı
   (below) Mosque of Şemsi Paşa

Note on Turkish Words and Spellings

One feature of this book may at first puzzle and irritate the reader: we have consistently used the modern Turkish spelling of Turkish proper names and we have employed many Turkish words for specifically Turkish things. Turkish spelling, however, is rigorously logical and phonetic and the traveller here for any length of time will have to accustom himself to it; the few letters which differ in pronunciation from English are indicated below. As for Turkish terms, chiefly for buildings of various sorts, these are useful words for the traveller to know, their meaning is frequently indicated in the course of the text, and is explained in detail in the appendix on Ottoman Architectural Forms.

TURKISH SPELLING

All letters have one and only one sound. No letters are silent.

Vowels have their short Continental value as in French, German, or Italian, i.e.: *a* as in *father, e* as in *get, i* as in *sit, o* as in *doll, u* as in *bull.* (In modern Turkish pronunciation there is little distinction between long and short vowels.) *Note: ı* (undotted) is between *i* and *u,* as the final *a* in Anna; *ö* as in German or the *u* in further; *ü* as in German or French *u* in *tu.*

Consonants as in English, except:

c as *j* in *jam:* e.g. *cami* (mosque) = *jahmy*

ç as *ch* in church, e.g. *çeşme* (fountain) = *cheshme*

g is always hard as in *give,* never soft as in *gem*

ğ is almost silent; it tends to lengthen the preceding vowel

s is always unvoiced as in *sit,* never like *z*

ş as *s* in sugar; e.g. *çeşme* = cheshme

Turkish is very lightly accented, most often on the last syllable, but all syllables should be clearly and almost evenly articulated.

Acknowledgements

I would like to acknowledge my gratitude to Selçuk Altun, whose very generous support made the publication of this new edition of *Strolling Through Istanbul* possible. I am grateful to Emre Gençer for all of the technical help he gave me in preparing the manuscript for publication. I would also like to thank Anthony E. Baker for the photographs I have used as illustrations.

Preface to the Revised Edition

This is the first thoroughly revised and updated edition of *Strolling Through Istanbul* since the book was first published in 1972. The senior author, Hilary Sumner-Boyd, passed away in the interim, and so I have taken the responsibility of revising our book and bringing it up to date, trying to live up to his standards of scholarship.

Istanbul has changed greatly since this book was first written. The population was then somewhat over 2 million and now, according to some estimates, it is more than 12 million, spread out over an area four times as great as it had been in 1972, with the addition of 25 new municipalities to the city to absorb the influx from the provinces of Turkey. New highways have been constructed in and around the city and two intercontinental bridges now span the Bosphorus, linking the European and Asian suburbs which have spread out along the coast of the Sea of Marmara and up both shores of the strait to within sight of the Black Sea, with sky-scraping office buildings creating a new skyline on the Thracian hills and satellite towns springing up in what were once virtually uninhabited woodlands and pastures.

But this explosive growth has in many respects spared the historic heart of the city, that is to say the seven-hilled peninsula bounded on the north by the Golden Horn, on the south by the Marmara, and on its landward side by the ancient Theodosian Walls, though in the areas frequented by most tourists its streets are now clogged with traffic and its sidewalks thronged with pedestrians, as I learned when I began revising this guide. But as I began strolling through the old city again I found that even in the busiest areas it was still the same enchanting place that I first came to know in the autumn of 1960. As I left the crowded avenues and stepped into the quiet courtyard of an old mosque or medrese, I found there the Istanbul of my first memories. Thus I have not changed the original itineraries, though I have updated the descriptions of the monuments and museums to reflect the changes that have taken place since the original edition was published. Along the way I have noted what has been lost forever, such as the little village that once flourished in the great Roman reservoir on the Fifth Hill, where the tree tops and chimneys and the minaret of the mosque came up only to the level of the surrounding streets, and where an old man raised peacocks for sale, perhaps to princes. Now I pass that scene on to those who might stroll that way with this guide in hand, along with other remembrances of things past that still linger on in the civic memory of Istanbul.

J.F.
Bosphorus University

Preface to the First Edition

This book is meant to be a useful and informative guide to the city of Istanbul. The first chapter gives a brief topographical description of Istanbul as seen from the Galata Bridge, followed by a short history of the city, largely with reference to the conspicuous monuments of the past which are visible from the bridge. Each of the subsequent chapters focuses on a particular part of the city and follows an itinerary which takes one to most of the ancient monuments in that area. Major monuments are described in some detail, principally in terms of their history, architecture and art; minor monuments are more briefly mentioned in passing. Although the main emphasis of the book is on the antiquities of Istanbul, the city is not treated as if it were merely an inhabited museum. Instead, the ancient monuments are described in the context of the living, modern town of which they are an integral part, that intimate juxtaposition of old and new which makes Istanbul such a fascinating city. The itineraries are designed so that each takes one to a different part of Istanbul, for the town itself is as interesting and picturesque as the antiquities it preserves. Each of the itineraries can easily be completed in a day or less, some in only a few hours.

On the other hand, tourists with restricted time should also find the book easy to use, for each of the principal monuments – the "musts" on anyone's list – has been given a chapter to itself: Haghia Sophia (Aya Sofya), the Topkapı Palace, the Süleymaniye Mosque, the Church of St. Saviour in Chora (Kariye Camii). Moreover, each chapter is provided with a map of the district covered so that the reader may find his way easily either on foot or by car to those monuments which seem most interesting while ignoring those of minor importance.

This book came into being as a result of many years of study of various aspects of the city and its history by both of the authors, each of whom had prepared a long and detailed work on the subject from a very different point of view. Both works proved too lengthy and elaborate for convenient publication, so it was decided to conflate the material from each that was suitable for a guide book, leaving for later independent publication matters likely to appeal to a different audience. Such, for example, are discussions of date and attribution of buildings, the details of architectural form and artistic style, the wealth of folklore, local custom, and dissenting sects with which the city abounds, or an account of the hundreds of foreign visitors to the city who have left us such fascinating descriptions of it in former times. Two of these, indeed, we have not been able to resist quoting fairly frequently: the Frenchman Pierre Gilles (Petrus Gyllius), resident here from 1544 to 1550, whose two books on *The Topography of Constantinople* and *The Thracian Bosphorus* give an unrivalled account of what the city was like toward the middle of the reign of Süleyman the Magnificent; and Evliya Çelebi, an Istanbullu by birth, who prefaces his *Seyahatname,* or *Book of Travels,* with a vivid and detailed description of his native city as it was in the mid-seventeenth century; these have been our constant companions.

Two works of a very different nature are frequently referred to: the so-called *Tezkeret-ül Ebniye* or *List of Buildings* by the great architect Sinan, drawn up soon after his death in 1588 by his friend the poet Mustafa Sa'i; and the *Hadikat-ül Cevami* or *Gardens of the Mosques* by Hafız Hüseyin Ayvansarayı, which is an account of all the mosques extant in Istanbul in his time (about 1780). Of modern guidebooks only two are of value: Ernest Mamboury, *Istanbul Touristique* (2nd ed. 1950), a pioneer work by a scholar of distinction; and Semavi Eyice, *Petit Guide a travers les Monuments Byzantines et Turcs* (1953), an invaluable little book by the leading Turkish authority on the city, prepared for the Third Congress of Byzantine Studies and never on public sale. But our work is based on a wide acquaintance with the authorities ancient and modern, Turkish and foreign; unfortunately a guidebook is not the place for detailed references and acknowledgements.

To our editors at the Redhouse Press, William Edmonds, C. Robert Avery and Robert Arndt, we owe more than an author's usual debt to his publisher. If this book is reasonably free from the tiresome errors of the press which often abound in English works published in foreign countries, the credit is almost wholly due to their skill and patience. We wish particularly to thank William Edmonds, for without his constant help and unremitting zeal it would not have been possible to produce this guide.

Our more personal debts are many. The elder collaborator remembers with delight and gratitude his first introduction to the antiquities of the city by two former colleagues on the staff of Robert College, the late Sven Larsen and Mr. Arthur Stratton, who has recently poured his enthusiasm for the city into his book about Sinan. The late Paul Underwood and his colleague Mr. Ernest Hawkins allowed him to follow their wonderful work of restoration at Kariye Camii as it progressed. Mr. Robert Van Nice not only allowed him the same privilege throughout his long years of investigations at Haghia Sophia but was a constant source of help and encouragement, as was also Mr. Cyril Mango who introduced him to many an important traveller of former days. To Dr. Aptullah Kuran, his former student at Robert College, later his colleague there, and the first rector at the University of the Bosphorus, most penetrating of Turkish historians of Ottoman architecture, his debts are too continuous and multifarious to be easily acknowledged or adequately repaid. And the same is true of Mr. Godfrey Goodwin, until recently professor of art history at Robert College, whose monumental *History of Ottoman Architecture* has revealed to the world for the first time in a western language the wealth and variety of its subject.

The younger author also owes a debt of gratitude to Godfrey Goodwin, who tried to teach him something of Byzantine and Ottoman architecture and who was his first companion-guide to the antiquities of Istanbul. The author fondly recalls the many friends who shared with him and his wife Dolores the pleasures of strolling through Istanbul on Saturday afternoons, picnicking on a Bosphorus ferry or on a tower of the Theodosian walls and later singing and dancing together at one of the now-vanished *tavernas* of old Pera. To list their names would be too poignant, since so many have left Istanbul and some he will never see again; he can only hope that this book will evoke for his dear friends some memories of the mad and happy days we spent together in this wonderful old town.

In the memorial dedication we have expressed our sense of gratitude to three of our dearest and most lamented colleagues. Lee Fonger, for many years Librarian of Robert College, not only made the College's unrivalled collection of books on the Near East easily available to us but did his best to supply us with whatever material was needed. Keith Greenwood, whose history of the founding and early years of Robert College still awaits publication, was a source of encyclopedic information and enthusiastic support. Their untimely deaths, and that of our very good friend David Garwood, deprived the College community of three of its most vital and creative men; for some of us Istanbul will never be the same without them. Our dedication of this book extends also to their wives, Carol Fonger, Joanne Greenwood and Mini Garwood, and to Dolores Freely, for they have been our companions on so many strolls through Istanbul across the years.

H.S.-B.
J.F.
Bosphorus University
June 1972

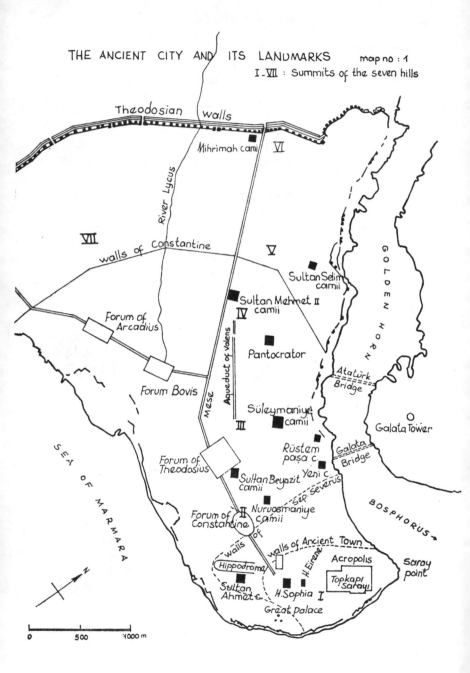

THE ANCIENT CITY AND ITS LANDMARKS   map no : 1

I - VII : Summits of the seven hills

Theodosian walls

Mihrimah camii   VI

River Lycus

VII

walls of Constantine   V

Sultan Selim
camii

Forum of
Arcadius

Sultan Mehmet II
camii

IV

Pantocrator

Aqueduct of Valens

Forum Bovis

Süleymaniye
camii

III

Rüstem
paşa c.

Forum of
Theodosius

Yeni c.

Sultan Beyazit
camii

Atatürk
Bridge

GOLDEN HORN

Galata
Bridge

Galata Tower

Nuruosmaniye
camii

Forum of
Constantine

II

Sep. Severus

BOSPHORUS

SEA OF MARMARA

walls of

walls of Ancient Town

Hippodrome

H. Eirene

Acropolis

Saray
point

Sultan
Ahmet c.

H. Sophia   I

Topkapı
Sarayı

N

Great palace

0   500   1000 m

1

The View from the Bridge

A poet writing 14 centuries ago described this city as being surrounded by a garland of waters. Much has changed since then, but modern Istanbul still owes much of its spirit and beauty to the waters which bound and divide it. There is perhaps nowhere else in town where one can appreciate this more than from the Galata Bridge, where all tours of the city should begin. There are other places in Istanbul with more panoramic views, but none where one can better sense the intimacy which this city has with the sea, nor better understand how its maritime situation has influenced its character and its history. So the visitor is advised to stroll to the Galata Bridge for his first view of the city. But you should do your sight-seeing there as do the Stamboullus, seated at a teahouse or café on the lower level of the Bridge, enjoying your *keyif* over a cup of tea or a glass of rakı, looking out along the Golden Horn to where it meets the Bosphorus and the Sea of Marmara.

Istanbul is the only city in the world which stands upon two continents. The main part of the city, which is located at the south-eastern tip of Europe, is separated from its suburbs in Asia by the incomparable Bosphorus. The Golden Horn then divides the European city into two parts, the old imperial town of Stamboul on the right bank and the port quarter of Galata on the left, with the more modern residential districts on the hills above Galata and along the European shore of the lower Bosphorus. Stamboul itself forms a more or less triangular promontory bounded on the north by the Golden Horn and on the south by the Sea of Marmara, the ancient Propontus. At Saray Point, the apex of this promontory, the Bosphorus and the Golden Horn flow together into the Marmara, forming a site of great beauty. So it must have appeared to Jason and the Argonauts when they sailed across the Propontus 3,000 years ago in search of the Golden Fleece, and so it still appears today to the tourist approaching the city on a modern oceanliner.

According to tradition, the original settlement from which the city grew was established on the acropolis above Saray Point in the seventh century B.C., although there is evidence that the site was inhabited much earlier than that. The legendary founder of the town of Byzantium was Byzas the Megarian, who established a colony on the acropolis in the year 667 B.C. We are told that Byzas had consulted the Delphic oracle, who advised him to settle "opposite the land of the blind". The oracle was referring to the residents of Chalcedon, a Greek colony which had been established some years before across the strait. The implication is that the Chalcedonians must have been blind not to have appreciated the much greater advantages of the site chosen by Byzas. Situated at the mouth of the Bosphorus, it was in a position to control all shipping from the Black Sea, the ancient Pontus, through to the Propontus and the Aegean, while its position on the boundary of Europe and Asia eventually attracted to it the great land routes of both continents. Moreover, surrounded as it is on three sides by water, its short landward exposure defended by strong walls, it could be made impregnable to attack. As the French writer Gyllius concluded four centuries ago: "It seems to me that while other cities may be mortal, this one will remain as long as there are men on earth."

From the very beginning of its history Byzantium was an important centre for trade and commerce, and was noted for its wine and fisheries. Not all of the wine was exported, apparently, for in antiquity the citizens of Byzantium had the reputation of being confirmed tipplers. Menander, in his comedy, *The Flute Girl*, tells us that Byzantium makes all of her merchants sots. Says one of the Byzantine characters in his play: "I booze it all the night, and upon my waking after my dose I feel that I have no less than three heads upon my shoulders." The character of a city is formed quite early in its career.

During its first millennium Byzantium had much the same history as the other Greek cities in and on the edge of Asia Minor. The city was taken by Darius in the year 512 B.C., and remained under Persian control until 479 B.C., when it was recaptured by the Spartan general Pausanias. Byzantium later became part of the Athenian Empire; although it revolted in 440 B.C. and again in 411 B.C., it was conquered on each occasion by the Athenians, the last time by Alcibiades. After the defeat of Athens in 403 B.C. Byzantium was captured by Lysander and was still under a Spartan governor when Xenophon's Ten Thousand arrived shortly afterwards. Xenophon and his men were so inhospitably treated that in retaliation they occupied the town, leaving only after they exacted a large bribe from its citizens. During the first half of the fourth century B.C. Byzantium was held in enforced alliance with Athens, but in the year 356 B.C. the city rebelled and won its independence. Despite this the Athenians, through the urgings of Demosthenes, sent aid to Byzantium when it was besieged by Philip of Macedon in 340 B.C. A contemporary Athenian writer informs us that the Byzantine commanders were forced to build taverns within the very defence walls in order to keep their tipsy soldiers at their posts. But the Byzantines fought well, for they successfully held off the Macedonians in a memorable siege.

Despite their spirited fight against King Philip, the Byzantines had enough good sense not to resist his son, Alexander the Great. Soon after Alexander's victory at the battle of the Granicus in 334 B.C. Byzantium capitulated and opened its gates to the Macedonians. Later, after Alexander's death in 323 B.C., Byzantium was involved in the collapse and dismemberment of his empire and the subsequent eastward expansion of Rome. In the year 179 B.C. the city was captured by the combined forces of Rhodes, Pergamum and Bithynia. A century later Byzantium was a pawn in the struggle between Rome and Mithridates, King of Pontus. After the final victory of Rome, Byzantium became its client state, and thereafter enjoyed nearly three centuries of quiet prosperity under the mantle of the Pax Romana. But eventually, in the closing years of the second century A.D., Byzantium was swept up once again in the tides of history. At that time Byzantium found itself on the losing side in a civil war and was besieged by the Emperor Septimius Severus. After finally taking Byzantium in the year 196 A.D., the Emperor tore down the city walls, massacred the soldiers and officials who had opposed him, and left the town a smouldering ruin. A few years afterwards, however, Septimius realized the imprudence of leaving so strategic a site undefended and then rebuilt the city and its walls. The walls of Septimius Severus are thought to have begun at the Golden Horn a short distance downstream from the present site of the Galata Bridge, and to have ended at the Marmara somewhere near where the lighthouse now stands. The area thus enclosed was more than double that of the ancient town of Byzantium, which had comprised little more than the acropolis itself.

At the beginning of the fourth century A.D. Byzantium was profoundly affected by the climactic events then taking place in the Roman Empire. After the retirement of the Emperor Diocletian in the year 305, his successors in the Tetrarchy, the two co-emperors and their Caesars, fought bitterly with one another for the control of the Empire. This struggle was eventually won by Constantine, Emperor of the West, who in the year 324 finally defeated Licinius, Emperor of the East. The last battle took place in the hills above Chrysopolis, just across the Bosphorus from Byzantium. On the following day, 18 September in the year A.D. 324, Byzantium surrendered and opened its gates to Constantine, now sole ruler of the Roman Empire.

During the first two years after his victory Constantine conceived the grand scheme which would affect world history for the next millennium: the re-establishment of the Roman Empire with Byzantium as its capital. After he made his decision Constantine set out to rebuild and enlarge and adorn the old town to suit its imperial role. Work began on 4 November in the year 326, when the Emperor personally traced out the limits of the new city. The defence walls with which Constantine enclosed the city on the landward side began at a point on the Golden Horn somewhat upstream from the present Atatiirk Bridge, and extended to the Sea of Marmara in a great circular arc, ending in the bay of Samatya. Constantine's city was thus more than five times as large as the town of Septimius Severus, and it was to be infinitely more grand.

The imperial building programme proceeded rapidly, and in less than four years the new capital was completed. On 11 May in the year

A.D. 330, in a ceremony in the Hippodrome, Constantine dedicated the city of New Rome, soon after to be called Constantinople. Three years thence the old town of Byzantine would have been 1,000 years old.

During the century following the reign of Constantine the city grew rapidly and soon expanded beyond the limits set by its founder. In the first half of the fifth century, during the reign of Theodosius II, a new and much stronger line of defence-walls was built nearly a mile farther out into Thrace, replacing the older walls of Constantine. These walls have delimited the size of the old city up to the present day, so that subsequent expansion was restricted to the suburban districts along the Marmara, the Golden Horn and the Bosphorus. The area thus enclosed included seven hills, the same number as in Old Rome, a matter of some mystical significance in Byzantium. Although the contours of these hills have been obscured by modern roads and buildings, they can still be discerned and form convenient reference-points for studying the old city. Six of the seven hills can be seen from the Galata Bridge, marching in stately line down the Golden Horn, each of them crowned with a Byzantine church or an Ottoman mosque, giving an imperial quality to the skyline of Stamboul.

Great changes took place in the Roman Empire in the two centuries following the reign of Constantine the Great. After the death of Theodosius I in 395, the Empire was divided between his two sons, with Honorius ruling the West from Rome and Arcadius the East, with his capital at Constantinople. The western part of the Empire was overrun by barbarians during the following century, and in the year 476 the last Emperor of the West was deposed, leaving the Emperor in Constantinople sole ruler of what was left of the Empire. This soon brought about a profound change in the character of the Empire, for it was now centred in lands populated largely by Greek-speaking Christians. And so, although Latin remained the official language of the court up until the beginning of the sixth century, the Empire was becoming more and more Greek and Christian in character, and began to sever its connections with the classical traditions of Athens and Rome. As the great churchman Gennadius was to write in later times: "Though I am a Hellene by speech yet I would never say that I was a Hellene, for I do not believe as Hellenes believed. I should like to take my name from my faith, and if anyone asks me what I am, I answer, 'A Christian'. Though my father dwelt in Thessaly I do not call myself a Thessalian, but a Byzantine, for I am of Byzantium."

A new epoch in the city's history began during the reign of Justinian the Great, who succeeded to the throne in the year 527. Five years after his accession Justinian was very nearly overthrown by an insurrection of the factions in the Hippodrome, the famous Nika Revolt, which was finally crushed only after widespread destruction and terrible loss of life. Immediately after the suppression of the revolt Justinian set out to rebuild the city on an even grander scale than before. When he had finished his reconstruction apparently within just a few years, the city of Constantinople was the greatest and most magnificent metropolis on earth, an imperial capital beginning the first of its golden ages. The crowning glory of Justinian's new city was the resurrected church of Haghia Sophia, whose venerable form can still be seen on the acropolis, a symbol of the ancient city of which it was so long the heart.

During the course of Justinian's reign his generals succeeded in reconquering many of the lost dominions of the Roman Empire, and by the time he died in 565 the borders of Byzantium stretched from the Euphrates to the Pillars of Hercules. But the golden age did not last long, for within a half-century after the death of Justinian his empire had fallen apart, assaulted from without by the Lombards, Slavs, Avars and Persians, ravaged from within by anarchy, plague and social unrest. The Empire was saved from total destruction by the Emperor Heraclius, who ruled from 610 till 641. In a series of brilliant campaigns, Heraclius defeated the Persians, the Avars and the Slavs, and succeeded in regaining much of the territory which had been lost in the previous half-century. Shortly after the death of Heraclius, however, much of the eastern part of the Byzantine Empire was overrun by the Arabs, who on several occasions in the seventh and eighth centuries besieged Constantinople itself. But Byzantium held off the Arab advance and prevented them from gaining a foothold in eastern Europe, just as they were finally stopped at about the same time in the West by Charles Martel. In the ninth and tenth centuries the Byzantine Empire was invaded by the Bulgars, who gained control of large areas of the Balkans and twice laid siege to Constantinople. But on both occasions they were defeated by the great Theodosian land-walls, which continued to shelter Byzantium from its enemies across the centuries.

Despite these numerous wars Byzantium was still strong and basically sound as late as the middle of the eleventh century, controlling an empire which stretched from western Persia through Asia Minor and the Balkans to southern Italy. But then in the year 1071 the Byzantine army, led by Romanus IV, suffered a catastrophic defeat by the Selçuk Turks at the battle of Manzikert and much of eastern Asia Minor was permanently lost to the Empire. In the same year the Normans captured Bari, thus bringing to an end Byzantine rule in Italy. The forces were now gathering which would eventually destroy the Empire.

A decade after these defeats Alexius Comnenus ascended the throne of Byzantium. For the next century he and his successors, the illustrious dynasty of the Comneni, successfully defended the Empire against the attacks of its numerous enemies. During that period the Empire was being subjected to increasing pressure by the Latins of western Europe, whose armies first passed through Asia Minor in the year 1097 during the First Crusade. As time went on it became increasingly apparent that the Latins were less interested in freeing the Holy Land from the Saracens than they were in seizing land and wealth for themselves. And the prize which attracted them most was the rich and magnificent city of Constantinople. By the time the Comneni dynasty came to an end in the year 1185, the Normans had already captured Thessalonica and were advancing towards the capital. Two decades later, in the year 1203, the Latin armies of the Fourth Crusade made their first assault upon Constantinople. Although they were not able to take the city at that time they did so in a second attack the following year. On 13 April 1204 the Crusaders breached the sea-walls along the Golden Horn and took the city by storm. They then proceeded to ruin and sack Constantinople, stripping it of its wealth, its art treasures and its sacred relics, most of which were shipped off to western Europe. As wrote the French knight Villehardouin, describing the sack of Constantinople by the Crusaders: "Of holy relics I need only say that it contained more than all Christendom combined; there is no estimating the quantity of gold silver, rich stuffs and other valuable things – the production of all the climates of the world. It is the belief of me, Geoffrey de Villehardouin, marechal of Champagne, that the plunder of this city exceeded all that had been witnessed since the creation of the world." And as the Byzantine historian Nicetas Choniates wrote in his lament: "Oh city, city, eye of all cities, subject of narratives all over the world, supporter of churches, leader of faith and guider of orthodoxy, protector of education, abode of all good. Thou hast drunk to the dregs the cup of the anger of the Lord, and hast been visited with fire fiercer than that which in days of yore descended upon the Pentapolis."

The Latin Kings ruled in Constantinople from 1204 till 1261, at which time Michael Palaeologus succeeded in recapturing the city and restoring the Byzantine Empire. But the Empire was now only a fragment of what it had been in former days, comprising parts of Thrace, Macedonia and the Peloponnesus, with most of its former possessions in Asia Minor occupied by the Ottoman Turks, and much of its land in Europe lost to the rapacious Latins. Within the next century even these dominions were lost, as the Turks crossed over into Europe and advanced far into the Balkans. By the beginning of the fifteenth century the Byzantine Empire consisted of little more than Constantinople and its immediate suburbs, with the old city decaying within the great walls which had protected it for so long. Nevertheless, the indomitable Byzantines hung on for another half-century, fighting off several attempts by the Turks to take the capital. But by the middle of the fifteenth century it became increasingly obvious that the city could not hold out much longer, for it was by then completely surrounded by the Ottoman Empire.

On 13 February 1451 the young Sultan Mehmet II ascended to the Ottoman throne and almost immediately began preparations for what would be the final siege of the city. During the summer of the following year, 1452, he constructed the fortress of Rumeli Hisarı on the Bosphorus, just across the narrow straits from the Turkish fortress of Anadolu Hisarı, which had been built around 1395 by Sultan Beyazit I. The two fortresses thus completely cut off Constantinople from the Black Sea, the first step in the blockade of the capital. In March of 1453 the Ottoman navy sailed into the Sea of Marmara, cutting off Byzantium from the West and completing the blockade. Then, in the first week of April in that year, Sultan Mehmet massed his armies in Thrace and marched them into position before the land walls of the city, thus beginning a siege which was to last for seven weeks. The Byzantines and their Italian allies, who were outnumbered more than ten to one, defended the city valiantly, until their strength and resources were nearly gone. Finally, on 29 May 1453, the Turks forced their way through a breach in the shattered land walls and poured into the city. Constantine XI Dragases, the last Byzantine Emperor, fought on bravely with his men until he was killed on the walls of his fallen city, thus bringing to an heroic end the long and illustrious history of Byzantium.

According to the custom of the age, Sultan Mehmet, now called Fatih, or the Conqueror, gave over the city to his soldiers to pillage for three days after it was captured. Immediately afterwards the Sultan began to restore the city, repairing the damage it had sustained during the siege and in the decades of decay before the Conquest. A year or so later, Sultan Mehmet constructed a palace on the Third Hill, on the site of which the Beyazit Fire Tower now stands. Some years afterwards he built a more extensive palace, Topkapı Sarayı, whose domes and spires still adorn the First Hill, the ancient acropolis of the city. By 1470 he had completed the great mosque which bears his name; Fatih Camii, the Mosque of the Conqueror. This mosque, which was comparable in size to Haghia Sophia, was the centre of a complex of pious foundations, religious and philanthropic institutions of one sort or another. Many of Fatih's vezirs followed his example, building mosques and pious foundations of their own, each of which soon became the centre of its local neighbourhood, together developing into the new Muslim town of Istanbul. Fatih also repeopled the city, which had lost much of its population in the decades preceding the

Conquest, bringing in Turks, Greeks and Armenians from Asia Minor and Thrace and settling them in Stamboul and Galata. Later in that century large numbers of Jewish refugees from Spain were welcomed to the Ottoman Empire by Fatih's son and successor, Beyazit II, and many of them settled in Istanbul. By the beginning of the sixteenth century, then, Istanbul was a thriving and populous city, once again the capital of a vast empire.

During the first century after the Conquest, Turkish armies swept victoriously through the Balkans and the Near East, while buccaneering Ottoman fleets dominated the Mediterranean. By the middle of the sixteenth century the Ottoman Empire stretched from Baghdad in the east to Algiers in the west, and from lower Egypt to the southern borders of Russia, rivalling in extent the Byzantine Empire in the days of Justinian. The Empire reached the peak of its power during the reign of Süleyman the Magnificent, who ruled from 1520 till 1566. Süleyman personally led his armies in a dozen victorious campaigns, failing only in his attempts to take Vienna and Malta, which thereafter set the limit to Turkish expansion to the north and west in Europe. The loot from these campaigns and the tribute and taxes from the conquered territories enormously enriched the Empire, and much of this wealth was used by Süleyman and his vezirs to adorn Istanbul with mosques, palaces and pious foundations. The grandest and most beautiful of these structures was the Süleymaniye, the mosque which was completed for Süleyman in the year 1557 by his Chief Architect, the great Sinan. This magnificent edifice stands on the crest of the ridge above the Golden Horn to the west of the Stamboul end of the Galata Bridge, dominating the whole skyline of the city. The Süleymaniye is the symbol of the golden age of the Ottoman Empire, just as Haghia Sophia represents the triumph of Byzantium in the days of Justinian. These two great buildings, separated in foundation by more than 1,000 years of history, stand only a mile apart in Stamboul. Looking at them both at once from the Galata Bridge, we are reminded that this old town was twice the capital of a world empire.

This second golden age lasted longer than did the first, for the Ottoman Empire was still vigorous and expanding as late as the middle of the seventeenth century, 100 years after the death of Süleyman. But by that time signs of decadence were already apparent in the Empire. During the century after Süleyman the Ottoman armies and navies suffered several defeats, and territory was lost in Transylvania, Hungary and Persia. There were also symptoms of decay within the Empire, whose subjects, both Muslims and Christians, were suffering from the maladministration and corruption which had spread to all levels of the government. One of the principal causes of this decay was to be found in the Sultanate itself, for the successors of Süleyman ceased to lead their armies in the field, preferring to spend their time with their women in the Harem. By the end of the sixteenth century the Empire was literally ruled by these women, the mothers of the sultans or their favourite concubines, who ran the country to satisfy their own personal ends, to its great detriment. The situation seemed to improve for a time during the reign of Sultan Murat IV, who ruled from 1623 till 1640. The young Sultan, who was only 14 when he ascended the throne, proved to be a strong and able ruler and checked for a time the decline of the Ottoman Empire. He was the first sultan since Süleyman to lead his army in battle and was victorious in several campaigns, climaxed by the recapture of Baghdad in 1638. But Murat's untimely death at the age of 30 ended this brief revival of the old martial Ottoman spirit, and after his reign the decay proceeded even more rapidly than before.

Nevertheless, the Ottoman Empire was still vast and prosperous and some of its institutions remained basically sound, so that it held together for centuries after it had passed its prime. And although the Ottoman armies suffered one defeat after another in the Balkans, Istanbul was little affected, for the frontiers were far away and wealth continued to pour into the capital. Members of the royal family and the great and wealthy men and women of the Empire continued to adorn the city with splendid mosques and pious foundations, while the Sultan continued to take his pleasure in the Harem.

But by the end of the eighteenth century the fortunes of the Empire had declined to the point where its basic problems could no longer be ignored, not even in the palace. The Empire gave up large portions of its Balkan territories in humiliating peace treaties after losing wars with European powers. Within, the Empire was weakened by anarchy and rebellion and its people were suffering even more grievously than before. This led to social and political unrest, particularly among the subject Christians, who now began to nourish dreams of independence.

During this period the Ottoman Empire was being increasingly influenced by developments in western Europe, particularly by the liberal ideas which brought about the French Revolution. This eventually led to a movement of reform in the Ottoman Empire. The first sultan to be deeply influenced by these western ideas was Selim III, who ruled from 1789 till 1807. Selim attempted to improve and modernize the Ottoman army by reorganizing and training it according to western models. By this he hoped to protect the Empire from encroachments by foreign powers and from rebellion and anarchy within its own borders. But Selim's efforts were resisted and eventually frustrated by the Janissaries, the elite corps of the old Ottoman army, who felt that their privileges were being threatened by the new reforms. The Janissaries were finally crushed in 1826 by Sultan Mahmut II, who thereupon instituted an extensive programme of reforms in all of the basic institutions of the Empire, reshaping them along modern western lines. This programme continued for a time during the reigns of Mahmut's immediate successors, Abdül Mecit I and Abdül Aziz. The reform movement, or Tanzimat, as it was called, culminated in 1876 with the promulgation of the first Ottoman constitution and the establishment of a parliament, which met for the first time on 19 March of the following year. But this parliament was very short-lived, for it was dissolved on 13 February 1878 by Sultan Abdül Hamit II, then in the second year of his long and oppressive reign. Nevertheless, the forces of reform had now grown too strong to be held down permanently. The pressures they generated eventually led, in 1909, to the deposition of Abdül Hamit and to the restoration of the constitution and the parliament in that same year. But the next decade, which seemed so full of promise at its beginning, was a sad and bitter one for Turkey. The country found itself on the losing side in the First World War, after which the victorious Allies proceeded to divide up the remnants of the

Ottoman Empire amongst themselves. Turkey was saved only by the heroic efforts of its people, who fought to preserve their homeland when it was invaded by the Greeks in 1919.

Their leader in this War of Independence, which was finally won by Turkey in 1922, was Mustafa Kemal Paşa, later to be known as Atatürk, the Father of the Turks. Even before the conclusion of the war, Atatürk and his associates had laid the foundations of the new republic which would arise out of the ruins of the Ottoman Empire. The Sultanate was abolished in 1922 and on 29 October of the following year the Republic of Turkey was formally established, with Kemal Atatürk as its first President. During the remaining 15 years of his life Atatürk guided his countrymen to a more modern and western way of life, a process which still continues in Turkey today. Kemal Atatürk died on 10 November 1938, profoundly mourned by his people then and revered by them still as the father of their country.

At the time of the establishment of the Turkish Republic in 1923, the Anatolian city of Ankara was chosen as the capital and the seat of parliament. Soon afterwards the embassies of the great European powers packed up and moved to new quarters in Ankara, leaving their old mansions along the Grand Rue de Pera in Istanbul. And so, for the first time in 16 centuries, Istanbul was no longer the capital of an empire. Now, more than eight decades later, history would seem to have passed Istanbul by, and no longer do wealthy and powerful emperors adorn her with splendid buildings. The old town is now running down at the heels, some say, living on her memories. But what memories they are!

Many monuments of the city's imperial past can be seen from the Galata Bridge, particularly those which stand on the six hills along the Golden Horn. On the First Hill, the ancient acropolis of Byzantium, we see the gardens and pavilions of Topkapı Sarayı and the great dome of Haghia Sophia, framed by its four minarets. The most prominent monument on the Second Hill is the baroque Nuruosmaniye Camii, while the Third Hill is crowned by the Süleymaniye, surrounded by the clustering domes of its pious foundations. On the foreshore between these two hills we see Yeni

Cami, the large mosque which stands at the Stamboul end of the
Galata Bridge, and Rüstem Paşa Camii, the smaller mosque which is
located in the market district just to the west. The Third and Fourth
Hills are joined by the Roman aqueduct of Valens; but to see this
we must bestir ourselves from our seat on the Galata Bridge and
walk some distance up the Golden Horn towards the inner span, the
Atatürk Bridge. The Fourth Hill is surmounted by Fatih Camii, the
Mosque of the Conqueror, whose domes and minarets can be seen
in the middle distance, some way in from the Golden Horn. The
mosque of Sultan Selim I stands above the Golden Horn on the Fifth
Hill. Far off in the distance we can just see the minarets of Mihrimah
Camii, which stands on the summit of the Sixth Hill, a mile inland
from the Golden Horn and just inside the Theodosian walls. Across
the Golden Horn the skyline is dominated by the huge, conical-
capped Galata Tower, the last remnant of the medieval Genoese town
of Galata.

Looking down the Golden Horn to where it joins the Bosphorus
and flows into the Marmara we see the fabled Maiden's Tower, the
little islet watchtower which stands at the confluence of the city's
garland of waters. Beyond, on the Asian shore, the afternoon sun is
reflected in the windows of Üsküdar, anciently called Chrysopolis,
the City of Gold. Farther to the south, out of sight from our vantage
point on the Galata Bridge, is the Anatolian suburb of Kadıköy, the
ancient Chalcedon, settled a decade or so before Byzantium. Sipping
our tea or rakı in our café on the Galata Bridge, we rest our eyes
once more on the gray and ruined beauty of Stamboul, crowned with
imperial monuments on its seven ancient hills. At times like this we
can agree with the Delphic oracle, for those who settled across the
straits from this enchanting place were surely blind.

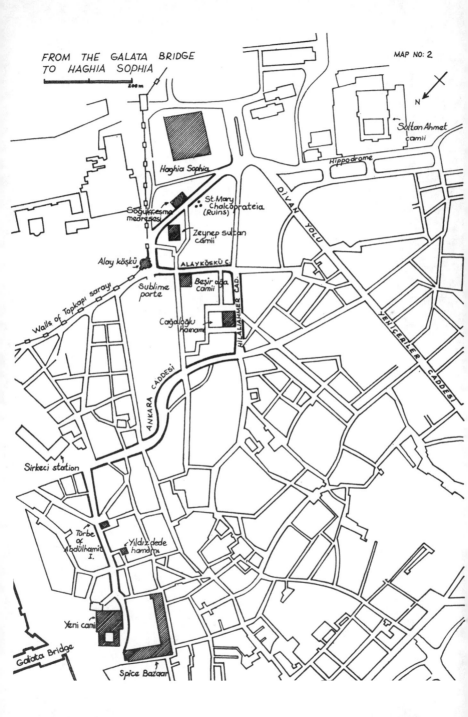

FROM THE GALATA BRIDGE
TO HAGHIA SOPHIA

MAP NO: 2

200 m

N

Sultan Ahmet
camii

Hippodrome

Haghia Sophia

St.Mary
Chalcoprateia
(Ruins)

Soğukçeşme
medresesi

Zeynep Sultan
camii

Alay köşkü

ALAY KÖŞKÜ C.

Sublime
porte

Beşir ağa
camii

Walls of Topkapı sarayı

Çağaloğlu
hamamı

DIVAN YOLU

HILÂLIAHMER CAD.

YENİÇERLER CADDESİ

ANKARA CADDESİ

Sirkeci station

Türbe
of
Abdülhamit
I.

Yıldız dede
hamamı

Yeni camii

Galata Bridge

Spice Bazaar

2

From the Galata Bridge to Haghia Sophia

The area around the Stamboul end of the Galata Bridge, known as Eminönü, is the focal point of Istanbul's colourful and turbulent daily life. Throughout the day and early evening a steady stream of pedestrians and traffic pours across the bridge and along the highway that parallels the right bank of the Golden Horn, while an endless succession of ferry-boats sail to and from their piers around and under the Galata Bridge, connecting the centre of the city to its maritime suburbs on the Bosphorus, the Marmara and the Princes' Isles, as well as to stops on both shores of the Golden Horn itself.

The quarter now known as Eminönü was during the latter period of the Byzantine Empire given over to various Italian city-states, some of which had obtained trading concessions here as early as the end of the tenth century. The area to the right of the Galata Bridge, where the markets are located, was the territory of the Venetians. The region immediately to the left of the bridge was given over to the Amalfians, and beyond them were the concessions of the Pisans and the Genoese, who also had extensive concessions across the Golden Horn in Galata. These rapacious Italians were as often as not at war with one another or with the Byzantines, though at the very end they fought valiantly at the side of the Greeks in the last defence of the city. After the Conquest the concessions of these Italian cities were effectively ended in Stamboul, although the Genoese in Galata continued to have a measure of autonomy for a century or so. Today there is virtually nothing left in Eminönü to remind us of the colourful Latin period in the city's history, other than a few medieval Venetian basements underlying some of the old hans in the market quarter around Rüstem Paşa Camii.

The area directly in front of the Galata Bridge, where Yeni Cami now stands, was in earlier centuries a Jewish quarter, wedged in between the concessions of the Venetians and the Amalfians. The Jews who resided here were members of the schismatic Karaite sect, who broke off from the main body of Orthodox Jewry in the eighth century. The Karaites seem to have established themselves on this site as early as the tenth century, at about the time when the Italians first obtained their concessions here. The Karaites outlasted the Italians though, for they retained their quarter up until the year 1660, at which time they were evicted to make room for the final construction of Yeni Cami. They were then resettled in the village of Hasköy, some three kilometres up the Golden Horn and on its opposite shore, where their descendants remain to this day.

YENİ CAMİ

The whole area around the Stamboul end of the Galata Bridge is dominated by the imposing mass of Yeni Cami, the New Mosque, more correctly called the New Mosque of the Valide Sultan. The city is not showing off its great age in calling new a mosque built in the seventeenth century: it is just that the present mosque is a reconstruction of an earlier mosque of the same name. The first mosque was commissioned in 1597 by the Valide Sultan (Queen Mother) Safiye, the mother of Sultan Mehmet III. The original architect was Davut Ağa, a pupil of the great Sinan, the architect who built most of the finest mosques in the city during the golden age of Süleyman the Magnificent and his immediate successors. Davut Ağa died in 1599, however, and was replaced by Dalgıç Ahmet Çavuş, who supervised the construction up until the year 1603. But in that year Mehmet III died and his mother Safiye was unable to finish her mosque. For more than half-a-century the partially completed mosque stood on the shore of the Golden Horn, gradually falling into ruins. Then in 1660 the whole area was devastated by fire, further adding to the ruination of the mosque. Later in that year the ruined and fire-blackened mosque caught the eye of the Valide Sultan Turhan Hadice, mother of Mehmet IV, who decided to rebuild it as an act of piety. The architect Mustafa Ağa was placed in charge of the reconstruction, which was completed in 1663. On 6 November of that year the New Mosque of the Valide Sultan was consecrated in a public ceremony presided over by the Sultan and his mother. The French scholar Grelot, writing when Turhan Hadice was still alive, tells us that she was one of the "greatest and most brilliant (*spirituelle*) ladies who ever entered the Saray," and that it was fitting that "she should leave to posterity a jewel of Ottoman architecture to serve as an eternal monument to her generous enterprises."

But time has dimmed the glitter of Safiye's jewel, and its walls and windows are blackened by the soot from the ferries which berth nearby. Then, too, Yeni Cami was built after Ottoman architecture had passed its peak, and it fails to achieve the surpassing beauty of Sinan's masterpieces of the previous century. Nevertheless, it is still a fine and impressive structure, and its graceful silhouette is an adornment to the skyline of Stamboul.

Yeni Cami, like many of the other imperial mosques in Stamboul, represents a variation on the basic plan of the great church of Haghia Sophia. Whereas in Haghia Sophia the central dome is flanked by two semidomes along the longitudinal axis, Yeni Cami is cruciform, with semidomes along both axes and smaller domes at each of the four corners. The resultant silhouette is a graceful flowing curve from dome to semidomes to minor domes, a symmetrical cascade of clustering spheres. The north and south façades of the building have two storeys of porticoed galleries which, with the pyramidal arrangement of the domes, give a light and harmonious effect. The two minarets each have three şerefes, or balconies, with superb stalactite carving. In olden times the call to prayer was given by six müezzins, one to each şerefe, but now they have been replaced by a single loudspeaker attached to a soulless tape-recorder.

Like all of the other imperial mosques in Stamboul, Yeni Cami is preceded by a monumental courtyard, or avlu. The courtyard is bordered by a peristyle of 20 columns, forming a portico which is covered with 24 small domes. At the centre of the courtyard there is a charming octagonal şadırvan, or ablution fountain, one of the finest of its kind in the city. At the şadırvan, which means literally "free-flowing fountain", the faithful would ordinarily perform their

YENİ CAMİ KÜLLİYESİ

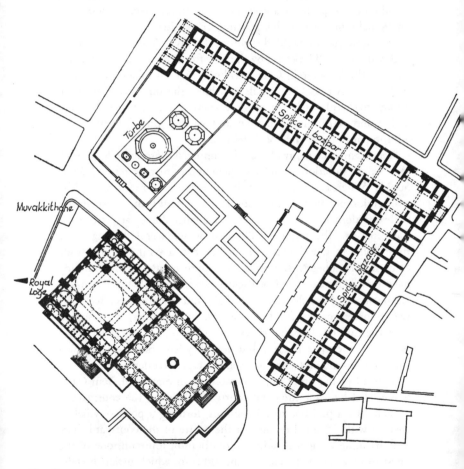

Plan no : 1

abdest, or ritual ablutions, before entering the mosque to pray. But in Yeni Cami the şadırvan serves merely a decorative purpose, and the ritual washings are performed at water-taps along the south wall of the mosque.

The stone dais on that side of the courtyard which borders the mosque is called the son cemaat yeri, literally the place of last assembly. Latecomers to the Friday noon service when the mosque is full often perform their prayers on this porch, usually in front of one of the two niches which are set to either side of the door. The façade of the building under the porch is decorated with tiles and faience inscriptions forming a frieze. The two central columns of the portico, which frame the entrance to the mosque, are of a most unusual and beautiful marble not seen elsewhere in the city.

The interior of Yeni Cami is somewhat disappointing, partly because the mosque is darkened by the soot which has accumulated on its windows. What is more, the tiles which decorate the interior are of a quality inferior to those in earlier mosques, the celebrated Iznik tiles of the period 1555–1620. Nevertheless, the interior furnishings of the mosque are quite elegant in detail. The most important part of the interior of Yeni Cami, as in all mosques, is the mihrab, a niche set into the centre of the wall opposite the main entrance. The purpose of the mihrab is to indicate the kıble, the direction of Mecca, towards which the faithful must face when they perform their prayers. (In Istanbul the direction of the kıble is approximately south-east, but for convenience we will refer to it as east, the general orientation of the Christian churches of the city.) In the great mosques of Istanbul the mihrab is invariably quite grand, with the niche itself made of finely carved and sculptured marble and with the adjacent wall sheathed in ceramic tiles. The mihrab in Yeni Cami is ornamented with gilded stalactites and flanked with two enormous golden candles, which are lighted on the holy nights of the Islamic year. To the right of the mihrab we see the mimber, or pulpit, which is surmounted by a tall, conical-topped canopy carried on marble columns. At the time of the noon prayer on Friday the imam, or preacher, mounts the steps of the mimber and pronounces the weekly sermon, or hutbe. To the left of the mihrab, standing against the main pier on that side, we see the kürsü, where the imam sits when he is reading the Kuran to the congregation. And to the right of the main entrance, set up against the main pier at that end, we find the müezzin mahfili, a covered marble pew. During the Friday services and other ceremonial occasions the müezzin kneels there, accompanied perhaps by a few other singers, and chants the responses to the prayers of the imam. During these formal occasions of worship, the faithful kneel in long lines and columns throughout the mosque, following the prayers attentively and responding with frequent and emphatic amens. The women, who take no part in the public prayers, are relegated to the open chambers under the gallery to the rear of the mosque.

The mosque interior is overlooked by an upper gallery on both sides and to the rear, with the two side galleries carried on slender marble columns. At the far corner of the left gallery we see the sultan's loge, or hünkâr mahfili, which is screened off by a gilded grille so that the sultan and his party would be shielded from the public gaze when they attended services. Access to the sultan's loge is gained from the outside by a very curious ramp behind the mosque. This ramp leads to a suite of rooms built over a great archway; from these a door leads to the hünkâr mahfili. This suite of rooms included a salon, a bedchamber and a toilet, with kitchens on the lower level, and served as a pied-à-terre for the Sultan.

Yeni Cami, like all of the imperial mosques, was the centre of a whole complex of religious and philanthropic institutions called a külliye. The original külliye of Yeni Cami included a hospital, a primary school, a public bath, two public fountains, a mausoleum and a market, whose profits were used towards the support of the other institutions in the külliye. The hospital, the primary school and the public bath have been destroyed but the other institutions remain.

The market of Yeni Cami is the handsome L-shaped building to the south and west of the mosque. It is called the Mısır Çarşısı, or the Egyptian Market, because it was once endowed with the Cairo imposts. In English it is more commonly known as the Spice Bazaar, for in former times it was famous for the spices and medicinal herbs which were sold there. Spices and herbs are still sold there today, but the bazaar now deals in a wide variety of commodities, which makes it perhaps the most popular market in the city. In the domed rooms above the arched entrance there is a very picturesque and excellent restaurant called Pandelis, or the Mısır Lokantası, which serves both Turkish and western dishes.

The mausoleum, or türbe, of the Yeni Cami külliyesi is the handsome building at the eastern end of the garden of the Egyptian Bazaar. Here are buried the foundress of Yeni Cami, Turhan Hadice, her son, Mehmet IV, and several later sultans, Mustafa II, Ahmet III, Mahmut I, Osman III and Murat V, along with countless royal princes and princesses. The small building to the west of the türbe is a kütüphane, or library, which was built by Turhan Hadice's grandson, Ahmet III, who ruled from 1703 till 1730. Ahmet III was known as the Tulip King, and the period of his reign came to be called the Lale Devri, the Age of Tulips, one of the most charming and delightful eras in the history of old Stamboul. It is entirely fitting that the tomb of the Tulip King should look out on a garden which is now the principal flower-market of the city.

Directly opposite the türbe, at the corner of the wall enclosing the garden of the mosque, is a tiny polygonal building with a quaintly-shaped dome. This was the muvakkithane, or the house and workroom of the müneccim, the mosque astronomer. It was the duty of the müneccim to regulate the times for the five occasions of daily prayer and to announce the exact times of sunrise and sunset during the holy month of Ramazan, beginning and ending the daily fast. It was also his duty to determine the date for the beginning of a lunar month by observing the first appearance of the sickle moon in the western sky just after sunset. The müneccim, like most astronomers of that period, also doubled as an astrologer, and the most able of them were often asked to cast the horoscopes of the Sultan and his vezirs. In more recent times the müneccim often served as the watch repairman for the people in the local neighbourhood.

At the next corner, on the same side of the street as the türbe, is the sebil of the Yeni Cami külliyesi. The sebil is an enclosed fountain which was used to distribute water free to thirsty passersby. Sebil means literally "way" or "path", and to construct a sebil was to build a path for oneself to paradise. There are some 80 sebils still extant in Istanbul, although that belonging to Yeni Cami is one of the very few still serving something like its original purpose (bottled water is now sold there rather than given away free). These sebils are often extremely attractive, with ornate bronze grilles and sculptured marble façades. The architects who designed the pious foundations of Istanbul were quite fond of using sebils to adorn the outer wall of a külliye, particularly at a street-corner. Although most of the sebils in town no longer distribute free water, they still gratify passers-by with their beauty. For that reason they should still provide a path to paradise for their departed donors.

TOWARDS THE FIRST HILL

The next street to the right beyond the sebil is a narrow alley which leads to the hamam, or public bath of Yıldız Dede. This gentleman, whose name was Necmettin, was an astrologer (Yıldız = Star) in the court of Sultan Mehmet II and won fame by predicting the fall of Constantinople from the celestial configurations at that time. According to tradition, Yıldız Dede built his hamam on the site of an ancient synagogue, probably one belonging to the Karaite Jews. The present bath, however, appears to date only from the time of Sultan Mahmut I, about 1730. It is now known as Yıldız Hamamı, but of old it was called Çıfıt Hamamı, the Bath of the Jews.

A little farther down the main street (Hamidiye Caddesi) and on the same side we come to the türbe of Sultan Abdül Hamit I. During his reign, from 1774 till 1789, the Ottoman armies suffered a series of humiliating defeats at the hands of the Russians and the Empire began to lose its dominions in the Balkans. By that time the reputation of the once proud Ottomans had sunk so low that Catherine the Great was heard to remark to the Emperor Joseph: "What is to become of those poor devils, the Turks?" Buried alongside Abdül Hamit in this türbe is his son, the mad Sultan Mustafa IV. Mustafa, the second imperial lunatic to bear that name, was responsible for the murder of his cousin, Selim III, and nearly succeeded in bringing about the execution of his younger brother, Mahmut II. Mustafa was eventually deposed on 28 July 1808 and was himself executed three months later.

Behind the türbe there is a medrese, or theological school, also due to Abdül Hamit I. The türbe and medrese were part of a külliye built for that sultan in 1778 by the architect Tahir Ağa. The remainder of the külliye has since disappeared except for the sebil, which has been moved to a different site.

A short distance beyond the türbe, Hamidiye Caddesi intersects Ankara Caddesi, a broad avenue which runs uphill. Ankara Caddesi follows approximately the course of the defence-walls built by Septimius Severus at the end of the second century A.D., a circuit of fortifications that extended from the Golden Horn to the Sea of Marmara along the course of the present avenue, enclosing the ancient town of Byzantium. Looking to the left at the intersection we see the recently refurbished Sirkeci Station, the terminus of the famous Orient Express, which made its first run through to Istanbul in 1888. There is an antique locomotive dated 1874 on view outside the station.

We now turn right along Ankara Caddesi and follow it as it winds uphill. The district through which we are now strolling is the centre of the publishing world of Istanbul; all of the major newspapers and magazines have their presses and offices here. There are also a number of bookshops along the avenue, with one of them built over a Byzantine basement that can be seen at the back of the store. Ahead and to the left we see the building that houses the Istanbul Governor's Office. The view down Hükümet Konağı Sokak past the governor's office is a good perspective of the west façade of Haghia Sophia.

CAĞALOĞLU HAMAMI

About half a kilometre along, we come on our left to Hilaliahmer Caddesi. If we follow this for about 100 metres, we see on our left the entrance to one of the most famous and beautiful public baths in Istanbul. This is the Cağaloğlu Hamamı, built in 1741 by Sultan Mahmut I. In Ottoman times the revenues from this bath were used to pay for the upkeep of the library which Sultan Mahmut built in Haghia Sophia, an illustration of the interdependence of these old pious foundations. There are well over a hundred Ottoman hamams in Istanbul, which tells us something of the important part which

CAĞALOĞLU HAMAMI

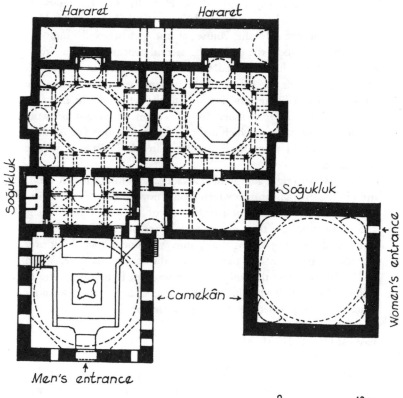

Hararet   Hararet

Soğukluk

←Soğukluk

Women's entrance

←Camekân→

↑
Men's entrance

0 _____ 10 m

Plan no: 2

they played in the life of the city. Since only the very wealthiest Ottoman homes were equipped with private baths, the vast majority of Stamboullus for centuries used the hamams of the city to cleanse and purify themselves. For many of the poorer people of modern Istanbul the hamam is still the only place where they can bathe.

Turkish hamams are the direct descendants of the baths of ancient Rome and are built to the same general plan. Ordinarily, a hamam has three distinct sections. The first is the camekân, the Roman apoditarium, which is used as a reception and dressing room, and where one recovers and relaxes after the bath. Next comes the soğukluk, or tepidarium, a chamber of intermediate temperature which serves as an ante-room to the bath, keeping the cold air out on one side and the hot air in on the other. Finally there is the hararet, or steam-room, anciently called the calidarium. In Turkish baths the first of these areas, the camekân, is the most monumental. It is typically a vast square room covered by a dome on pendentives or conches, with an elaborate fountain in the centre; around the walls is a raised platform where the bathers undress and leave their clothes. The soğukluk is almost always a mere passageway, which usually contains the lavatories. In Cağaloğlu, as in most hamams, the most elaborate chamber is the hararet. Here there is an open cruciform area, with a central dome supported by a circlet of columns and with domed side-chambers in the arms of the cross. In the centre there is a large marble platform, the göbektaşı, or belly-stone, which is heated from the furnace room below. The patrons lie on the belly-stone to sweat and be massaged before bathing at one of the wall-fountains in the side-chambers. The light in the hararet is dim and shimmering, diffusing down through the steam from the constellation of little glass windows in the dome. Lying on the hot belly-stone, under the glittering dome, and lazily observing the mists of vapour condensing into pearls of moisture on the marble columns, one has the voluptuous feeling of being in an undersea palace, in which everyone is his own sultan.

Cağaloğlu, like many of the larger hamams in Istanbul, is a double bath, with separate establishments for men and women. In the smaller hamams there is but a single bath and the two sexes are assigned different days for their use. In the days of old Stamboul, when Muslim women were more sequestered than they are now, the hamam was the one place where they could meet and exchange news and gossip. Even in modern Istanbul the weekly visit to the hamam is often the high point of feminine social life among the lower classes. And we are told by our lady friends that the women of Stamboul still sing and dance for one another in the hararet – another old Osmanlı custom.

BEŞİR AĞA CAMİİ

Leaving the Cağaloğlu Hamamı, presumably cleansed and purified, we continue on along Hilaliahmer Caddesi for another 100 metres and then turn left on Alay Köşkü Caddesi. About 100 metres along we come on our left to a small mosque with an elegant sebil at the street corner. This mosque and its külliye were built in 1745 by Beşir Ağa, Chief of the Black Eunuchs in the reign of Sultan Mahmut I. In addition to the mosque and sebil, the külliye of Beşir Ağa includes a library, a medrese and a tekke, or dervish monastery. The tekke is no longer occupied by dervishes, of course, since their various orders were banned in the early years of the Republic.

THE SUBLIME PORTE

A block beyond the mosque we come to Alemdar Caddesi, the avenue which skirts the outer wall of Topkapı Sarayı. Just to the left at the intersection we see a large ornamental gateway with a projecting roof in the rococo style. This is the famous Sublime Porte, which in former days led to the palace and offices of the Grand Vezir, where from the middle of the seventeenth century onwards most of the business of the Ottoman Empire was transacted. Hence it came to stand for the Ottoman government itself, and ambassadors were accredited to the Sublime Porte rather than to Turkey, just as to this day ambassadors to England are accredited to the Court of St. James. The present gateway, in which it is hard to discover anything of the sublime, was built about 1843 and now leads to the various buildings of the Vilayet, the government of the Province of Istanbul. The only structure of any interest within the precinct stands in a corner to the right of the gateway. This is the dershane, or lecture-hall of an ancient medrese; dated 1565, it is a pretty little building in the classical style of that period.

THE ALAY KÖŞKÜ

Opposite the Sublime Porte, in an angle of the palace wall, is a large polygonal gazebo. This is the Alay Köşkü, the Review or Parade Pavilion, from whose latticed windows the Sultan could observe the comings and goings at the palace of his Grand Vezir. One sultan, Crazy Ibrahim, was said to have used it as a vantage point from which to pick off passing pedestrians with his crossbow. The present kiosk dates only from 1819, when it was rebuilt by Sultan Mahmut II, but there had been a Review Pavilion at this point from much earlier times. From here the Sultan reviewed the great official parades which took place from time to time. The liveliest and most colourful of these was the Procession of the Guilds, a kind of peripatetic census of the trade and commerce of the city which was held every half-century or so. The last of these processions was held in the year 1769, during the reign of Sultan Mustafa II.

It might be worthwhile to pause for a few moments at this historic place to read a description of one of these processions, for it reveals to us something of what Stamboul life was like three centuries ago. This account is contained in the *Seyahatname*, or *Book of Travels*, written in the mid-seventeenth century by Evliya Çelebi, one of the great characters of old Ottoman Stamboul. Evliya, describing the Procession of the Guilds which took place in the year 1638, during the reign of Sultan Murat IV, tells us that it was an assembly "of all the guilds and professions existing within the jurisdiction of the four Mollas (Judges) of Constantinople," and that "the procession began its march at dawn and continued till sunset... on account of which all trade and work in Constantinople was disrupted for a period of three days. During this time the riot and confusion filled the town to a degree which is not to be expressed by language, and which I, poor Evliya, only dared to describe."

Evliya tells us that the procession was distributed into 57 sections and consisted of 1,001 guilds. Representatives of each of these guilds paraded in their characteristic costumes or uniforms, exhibiting on floats their various enterprises, trying to outdo one another in amusing or amazing the crowd. The liveliest of the displays would seem to have been that of the Captains of the White Sea (the Mediterranean), who had floats with ships mounted on them, in which, according to Evliya, "are seen the finest cabin-boys dressed in gold, doing service to their masters who make free with drinking. Music is played on all sides, the masts and oars are adorned with pearls, the sails are of rich stuffs and embroidered muslin. Arrived at the Alay Köşkü they meet five or ten ships of the Infidels with whom they engage in battle in the presence of the Emperor. Thus the show of a fight is represented with the roaring of cannons, the smoke covering the sky. At last, the Moslems becoming victors, they board the enemy ships, take booty and chase the fine Frank boys, carrying them off from the old bearded Infidels, whom they put in chains, upset the crosses of their flags, dragging them astern of their ships, crying out the universal Moslem shout, Allah!, Allah!"

Besides the respectable tradesmen, artisans and craftsmen of the city, the procession included less savoury groups such as, according to Evliya, "the corporation of thieves and footpads who might be here mentioned as a very numerous one and who have an eye to our purses. But far be they from us. These thieves pay tribute to the two chief officers of the police and get their subsistence by cheating foreigners."

The last guild in the procession was that of the tavern keepers. Evliya tells us that there were "one thousand such places of misrule, kept by Greeks, Armenians and Jews. In the procession wine is not produced openly, but the inn-keepers pass all in disguise and clad in armour. The boys of the taverns, all shameless drunkards, and all the partisans of wine pass, singing songs, tumbling down and rising again." The last of all to pass were the Jewish tavern keepers, "all masked and wearing the most precious dresses... bedecked with jewels, carrying in their hands crystal and porcelain cups, out of which they pour sherbet instead of wine for the spectators."

Evliya then ends his account by stating: "Nowhere else has such a procession been seen or shall be seen. It could only be carried into effect by the imperial orders of Sultan Murat IV. Such is the crowd and population of that great capital, Constantinople, which may God guard from all celestial and earthly mischief and let her be inhabited till the end of the world." But the last procession of the guilds passed by more than two centuries ago, and the Alay Köşkü now looks down upon a drab and colourless avenue. Nevertheless, the guilds and professions which Evliya so vividly described are still to be seen in the various quarters of the town, looking and behaving much as they did when they passed the Alay Köşkü in the reign of Murat IV.

ZEYNEP SULTAN CAMİİ

Following the Saray wall to the right of the Alay Köşkü we soon come to Soğuk Çeşme Kapısı, the Gate of the Cold Fountain, which leads to the public gardens of Topkapı Sarayı and to the Archaeological Museum. After passing the gate, we continue to follow Alemdar Caddesi, which now bends to the right, leaving the Saray walls. Just around the bend, on the right side of the avenue, we come upon a small baroque mosque, Zeynep Sultan Camii. This mosque was erected in 1769 by the Princess Zeynep, daughter of Ahmet III, and is a rather pleasant and original example of Turkish baroque. In form it is merely a small square room covered by a dome, with a square projecting apse to the east and a porch with five bays to the west. The mosque looks rather like a Byzantine church, partly from being built in courses of stone and brick, but more so because of its very Byzantine dome, for the cornice of the dome undulates to follow the extrados of the round-arched windows, a pretty arrangement generally used in Byzantine churches but hardly ever in Turkish mosques. The little sibyan mektebi at the corner just beyond the mosque is part of the foundation and appears to be still in use as a primary school. The elaborate rococo sebil outside the gate to the mosque garden does not belong to Zeynep's foundation, but was built by Abdül Hamit I in 1778 as part of the külliye which we passed earlier. The sebil was moved here some years ago when the street past Abdül Hamit's türbe was widened.

TOWARDS HAGHİA SOPHİA

Just beyond Zeynep Sultan Camii and on the same side of the avenue we see a short stretch of crenellated wall, almost hidden behind an auto-repair shop; this is all that remains of the apse of the once-famous church of St. Mary Chalcoprateia. This church, which is thought to date from the middle of the fifth century, was one of the most venerated in the city, since it possessed as a relic the girdle of the Blessed Virgin. After the Nika Revolt in the year 532, when the church of Haghia Sophia was destroyed, St. Mary's served for a time as the patriarchal cathedral. It was built on the ruins of an ancient synagogue which since the time of Constantine had been the property of the Jewish copperworkers, hence the name Chalcoprateia, or the Copper Market.

The handsome though forbidding building that occupies most of the opposite side of the avenue here is the Soğuk Kuyu Medresesi. This theological school was founded in the year 1559 by Cafer Ağa, Chief White Eunuch in the reign of Süleyman the Magnificent, and was built by the great Sinan. The hillside slopes quite sharply here, so Sinan first erected a vaulted substructure to support the medrese and its courtyard. The entrance to the medrese is approached from the street running parallel to the west end of Haghia Sophia, where an alleyway leads down to the inner courtyard of the building. The student cells of the medrese are arrayed around the courtyard, with the dershane, or lecture hall, in the large domed chamber to the left as you enter. The medrese now serves as a bazaar of old Ottoman arts and crafts, as well as a restaurant serving traditional Turkish food in a picturesque setting.

Alemdar Caddesi now brings us out into the large square which occupies the summit of the First Hill. On our left we see the great edifice of Haghia Sophia, flanked by a wide esplanade shaded with chestnut and plane-trees. Straight ahead is Sultan Ahmet I Camii, the famous Blue Mosque, its cascade of domes framed by six slender minarets. In front of the Blue Mosque is the At Meydanı, the site of the ancient Hippodrome, three of whose surviving monuments stand in line in the centre of a park. This is the centre of the ancient city, and the starting-point for our next five strolls through Stamboul.

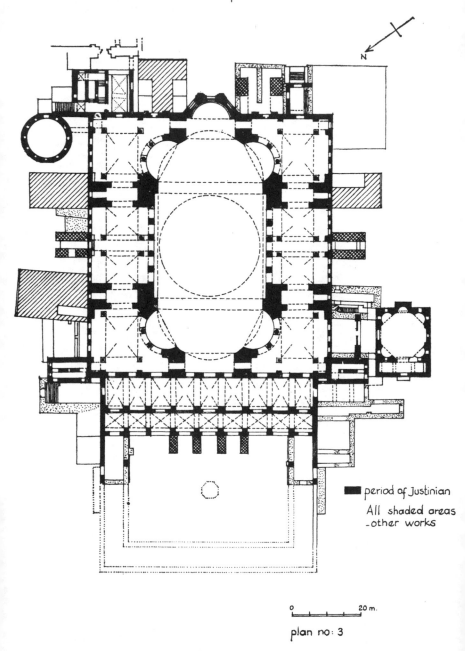

HAGHIA SOPHIA - Ground plan -

N

■ period of Justinian

All shaded areas
- other works

0   20 m.

plan no: 3

3

Haghia Sophia

"The church presents a most glorious spectacle, extraordinary to those who behold it and altogether incredible to those who are told of it. In height it rises to the very heavens and overtops the neighbouring houses like a ship anchored among them, appearing above the city which it adorns and forms a part of ... It is distinguished by indescribable beauty, excelling both in size and the harmonies of its measures." So wrote the chronicler Procopius more than 14 centuries ago, describing Haghia Sophia as it appeared during the reign of its founder Justinian I. Haghia Sophia, the Church of the Divine Wisdom, was dedicated by Justinian on 26 December 537. For more than nine centuries thereafter Haghia Sophia served as the cathedral of Constantinople and was the centre of the religious life of the Byzantine Empire. For 470 years after the Turkish Conquest it was one of the imperial mosques of Istanbul, known as Aya Sofya Camii. It continued to serve as a mosque during the early years of the Turkish Republic, until it was finally converted into a museum in 1935. Now, emptied of the congregations which once worshipped there, Christians and Muslims in turn, it may seem just a cold and barren shell, devoid of life and spirit. But for those who are aware of its long and illustrious history and are familiar with its architectural principles, Haghia Sophia remains one of the truly great buildings in the world. And it still adorns the skyline of the city as it did when Procopius wrote of it 14 centuries ago.

The present edifice of Haghia Sophia is the third of that name to stand upon this site. The first church of Haghia Sophia was dedicated on 15 February in the year A.D. 360, during the reign of Constantius, son and successor of Constantine the Great. This church was destroyed by fire on 20 June 404, during a riot by mobs protesting the exile of the Patriarch John Chrysostom by the Empress Eudoxia, wife of the Emperor Arcadius. Reconstruction of the church did not begin until the reign of Theodosius II, who succeeded his father Arcadius in the year 408. The second church of Haghia Sophia was completed in 415 and was dedicated by Theodosius on 10 October of that year. The church of Theodosius eventually suffered the same fate as its predecessor, for it was burned down during the Nika Revolt on 15 January 532.

The chronicler Procopius, commenting on the destruction of Haghia Sophia in the Nika Revolt, observed that "God allowed the mob to commit this sacrilege, knowing how great the beauty of this church would be when restored." Procopius tells us that Justinian immediately set out to rebuild the church on an even grander scale than before. According to Procopius: "The Emperor built regardless of expense, gathering together skilled workmen from every land." Justinian appointed as head architect Anthemius of Tralles, one of the most distinguished mathematicians and physicists of the age, and as his assistant named Isidorus of Miletus, the greatest geometer of late antiquity. Isidorus had been the director of the ancient and illustrious Academy in Athens before it was closed by Justinian in the year 529. Isidorus, who was placed in charge of the building of Haghia Sophia after the death of Anthemius in the year 532, is thus a link between the worlds of ancient Greece and medieval Byzantium. Just as the Academy of Plato had been one of the outstanding institutions of classical Greek culture, so would the resurrected Haghia Sophia be the symbol of a triumphant Christianity, Byzantine-style.

The new church of Haghia Sophia was finally completed late in 537 and was formally dedicated by Justinian on 26 December of that year, St. Stephen's Day. Hardly had the church come of age, however, when earthquakes caused the collapse of the eastern arch and semidome and the eastern part of the great dome, crushing beneath the debris the altar with its ciborium and the ambo. Undaunted, Justinian set out to rebuild his church, entrusting the restoration to Isidorus the Younger, a nephew of Isidorus of Miletus. The principal change made by Isidorus was to make the dome somewhat higher than before, thereby lessening its outward thrust. Isidorus' solution for the dome has on the whole been a great success for it has survived, in spite of two later partial collapses, until our own day. Restorations after those collapses, in the years 989 and 1346, have left certain irregularities in the dome; nevertheless it is essentially the same in design and substantially also in structure as that of Isidorus the Younger.

The doors of Haghia Sophia were opened once again at sunrise on Christmas Eve in the year 563, and Justinian, now an old man in the very last months of his life, led the congregation in procession to the church. Here is a poetic description of that occasion by Paul the Silentiary, one of Justinian's court officials: "At last the holy morn had come, and the great door of the newly-built temple groaned on its opening hinges, inviting Emperor and people to enter; and when the interior was seen sorrow fled from the hearts of all, as the sun lit the glories of the temple. 'Twas for the Emperor to lead the way for his people, and on the morrow to celebrate the birth of Christ. And when the first glow of light, rosy-armed, leapt from arch to arch, driving away the dark shadows, then all the princes and people with one voice hymned their songs of praise and prayer; and as they came to the sacred courts it seemed as if the mighty arches were set in heaven."

Although Haghia Sophia has been restored several times during the Byzantine and Ottoman periods, the present edifice is essentially that of Justinian's reign. The only major structural additions are the huge and unsightly buttresses which support the building to north and south. Originally erected by the Emperor Andronicus II Palaeologus in 1317, when the church seemed in imminent danger of collapse, they were restored and strengthened in Ottoman times. The four minarets at the corners of the building were placed there at various times after the Conquest: the south-east minaret by Sultan Mehmet II, the one to the north-east by Beyazit II, and the two at the western corners by Murat III, the work of the great Sinan. The last extensive restorations were commissioned by Sultan Abdül Mecit and carried out by the Swiss architects, the brothers Fossati, in the years 1847–9. As a result of this and later minor restorations and repairs, Haghia Sophia is today structurally sound, despite its great age, and looks much as it did in Justinian's time.

THE CHURCH

The original entrance to Haghia Sophia was at its western end, where the church was fronted by a great atrium, or arcaded courtyard, now vanished. The present entrance to the precincts of Haghia Sophia brings one in through the southern side of this atrium, now a garden-courtyard filled with architectural fragments from archaeological excavations in Istanbul. From the eastern side of this atrium five doorways gave entrance to the exonarthex, or outer vestibule, and from there five more doorways led to the inner vestibule, the narthex. The central and largest door from the atrium to the exonarthex was known as the Orea Porta, or the Beautiful Gate, and was reserved for the use of the Emperor and his party. (Just to the left of this portal one can see the excavated entryway to the so-called Theodosian church, the predecessor of the present edifice, which is described in the section on the Precincts of Haghia Sophia.) In addition to the Orea Porta, the Emperor also used an entryway which led into the southern end of the narthex, where the present public exit from the edifice is located, passing through a long and narrow passageway which in Byzantium was called the Vestibule of the Warriors. Here according to the *Book of Ceremonies,* the manual of Byzantine court-ritual, the Emperor removed his sword and crown before entering the narthex, and here the troops of his bodyguard waited until his return.

While passing through the vestibule we should notice the gold mosaics glittering on the dark vault; these are part of the original mosaic decoration from Justinian's church. The great dome, the semidomes, the north and south tympana and the vaults of narthex, aisles and gallery – a total area of more than four acres – were covered with gold mosaics, which, according to the Silentiary, resembled the midday sun in spring gilding the mountain heights. It is clear from his description and that of Procopius that in Justinian's time there were no figural mosaics in the church. A great deal of the Justinianic mosaic still survives – in the vaults of the narthex and the side aisles, as well as in the 13 ribs of the dome of Isidorus which have never fallen. It consists of large areas of plain gold ground, adorned round the edges of architectural forms with bands of geometrical or floral designs in various colours. Simple crosses in outline on the crowns of vaults and the soffits of arches are constantly repeated, and the Silentiary tells us that there was a cross of this kind on the crown of the great dome. This exceedingly simple but brilliant and flashing decoration must have been very effective indeed.

Whatever figural mosaics may have been introduced into the church after Justinian's time were certainly destroyed during the iconoclastic period, which lasted from 729 till 843. The figural mosaics which we see in Haghia Sophia today are thus from after that period, although there is far from being unanimous agreement among the experts as to the exact dates. Most of them would appear to belong to the second half of the ninth century and the course of the tenth century, although some are considerably later.

In the lunette above the doorway at the inner end of the Vestibule of the Warriors, we see one of the two mosaic panels which were rediscovered in 1933, after having been obscured for centuries by whitewash and plaster. Since that time other mosaics in the nave and gallery have been uncovered and restored, and their brilliant tesserae now brighten again the walls of Haghia Sophia, reminding us of the splendour with which it was once decorated throughout. The mosaic in the Vestibule of the Warriors is thought to date from the last quarter of the tenth century, from the reign of Basil II, the Bulgar-Slayer. It depicts the enthroned Mother of God holding in her lap the Christ-Child, as she receives two emperors in audience. On her right "Constantine the Great Emperor among the Saints" offers her a model of the city of Constantinople; while "Justinian the illustrious Emperor" on her left presents her with a model of Haghia Sophia: neither model remotely resembles its original!

We now enter the narthex, a long vestibule of nine vaulted bays. Five great doors on the left lead to the exonarthex and nine on the right give entrance to the nave. Many of these doors are splendid and interesting and most of them appear to date from the time of Justinian. The monumental central door to the nave was known anciently as the Imperial Gate. The frame of the door is covered with brass, replacing the silver with which it was sheathed in the days of Justinian, and is surmounted by a casket-like cornice in brass. According to an old

Byzantine legend, the doors of the Imperial Gate were made of wood which had originally been part of Noah's Ark and the cornice was the sarcophagus of St. Eirene.

In the lunette above the Imperial Gate we see the second of the two mosaics which were uncovered in 1933. The mosaic shows Christ seated upon a jewelled throne, his feet resting on a footstool. He raises his right hand in a gesture of blessing, and in his left he holds a book in which we may read this inscription in Greek: "Peace be with you. I am the Light of the World." On Christ's right an emperor prostrates himself, his hands outstretched in supplication. Above, on either side of the throne, are two roundels: the one above the emperor containing a bust of the Blessed Virgin; that on the other side, an angel carrying a staff or wand. It is thought that the imperial figure represents the Emperor Leo VI, the Wise, and the mosaic is dated to the period of his reign, 886–912. If so, it is probable that the Emperor is pleading with Christ to forgive him for what Gibbon so aptly called "the frequency of his nuptials." For the Emperor had lost his first three wives without producing a male heir, and wished to take a fourth mate, ordinarily forbidden by the Orthodox Church. After a long and bitter dispute, the famous Scandal of the Tetragamy, Leo finally obtained permission to marry his mistress, Zoe, and legitimized his bastard son, the future Constantine VII Porphyrogenitus. Although the affair of the Tetragamy may have scandalized Byzantium, we are fortunate that it was resolved in Leo's favour. For his son Constantine would later write the *Book of Ceremonies,* which recreates the pomp and splendour of the rituals and liturgies performed in Haghia Sophia in the days of Byzantium.

The Imperial Gate was reserved for the use of the Emperor and his procession, which passed through there into the nave of the church. According to the *Book of Ceremonies*: "The princes remove their crowns, kiss the holy Gospel carried by the archdeacon, greet the patriarch and proceed to the Imperial Gate. Bearing the candles and bowing thrice, they enter the church after a prayer is pronounced by the patriarch."

As we walk through the Imperial Gate into the nave, we notice the deep hollows worn into the pavement on either side of the entrance.

We learn from the *Book of Ceremonies* that in the days of Byzantium the imperial chamberlains called *praepositii* stood there, and we are reminded once again of the great antiquity of this place.

The first and abiding impression created by the interior of Haghia Sophia is that of a vast contained space, pierced by shafts of moted sunlight. Walking forward, we can now see the whole of the immense interior at once and appreciate its beauty and its grandeur: the fabled dome, which the ancients pictured as being suspended from heaven by a golden chain; the enormous expanse of the nave, its central area flanked by the graceful two-tiered colonnade which Procopius likened to a line of dancers in a chorus; all elements of the vast structure interrelated in perfect harmony.

Justinian and his architects, Anthemius and Isidorus, chose to disregard the plan or the earlier churches on this site and, indeed, all earlier plans of which any trace or record has come down to us. The essential structure of their astonishingly original building can be briefly described. Four enormous and irregularly shaped piers, built of ashlar stone bound together with lead, stand in a square approximately 31 metres on a side. From these piers rise four great arches between which four pendentives make the transition from square to circle. Upon the cornice of the circle so formed rests the slightly elliptical dome, of which the east-west diameter is about 31 metres, the north-south diameter about 33 metres, the crown being 56 metres above the floor – that is, about the height of a 15-storey building. The dome has 40 ribs which radiate out from the crown, separated at the base by 40 windows, of which four towards the west were blocked up during repairs in the tenth century. To east and west, pairs of subsidiary piers support the two great semidomes, each with five windows, which give the nave its vast length, a full 80 metres. The central arches to north and south are filled with tympanum walls pierced by 12 windows, seven in the lower row, five in the upper, of which the three central ones originally formed a kind of triple arcade. All these windows have in Turkish times been considerably reduced in size, probably by the architect Sinan in the sixteenth century. Between the great piers on the north and south, four monolithic columns of verd antique support the galleries, while above six columns of the same type carry the tympana. At the eastern and western ends, to north and south, semicircular exedrae prolong the nave, with two massive monolithic columns of porphyry below and six of verd antique above, on which rest smaller semidomes. At the east, beyond the subsidiary piers, a semicircular apse projects beyond the east wall; it too is covered by a semidome or conch. Finally, four great buttresses projecting from the north and south walls opposite the central piers help to consolidate the whole fabric.

If the plan is to all intents and purposes that of a basilica, the originality consists in covering it with a dome and two semidomes. Glorious as is the dome, it is the introduction of the semidomes which constitutes the real triumph of genius. For in addition to lengthening the nave, they make it possible to appreciate from the very threshold the soaring, hovering height; they allow the dome, in short, to play its true and full part in the total effect. Contrast the relative ineffectiveness of such a dome as that of St. Peter's, from which radiate barrel-vaults along the axes of the building. That dome, though higher and somewhat greater in diameter than Haghia Sophia's, is almost insignificant, for it can only be seen when one is very nearly underneath it, so that one must crane back one's neck to get a view of it at all. How very different here, where from every point of view the dome dominates the whole interior!

THE COLUMNS AND MARBLES

Much has been written about the provenance of the various columns in the church. The Anonymous of Banduri, that Baron Munchausen among Byzantine writers, is the chief source of various legends that have grown up and are still repeated about where the great columns of the nave came from: the Temple of the Sun at Heliopolis, some buildings at Rome, the Temple of Diana at Ephesus, or one of those at Baalbec, the tales differ with the tellers. But there seems to be no foundation for these stories and there is every reason to believe that most of the columns, if not all, were specially quarried for Haghia Sophia. From the Silentiary's description, there can be little doubt that the eight monolithic verd antique columns of the nave, the 16 columns of the aisles, the 40 columns of the gallery arcade, and all the other verd antique of the building were expressly hewn for Haghia Sophia from the famous quarries in Thessaly near Molossis. But about the eight porphyry columns in the exedrae, there is a problem, for there is some evidence that the porphyry mountain at Djebel Dochan near Thebes had ceased to be quarried in the fifth century. If this is true, the eight exedra columns – which, by the way, differ very appreciably in height and diameter – must have been taken from some older building. But there is no evidence to connect them to any particular ancient building; we simply do not know where they came from.

The only other kind of marble used for columns in the church is that from the island of Proconnesus in the Marmara. It is a soft white, streaked with grey or black, and is used for the 24 aisle columns of the gallery and the eight rectangular pillars at the ends of the ground floor aisles. The floor of the church, too, the frames of doors and windows, and parts of the wall surfaces are also of this marble. It is very common to this day in Istanbul, and is used for everything from tombstones to toilets.

For the superb revetment of the piers and walls, a great variety of rare and beautiful marbles was used. Besides those already discussed, the Silentiary mentions at least eight different varieties: the deep green porphyry from Mount Taygetus near Sparta; a "fresh green" from Carystus in the island of Euboea; the rose-red Phyrygian marble from Synnada and a variegated one from Hierapolis in Asia Minor; "Iassian, with slanting veins of blood red on livid white," probably from Lacedaemon; a marble "of crocus yellow glittering like gold," from Simittu Colonia near Tunis; and one from the Pyrenees, "the product of the Celtic crags, like milk poured on a flesh of glittering black"; and finally the precious onyx, like alabaster honey-coloured and translucent. In order to obtain the elaborate symmetrical patterns of each panel, the thin blocks of marble were sawn in two, sometimes in four, and opened out like a book so that the natural veining of the stone was reduplicated, very much like the ink blots of a Rorschach test. And spectators, both ancient and modern, respond as patients do to the Rorschach test by finding in the veined panels likenesses of men and animals, devils and angels, giving form to the ghosts and legends which attach themselves to every stone of this ancient building.

Other types of decoration in rare marbles are also found in the church. The great square of *opus Alexandrinum* in the pavement towards the south-east of the nave always attracts attention. It is chiefly composed of circles of granite, red and green porphyry and verd antique. According to Antony, Bishop of Novgorod, who visited the church in 1200, the Emperor's throne stood upon this square, surrounded by a bronze enclosure. There are some equally interesting marble panels above the imperial door: slabs of verd antique alternate with inlaid panels of various marbles. At the top is an elaborate ciborium with drawn curtains revealing a cross on an altar; lower down are other panels with ovals of porphyry, those at the bottom surrounded by pairs of stylized dolphins with foliate tails gobbling up tiny squid with waving tentacles. Finally, in the spandrels above the nave and gallery arcades is a rich and magnificent frieze of sectile work with scrolls of leaves and flowers, and birds "perched on the twigs".

The capitals of the columns are famous and splendid. There are several different types, but all are alike in having the surface decoration of acanthus and palm foliage deeply undercut so that they produce an effect of white lace on a dark ground; it is possible that they were once gilded. The commonest of the capitals – those of the nave and gallery arcades – are generally known as the bowl type: Ionic volutes support a decorated abacus beneath which the bowl-shaped body of the capital is adorned with acanthus leaves, in the centre of which in front and back is a medallion containing a monogram. These monograms are extremely tricky to read, but when deciphered they give the names Justinian and Theodora and the titles Basileus and Augusta. The capitals of the 16 verd antique columns of the aisles are of similar type but smaller in scale. Those of the eight rectangular pillars at the ends of the aisles are closely related, only here the bowl, instead of becoming circular towards its base, remains square throughout since the column itself is square. One of these rectangular pillars, the north-west one in the north aisle, is the subject of ancient legend. Antony of Novgorod reports it thus: "One sees at the side the column of St. Gregory the Miracle-Worker, all covered with bronze plates. St. Gregory appeared near this column, and the people kiss it and rub their breasts and shoulders against it to be cured of their pains." Centuries of credulous pilgrims have worn a hole in the metal plate and into the column itself, for the moisture contained in the cavity has always been considered specific against eye diseases and a nostrum for fertility. It is often said that the moisture in this little hole is drawn up through the column from the cisterns supposed to be under the church. But these cisterns are themselves a legend, for a recent study has shown that they do not exist.

THE MOSAICS IN THE NAVE

Little now remains of the mosaics which once adorned the nave of Haghia Sophia. The largest and most beautiful of those which have survived is contained in the conch of the apse. This mosaic depicts the Mother of God with the Christ-Child on her knees; she is dressed in flowing robes of blue with a small cross on the fold of the mantle over her head and one on each shoulder; her right hand rests on the Child's shoulder and her left upon his knee. The Child is dressed in gold and wears sandals on his feet; his right hand is raised in blessing while his left holds a scroll. The Virgin sits on a simple bench-like throne adorned with jewels; under her are two cushions, the lower green, the upper embroidered with clubs like those on playing cards; beneath her feet is a plinth-like footstool, also bejewelled. At the bottom of the arch which frames the apse we see a colossal figure of the Archangel Gabriel; he wears a divitision, or undergarment, over which is thrown a chlamys, or cloak of white silk; his great wings, reaching nearly to his feet, are of brightly-coloured feathers, chiefly green, blue and white. In his right hand he holds a staff, in his left a crystal globe through which can be seen his thumb. Although the upper part of his left side and the top of his right wing are lost, he is nevertheless a fine and striking figure. Opposite, on the north side of the arch, can be seen only a few sad feathers of the wings of the Archangel Michael. Finally, on the face of the apse conch we read the first three and the last nine letters of an inscription in Greek, of which the whole of the middle part is now missing. The inscription was an iambic distich which once read in full: "These icons the deceivers once cast down / The pious emperors have again restored." The apse mosaic was first unveiled by the Patriarch Photius on Easter Sunday in the year 867: a most momentous occasion, for it signified the final triumph of the Orthodox over the Iconoclasts, and celebrated the permanent restoration of sacred images to the churches of Byzantium. The two pious sovereigns referred to here are Michael III, the Sot, and his protege, Basil I, whom Michael had made co-emperor the previous May, and who would the following September murder his benefactor and usurp the throne for himself.

Three other mosaic portraits are located in niches at the base of the north tympanum wall and are visible from the nave. They portray three sainted bishops of the early church. In the first niche from the west we have St. Ignatius the Younger, in the central niche St. John Chrysostomos, and in the fifth from the west St. Ignatius Theophorus. All three figures are nearly identical except for the faces; each is clad in sacerdotal robes, the most striking item of which is the wide omophorion, or stole, with two large crosses below the shoulders and a third just below the knee; each holds in his left hand, which is concealed below his cloak, a large book with bejewelled binding; the younger St. Ignatius appears to be touching the top of the book with his right hand, while the other two have their right hands raised in blessing. The faces get older the farther east one goes: the first Ignatius, as his name suggests, is a young man but with a very ascetic face; St. John is in early middle age and his small, compressed lips hardly suggest the"Golden Mouth" from which he receives his name, Chrysostomos; St. Ignatius Theophorus is an old man with white hair and a beard. Chrysostomos and the elder Ignatius were two of the most powerful and contentious patriarchs in the history of Byzantium; each would have seen both Church and Empire wrecked rather than compromise his principles. It was said of Chrysostomos in his time that "he was merciless to sin but full of mercy for the sinner."

The only other mosaics which are visible from the nave are the famous six-winged seraphim or cherubim in the eastern pendentives. (Those in the western pendentives are imitations in paint done by the

Fossatis at the time of their restorations in 1847–9.) These have never been covered; we see them in pictures of Haghia Sophia across the centuries, hovering eerily over the nave. Evliya Çelebi believed them to be talismans, albeit moribund ones, as he tells us in his *Seyahatname*: "Before the birth of the Prophet these four angels used to speak, and gave notice of all the dangers which threatened the Empire and the city of Istanbul; but since his highness appeared all talismans have ceased to act." Their faces are sometimes exposed, sometimes covered, most recently by the Fossatis' gold-starred medallions, which are still in place. Unfortunately, these mosaics have not yet been cleaned and restored and are a bit dirty and discoloured. It is not certain whether these heavenly creatures are intended to be seraphim or cherubim; the former are said by Isaiah to have, like these, six wings: "With twain he covered his face, and with twain he covered his feet, and with twain he did fly," while Ezekiel informs us that cherubim had only four (or eight) wings. But as Cyril Mango amusingly shows, Byzantine artists do not seem to have understood or observed the distinction between the two Orders; he suggests that perhaps we have here one of each. As to date, Mr. Mango points out that since both pendentives were largely destroyed in the collapse of 1346, the mosaics must be subsequent to that time; they doubtless belong to the period of restoration after the collapse, between 1346 and 1355. But they certainly replace, and may closely copy, older mosaics of the same subject.

THE GALLERIES

All of the remaining mosaics are in the galleries and in the rooms adjacent to them. The public entryway to the galleries is at the northern end of the narthex, where an inclined labyrinth leads us to the angle of the western and northern galleries. Before we examine the mosaics we might walk to the central or western gallery, from whence we can orient ourselves and enjoy a splendid view of the nave. Just next to the balustrade at the centre of this gallery we see the spot where the throne of the Empress was located; it is marked by a disc of green Thessalian marble set into the pavement and framed by a pair of coupled columns in green marble. Although Procopius and the Silentiary tell us that in their time the entire gallery was used as the women's quarter, or gynaeceum, it appears that in later centuries most of the southern gallery was reserved for the use of the royal family, and, on occasion, for synods of the Orthodox Church.

Let us now return to the northern gallery, where the earliest of the visible mosaics is located. This mosaic, the last of those in the church to be uncovered and restored, is found high on the east face of the north-west pier. This panel represents the Emperor Alexander, who came to the throne in May of the year 912, succeeding his elder brother, Leo VI. "Here comes the man of thirteen months," said Leo with his dying breath, as he saw his despised brother coming to pay his last respects. This cynical prophecy was fulfilled in June of the following year, when Alexander died of apoplexy during a drunken game of polo. This mosaic portrait must surely have been done during Alexander's brief reign, for so incompetent and corrupt was this mad and alcoholic despot that no one would have honoured him other than in the single year when he was sole ruler. Alexander's portrait shows him standing full length, wearing the gorgeous ceremonial costume of a Byzantine emperor: crowned with a camelaucum, a conical, helmet-shaped coronet of gold with pendant pearls; draped in a loros, a long, gold-embroidered scarf set with jewels; and shod in gem-studded crimson boots. Four medallions flanking the imperial figure bear this legend: "Lord help thy servant, the orthodox and faithful Emperor Alexander."

On the west face of the same pier we find one of the most elaborate of the many graffiti which are carved on the walls of Haghia Sophia; it shows a medieval galleon under full sail. Anyone who has ever sat through the whole of a long Greek Orthodox service can appreciate how the artist had plenty of time to complete this sketch. Most of the other graffiti consist merely of names and dates, many of them carved on the marble balustrade. On the inner balustrade of the north gallery we find this inscription: "Place of the most noble Patrician, Lady Theodora." A short distance farther along there is one which reads: "Timothy, Keeper of the Vessels." What was Timothy doing in the gynaeceum, we wonder?

We now retrace our steps to view the other visible mosaics, all of which are located in the southern gallery. Before we turn into the gallery, we might pause for a moment at a closed door in the south end of the central gallery. This door leads into a large chamber directly over the Vestibule of the Warriors, and this in turn leads into a suite of rooms on either side. These rooms contain a large number of mosaics, which are thought to date from the second half of the ninth century, just after the end of the iconoclastic period. These fascinating rooms are almost certainly the large and small secreta of the Patriarchal Palace, which adjoined Haghia Sophia to the south. Unfortunately, they are not open to the public.

In the south gallery, between the western pier and buttress, there stretches a marble screen in the form of two pairs of false double doors with elaborately ornamented panels, the so-called Gates of Heaven and Hell. Between them is the actual doorway with a slab of translucent Phrygian marble above it; a sculpted wooden beam forms a kind of cornice to the whole. Neither the date nor the purpose of this screen is known. It is certainly not an original part of the church but a later addition, and it has been suggested that it may have been erected to screen off the portion of the south gallery used for Church synods.

The second in date of the imperial portraits is located at the east end of the south gallery, next to the apse; it depicts the famous Empress Zoe and her third husband, Constantine IX Monomachos. At the centre of the composition we see the enthroned figure of Christ, his right hand raised in a gesture of benediction, his left holding the book of Gospels. On Christ's right stands the Emperor holding in his hands the offering of a moneybag, and to his left is the Empress holding an inscribed scroll. Above the Emperor's head an inscription reads: "Constantine, in Christ the Lord Autocrat, faithful Emperor of the Romans, Monomachus." Above the head of the Empress we read: "Zoe, the most pious Augusta." The scroll in her hand has the same legends as that over the Emperor's head, save that the words Autocrat and Monomachus are omitted for want of space.

Now the curious thing about this mosaic is that all three heads and the two inscriptions concerning Constantine have been altered. A possible explanation for this is furnished by a review of the life and loves of the extraordinary Empress Zoe, daughter of Constantine VIII and one of the few women to rule Byzantium in her own right. A virgin till the age of 50, Zoe was then married by her father to Romanus Argyros so as to produce a male heir to the throne. Though it was too late for Zoe to produce children, she enjoyed her new life to the full, taking a spectacular series of lovers in the years that were left to her. After the death of her first husband, Romanus III (r. 1028–34), Zoe married Michael IV (r. 1034–41), and after his death she wed Constantine IX (r. 1042–55). It has been suggested that the mosaic in the gallery of Haghia Sophia was originally done between 1028 and 1034 and portrayed Zoe with her first husband, Romanus III, and that the faces were destroyed during the short and fanatically anti-Zoe reign of Michael V, the adopted son of the Empress. When Zoe ascended the throne in 1042 with her third husband, Constantine IX, she presumably had the faces restored, substituting that of Constantine for Romanus and altering the inscriptions accordingly. Zoe died in 1050, aged 72; Michael Psellus tells us that to the end, though her hand trembled and her back was bent with age, "her face had a beauty altogether fresh." So she still appears today in her mosaic portrait in Haghia Sophia.

The third and last of the imperial portraits is just to the right of the one we have been dealing with. Here we see the Mother of God holding the infant Christ; to her right stands an emperor offering a bag of gold and to her left a red-haired empress holding a scroll. The imperial figures are identified by inscriptions as: "John, in Christ the Lord faithful Emperor, Porphyrogenitus and Autocrat of the Romans, Comnenus", and "Eirene, the most pious Augusta." The mosaic extends onto the narrow panel of side wall at right angles to the main composition; we see there the figure of a young prince, identified by an inscription as "Alexius, in Christ, faithful Emperor of the Romans, Porphyrogenitus." These are the portraits of the Emperor John II Comnenus (r. 1118–43); his wife, the Empress Eirene, daughter of King Ladislaus of Hungary; and their eldest son, Prince Alexius. The main panel has been dated to 1118, the year of John's accession, and the portrait of Alexius to 1122, when at the age of 17 he became co-emperor with his father. Young Alexius did not live to succeed

John, for he died not long after his coronation; we can almost see the signs of approaching death in his pale and lined features. The Emperor was known in his time as Kalo John, or John the Good. The Byzantine historian Nicetas Choniates wrote of John that "he was the best of all the emperors from the family of the Comneni who ever sat upon the Roman throne." Eirene was noted for her piety and for her kindness to the poor, for which she is honoured as a saint in the Orthodox Church. John and Eirene were full of good works; together they founded the monastery of the Pantocrator, the triple church of which is still one of the principal monuments on the Fourth Hill of the city.

The latest in date of the mosaics in the gallery is the magnificent Deesis, which is located in the east wall of the western buttress in the south gallery. This mosaic, one of the very greatest works of art produced in Byzantium, is thought to date from the beginning of the fourteenth century. It is a striking illustration of the cultural renaissance which took place in Constantinople after the restoration of the Byzantine Empire by Michael VIII Palaeologus in 1261. Although two-thirds of the mosaic is now lost, the features of the three figures in the portrait are still completely intact and unmarred. Here we see Christ flanked by the Virgin and St. John the Baptist; they lean towards him in suppliant attitudes, pleading, so the iconographers tell us, for the salvation of mankind. John looks towards Christ with an expression of almost agonized grief on his face, while the young and wistful Virgin casts her gaze shyly downwards. Christ, holding up his right hand in a gesture of benediction, looks off into space with a look of sadness in his eyes, appearing here as if he partook more of the nature of man than of God, whatever the medieval theologians may have decided about him. The Deesis is a work of great power and beauty, a monument to the failed renaissance of Byzantium and its vision of a humanistic Christ.

Set into the pavement just opposite to the Deesis is the tomb of the man who ruined Byzantium. Carved in Latin letters on the broken lid of a sarcophagus there, we see the illustrious name, HENRICUS DANDALO. Dandalo, Doge of Venice, was one of the leaders of the Fourth Crusade and was the one chiefly responsible for persuading the Latins to attack Constantinople in the years 1203–4. After the final capture of Constantinople on 13 April 1204, Baldwin of Flanders was crowned in Haghia Sophia as Emperor of Rumania, as the Latins called the portion of the Byzantine Empire which they had conquered. But the Latin Emperor did not reign supreme even in his capital city, for three-eighths of Constantinople, including the church of Haghia Sophia, was awarded to the Venetians and ruled by Dandalo. The old Doge now added the title of Despot to his name and thereafter styled himself "Lord of the fourth and a half of all the Roman Empire." But proud Dandalo had little time to lord it over his fractional kingdom, for he died the following year, 16 June 1205, and was buried in the gallery of Haghia Sophia. After the Conquest, according to tradition, Dandalo's tomb was broken open and his bones thrown to the dogs.

After the Palaeologian renaissance of the thirteenth and fourteenth centuries the fortunes of the Empire declined rapidly, and in the last decades of Byzantine rule Haghia Sophia shared in the general decay of the dying capital. Travellers to Constantinople in that period report that the church showed signs of grievous neglect and was beginning to fall into ruins. Then, towards the very end, Haghia Sophia was all but deserted by its congregation, who stayed away in protest over the Emperor's attempted union with the Church of Rome. The people of the city began returning to their church only in the very last days before Constantinople fell to the Turks, when doctrinal differences no longer seemed important, not even to a Byzantine.

The final Christian liturgy in Haghia Sophia began shortly after sunset on Monday 28 May 1453. The Emperor Constantine XI Dragases arrived in Haghia Sophia an hour or so before midnight, and there made his peace with God before returning to his post on the city walls. The prayers continued in Haghia Sophia throughout the night, and the church filled with crowds of refugees as the sound of the Ottoman artillery grew more intense. Shortly after dawn word came that the defence walls had been breached and that the city had fallen. Then the doors of the church were barred and the congregation huddled inside, praying for a miraculous deliverance which never came. Soon afterwards the vanguard of the Turkish soldiery forced its way into Haghia Sophia, bringing to an end the last tragic hour of Byzantium.

THE CHURCH AS A MOSQUE

Sultan Mehmet the Conqueror entered the city late in the afternoon of that same day, Tuesday 29 May, and rode slowly through the streets of the city to Haghia Sophia. He dismounted at the door of the church and bent down to take a handful of earth, which he then sprinkled over his turban as an act of humility before God. Let us read Evliya Çelebi's account of this historic occasion: "Sultan Mehmet II, on surveying more closely the church of Aya Sofya, was astonished at the solidity of its construction, the strength of its foundations, the height of its cupola, and the skill of its builder. He caused the ancient building to be cleared of its idolatrous objects and purified from the blood of the slain, and having refreshed the brains of the victorious Moslems by fumigating it with amber and lion-aloes, converted it that very hour into a mosque."

Immediately after the Conquest, Sultan Mehmet thoroughly repaired the fabric of Haghia Sophia. Later sultans refurbished and adorned the interior of the building in various ways, so as to restore something of its ancient beauty. Evliya Çelebi describes some of these benefactions: "Sultan Murat III brought from the island of Marmara two princely basins of white marble, each of them resembling the cupola of a bath. They stand inside the mosque, full of living water, for all the congregation to perform their ablutions and quench their thirst. The same sultan caused the walls of the mosque to be cleansed and smoothed; he increased the number of lamps and built four raised stone platforms for the readers of the Kuran, and a lofty pulpit on slender columns for the müezzins. Sultan Murat IV, the Conqueror of Baghdad, raised upon four marble columns a marble throne for the preacher."

All of these objects can still be seen in the nave of Haghia Sophia, along with the gifts of later sultans. The two lustration urns which Evliya mentions are located in the western exedrae. They are late classical or early Byzantine urns to which have been added Turkish lids. An English traveller in the seventeenth century reported that they were always kept full of water "to cool the Mohammedans overheated by their pious gesticulations." The marble preacher's throne is located in the middle of the northern arcade. The four marble platforms for the readers of the Kuran are the large one next to the south-east pier and the three smaller ones that are built up against the other piers. The most noteworthy of the later Ottoman additions are the very elegant library built beyond the south aisle by Sultan Mahmut I in 1739, and the imperial loge to the left of the apse, constructed by the Fossatis for Sultan Abdül Mecit in 1847–9.

Of the Fossatis' decorations the most obtrusive and regrettable are the eight huge green levhas, or medallions, which hang from the piers at gallery level. These were done by the calligrapher Mustafa Izzet Efendi and contain in golden letters the Holy Names; that is, those of Allah, the Prophet Muhammed, and the first Caliphs and Imams. The great inscription in the dome is also by Mustafa Izzet Efendi. This replaces an earlier inscription with the same text, Surah 24:35 from the Kuran.

For a vivid picture of what Haghia Sophia was like as a mosque we turn to the *Seyahatname*, where Evliya Çelebi describes the building as it was in the reign of Sultan Murat IV, in the middle of the seventeenth century. From Evliya's description we see that Haghia Sophia partook once again of the glories of the age, just as it had 11 centuries before in the reign of Justinian:

> This mosque, which has no equal on earth, can only be compared to the tabernacle of the seventh heaven, and its dome to the cupola of the ninth. All of those who see it remain lost on contemplating its beauties; it is the place where heavenly inspiration descends into the minds of the devout and which gives a foretaste even here below of the Garden of Eden. Sultan Murat IV, who took great delight in this incomparable mosque, erected a wooden enclosure within it near the southern door, and when he went to prayer on Friday caused cages containing a great number of singing birds, and particularly nightingales, to be hung there, so that their sweet notes, mingled with those of the müezzins' voices, filled the mosque with a harmony

approaching to that of paradise. Every night in the month of Ramazan, the two thousand lamps lighted there and the lanterns containing wax tapers perfumed with camphor pour forth streams of light upon light; and in the centre of the dome a circle of lamps represents in letters as finely formed as those of Yakut Musta'sime, that text of the Kuran: "God is the light of the heavens and of the earth."

And so, for nearly five centuries after the Conquest, Haghia Sophia served the faithful Muslims of the city, just as it had served devout Christians for more than nine centuries before the Fall. These words which Evliya Çelebi wrote of Haghia Sophia would have been a true description of it in either period, as church or mosque: "Aya Sofya is in itself, peculiarly the place of God. It is always full of holy men who pass the day there in fasting and the night in prayer. Seventy lectures well pleasing to God are given there daily, so that to the student it is a mine of knowledge, and it never fails to be frequented by multitudes every day."

THE PRECINCTS OF HAGHİA SOPHİA

Something of the reverence which was accorded to Haghia Sophia in Ottoman times can be gathered from the fact that five sultans are buried in its precincts. These royal sepulchers are located in the garden just to the south of Haghia Sophia. The oldest of these structures is the türbe of the two mad sultans, Mustafa I and Ibrahim, who ruled briefly in the first half of the seventeenth century. This building, which stands at the south-west corner of Haghia Sophia, just to the right of the entrance, was formerly the Baptistry, and is part of the original structure of Justinian's church. We learn from Evliya Çelebi that when Mustafa I died in 1623 no place had been prepared for his burial and on the suggestion of Evliya's father it was decided to turn the Baptistry into a türbe for the dead sultan. Beside Mustafa lies his nephew, Crazy Ibrahim, who ruled from 1640 till 1648. Evliya tells us that Ibrahim's tomb was much visited by women, "because he was much addicted to them." But, alas, the women of Stamboul can no longer visit the tomb of Crazy Ibrahim, because the Baptistry is not open to the public.

The other imperial türbes are located in the garden beside the Baptistry; all of these are open to the public. The earliest in date is that of Sultan Selim II, which was completed in 1577. This türbe is important because it is a work of the great Ottoman architect Sinan, and also because both the exterior entrance façade and the whole of the interior are covered with superb Iznik tiles. The building is square, with an outer dome resting directly on the exterior walls; within, a circlet of columns supports an inner dome. The largest of the catafalques which we see there covers the grave of Selim II, who became sultan in 1566, after the death of his father, Süleyman the Magnificent. As Evliya Çelebi wrote of him: "He was an amiable monarch, took much delight in the conversations of poets and learned men, and indulged in wine and gaiety. He was a sweet-natured sovereign but much given to women and wine." Selim II died in 1574 at the age of 54, after having fallen in his bath while in a drunken stupor. Beside Selim's catafalque we see that of his favourite wife, Nurbanu. Arrayed around them are the tiny catafalques covering the graves of five of Selim's sons, three of his daughters, and 32 children of his son and successor, Murat III. Selim's sons were murdered on the night of 21 December 1574, assassinated according to Ottoman law, to ensure the peaceful accession of Murat, the eldest son.

Murat's own türbe stands just beside that of his father; it was completed in 1599 by Davut Ağa, the successor to Sinan as Chief of the Imperial Architects. It is hexagonal in plan, also with a double dome, and is adorned with Iznik tiles comparable in quality to those in Selim's türbe. The türbe contains the remains of Murat III as well as those of his favourite wife, Safiye, four of his lesser concubines, 23 of his sons and 25 of his daughters. The Sultan himself died on 16 January 1595, when he was only in his 49th year. Murat's türbe was not finished at the time of his death and so his coffin was placed under a tent in the garden of Haghia Sophia. The following morning 19 more coffins were placed there around him, for that night all but one of his surviving sons were executed to ensure the succession of the heir, Mehmet III. This was the last application of what Evliya called the bloody code of the Ottomans; thenceforth the younger brothers of a succeeding sultan were confined in the Saray rather than murdered.

Built up against Murat's türbe is the little building called the Türbe of the Princes, which contains only the tiny catafalques of five sons of Murat IV. These five princelings died natural deaths, succumbing to one of the many plagues which ravaged the Harem.

The latest in date of the türbes in this necropolis beside Haghia Sophia is that of Mehmet III, son and successor of Murat III. This türbe is octagonal in plan and, like the others, is covered with superb Iznik tiles. Mehmet became sultan in the year 1595 and ruled for only eight years, dying in 1603 at the age of 36. Like his father and his grandfather before him, Mehmet's world was bounded by the walls of the Harem. Even there he was of no great distinction and sired only 11 children, barely a tenth the homeric output of his father, who is officially credited with 103 offspring. Nine of Mehmet's children are buried with him, as is his favourite wife, Handan. Mehmet and his family hardly half fill the türbe, leaving room for 16 daughters of Murat III, all of whom died of plague in the same year, 1598.

The other Ottoman structures in the precincts of Haghia Sophia are of minor importance. The building just to the left of the entrance is a primary school built by Sultan Mahmut I in 1740. It is very typical of the little Ottoman one-room schoolhouses of that period, consisting of just a porch and a square chamber covered by a dome. To the right of the entrance there is a little domed structure built by the Fossatis in 1847–9. This was the muvakkithane, the house and workshop of the mosque astronomer, whose sundial can still be seen on the façade of Haghia Sophia to the left of the entrance. In the centre of the courtyard to the left we see the şadırvan, or ablution fountain, built by Sultan Mahmut I in about 1740. It is one of the most rococo of all mosque şadırvans, but in spite of its extravagance – or perhaps because of it – it is extremely attractive, with its widely projecting roof gaily painted in decorative motifs, its fine bronze grilles, and its marble panels carved in low relief.

Beyond the fountain, a forest of marble columns interspersed with rose bushes and other flowers forms a quaint but attractive garden, which is actually a morgue for stray columns dug up here and there around the city in the course of excavations for roads and buildings. This columnar garden leads along the west front of the building, in what was once the atrium, and brings us to the excavations which in 1935 uncovered the entryway to the Theodosian church, the predecessor of the present edifice. What remains in situ is chiefly the foundation of a monumental entrance-porch. It is essentially in the classical manner – a colonnaded porch with the traditional entablature and coffered ceiling above the columns, although at least above the central columns above the main door the entablature appears to have been arched instead of trabeated (i.e. with a horizontal lintel), as was always the case in pure classical buildings. Vast fragments of this superstructure can be examined close at hand as they lie scattered about here and there in front of the building: it is interesting to see the predominantly Hellenistic decorative motifs giving place from time to time to some distinctively Christian symbol. Through this temple-like porch one entered a great basilical church, probably with five aisles rather than the more usual three. Such a plan, with a wide central nave flanked on either side by two rows of columns forming a double aisle, was occasionally used in early times for the largest churches, as may still be seen, for example, at the Lateran and St. Paolo fuori le Mura in Rome or at St. Demetrius in Thessalonica. A similar plan was probably used for the earlier church built by Constantius. The still remaining fragments of the Theodosian church testify well enough that this too was a building of monumental proportions; it well deserved the name by which it was generally known and which it passed on to its successor; *Megale Ekkiesia*, the Great Church.

One might now sit and rest for awhile in the columnar garden behind Haghia Sophia, perhaps to reflect upon the past of the magnificent edifice one has just visited.

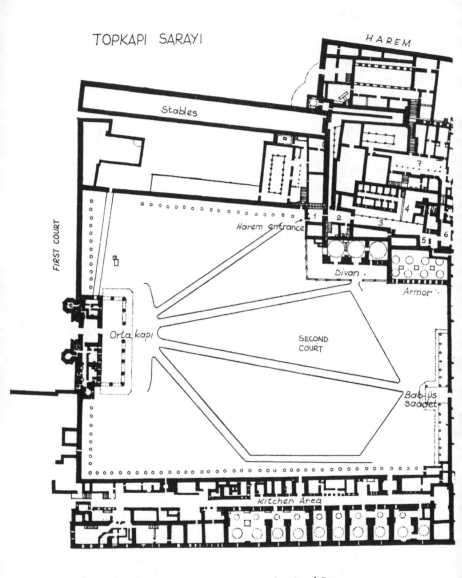

TOPKAPI SARAYI

HAREM

Stables

FIRST COURT

Harem entrance

Orta kapı

SECOND COURT

Divan

Armor

Bab-üs Saadet

Kitchen Area

1. Room with Cupboards
2. Guard Room
3. Courtyard of the Black Eunuchs
4. Quarters of the Black Eunuchs
5. Cümle Kapısı (Main Entrance to the Harem)
6. Guard Room
7. Courtyard of Women Slaves
8. Courtyard of the Valide Sultan
9. Room with the Fireplace
10. Room with the Fountain

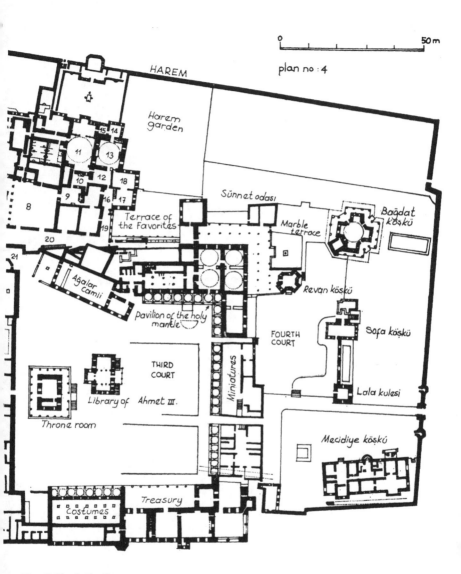

plan no : 4

11. Hall of the Emperor
12. Antechamber
13. Salon of Murat III
14. Library of Ahmet I
15. Fruit-Room of Ahmet III

16. Passage
17.-18. Double Pavillion
19. Consultation Place of the Jinns
20. Golden Road
21. Birdcage Gate (Harem Exit)

4

Topkapı Sarayı

Topkapı Sarayı, the Great Palace of the Osmanlı Sultans, is the most extensive and fascinating monument of Ottoman civil architecture in existence. In addition to its architectural and historical interest, it contains, as a museum, superb and unrivalled collections of porcelains, armour, fabrics, jewels, illuminated manuscripts, calligraphy, and many objects of art formerly belonging to the sultans. A cursory visit requires several hours; to know it thoroughly many weeks would hardly suffice.

When Mehmet the Conqueror, known to the Turks as Fatih Sultan Mehmet, captured Constantinople in 1453, he found the former palaces of the Byzantine Emperors in such ruins as to be uninhabitable. He therefore selected a large overgrown area on the Third Hill as the site of his palace, the district where now stand the central buildings of the University of Istanbul and the great complex of the Süleymaniye. Here he erected an extensive palace which later came to be known as Eski Saray, or the Old Palace. For only a few years later, in 1459, he decided to build a new palace at the northern end of the First Hill; the area once occupied by the ancient acropolis of Byzantium. To do so he cut off the point of the Constantinopolitan triangle by building a massive defence-wall, guarded by towers, which extended from the Byzantine sea-walls along the Golden Horn to those along the Marmara. (The palace eventually took its name from the main sea-gate in these defence-walls; this was Topkapı, the Cannon Gate, so-called because it bristled with armaments. This twin-towered gateway formerly stood at Saray Point, but it was destroyed in the nineteenth century.) The area thus enclosed must be approximately identical with the ancient city of Byzantium before its successive enlargements. Fatih Mehmet constructed his palace on the high ground, or acropolis; on the slopes of the hill and along the seashore he laid out extensive parks and gardens. He could not have chosen a more magnificent site in the city. As Evliya Çelebi remarked of it more than three centuries ago: "Never hath a more delightful residence been erected by the art of man."

Of the Palace as we know it today, almost the entire plan, with the exception of the Harem and the so-called Fourth Court, was laid out and built by Fatih between 1459 and 1465. The Harem in its present state belongs largely to the time of Murat III (r. 1574–95), with extensive reconstructions and additions chiefly under Mehmet IV (r. 1648–87) and Osman III (r. 1754–7); while the isolated pavilions of the Fourth Court date from various periods. On three occasions, in 1574, 1665 and 1856, very serious fires devastated large sections of the Palace, so that while the three main courts have preserved essentially the arrangement given them by Fatih, many of the buildings have either disappeared (as most of those in the First Court) or been reconstructed and redecorated in later periods.

The Palace of Topkapı must not be thought of merely as the private residence of the Sultan and his court, for it was much more than that. It was the seat of the supreme executive and judicial council of the Empire, the Divan, and it housed the largest and most select of the training schools for the imperial civil service, the Palace School. The various divisions of the Saray correspond pretty clearly with these various functions. The First Court, which was open to the public, was the service area for the Palace. It contained a hospital, a bakery, an arsenal, the mint and outer treasury, and a large number of storage places and dormitories for guards and domestics of the Outer Service, those whose duties did not ordinarily bring them into the private, residential areas of the Palace. The Second Court was the seat of the Divan, devoted to the public administration of the Empire; it could be entered by anyone who had business to transact with the Council. Beyond this court to right and left were certain other service areas: the kitchens and privy stables. The Third Court, strictly reserved for officials of the Court and Government, was largely given over to various divisions of the Palace School, but also contained some of the chambers of the selamlık, or reception rooms of the Sultan. The Harem, specifically the women's quarter of the Palace, had additional rooms of the selamlık, the men's quarter of the palace, and the

Sultan's private apartments, as well as quarters for the Black Eunuchs. The Fourth Court was a large enclosed garden on various levels with occasional pleasure domes. The total number of people permanently resident in the Saray was between 4,000 and 5,000.

THE FIRST COURT

The main entrance to the Palace, now as always, is through the Imperial Gate, Bab-ı Hümayun, opposite the north-east corner of Haghia Sophia and the fountain of Ahmet III (see Chapter 5). The great gatehouse is basically the work of Fatih Mehmet, though it has radically changed its appearance in the course of the centuries. Originally there was a second storey, demolished in 1867 when Abdül Aziz surrounded the gate with the present marble frame and lined the niches on either side with marble. The side niches were once used for the display of the severed heads of offenders of importance. The rooms in the gateway were for the Kapıcıs, or corps of guards, of whom 50 were perpetually on duty. The older part of the arch contains four beautiful inscriptions, one recording the erection of the gate by Mehmet the Conqueror in 1478, the other three quotations from the Kuran. The tuğra, or imperial monogram, is that of Mahmut II, and other inscriptions record the remodelling by Abdül Aziz in 1867.

On entering through the Bab-ı Hümayun, we find ourselves in the First Court, often called the Courtyard of the Janissaries. On the right as one enters, there once stood the famous infirmary for the pages of the Palace School. Beyond this, a road leads down to the gardens of the outer palace, filled with Byzantine substructures and modern military installations. The rest of the right-hand side of that Court consists of a blank wall behind which were the palace bakeries, famous for the superfine white bread baked for the Sultan and the chosen few on whom he bestowed it; these buildings, several times burned down and reconstructed, now serve as workrooms for the museum.

On the left or west side of the Court, between the outer wall and the church of Haghia Eirene, once stood a quadrangle which housed the Straw Weavers and the Carriers of Silver Pitchers, and whose courtyard served as a storage place for the firewood of the Palace.

Part of this has been excavated, revealing Byzantine substructures; these and the church of Haghia Eirene, converted by Fatih into an arsenal, are described in Chapter 5. North of the church, behind a high wall, are buildings once used as the Imperial Mint and the Outer Treasury. Beside these a road runs down to the museums and the public gardens of the Saray. The rest of this side of the Court was occupied by barracks for domestics of the Outer Service, a mosque, and storerooms; these, doubtless largely constructed of wood, have completely disappeared.

We now approach the Bab-üs Selam or Gate of Salutations, generally known as Orta Kapı, or the Middle Gate. This is a much more impressive gateway than the first, very typical of the military architecture of Fatih's time with its octagonal towers and conical tops. This was the entrance to the Inner Palace where everyone had to dismount, for no one but the Sultan was allowed to ride beyond this point. In the wall to the right of the gate is the Executioner's Fountain (Cellat Çeşmesi); here the executioner washed his hands and sword after a decapitation, which usually took place just outside the gate. Nearby are two Example Stones (İbret Taşları) for displaying the heads of important culprits. Here one comes to the public entrance to the Topkapı Sarayı Museum where, after purchasing a ticket, one enters the Second Court.

THE SECOND COURT

This Court, still very much as it was when Fatih laid it out, is a tranquil cloister of imposing proportions, planted with venerable cypress trees; several fountains once adorned it and mild-eyed gazelles pastured on the glebe. Except for the rooms of the Divan and the Inner Treasury in the north-west corner there are no buildings in this court, which consists simply of blank walls faced by colonnaded porticoes with antique marble columns and Turkish capitals. Beyond the colonnade the whole of the eastern side is occupied by the kitchens of the palace, while beyond the western colonnade are the Privy Stables and the quarters of the Halberdiers-with-Tresses.

The Court of the Divan seems to have been designed essentially for the pageantry connected with the transaction of the public business of the Empire. Here four times a week the Divan, or Imperial Council, met to deliberate on administrative affairs or to discharge its judicial functions. On such occasions the whole courtyard was filled with a vast throng of magnificently dressed officials and the corps of Palace guards and Janissaries, at least 5,000 on ordinary days, but more than 10,000 when ambassadors were received or other extraordinary business was transacted. Even at such times an almost absolute silence reigned throughout the courtyard, a silence commented on with astonishment by the travellers who witnessed it.

The inside of the Bab-üs Selam has an elaborate but oddly irregular portico of ten columns with a widely overhanging roof, unfortunately badly repainted in the nineteenth century. To the right is a crude but useful bird's-eye view of the Saray which helps one to get one's bearings. The rooms on either side of the gate had various uses: guardrooms, the executioner's room with a prison attached, waiting-rooms for ambassadors and others attending an audience with the Grand Vezir or Sultan.

From the gate, five paths radiate to various parts of the Court. Let us first visit – as is only right – the Divan. This, together with the Inner Treasury, projects from the north-west corner and is dominated by the square tower with a conical roof which is such a conspicuous feature of the Saray from many points in the city. This complex dates in essentials from Fatih's time, though much altered at subsequent periods. The tower was lower in Fatih's day and had a pyramidal roof, the present structure with its Corinthian columns having been added by Mahmut II in 1820.

The complex consists of the Council Chamber or Divan proper, the Public Records Office and the Office of the Grand Vezir. The first two open widely into one another by a great arch; each is square and domed. Both were redecorated in the time of Ahmet III in a rather charming rococo style, but the Council Chamber was restored in 1945 to its appearance in the reign of Murat III, who had restored it after the great fire of 1574. The lower walls are revetted in Iznik tiles of the best period, while the upper parts, the vaults and the dome, retain faded traces of their original arabesque painting. Around three sides of the room run low couches covered with carpets. Here sat the members of the Council; the Grand Vezir in the centre opposite the door, the other Lords of Council on either side of him in strict order of rank. Over the Grand Vezir's seat is a grilled window giving into a small room in the tower; here the sultans, after they had ceased to attend meetings of the Divan, could overhear the proceedings unseen. The Records Office has retained its eighteenth-century decor; here were kept records that might be needed at Council meetings. From here a door led to the Grand Vezir's office, though the present entrance is from under the elaborate portico with richly painted rococo ceiling.

Adjacent to these three rooms is the Inner Treasury, a long room with eight domes in four pairs supported by three massive piers. Here and in the vaults below was stored the treasure of the Empire as it arrived from the provinces, and here it was kept until the quarterly pay-days for the use of the Council, the payment of officials, Janissaries and others; at the end of each quarter what remained unspent was transferred to the Imperial Treasury in the Third Court. In this room is now displayed the Saray's collection of arms and armour. As one would expect, this is especially rich in Turkish armour of all periods, including much that belonged to the sultans themselves, and outstanding pieces of booty from foreign conquests in Europe, Asia and Africa.

Retracing our steps under the loggia of the Divan, we come to a door almost underneath the tower. This is the Carriage Gate, one of the two main entrances to the Harem; we shall return to it later after visiting the rest of the palace first. The remainder of the west side of the Court is occupied by a long portico where are displayed various Turkish inscriptions assembled from different places. A small door in this wall near the Carriage Gate leads to the quarters of the Halberdiers-with-Tresses (Zülüflü Baltacılar), so called because two false curls or tresses hung down from their tall hats in front of their eyes. This strange headgear was devised so that the Halberdiers, who on occasion delivered firewood to the Harem, could not get a good view of the odalisques! The quarters of the Halberdiers-with-Tresses are as picturesque as their name, but they are not open to the public.

At the south end of this portico, a door called the Gate of the Dead (Meyyit Kapısı), because through it were borne the bodies of those who died in the Saray, leads down to the area of the Privy Stables on the lower slope of the hill. We come first to the mid-eighteenth-century mosque of Beşir Ağa. This is chiefly interesting for its curious minaret corbelled out from a corner of the building; the minaret has no balcony but, instead, an enclosed space at the top with openings for the müezzin to make the call to prayer. The Privy Stables (Has Ahır), which housed only 20 or 30 horses for the use of the Sultan and his favourite pages, occupied the long building which runs from end to end of this area. Built by Fatih, it consists of two parts, the long stables themselves and at the far end two smaller rooms, that of the Imrahor, or Master of the Horse, and the Raht Hazinesi, or Harness Treasury, for the bejewelled harnesses and trappings. These are very pretty rooms, one with a charming eighteenth-century painted ceiling, the other domed and with a quaint gallery. In both are now displayed the valuable imperial harnesses, while the long stable now houses carriages, mostly of the nineteenth century and not very interesting.

Returning to the Orta Kapi, we now take the right-hand path towards the kitchens. On the way we notice an enormous fifth- or sixth-century Byzantine capital, dug up here in the 1960s. If we enter the kitchen area by the southernmost gate, we find another capital of the same type, slightly smaller but more interestingly carved. Both capitals obviously bore statues, but whose statues and why they came to be buried in the Saray are still unanswered questions.

Beyond the three gates a long, narrow courtyard or open passageway runs the entire length of the area. The palace kitchens open off from this on the right; on the left are the storerooms for food and utensils and rooms for the various categories of cooks, as well as two mosques. The southern part of the area and rooms on the left have been much reconstructed in modern times and are used as museum storehouses and offices. The kitchens consist of a long series of ten spacious rooms with lofty domes on the Marmara side – a conspicuous feature of the Istanbul skyline – and equally lofty dome-like chimneys on the side of the courtyard. The two southernmost

domes go back to Fatih's time, the other eight to that of Beyazit
II, while the cone-like chimneys in front of them are additions by
Sinan, who reconstructed much of this area for Murat III after the
devastating fire of 1574. Each kitchen had a separate use: for the
Sultan, for the Valide, the eunuchs, the harem ladies, the Divan, and
so on; but the assignments varied from time to time.

Today the kitchens are used for the display of the Saray's
incomparable collection of Chinese porcelain and other china and
glass. The Chinese collection is said to be the third richest and most
varied in the world, surpassed only by those at Beijing and Dresden.
Begun by Beyazit II, augmented by Selim I and above all by Süleyman
the Magnificent, the pieces date from the wonderful celadons of the
Sung and Yuan dynasties (A.D. 960–1368) to the later Ming of
the eighteenth century. The European specimens, Limoges, Sèvres,
Meissen and others, are less impressive. In the last two kitchens
there is a fascinating collection of antique kitchen utensils, including
platters, bowls, ladles and kazans, or bronze cauldrons of prodigious
size, all of which were once used in the Saray kitchens. The small
building with three domes at the north end of the courtyard is
variously described as the confectioner's mosque or as an olive-oil
refinery and soap manufactory; doubtless it served different purposes
at different times. It now houses an interesting collection of Turkish
glass from the Beykoz and other Istanbul factories of the eighteenth
and nineteenth centuries, some of it very lovely.

Leaving the kitchen precincts, we approach the third gate, the
Bab-üs Saadet, or Gate of Felicity, the entrance to the strictly
private parts of the Palace. The gate itself must go back to the time
of Fatih, though it was reconstructed in the later sixteenth century
and thoroughly redecorated in a rococo style in the eighteenth.
At the time of his accession and on bayrams, the Sultan sat here on
his gold and emerald throne to receive the homage of his subjects
and officials.

THE THIRD COURT

Just beyond the inner threshold of the Bab-üs Saadet stands the Arz
Odası, or Throne Room. Although in the Third Court, it belongs by

function and use rather to the Second, for here was played out the last act of the ceremonies connected with the meetings of the Divan. Here, at the end of each session of the council, the Grand Vezir and the other high functionaries waited on the Sultan and reported to him upon the business transacted and the decisions taken, which could not be considered final until they had received the royal assent. Here also the ambassadors of foreign powers were presented at their arrival and leave-taking. The Throne Room occupies a small building with a heavy and widely overhanging roof supported on a colonnade of antique marble columns. The foundations date from Fatih's time, but most of the superstructure belongs to that of Selim I; inscriptions record restorations by Ahmet III and Mahmut II. The room was restored yet again in more recent times, after being badly damaged in the fire of 1856. On either side of the entrance portal are panels of yellow and green tiles in the charming *cuerda seca* technique of the early Iznik period in the sixteenth century, and nearby is a fountain placed there by Süleyman. The building is divided into a small antechamber on the right and the throne room proper on the left. The magnificent canopy of the throne, dated by an inscription to A.H. 1005 (A.D. 1596) in the reign of Mehmet III, and a gilt-bronze chimney-piece nearby, are the only parts of the decoration that survived the nineteenth-century fire. The throne was hung with magnificent bejewelled embroideries for different occasions; some of these are on display in the Treasury.

Apart from the Throne Room, the Treasury and the Pavilion of the Holy Mantle, all the buildings in and around this Third Court were devoted to the Halls of the Palace School. The School was organized in six divisions or Halls: the two introductory schools, Küçük Oda (Small Hall) and Büyük Oda (Large Hall), occupied the entire southern side of the court to left and right, respectively, of the Bab-üs Saadet. Here were the quarters of the White Eunuchs and their Ağa, who were in charge of the administration and discipline of the School. If a youth was talented in any direction, he would pass from this introductory school to one of the four vocational Halls. The Seferli Koğuşu, or Campaign Hall, stands on the raised part of the east side of the Court, formerly surrounded on the sides and back by

the baths of Selim III, the principal hamam of the school. The northen
side of the Court, opposite the Bab-üs Saadet, was occupied by the
Hazine Koğuşu, the Hall of the Treasury, next to the Treasury itself,
and the Kiler Koğuşu, the Hall of the Commissariat. Finally, the last
and highest of the vocational schools, the Has Oda Koğuşu, the Hall
of the Privy Chamber, occupies a large building on the west side of the
Court between the Pavilion of the Holy Mantle and Ağalar Camii.

This elaborately organized school for the training of the Imperial
Civil Service appears to be unique in the Islamic world. It was founded
and its principles laid down by Fatih, though later sultans added
to and modified it. The pages who attended the school came from
the Christian minorities of the Empire and likely youths captured
in war. They entered at various ages from 12 to 18 and received a
vigorous training, intellectual and physical, which in contrast to the
usual Islamic education was largely secular and designed to prepare
the students for the administration of the Empire. There can be no
doubt that the brilliant success of the Ottoman state in the earlier
centuries of its existence was to a large extent due to the training its
administrators received in this school.

Tuning to the right from Bab-üs Saadet, we pass the building
which was once the Büyük Oda. This building burned down in 1856
but has since been reconstructed and is now used for museum offices.
We then come to Seferli Koğuşu, preceded by a domed colonnade
supported by a row of very handsome Byzantine columns in verd
antique. The Hall is a long room divided into three aisles by two
rows of pillars and barrel-vaulted. It houses the Imperial Wardrobe,
a fascinating collection of costumes of the sultans from Fatih's time
onward. There are over 1,300 of them, of which many of the most
interesting are on display. All of the older ones are of the kaftan type,
a long robe reaching to the feet made of silk, satin or velvet brocade
in brilliant colours and bold design, often lined or trimmed with
fur; many are of outstanding beauty and nearly all are in perfect
condition.

The rest of the eastern side of the Court is taken up with the
rooms, on a slightly lower level, of the köşk or pavilion of Mehmet the
Conqueror, which served him and several later sultans as a selamlık,

or suite of reception rooms. The vaults below were used as the Privy Treasury and gradually the rooms themselves were turned over to the Treasury as storerooms. It is curious that these rooms, some of the finest in the Palace and with an unrivalled view, should from the seventeenth century onwards have been used as mere storerooms, even the superb open loggia at the corner having at one time been walled in. The loggia has been opened again and the rooms are used for the display of the Palace treasures: four great thrones encrusted with precious stones, of which the huge golden one studded with emeralds (actually chrysolites) was used on bayrams and other state occasions right down to the end of the Empire; bejewelled swords and daggers, objects of jade and other semi-precious stones often mounted in gold, caskets overflowing with uncut emeralds and rubies, and hundreds of other precious objects of gold and jewels. It is altogether an astonishing collection, admirably mounted and displayed.

In the centre of the Court, standing by itself, is the Library of Ahmet III, erected in 1719 near the site of an older pavilion with a pool. It is an elegant little building of Proconnesian marble consisting of a domed area flanked by three loggias with sofas and cupboards for books, and though of the eighteenth century the decoration is still almost wholly classical.

The two main buildings on the north side of the Court were both damaged in the fire of 1856; the nearer one was entirely reconstructed and now serves as offices for the Director of the Museum. The farther one, beyond a passage leading to the Fourth Court, houses the exhibition of Turkish and Persian miniatures. From an artistic point of view this is perhaps the supreme treasure of the Saray; the collection of miniatures is said to number more than 13,000. Here one finds exhibited, in addition to the celebrated paintings of the Fatih Album and examples of the various Persian schools, a large collection of the Turkish school, including a beautiful and touching portrait of Süleyman in old age by Nigâri and portraits by the same artist of Barbarossa and of Selim II. The *Hünername* and the *Surname* manuscripts are justly celebrated: the former deals with the hunting prowess of the sultans, the latter with the fabulous circumcision ceremonies of Prince Mehmet, son of Mehmet III, which lasted for

52 days in the Hippodrome; both are lavishly illustrated. Among the later works the single figures of men and women by Levni are bewitching for their elegance and wit.

The west side of the Court is occupied by the following buildings: the Pavilion of the Holy Mantle, the Hall of the Privy Chamber, the Mosque of the Ağas, and one of the two main entrances to the Harem. The first and last of these we shall visit presently; meantime a few words will suffice for the two middle ones. The Has Oda Koğuşu, or Hall of the Privy Chamber, was the highest of the vocational divisions of the Palace School, limited to 40 pages in immediate attendance upon the Sultan, including the highest of the officials in the Inner Palace. Here is displayed a part of the collection of manuscripts, not miniatures this time but admirable calligraphy, of all periods and all schools. Beyond the Has Oda, the building that juts out at an angle is Ağalar Camii, the principal mosque of the Palace School. Though dating in origin from the time of Fatih, it has been much remodelled and now houses the Library of the Saray.

We now return to the Pavilion of the Holy Mantle, or Hırka-i Saadet Dairesi, where are preserved the relics of the Prophet Muhammed. These relics, of which the Prophet's Mantle is the most sacred, were brought from Egypt by Selim I after his conquest of that country in 1517, when he assumed the title of Caliph. For centuries they were guarded here religiously and displayed on state occasions only to the Sultan, his family and his immediate entourage; in 1962 the present exhibit was arranged and opened to the public. The Pavilion itself consists of four domed rooms forming a square, with a fifth domed room opening off to the left. In foundation and plan at least, it goes back to Fatih's time; at that time and until the nineteenth century it formed part of the Has Oda, or selamlık. Murat III partly reconstructed the rooms and embellished them with tiles, and Mahmut II added some not very happy touches.

One enters into a room with a pretty fountain under the dome, which opens by a huge arch into the second room. Here are displayed the bow of the Prophet Muhammed and the swords of the first four Caliphs, Abu Bekr, Umar, Othman and 'Ali; farther on is one of the doors of the great mosque at Mecca. In the room to the left are some beautiful ancient Kurans; the solid gold covering for the Hacer-i Esved, the stone which fell from heaven and is built into the Kaaba at Mecca; also water-gutters from Mecca of chased and moulded silver-gilt, and other precious objects. Returning to the room with the fountain, we pass into another chamber where are preserved the more personal relics of the Prophet: hairs from his beard, one of his teeth, his footprint, his seal, and so on. Through a grilled door in this room one looks into (one cannot enter) the room where the Holy Mantle itself is preserved in a golden coffer under a magnificent golden baldachino, and in another coffer is the Holy Standard, unfurled at times when a holy war was declared against the infidel. This room has the most superb tiles of the greatest Iznik period, but has been somewhat marred by the heavy rococo fireplace added by Mahmut II.

Leaving the room by the door opposite that by which we entered, we find ourselves in the open L-shaped Portico of Columns. This portico surrounds two sides of the Pavilion of the Mantle and opens onto a marble terrace bordering a pool with a fountain; at one end is the Rivan Köşkü, at the other the Circumcision Room. This is one of the most charming parts of the Palace and commands excellent views of Pera and the Golden Horn. It was here that Thomas Dallam set up the famous mechanical organ which Queen Elizabeth I had sent as a gift to Sultan Mehmet III. The Rivan Köşkü at the east end of the portico was built in 1636 by Murat IV to commemorate his capture of Rivan, or Arivan, in Persia. It is a cruciform room entirely revetted with Iznik tiles dating from just after the greatest period but still beautiful; the outside has a polychrome revetment of marble. At the other end of the portico is the Circumcision Room (Sünnet Odası) built by the mad Sultan Ibrahim in 1641; it is entirely sheathed inside and out in tiles. They are rather a puzzle, for they date from several different periods from the greatest Iznik style in *cuerda seca* technique through the great period in the second half of the sixteenth and early seventeenth centuries; few if any belong to the time of Ibrahim himself; as it is they form a sort of museum of Turkish tiles of the best periods. The marble terrace with the pool is the meeting place of the Third and Fourth Courts.

THE FOURTH COURT

The Fourth Court is not really a courtyard but a garden on various levels, adorned with köşks or pavilions. In the centre of the balustrade of the marble terrace stands the Iftariye, a baldachino with a magnificent gilt-bronze canopy erected by Sultan Ibrahim in 1640. The balcony receives its name from the *iftar,* or evening meal, which is taken after sunset in the holy month of Ramazan. Beyond it stands the famous Baghdad Köşkü, a sort of grander replica of the Rivan Köşkü, built by Murat IV in 1639 to commemorate his capture of Baghdad. Cruciform like the other, it, too, is sheathed in tiles both within and without and is surrounded by a columned portico. The tiles are chiefly blue and white and some may antedate the köşk itself. Its enormous bronze chimney-piece is very fine and its dome splendid with elaborate arabesques on a crimson ground, painted on leather.

A staircase beside the pool leads down into what was once the tulip garden of Ahmet III. This garden was the site of the famous tulip festivals of the Lâle Devri, the Age of Tulips, that delightful epoch in the first half of the eighteenth century. It is still a pretty garden and on the north side is a charming rococo köşk called Sofa Köşkü, or sometimes, for no good reason, the Köşk of Kara Mustafa Paşa. It seems to have been built or thoroughly reconstructed by Ahmet III, doubtless to enjoy his tulips from, and again redecorated in 1752 by Mahmut I; it is a very pretty example of Turkish rococo. Farther on is a low tower called variously Başlala Kulesi and Hekimbaşı Odası, the Tower of the Head Tutor or the Chamber of the Head Physician; it doubtless served different purposes at different periods. Across a road that leads down to the outer gardens, there stands on a marble terrace the Mecidiye Köşkü, the latest addition to the buildings of the Saray. This was constructed in about 1840 by Abdül Mecit I, not long before he built the Palace of Dolmabahçe on the Bosphorus; it is entirely western in style. On its lower floor and terrace, overlooking the Marmara, there is an excellent restaurant; if one has spent the morning in the Saray one would do well to fortify oneself here before visiting the Harem.

THE HAREM

We now return to the Court of the Divan to visit the Harem, the public entrance to which is through the Carriage Gate under the Divan tower. The Harem is a veritable labyrinth of passages, courtyards, gardens, staircases and rooms – some 300 of them almost all surprisingly small – on half a dozen levels. It includes not only the women's quarters or Harem proper, but also the quarters of the Black Eunuchs who were in charge of the Harem, rooms and schoolhouses for the young princes, the Sultan's private apartments, and the apartments called the Cage (Kafes) where the Sultan's brothers lived in relatively honourable confinement. To inspect it all even cursorily would take many days of arduous exploration. Perhaps fortunately, only about two dozen rooms, passages and courtyards are at present open to the public, including most of the more important and impressive ones; the rest of the area is still undergoing restoration. We shall therefore confine this account principally to those rooms which are now open.

The Harem was not an original part of the Palace as laid out by Fatih Mehmet. Fatih seems to have designed Topkapı Sarayı as a kind of glorified office-building for the transaction of the public business of the Empire and for the training of the Civil Service, reserving the Eski Saray on the Third Hill for his domestic life, his wives and concubines. His immediate successors, Beyazit II, Selim I and Süleyman the Magnificent for most of his reign, maintained this arrangement. Süleyman is said to have allowed his wife Roxelana (Haseki Hürrem) to install herself in Topkapı Sarayı, but probably in wooden pavilions, like many of those at the Eski Saray; and their son, Selim II, seems to have followed suit. At all events, the earliest buildings in the Harem which can be definitely dated belong to the reign of Selim's son and successor, Murat III (r. 1574–95).

The Carriage Gate receives its name from the fact that the Harem ladies here entered their carriages whenever they were allowed to go for an outing. Above the gate there is an inscription giving the date A.H. 996 (A.D. 1588). The gateway opens into a small, dark room called Dolaplı Kubbe, the Dome with Cupboards, and this is followed by a room revetted with quite fine tiles, which served as a

guard room. On the left a door opens to a long passage leading down
to the gardens of the Saray, and another gives access to the mosque of
the Black Eunuchs; while on the right a door opens into the Divan
tower. We now enter the long, narrow, open Courtyard of the Black
Eunuchs, also revetted with tiles and with a colonnade on the left,
behind which are the rooms of the eunuchs. Both the guard room
and the courtyard have inscriptions dated A.H. 1079 (A.D. 1668–9),
showing that these areas were reconstructed or redecorated by Mehmet
IV after the great fire of 1665. The living quarters of the Black Eunuchs
are arranged around an inner covered courtyard in three storey with a
tall fireplace at one end. There are ten or twelve little rooms on each
floor, but even so they must have been very crowded since there were
several hundred of them; doubtless they served in watches and slept in
relays. Returning to the open courtyard, we pass on the left a staircase
that leads up to the Princes' Schoolrooms where the young sons of
the Sultan received their instruction; these are pretty rooms with good
tiles, but they are not now open to the public. Just beyond, a door leads
to the apartments of the Chief Black Eunuch or Kızlar Ağası (literally
Lord of the Girls); he was a most important and powerful official in the
Harem, but his apartments (also closed) are very small and gloomy.

At the far end of the open courtyard is the Cümle Kapısı, or Main
Gate, into the Harem proper. It leads into a second guard room,
from the left side of which a long, narrow corridor stretches to the
open Courtyard of the Cariyeler, or women slaves. This courtyard is
a pleasant one with a colonnade on one side; round the far end of it
stretch the dormitories of the slaves on two floors. On the right are
three suites of rooms for the chief women officials of the Harem;
the Kahya Kadın, or Head Stewardess, an important functionary
who under the Sultan's mother ruled over the Harem; the Harem
treasurer; and the Harem laundress. Their rooms are very attractive,
domed and tiled, and with a good view over the gardens, not at all
like the stuffy rooms of the eunuchs. (One of these suites is open to
the public.) The long staircase just beyond the three suites leads down
to a large courtyard on a much lower level occupied by the Harem
hospital. It is very picturesque, but unfortunately it is not yet open
to the public.

Retracing our steps a little way we come to a short passage that leads to the large open Courtyard of the Valide Sultan. At the north-west corner of the courtyard a doorway leads into Ocaklı Oda, the Room with a Hearth, a tiled chamber dominated by a splendid bronze ocak, or chimney-piece. On the right a door leads into the apartments of the First and Second Kadıns, the two highest ranking wives of the Sultan. On the left a door opens into a smaller chamber called Çeşmeli Oda, the Room with a Fountain, named for the pretty çeşme that adorns one of its walls. This and Ocaklı Oda served as ante-rooms between the Harem and the Sultan's own apartments.

The apartments of the Valide Sultan occupy most of the west side of the courtyard that bears her name, with four rooms on the ground floor and four more above, all of them dating to 1666–7. The rooms on the ground floor, the only ones open to the public, are her salon, reception room, bedroom and sitting room. Her bedroom has Iznik tiles dated 1667, with floral panels of quite magnificent design for this reatively late date. A long and narrow hall known as the Corridor of the Baths leads north from the Valide's sitting room to the Sultan's apartments. This passes through an elaborate suite of rooms and baths, partly on two floors, separating the baths to the east from the living rooms to the west. There are two baths, the one on the south belonging to the Valide and the other to the Sultan. Only the Sultan's bath is open to the public. The two baths are almost identical, their decoration baroque but simple; the actual bathing place screened off by a gilt-bronze grille.

At its north end the Corridor of the Baths leads to the imperial reception room known as Hünkâr Sofası, the Hall of the Emperor, the largest and grandest room in the Palace. Divided by a great arch into two unequal sections, the larger section is domed, the smaller, slightly raised, with a balcony above. The upper part of the room – dome, pendentives and arches – has been restored to its original appearance in the late sixteenth century, while the lower part retains the baroque decorations with which Osman III (r. 1754–7) unfortunately adorned the entire room; the contrast is not altogether happy. This Hall was a reception room where the Sultan gave entertainments for the women of the Harem, the balcony being used by the musicians.

It was evidently built somewhat later than the adjacent Salon of Murat III, which is dated by an inscription to 1578. The tradition that this room, like Murat's, is by Sinan is not impossible; Murat may well have decided to add an even grander room to his already very beautiful suite. This great room is certainly worthy of Sinan and if not built by him cannot at all events be very much later.

We pass through a small but lavishly tiled antechamber into the Salon of Murat III, often but erroneously called his bedroom. This is undoubtedly the most beautiful room in the Saray, retaining the whole of its original decoration. The walls are sheathed in Iznik tiles at the apogee of their greatest period; the panel of plum blossoms surrounding the elegant bronze ocak is especially noteworthy, as is the calligraphic frieze that runs around the room. Opposite the ocak is an elaborate three-tiered fountain of carved polychrome marble set in a marble embrasure. But it is the perfect and harmonious proportions of the room as much as its superb decoration that lend it distinction and charm. As we have said, it was created by Sinan in 1578. Early in the next century (1608–9) Ahmet I added a pendant to it on the west, a much smaller room but domed and tiled almost as beautifully as Murat's. It looks out over the pool and garden and the much later marble terrace of Osman III, and the light reflected from the predominately blue-green tiles gives it a cool and aqueous atmosphere. A century later still (1705–6) Ahmet III added or re-decorated another tiny room to the south, called Yemiş Odası, or the Fruit Room, because of the painted panels of fruit with which the walls are decorated. This belongs to the high Tulip period and shows the first beginnings of European rococo influence; but of all the rococo rooms in the Palace this is surely the most bewitching.

We now retrace our steps through Murat's Salon and antechamber and come on the left to a pair of very beautiful rooms until recently identified as the Cage, the place of confinement of the Sultan's brothers. This was never a very convincing identification and has at last been definitely abandoned, the Cage being now identified with the many small and dark rooms on the upper floor over the Council Place of the Jinns, from the west end of which opens the first of the rooms we have come to. It is not known exactly when or why they were built, but they must date from the end of the sixteenth century or the first years of the seventeenth, for their tiles are of the very greatest period, indeed perhaps the most beautiful anywhere in the Palace. The first room has a dome magnificently painted on canvas; the ceiling of the inner room is flat but also superbly painted. And it has a wonderful brass-gilt fireplace, on each side of which, above, are two of the most gorgeous tile panels in existence. Beyond the fireplace the paving stones have been removed to reveal at a depth of 30 cm. or so another pavement and a surface of tiles, also of the great period but of a totally different design and colour from those which now line the room. This was the level of the antechamber to Murat's Salon, which was cut in half to provide space for this room. This chopping up of rooms in order to fit in new ones occurs frequently in the Harem, and although one would not willingly lack this room with its wonderful tiles, it does seem wanton to have so badly botched Sinan's antechamber.

We come out again into the colonnade known as the Council Place of the Jinns, a name which seems to have no traditional origin – perhaps the Sultan felt that since the incarcerated princes lived above it they might be taking council with the Jinns for his overthrow. The colonnaded way leads to a large open courtyard known as the Gözdeler Taşlığı, the Terrace of the Favourites, which overlooks the lower gardens of the palace. The apartments of the Sultan's favourites were in the long suite of rooms on the upper floor of the building to the rear of the courtyard. These rooms are still undergoing restoration and are not open to the public. When we first saw them in the early 1960s these apartments looked as if they had been untouched since their last occupants left when the Harem was officially closed in 1909, deserted and hung with cobwebs, inhabited with the ghosts of those who lived there in the past. The windows were shuttered and the rooms were in almost total darkness; we could see the dull gleam of an old brass bedstead under a tottering canopy, and discern the forms of sagging divans draped in rotting cloth. The dust-covered mirror of an old dressing-table reflected the dark image of a deserted room.

At the far end of the Hall of the Favourites there is a sitting-room once used by the Sultan when he came to call on his ladies. It has a pleasant balcony from which the Sultan could look out over the gardens of the Saray and across the Golden Horn to the green hills of Pera on the other side. In all the Saray there could have been no more agreeable place for the Sultan to enjoy his *keyif* than there, cooled by gentle breezes from the Bosphorus, watching the lights twinkling like captive constellations on the hills of his beautiful city, listening to the soft voices of his women whispering along the Hall of the Favourites. It is no wonder that they once called this place Darüssaadet, or the House of Felicity.

Tours of the Harem end at the Gözdeler Taşlığı, and from there we head back to the exit. We follow the Golden Road, passing the staircase where in the year 1809 the slave girl Cevri Khalfa fought off the assassins who were trying to kill Prince Mahmut, the future Sultan Mahmut II. We then pass through the Cümle Kapısı, the main gate of the Harem, and turn left twice to pass through Kuşhane Kapısı, the Birdcage Gate, where in 1651 the Sultan Valide Kösem was killed by the Chief Black Eunuch, Tall Süleyman. Here we leave the Harem and return to the Third Court, having completed our stroll through the House of Felicity.

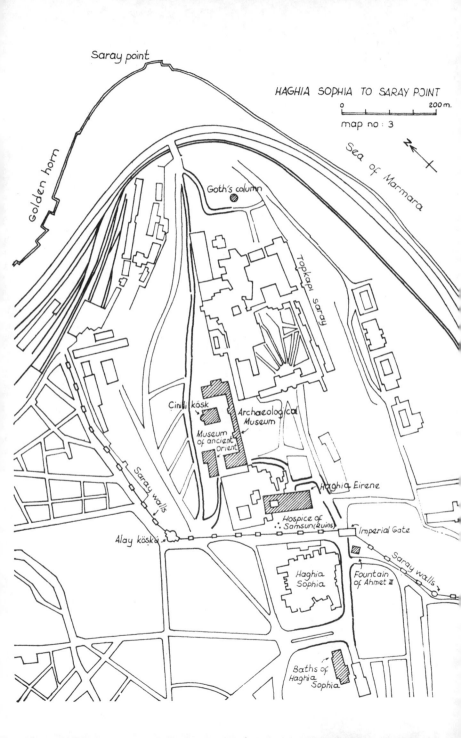

Saray point

Golden horn

HAGHIA SOPHIA TO SARAY POINT

0   200 m.

map no: 3

Sea of Marmara

Goth's column

Topkapi Saray

Çinili kösk

Archaeological Museum

Museum of ancient Orient

Saray walls

Haghia Eirene

Hospice of Samsun (ruins)

Alay köskü

Imperial Gate

Saray walls

Haghia Sophia

Fountain of Ahmet III

Baths of Haghia Sophia

5

Through the Outer Gardens of the Saray

Our present stroll will take us from Haghia Sophia through the outer courtyard of the Saray and its lower gardens. This area, at the very apex of the old city, is almost totally cut off from the turbulent life of modern Stamboul, shielded as it is by outer walls of the Saray. Walking through these quiet gardens, it is difficult to imagine that this was the site of the ancient town of Byzantium.

We shall begin our stroll in the great square before Haghia Sophia, the heart of the ancient town. Before we leave the square we should at least glance at a building which most tourists miss, prominent as it is, probably because it is dwarfed by the imposing monuments around it. This is the Hamam of Haseki Hürrem, which stands at the eastern side of the park between Haghia Sophia and the Blue Mosque. This splendid bath was commissioned by Süleyman the Magnificent in the name of his wife Haseki Hürrem, better known in the West as Roxelana. The hamam was designed by Süleyman's Chief Architect, the great Sinan, and completed by him in the year 1556; it is perhaps the finest bath which Sinan built in his long and illustrious career. It is a double hamam, one end being for men, the other for women. Each end consists of a great entrance hall with a vast dome; from here one passes through a corridor with three small domes to the hararet, also domed and surrounded by a series of little chambers for washing. Notice the charming symmetry of the building and its gracious lines; it is the most attractive and one of the most elaborate of the Turkish baths in the city. The hamam has been splendidly restored, and it is now open to the public as a gallery for the display of modern Turkish carpets.

It is interesting to learn that the Hamam of Haseki Hürrem stands near the site of the ancient Baths of Zeuxippus, first built by Septimius Severus in about A.D. 196 and later enlarged by Constantine the Great. Excavations carried out in this area in the years 1927–8 brought to light early Byzantine foundations which some scholars have identified as belonging to this bath, the most celebrated in ancient Constantinople. These remains, which have since been covered up, are about midway between Haghia Sophia and the Blue Mosque.

We now leave the square and pass behind the apse of Haghia Sophia. The street on which we are now walking was known in Byzantium as the Embolos of the Holy Well. This was a porticoed way by which the Emperor could walk from the Palace of Chalke to the Holy Well, which was located at the south-east corner of Haghia Sophia. From there the Emperor could enter Haghia Sophia, passing through the large gate which we can still see in the east bay of the south aisle. The area to the right of this street is now under excavation by the Archaeological Museum, where extensive remains of the Great Palace of Byzantium (see Chapter 6) have been unearthed. The site will soon be open to the public.

Farther along this street, at the north-east corner of the church, we come to a large Turkish gate in rococo style. This is the back door to the precincts of Haghia Sophia and leads to a building which was once the skeuophylakion, or treasury of the church. The building is not open to the public. To the left is Soğuk Çeşme Sokağı, the Street of the Cold Fountain, where a row of elegant nineteenth-century Turkish houses is built up against the outer defence wall of Topkapı Sarayı. These houses were restored from near ruin in 1984–6 by the Turkish Touring and Automobile Association (TTAA), headed by Çelik Gülersoy, and now form the Aysofya Pansoyonlar. One of the houses is now the library of the Çelik Gülersoy Foundation, an extraordinary collection of books, maps, engravings and paintings of Istanbul in Ottoman times.

FOUNTAIN OF AHMET III

We are now in the square before the Imperial Gate of Topkapı Sarayı. In the centre of this square we see the grandest and most handsome of all the street-fountains in Istanbul. This fountain was built by Sultan Ahmet III in 1728 and is a particularly fine example of Turkish rococo architecture. It is a square structure with an overhanging roof surmounted by five small domes. On each of the four sides there is a çeşme, or wall-fountain, and at each of four corners a sebil. Each of the wall-fountains is set into a niche framed in an ogival archway. The voussoirs of the arches are in alternating red and pink marble and the façade is richly decorated with floral designs in low relief. The corner sebils are semicircular in form, each having three windows framed by engaged marble columns and enclosed with ornate bronze grilles. The curved wall above and below each sebil is delicately carved and elaborately decorated with relieved designs and ornate inscriptions. Above each of the four fountains there is a long and beautiful inscription in gold letters on a blue-green ground; the text is by the celebrated poet Seyit Vehbi, who is here praising the fountain and comparing its waters with those of the holy spring Zemzem and of the sacred selsebils of Paradise. The inscription ends with these modest lines: "Seyit Vehbi Efendi, the most distinguished among the word-wizards of the age, strung these pearls on the thread of his verse and joined together the two lines of the chronographic distich, like two sweet almonds breast to breast: With what a wall has Sultan Ahmet dammed the waters / For astonishment stopped the flood in the midst of its course!"

HAGHİA EİRENE

Passing through the Imperial Gate into the first courtyard of the Saray, we see a little way forward on the left the rose-red apse of a Byzantine church. This is Haghia Eirene, the former church of the Divine Peace. According to tradition, the original church of Haghia Eirene was one of the first Christian churches in the old town of Byzantium. The church was rebuilt on a larger scale by Constantine the Great or his son Constantius, and it served as the patriarchal cathedral until the completion of the first church of Haghia Sophia. During the reign of Constantius, Haghia Eirene was at the centre of the violent disputes then taking place between the Arians and the Orthodox party, the upholders of the Nicene Creed, and in the year

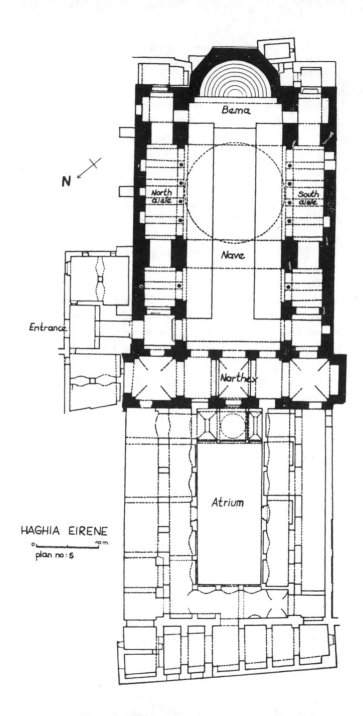

Bema

N

North aisle

South aisle

Nave

Entrance

Narthex

Atrium

HAGHIA EIRENE

0 ⌊————⌋ 10 m.

plan no: 5

346 more than 3,000 people were killed in a religious riot in the courtyard of the church. The final triumph of the Orthodox party came in Haghia Eirene in the year 381, when the Second Ecumenical Council there reaffirmed the Nicene Creed and condemned the Arians as heretics. Haghia Eirene again came into prominence after the destruction of Haghia Sophia in the year 404, when for a decade it again served as the patriarchal cathedral. But then, after the reconstruction of Haghia Sophia by Theodosius II, Haghia Eirene took its accustomed second place and seldom thereafter played a leading role in the religious life of the city. At the time of the Nika Revolt in 532, Haghia Eirene shared the fate of Haghia Sophia, when the two churches were totally destroyed by fire. Justinian immediately afterwards began to rebuild Haghia Eirene along with Haghia Sophia, and both churches were rededicated at about the same time, in the year 537. The new churches of the Divine Wisdom and the Divine Peace were thenceforth closely linked together and formed two parts of what was essentially one religious establishment. Although Haghia Eirene was dwarfed in size and eclipsed in importance by its great neighbour, its ancient origins were always honoured by the people of Byzantium, who called it Palaia Ekklesia, or the Old Church.

Haghia Eirene was almost destroyed in the year 564, when a fire ruined the atrium and part of the narthex, but it was soon afterwards repaired by Justinian, then in the last year of his life. In October 740 the church was severely shaken by a violent earthquake and was once again restored, either by Leo III or his son Constantine V. It appears that since that date no further major catastrophe has befallen the church, so that the building we see today is essentially that of Justinian, except for the eighth-century repairs and minor Turkish additions. After the Conquest, Haghia Eirene was enclosed within the outer walls of Topkapı Sarayı. The outermost court of the Saray, where Haghia Eirene was located, was principally given over to the Janissaries and the church was used by them as an arsenal. Later, some years after the destruction of the Janissaries in 1826, Haghia Eirene became a storehouse for antiquities, principally old Ottoman armaments. Beginning in the 1950s, the interior of Haghia Eirene was cleared of its military exhibits and thoroughly restored, and since then it has been used for concerts and exhibitions.

The ground around the church has risen some five metres above its ancient level and the present entry is through a Turkish porch and outbuildings towards the western end of the north aisle. Entering the church, we descend in semi-darkness along a stone ramp to the level of the interior. At the end of the ramp we pass through the north aisle and find ourselves at the rear of the church, looking down the length of the nave. From here we can see that the church is a basilica, but a basilica of a very unusual type. The wide nave is divided from the side aisles by the usual columned arcade, but this arcade is interrupted towards the west by the great piers that support the dome to the east and the smaller elliptical domical vault to the west. The eastern dome is supported by four great arches which are expanded into deep barrel-vaults on all sides except the west. Here we see the transition from a pure domed basilica to a centralized Greek-cross plan, which was later to supersede the basilica. The apse, semicircular within, five-sided without, is covered by a semidome. Below there is a synthronon, the only one in the city surviving from Byzantine times; this consists of six tiers of seats around the periphery of the apse facing the site of the altar, with an ambulatory passage beneath the top row, entered through framed doorways on either side.

In the semidome of the apse there is an ancient mosaic of a simple cross in black outline standing on a pedestal of three steps, against a gold ground with a geometric border. The inscription here is from Psalm lxv, 4 and 5; that on the bema arch perhaps from Amos ix, 6, with alterations, but in both cases, parts of the mosaic have fallen away and the letters were painted in by someone who was indifferent both to grammar and sense. There is some difference of opinion concerning the dating of these mosaics, one opinion being that they are to be ascribed to the reconstruction by Constantine V after the earthquake of 740, the other holding that they are from Justinian's time. The decorative mosaics in the narthex, which are not unlike those in Haghia Sophia, are almost certainly from Justinian's period.

At the western end of the nave, five doors lead from the church into the narthex and formerly five more led thence into the atrium, but three have been blocked up. This atrium and the scanty remains of that at St. John of Studius (see Chapter 16) are the only ones that are now extant in the city. Unfortunately, the one here has been rather drastically altered, for the whole of the inner peristyle is Turkish as well as a good many bays of the outer. But most of the outward walls are Byzantine; and curiously irregular they are, the northern portico being considerably longer than the southern so that the west wall runs at an angle. In the south-east corner, a short flight of steps leads to a door that communicated with buildings to the south, the ruins of which will be described presently. Haghia Eirene now serves as a concert hall for many of the musical events produced in the Istanbul International Festival; it makes a superb setting for these performances, and the acoustics of the old church are excellent.

If we leave Haghia Eirene and walk back through the garden behind the apse we can examine the ruins to the south of the church. (These are obscured by a fence and are not officially open to the public, but one can still view the ruins discreetly.) These ruins, which were first excavated in 1946, are almost certainly the remains of the once-famous Hospice of Samson. Procopius informs us that between Haghia Sophia and Haghia Eirene "there was a certain hospice, devoted to those who were at once destitute and suffering from serious illness, namely those who were suffering the loss of both property and health. This was erected in early times by a certain pious man, Samson by name." Procopius then goes on to say that the Hospice of Samson was destroyed by fire during the Nika Revolt, along with the two great churches on either side of it, and that it was rebuilt and greatly enlarged by Justinian. Unfortunately, the excavations were never carried far enough to make clear the plan of the Hospice. One can make out a courtyard opposite the atrium of Haghia Eirene, where some columns and capitals (which don't seem to fit) have been set up again. To the east is a complex series of rooms, including a nympheaeum and a small cistern, some of them with *opus sectile* floors. There is a broad corridor between the Hospice and Haghia Eirene and to the east a vaulted ramp which may have given access to the galleries of the church. From the masonry and the capitals it would appear that the major part of the work is of the time of Justinian and doubtless belongs to the reconstruction mentioned by Procopius. It is clear that this building connected directly with the atrium of Haghia Eirene, which is only a few feet higher than the level of the courtyard. One may hope that more serious and competent excavations will soon be carried out.

We now leave the precincts of Haghia Eirene and take the path which leads to the gate on the left side of the First Court. The building complex to the left of the gate is the Darphane, the former Imperial Mint and Treasury. This has been restored and is now open to the public; there is little of great interest to be seen except when there are special exhibitions or cultural events. At the lower entrance to the Darphane we see on the right the general entrance to the Archaeological Museum, the Museum of the Ancient Orient and the Çinili Köşk.

As we enter the courtyard the first building on our left is the Museum of the Ancient Orient. The entrance to the museum is flanked by two basalt lions of the neo-Hittite period (ca. 800 B.C.). The museum houses a unique collection of pre-Islamic Arab artifacts mostly from the Yemen, along with Babylonian, Neo-Hittite and Assyrian antiquities, including a series of the superb faience panels of lions and monsters, yellow on a blue ground, that once adorned the processional way to the Isthar gate at Babylon. Notable exhibits include the statue of a deified Babylonian king from the beginning of the second millennium B.C.; inscribed tablets with the Code of Hammurabi (1750 B.C.) and the Treaty of Kadesh (1286 B.C.); reliefs and colossal statues of the neo-Hittite period; a small Egyptian collection; and a selection of cuneiform cylinders for which the museum is famous. The collection as a whole is not large but is of the greatest historical importance. The building has recently been restored and the collection reorganized, thus making this one of the most interesting and attractive museums of antiquities in Europe.

THE ARCHAEOLOGICAL MUSEUM

The Archaeological Museum occupies the whole right side and far end of the courtyard. The modern history of the museum can be said to date from 1881, when Osman Hamdi Bey was made director. Over the next three decades, until his death in 1910, Osman Hamdi Bey succeeded in establishing the modern institution which we see today, one of the great museums of Europe. One of the most dramatic events in this development came in 1887 during Osman Hamdi Bey's excavation of the royal necropolis at Sidon, when he unearthed the magnificent group of sarcophagi which are the pride of the museum. Since the Çinili Köşk, where antiquities were first stored, proved too small to house these new acquisitions, a new museum was built directly opposite and opened to the public in 1896. Later discoveries by Osman Hamdi Bey and other archaeologists soon filled this museum to overflowing and it became necessary to build two additional wings, which were opened in 1902 and 1908. A new four-storey annexe was begun behind the museum in 1988 and completed in 1992.

On entering the museum notice the colossal porphyry sarcophagi arrayed along the side of the building between the two stairways. These contained the remains of early Byzantine emperors of the fourth and fifth centuries and were originally in the crypt of the church of the Holy Apostles on the Fourth Hill, now the site of Fatih Camii (see Chapter 12).

On entering from the first stairway we will first turn left to see the exhibits in the northern half of the museum; after which we will then retrace our steps to see the southern half; we will then go on to look at the antiquities in the annexe, whose entrance is opposite the museum shop between the two stairways. In the lobby we see a colossal statue of Bes, the Cypriot Hercules, holding up a headless lioness by her hind paws. A great hole gapes from the god's loins; it has been politely suggested that this once served as a fountain, but it was perhaps more likely the seat of an appropriately gigantic phallus. The statue is from Cyprus and dates from the imperial Roman era, first to third century A.D.

The first two rooms beyond the museum shop contain a number of the extraordinary sarcophagi discovered by Osman Hamdi Bey in the royal necropolis at Sidon in Syria. These sarcophagi belonged to a succession of kings who ruled in Phoenicia between the mid-fifth century B.C. and the latter half of the following century. Just inside the doorway of the first room we see the Tabit Sarcophagus, made in the sixth century B.C. for an Egyptian general and reused

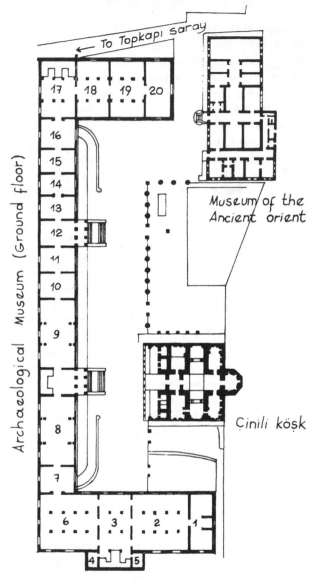

THE MUSEUMS

PLAN NO: 6

in the following century by Tabnit, King of Sidon, whose remains are displayed in the glass case just beyond. Also on exhibit here are the Lycian Sarcophagus and the Satrap Sarcophagus, both from the latter part of the sixth century B.C. and found in the region known as Lycia on the Mediterranean coast of Turkey. Beyond these rooms is the lobby inside the second staircase, which is devoted to Osman Hamdi Bey, with photographs illustrating his career.

The next room exhibits some of the sarcophagi discovered at Sidon by Osman Hamdi Bey in 1887. The most famous of these is the magnificent Alexander Sarcophagus, so-called not because it is that of Alexander himself (as is so often said), but because it is adorned with sculptures in deep, almost round relief showing Alexander in scenes of hunting and war. The sarcophagus was made for King Abdalonymos of Sidon, who began his reign in 333 B.C. after Alexander defeated the Persians at the battle of Issus, which may be represented in the reliefs of battle scenes on the sarcophagus. Also exhibited here are two other outstanding funerary monuments, the Satrap Sarcophagus and the Sarcophagus of Mourning Women. The Satrap Sarcophagus, which is dated to the second half of the fifth century B.C., takes its name from the fact that it was the tomb of a satrap, or Persian viceroy, who is shown reclining on a couch in a relief on one side of the monument, while on the other side he appears in a hunting scene. The Sarcophagus of Mourning Women dates from mid-fourth century B.C. It takes its name from the statues of the mourning women framed between Ionic columns on its sides and ends, 18 in all. A funeral procession is shown in a frieze on the lid of the sarcophagus, which is thought to have belonged to King Straton of Sidon, who died in 360 B.C.

The rooms beyond are principally devoted to sarcophagi and other funerary monuments, the finest of which are perhaps the Meleager Sarcophagus, the Sarcophagus of Phaedra and Hippolytus, and the Sidamara Sarcophagus, which date from the third and second centuries B.C. Other outstanding exhibits include reliefs from two Hellenistic temples in western Asia Minor, the temple of Hecate at Lagina and the temple of Artemis at Magnesia on the Maeander. The two stone lions which flank the foot of the staircase once stood on the façade of the Byzantine palace of Bucoleon (see Chapter 6), and were removed to the museum during the construction of the railway line along the Marmara in 1871.

Returning to the entrance lobby, we now stroll through the southern half of the museum. The first room has sculptures of the archaic period (700–480 B.C.). The free-standing statues here are idealized representations of a young man, known in Greek as a kouros, or a young woman, or kore, which were placed as dedicatory offerings in temples of Apollo and Artemis. The most notable are a legless kouros and a kouros from Samos, the face in both cases showing the haunting archaic style characteristic of Greek sculpture of this period. The finest relief is from Cyzicus, showing a long-haired youth driving a chariot drawn by two horses.

The next room contains sculptures dating from the period of Persian rule in Asia Minor (546–333 B.C.). The two best examples are from Daskylion, both with reliefs showing funeral processions in which mourners are following a cart carrying a sarcophagus.

The room beyond this is devoted to Attic grave stelae with reliefs, along with other sculptures of the classical period (480–323 B.C.). The finest stelae are those of a young athlete from Nisyros, a young warrior from Pella, and one from Amisus (Samsun) showing the deceased bidding farewell to his two young sons. The two most notable sculptures in the round are the head of a horse, provenance unknown, and a statue of Athena from Leptus Magna in Libya, a Roman copy of the Greek original.

The following room has sculptures of the Hellenistic period (323–129 B.C.), the two most famous being representations of Alexander the Great. One, from Pergamum, is a head of Alexander, a third century B.C. copy of the original by Lyssipus. Alexander is here represented in the classic pose which became the archetype for all later representations of him: what Plutarch called his swimming eye and lion's mane of hair, his mouth slightly open and his head inclined to the left, a strange lost look on his handsome face. The other, from Magnesia-ad-Sipylum, is a statue of Alexander in which he is shown as a young Hercules, another archetypal representation of the young god-king.

The next room has sculptures from Tralles and Magnesia on the Maeander. Here we see the famous Ephebos of Tralles, from the late first century B.C. or early first century A.D. This statue represents a youth resting after exercise; he is standing in a relaxed attitude with a cape draped round him to protect him from the cold, a wistful half-smile on his downcast face.

We now enter the first room of the south wing, devoted to Hellenistic and Roman sculpture. The most noteworthy is a statue of Hermes, a copy of the original by Alcamenes, which stood just outside the Propylaion on the Acropolis of Athens. In the centre of the room there is a large head of the poetess Sappho from Smyrna (Izmir), a Roman copy of the Hellenistic original. The left side of the room is devoted to Roman portrait busts of the first to fourth century A.D., including those of ten emperors ranging from Augustus to Constantine the Great.

The next room has sculptures from Ephesus, Miletus and Aphrodisias. The principal work from Ephesus is a large reclining statue of a river god from the second century A.D. The most outstanding exhibit from Miletus is a statue of Apollo Kitharados, also from the second century A.D. The most notable work from Aphrodisias is a statue of the emperor Valentinian II from the late fourth century A.D.

The last room in this wing is devoted to sculptures of the Roman imperial period. The most striking work here is just to the left inside the doorway. This is a colossal statue of Tyche, the Goddess of Fortune, who is shown holding the child Plutos, God of Wealth, while above them there is a cornucopia filled with fruit and flowers; this was found at Prusias-ad-Hypium and is from the second century A.D.

We now make our way to the new annexe. The ground floor is devoted to Byzantium and its Neighbours, as well as to an exhibition of antiquities found during excavations for the Marmararay Project, a new commuter railway line that will go under the southern end of the Bosphorus from Istanbul to Üsküdar. The exhibit on the first floor is called Istanbul Through the Age; on the second floor is Anatolia and Troy Through the Ages; and on the third floor the theme is the Cultures of Anatolia's Neighbours.

Byzantium and its Neighbours has exhibits from archaeological sites in Thrace and Bithynia, the regions that bordered the ancient city of Byzantium on its European and Asian sides, respectively. The most fascinating exhibits from Thrace were found in tumuli covering royal graves, particularly a superb bronze head of a warrior with a tightly-fitting helmet, from the fourth century B.C. A notable exhibit from Bithynia is a colossal head of Oceanus from Nicomedeia (Izmit), dating from the second century A.D. Other exhibits are from the ancient Thracian cities of Selymbia (Silivri), Perinthos and Eleonte, and from the Bithynian cities of Chalcedon (Kadıköy), Nicomedeia and Claudiopolis (Bolu), including funerary reliefs, portait busts and marble statues. The exhibits from Byzantine Constantinople include two large marble pedestals, monuments to the famous charioteer Porphyrios commemorating his victories in the Hippodrome. These pedestals, each of which once bore a bronze statue of Porphyrios, were commissioned by the Emperor Anastasius (r. 491–518), and give some measure of the enormous popularity which this charioteer once enjoyed in the Roman era. The pedestals are chiefly of interest because of the sculptures in low relief on their sides, in which are represented lively scenes from the ancient Hippodrome of Constantinople.

The exhibits from the Marmaray Project include objects found in both the old city and in Üsküdar. The main area of excavation has been in the Yeni Kapı district on the Marmara shore of the old city, where a large harbour was established when Constantine the Great founded Constantinople in A.D. 330, and which eventually silted up through alluvial earth deposited by the Lycus River. A team of archaeologists led by Professor Ismail Karamut, head of the Istanbul Archaeological Museum, has discovered the well-preserved remains of more than 30 ships, along with the remnants of piers, warehouses and other structures, including part of the city walls built by Constantine. The most spectacular find was made in 2008, when the skeletons of two adults and two children were unearthed along with the remains of a small Neolithic settlement on the harbour dating from between 6400 B.C. and 5800 B.C., predating the formation of the Bosphorus strait by several centuries. The exhibit includes numerous objects of all types found in the excavations, along with photographs of the sites and exciting videos of the archaeological work in progress, including the preservation of the ancient ships discovered in the harbour.

The first gallery of the Istanbul Through the Ages exhibit is arranged chronologically, beginning with the founding of the ancient Greek city-state of Byzantium in the seventh century B.C. and ending with the Turkish Conquest in 1453. The first part of the exhibit that one sees includes objects ranging from the archaic period through the Roman era, including tools, pottery, household artifacts and funerary monuments. Looking over the balcony here one sees a reconstruction of the façade of the temple of Athena at Assos, dating from the late sixth century B.C. The remaining galleries of the exhibit are arranged topographically, with objects found in various parts of the city and its most important Byzantine monuments. One of these shows the works of art discovered during the restoration of Kalenderhane Camii, the former church of the Kyriotissa (incorrectly identified as St. Saviour Akataleptos); these include frescoes of the life of St. Francis dating from the Latin Occupation of 1204–61, and a beautiful mosaic portait of the Virgin from the pre-iconoclastic period, the only work of this era extant in the city. One particularly fascinating exhibit is a fragment of the porphyry group of the Tetrarchs, a statue of the Emperors of East and West and their Caesars that originally stood in the square known as the Philadelphion on the Marmara slope of the Third Hill. The statue was carried off by the Venetians when the Latins sacked Constantinople in 1204, leaving beyond this fragment, which was rediscovered in 1965 by the Turkish archaeologist Nezih Fıratlı. Another interesting exhibit is a fragment of the so-called Serpent Column in the ancient Hippodrome (see Chapter 6). One of the three intertwined bronze serpents that form the column lost its head during the Ottoman period, but a fragment of it was found in 1847 and eventually preserved in the museum. The penultimate gallery has exhibits from Genoese Galata dating from the last two centuries of the Byzantine period, including coats-of-arms of Latin knights who were buried in the church of SS. Paul and Domenic, now known as Arap Camii (see Chapter 20). In the last gallery we see a length of the huge chain that was used by the Byzantines to close the Golden Horn in times of siege. There is also an exhibition of coins from ancient Byzantium and Byzantine Constantinople.

The exhibit on Anatolia and Troy Through the Ages is arranged chronologically, with the various levels in the archaeological site at Troy on one side of the room, ranging from Troy I (3000–2500 B.C.) to Troy IX (250 B.C.–A.D. 400), while on the other side are exhibits from other archaeological sites in Anatolia ranging from the earliest prehistoric periods up to the archaic age.

The exhibit on the Cultures of Anatolia's Neighbours is dedicated to ancient Syria, Palestine and Cyprus. The most striking exhibit is a recreated hypogeum, or subterranean tomb, from ancient Palmyra in Syria, dated A.D. 108. The sculptural portraits in the hypogeum are originals, taken from a number of funerary monuments in Palymyra's Valley of the Tombs.

In leaving the new annexe we pass through a room on the second floor of the old museum. The glass cases here contain votive figurines of the classical and Hellenistic periods. In the centre of the room is a colossal bronze statue of the emperor Hadrian from Nicomedeia, dated mid-second century A.D. From the window there is a good view of Çinili Köşk, the next stop on our itinerary.

ÇİNİLİ KÖŞK

We now leave the Archaeological Museum and cross over to Çinili Köşk, the Tiled Pavilion. This is the oldest Ottoman secular building in Istanbul, built by Sultan Mehmet II in 1472 as an outer pavilion of Topkapı Sarayı. It is Persian in design and decoration, a derivation which is emphasized by its long and beautifully written Persian inscription giving the date of construction. In front of the building before the museum was built, there was a large jirit field (jirit was a kind of polo game much favoured by the pages of the Saray), and Çinili Köşk seems to have been built as a kind of viewing pavilion. It is in two storeys, almost identical in plan, that is to say, cruciform, with chambers in the corners of the cross. It has a deeply recessed entrance alcove on the main floor, entirely revetted in tiles of various kinds, most of them tile mosaic in turquoise and dark blue. On the back wall these form simple geometric designs, but in the deep soffit of the arch, they display an inscription in an incredibly stylized, one might say geometricized, type of Cufic calligraphy. On the three faces of the vault at the height of the lintel of the door, there is a long double Persian inscription in the beautiful *cuerda seca* technique. The main inscription is in white letters on a dark blue ground. Above and entwined with this is a subordinate inscription in yellow, with the tendrils of a vine meandering in and out between the letters, the whole encased in a frame of deep mauve with flowers of dark blue, turquoise and white. Appropriately, Çinili Köşk now serves as a museum to exhibit Turkish tiles and ceramics.

The interior consists of a central salon in the shape of an inverted Latin cross with a dome over the crossing. The cross is extended by a vestibule at the entrance end, an apse-like room at the far end, and two eyvans, or open alcoves (now glazed in), at the ends of the shorter arms; additional chambers occupy the corners of the cross. All these rooms were once tiled and many of them still are, with triangular and hexagonal tiles of turquoise and deepest blue, sometimes with superimposed gold designs; these tiles are very similar to those in the Yeşil Cami at Bursa.

Until the present age of nationalism, foreign wares tended to be more highly prized than domestic products. Such appears to have been the case in the Ottoman court as regards the local pottery of Iznik – with the exception of wall tiles. At all events, the exhibition of china in the Çinili Köşk, though interesting, is far less extensive and varied than several of those in foreign museums and private collections, especially the Victoria and Albert and the unrivalled Godman collection; and most of the present display did not belong to the sultans, but was subsequently acquired by the museum. In the first room, to the left of the entrance vestibule, is a small collection of Selçuk tiles – mostly wall tiles of enamel and majolica ware – of the twelfth to fourteenth centuries. Entering the central salon, one is at once struck by the superb mihrab from the mosque of Ibrahim Bey at Karaman, one of the most splendid works from the height of the great Iznik period. Also in this room are two fine lunette panels in the *cuerda seca* technique from the medrese of Haseki Hiirrem, dated 1539. The second room, to the left, has tiles of the transition period from Selçuk to Ottoman of the fourteenth and fifteenth centuries, while the third and fourth contain some of the best Iznik ware of the sixteenth and early seventeenth centuries. Notice in the third room a charming eighteenth-century baroque fountain, partly tiled and partly painted, set into a niche in the wall. These last two rooms also contain a pair of magnificent kandils, or mosque lamps; they are both from Sokollu Mehmet Paşa Camii (see Chapter 6) and are therefore to be dated about 1577. The next two rooms contain pottery of the eighteenth and nineteenth centuries, some of it pretty but Europeanized and lacking in the brilliance and mastery of the earlier work. But in the last one should notice some very charming nineteenth-century plates from Çanakkale, painted with a very restricted palette in a sort of expressionist style with fish, birds, and especially boats.

Leaving the Çinili Köşk we walk back again through the courtyard. As we do so we might be tempted to wander through the gardens in the museum precincts. In the gardens opposite to the museum and beside the Çinili Köşk, there is a fascinating collection of antique fragments which one can examine leisurely while having a drink in the café there. The most extraordinary object there is a block of marble carved into the form of two colossal Gorgon heads, identical to another pair we will subsequently see in the Basilica Cistern (see Chapter 7). All four of these heads were apparently part of a frieze in the Forum of Constantine (see Chapter 7) on the Second Hill, and probably originated in a temple in Asia Minor.

Passing through the courtyard exit we turn right on the road outside and follow it downhill, flanked by ancient columns and capitals. This road takes us almost to Soğuk Çeşme Kapısı, the entrance to Gülhane Park, through which we will now stroll.

GÜLHANE PARK

Gülhane Park was once part of the outer gardens of the Saray. Originally this area would have been the lower town of the ancient Greek city of Byzantium, whose defence walls followed the same line as the outer walls of Topkapı Sarayı that we see to our left. The acropolis of ancient Byzantium was on the present site of the Saray, whose high retaining wall we see on our right. The kiosk just above the retaining wall is that of Osman III, built in the mid-eighteenth century in a baroque style. In the park below the kiosk we see an ancient structure that has been restored and is now open to the public. This is a Roman cistern dated to the early fourth century, its brick roof supported by 12 columns in three rows of four each.

On the left side of the park we now come to the new Museum of Islamic Science and Technology, which opened in 2008. The museum, which was conceived by the Turkish historian of science Fuat Sezgin, is devoted to the history of Islamic science and technology from the ninth through the sixteenth century. The instruments and other objects on display here were reconstructed by the Institute for the History of Arabic-Islamic Science at Goethe University in Frankfurt, based predominately on illustrations and descriptions found in original sources and, to a lesser extent, on surviving originals.

Once past the walls of the inner palace, we follow the path leading uphill to the right and come to one of the very oldest monuments in the city. This is the so-called Goth's Column, a granite monolith 15 metres high surmounted by a Corinthian capital. The name of the column comes from the laconic inscription on its base: FORTUNAE REDUCI OB DEVICTOS GOTHOS, which means: "To Fortune, who returns by reason of the defeat of the Goths." The column has been variously ascribed to Claudius II Gothicus (A.D. 268–70) or to Constantine the Great, but there is no firm evidence either way. According to the Byzantine historian Nicephorus Gregoras, this column was once surmounted by a statue of Byzas the Megarian, the eponymous founder of Byzantium.

Taking a path leading off from the column towards the park exit, we pass the ruins of what appears to be an early Byzantine structure, consisting of a series of small rooms fronted by a rather irregular colonnade. These ruins have never been thoroughly investigated and their date and identity have not been established.

Passing through the park exit we cross the highway and walk out to Saray Point. As we do so we pass a large bronze statue of Kemal Atatürk, the father of modern Turkey and the first President of the Turkish Republic. This monument, which was made in 1926 by the

Austrian sculptor Kripple, was the first statue of a Turk ever to be erected in this country.

Walking out onto Saray Point itself, we find ourselves at the confluence of the Bosphorus and the Golden Horn, as they flow together into the Sea of Marmara. Seated here at one of the seaside cafés, we command one of the most sweeping views in the city. From Saray Point we can stroll back to the Galata Bridge along the shore road. Along the way, we pass on our right the recently-reconstructed Sepetçiler Köşkü, a rather handsome Ottoman structure standing on the seashore. The kiosk was built in 1647 by the guild of the Sepetçiler, or Basket-Weavers, fot Sultan Ibrahim the Mad, and served as a sea-pavilion and boat-house of Topkapı Sarayı. In Ottoman times there was a line of such pavilions stretching from Saray Point to where the outer walls of the palace came down to the Golden Horn, but now only the Sepetçiler Köşkü remains.

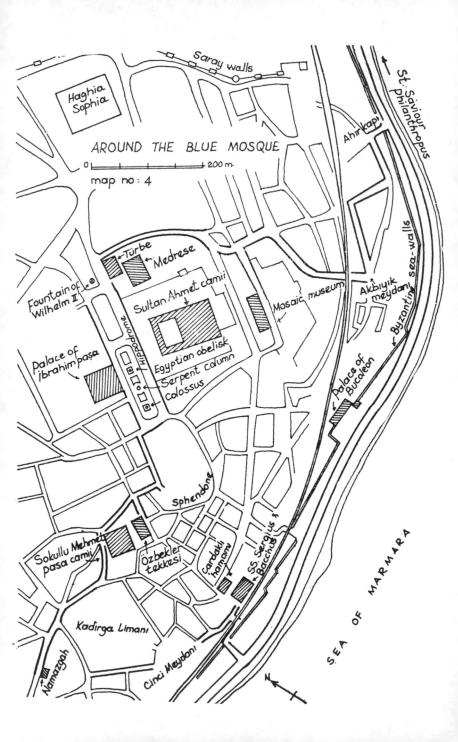

6

Around the Blue Mosque

The east side of the At Meydanı, the ancient Hippodrome, is occupied by Sultan Ahmet Camii, usually known to tourists as the BlueMosque. The Blue Mosque is thought by many to be the most splendid of the imperial mosques in the city, with its graceful cascade of domes and semidomes, its six slender minarets accentuating the corners of the courtyard and the building, the lovely grey colour of the stone set off by gilded ornaments on domes and minarets, and its generally imposing but gracious proportions. It is one of the principal adornments on the skyline of the old city, particulary when one sees it from a ship approaching Istanbul across the Sea of Marmara.

The Blue Mosque was founded by Sultan Ahmet I and constructed by the architect Mehmet Ağa between 1609 and 1616. Tradition has it that the young Sultan was so enthusiastic about his mosque that he often pitched in himself, to hurry along the construction. The same tradition tells us that the Sultan appeared at the dedication ceremony wearing a hat shaped like the Prophet's foot, in token of his humility. But Ahmet was given little time to enjoy his mosque, for he died the year after its completion, when he was only 27 years of age.

Sultan Ahmet Camii is preceded by a courtyard as large as the interior of the mosque itself, with monumental entryways at each of three sides. The central or western gate is the grandest of these; its outer façade is decorated with a calligraphic inscription by Dervish Mehmet, the father of Evliya Çelebi. The courtyard is in the classic style, bordered by a peristyle of 26 columns forming a portico covered by 30 small domes. At the centre of the courtyard there is a handsome octagonal şadırvan which, like the one at Yeni Cami, now serves only a decorative purpose. The ritual ablutions are actually performed at

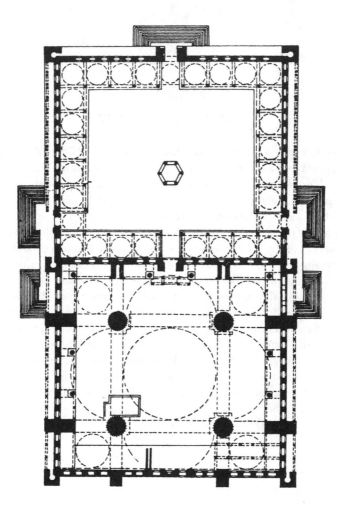

SULTAN AHMET · CAMii

0   20 m.

plan no : 7

water taps in the outer courtyard, beneath the graceful arcade which forms part of the north and south walls of the avlu.

The main entrance to the mosque itself is at the eastern side of the courtyard, with smaller entrances from the outer courtyard beside the central minarets on the north and south sides. (Tourists are asked to enter through the south door and are restricted to the west end of the prayer hall.)

The interior plan of Sultan Ahmet Camii, like that of Yeni Cami and other imperial mosques, recalls in a general way that of Haghia Sophia; but in this case the differences are greater than the resemblance. It is very nearly a square (51 metres long by 53 metres wide) covered by a dome (23.5 metres in diameter and 43 metres high), resting on four pointed arches and four smooth pendentives. To east and west are semidomes, themselves flanked by smaller ones. So far, it is not unlike Haghia Sophia. But in Sultan Ahmet, instead of tympanic arches to north and south, there are two more semidomes, making a quatrefoil design. This so-called "centralized" plan would seem to have two disadvantages: the reiterated symmetry becomes lifeless and tedious, and it gives too much prominence to the necessarily bulky piers that support the dome. In this case, the architect has gone out of his way to call attention to these supports by making them colossal, clear-standing columns, five metres in diameter, and has emphasized their squatness by dividing them in the middle by a band and then ribbing them above and below with convex flutes. The effect is somewhat disconcerting; nevertheless one has the impression that the mosque interior is in general the most admired in the city.

The mosque is flooded with light from its 260 windows. These were once filled with coloured glass which would have tempered the too-crude brightness; now they are slowly being replaced with modern imitations. The painted arabesques in the domes and upper parts of the building are feeble in design and crude in colouring, as almost always in these modern imitations of a type of decoration that was in the sixteenth and seventeenth centuries richly elaborate in design and somberly magnificent in colour. Here the predominant colour is a rather blatant blue, from which the building derives its popular name of the Blue Mosque. What is original and very beautiful in the decoration of the interior is the revetment of tiles on the lower part of the walls, especially in the galleries. They are Iznik tiles of the best period and they deserve study. The magnificent floral designs display the traditional lily, carnation, tulip and rose motifs, also cypresses and other trees, all in exquisite colours; subtle blues and greens predominating. The mihrab and mimber, of white Proconnesian marble, are also original; they are fine examples of the carved stonework of that period. Of equal excellence is the bronzework of the great courtyard doors and the woodwork, encrusted with ivory and mother-of-pearl, of the doors and window-shutters of the mosque itself. Under the sultan's loge, which is in the upper gallery to the left of the mihrab, the wooden ceiling is painted with floral and geometrical arabesques in that exquisite early style in rich and gorgeous colours, of which so few examples remain.

A ramp at the north-east corner of the mosque leads up to the hünkâr kasrı, a suite of rooms used by the Sultan whenever he came here for services, with an internal passageway leading to the hünkar mahfili, or imperial loge, within the mosque. The hünkâr kasrı is now used to house the Vakıflar Carpet Museum, a remarkable collection of Turkish carpets from all over Turkey and covering all periods of Ottoman history, including a number that were made for use in the Sultan's tent when he was on campaign.

Beneath the kıble end of the prayer room of the mosque there were storerooms and stables, and these have been restored to house the Vakiflar Kilim Museum, whose collection includes works ranging in date from the fifteenth to the nineteenth century, including rare and beautiful examples. This museum has a separate entryway from the courtyard below the mosque on that side, just above the restored Ottoman market-street (see p. 129) on Kaba Sakal Sokağı, the Street of the Bushy Beard.

The külliye of Sultan Ahmet was appropriately extensive, including a medrese, türbe, hospital, kervansaray, primary school, public kitchen and market. The hospital and the kervansaray were destroyed in the nineteenth century, and the public kitchen was incorporated into one of the buildings of the School of Industrial Arts, which stood at the southern end of the At Meydanı before it burned down in the late 1970s. It has since been restored and serves as the office of the rector of Marmara University. The primary school, which has recently been restored, is elevated above the northern wall of the outer precinct of the mosque.

The large medrese, dwarfed somewhat by the great scale of the mosque itself, is just outside the precinct wall towards the north-west. It is rectangular in plan, with 24 cells arrayed around the four sides of a portico, with its entrance at the west end of the north portico. The lavatories are located at the south-eastern corner of the building.

The large square türbe is just beside the medrese to the south. Here are buried, besides Ahmet I, his wife Kösem and three of his sons, Murat IV, Osman II and Prince Beyazit. Prince Beyazit, the Bajazet of Racine's great tragedy, was killed by his brother, the terrible Murat IV, who now shares the türbe with him. Osman II, as Evliya Çelebi tells us, was "put to death in the Castle of the Seven Towers by the compression of his testicles, a mode of execution reserved by custom to the Ottoman Emperors." And Kösem, as we know, was strangled to death in the Harem. This extraordinary woman had dominated the Harem for half a century during the reigns of her husband, Ahmet I, two of her sons, Murat IV and Ibrahim, and the early years of that of her grandson, Mehmet IV. She was originally named Anastasia, the daughter of a Greek priest on the Aegean isle of Tinos, and was sold into the Harem when she was only 13. Sultan Ahmet renamed her Kösem, or Leader of the Flock, since she was first in a group of slave girls presented to him one morning. She was also known as Mahpeyker, or Visage of the Moon, because of her great beauty.

THE HIPPODROME

As we have noted previously, the square in front of Sultan Ahmet Camii is located on the site of the ancient Hippodrome. It has often been remarked that just as Haghia Sophia was the centre of the religious life of Constantinople, so the Hippodrome was the centre of its civil activities. The interests and the passions of the populace were about equally divided between theological controversy and the chariot races of the Hippodrome. Frequently, indeed, the two became involved together, since the Blues and the Greens, the rival circus factions, would generally adopt different sides in religious disputes, which constantly served as a convenient mask for political and economic struggles. Thus on many occasions, riots and insurrections began in the Hippodrome, the most famous being the Nika rebellion in January 532. This revolt ended when Justinian's general, Belisarius, trapped the rebels in the Hippodrome and there slaughtered 30,000 of them. There is an ancient tradition that the partisans were buried where they fell and that their bones still inhabit the site.

The Hippodrome was an immense structure begun in 203 by the Emperor Septimius Severus; later Constantine the Great extended and remodelled it. It was 480 metres in length and 117.5 metres wide; it could seat, according to one estimate, about 30,000 spectators. The central line, or *spina*, of the course was marked by obelisks and columns, three of which are still the outstanding monuments of the At Meydanı. The royal enclosure, the *kathisma*, was probably situated midway along the eastern side of the arena. The straight northern end of the arena, where the spectators and chariots entered through vaulted passageways, was located about where is now the fountain of Kaiser Wilhelm II. The semi-circular southern end, or *sphendone*, is today concealed far beyond the buildings at the south end of the square. The great vaulted substructures at this end of the Hippodrome are visible from the streets below the At Meydanı on the Marmara slope of the First Hill. At the top of the outer wall there ran all around the structure an arcade of columns with an epistyle in the classical manner. Many of these were still standing nearly a century after the Turkish Conquest, but in 1550 they were pulled down and used for building material.

Some idea of the substructures and the internal anatomy of the Hippodrome may be obtained from the excavations made in the 1960s on the western side. Here we see various sustaining arches, remains of staircases leading to the seats, and a few of the seats themselves. Unfortunately the excavations were very badly done, being merely diggings for the foundations of the Law Courts which it was originally proposed to build there.

The first of the monuments on the *spina,* beginning at the northern end, is the Egyptian Obelisk. This was originally commissioned by the Pharaoh Thutmose III (1549–1503 B.C.), who erected it at Deir el Bahri opposite Thebes in Upper Egypt to commemorate one of his campaigns in Syria and his crossing of the Euphrates River. As can be seen, the shaft of the Obelisk, which is now nearly 20 metres high, has been broken off; according to Sir Flinders Petrie, it was originally 30 metres in height and weighed about 800 tonnes. The Obelisk was brought to Constantinople some time during the fourth century A.D., perhaps by Constantine the Great, but, though a mere fragment, it could not be raised and lay for some years on the seashore. It was finally erected on its present site by Theodosius the Great in 390. The Obelisk is mounted on four brazen blocks which rest on a marble basis with sculptured reliefs. These represent the Emperor and his family in the imperial box in the Hippodrome: on the south side he is watching the races depicted in the lower block; on the east he is crowning the victors; on the north he is assisting in the erection of the Obelisk itself, the method of which is represented in the lower block; and on the west he is receiving homage from vanquished enemies. Inscriptions in Greek and Latin on the base praise Theodosius and his Prefect Proclus for erecting the Obelisk; the Latin inscription tells us that 30 days were required to do the job, while the one in Greek says that it took 32. (Were the Greek and Latin scribes not on speaking terms?) The total height of the monument including the base is about 26 metres and the bottom of it represents approximately the original level of the race-course, some 4.5 metres below the present surface of the ground.

The second of the three monuments on the *spina* is the Serpent Column. The three intertwined bronze serpents which form the column were the base of a trophy that once stood in the Temple of Apollo at Delphi. This trophy was dedicated to Apollo as a token of gratitude by the 31 Greek cities which defeated the Persians in the battle of Plataea (479 B.C.); according to tradition the bronze serpents were cast from the shields of the fallen Persian warriors. The names of the 31 cities are inscribed on the coils of the serpents near the bottom. The column was brought from Delphi by Constantine the Great; it seems to have stood at first in the courtyard of Haghia Sophia and to have been moved to the Hippodrome only at a later date. There are several stories about what became of the missing serpent heads, but the most likely one is that they were chopped off by a member of the Polish Embassy one night in April of the year 1700. The upper part of one of the serpent heads was found in 1847 and is now, as we have seen, on exhibit at the Archaeological Museum. Like the serpents themselves, it is a very beautiful and finished piece of bronze sculpture, as is to be expected of a Greek work of that period.

The third of the ancient monuments on the *spina* is a roughly built pillar of stone 32 metres high which stands near the southern end of the At Meydanı. The sixteenth-century French traveller, Gyllius, called it the Colossus, but most modern writers refer to it, incorrectly, as the Column of Constantine Porphryogenitus. Both names stem from the Greek inscription on its base, where the pillar is compared to the Colossus of Rhodes, and where it is recorded that the pillar was restored and sheathed in bronze by the Emperor Constantine VII Porphyrogenitus (r. 912–59). But the inscription also says that the pillar was decayed by time, so that it must date to an earlier period, perhaps to that of Theodosius the Great or Constantine the Great. It seems to have been a favourite pastime in the early Turkish period to climb this column as an acrobatic feat – at least if one can judge by a Turkish miniature which shows a man at the top of it, another in the act of climbing the obelisk, and a monkey on a pole higher than both! And Gyllius tells a rather grim story of having, himself, seen two young men climb the pillar one after the other; the first came down safely but the second lost his nerve, jumped, and was, of course, instantly killed.

PALACE OF IBRAHİM PAŞA

Occupying a large part of the west side of the Hippodrome, but partly concealed by an ugly nineteenth-century building, are the remains of the vast palace of Ibrahim Paşa, built around 1520. Ibrahim Paşa was a Greek convert to Islam who became an intimate companion of Süleyman the Magnificent during the early years of his reign. In 1523, Ibrahim was appointed Grand Vezir and the following year he married Süleyman's sister Hadice, at which time he was given this palace on the Hippodrome. Some idea of the enormous wealth and influence which Ibrahim had at this time can be gained from even a casual view of the palace, the grandest private residence ever built in the Ottoman Empire, far greater in size than any of the buildings in Topkapı Sarayı itself. But the very magnitude of this wealth and power was the ultimate cause of Ibrahim's ownfall. Later in Süleyman's reign, when he fell under the influence of his wife Roxelana, the Sultan was persuaded that Ibrahim must be eliminated, for he was taking on the airs of royalty. And so one night in the year 1536, after having dined alone with the Sultan, as he had so often in the years of their intimacy, Ibrahim retired to an adjacent room in the Saray and was there murdered while he slept. Immediately afterwards all of Ibrahim's wealth and possessions were confiscated by the state, including the palace on the Hippodrome. For a time, Ibrahim's palace seems to have been used as a dormitory and school for the apprentice pages in the Saray. The great hall, that part of the palace which fronts on the Hippodrome, was in Ibrahim's time the Audience Room of the Grand Vezir, and afterwards it was probably the High Court of Justice. In later times it seems to have been used as a barracks for unmarried Janissaries and also as a prison. By the beginning of the nineteenth century much of the palace was in ruins, but then it was restored and opened to the public in 1983 as the Museum of Turkish and Islamic Art.

After passing through the entrance lobby, one enters the northeast corner of the great central courtyard; this has been restored very attractively, with marble paving around a garden and with a balcony overlooking the Hippodrome. Part of the north wing has been fitted out as an old-fashioned Istanbul coffee-house, an ideal place to relax before or after seeing the exhibits in the museum.

Before going through the galleries, one might pause to survey the structure of the palace. What one sees here is the main part of the original palace of Ibrahim Paşa. In addition to this there was another section of almost equal size adjoining the present structure to the north-west, apparently an enormous han-like edifice, which has vanished except for the wing nearest the Hippodrome. The most important part of the present structure is the great hall, which takes up most of the upper level of the south wing on the side overlooking the Hippodrome; this would have been Ibrahim Paşa's Hall of the Divan, and the two large rooms to its west would have been antechambers to this. The long western or inner side of the palace on the upper floor has at its rear a row of 13 cell-like cubicles opening onto a long corridor with a stone sofa overlooking the garden. This corridor turns the corner to pass along the north wing, which is only half as long as the south wing, with five cells along the inner side and a sixth overlooking the courtyard. The southern end of the corridor here is connected with the coutyard by a stairway, the entrance below being through a foyer with a great round-arched entryway. The lower level of the palace around the courtyard consists of a series of splendid vaults, supported by a single row of piers in the north and south wings, creating two aisles, while in the south wing there is a triple row of piers, one row engaged in the walls on the courtyard side, thus creating three aisles there. Some of these vaults are used to house the ethnographical collection of the museum, while the other exhibits are on the upper level of the palace.

The main collections on the upper level include rare and beautiful works from all periods of the Turkish and Islamic world, including objects from the Ummayid, Abbasid, Mamluk, Selçuk, Beylik and Ottoman periods, ranging in date from the seventh century to the nineteenth. The collections include carpets, manuscripts and calligraphy, miniatures, woodwork, ceramics and glassware, metalwork and folk-arts, altogether an extraordinary exhibit, superbly displayed. The ethnographical collection consists principally of objects belonging to the Yürük, the nomadic Turkish people of Anatolia, whose way of life has not changed in its essentials since the first Turcoman tribes made their way into Asia Minor after the battle of Manzikert in 1071. The most fascinating exhibits here are the black goat-hair tents of the Yürük, furnished with objects that these nomads still use in their daily life, a living heritage of Anatolian Turkish culture.

We now leave the At Meydanı by the street at the south-western end, walking alongside the building there, now the Rectorate of Marmara University. At the first turning we pass through a gate and enter the garden behind the school (the gateman never objects to visitors). This garden occupies part of the *sphendone,* the southern, semicircular end of the Hippodrome. The chief reason for coming here is the view, which is very fine. The Marmara coast of the city can be seen in all its extent, from Saray Point to the Marble Tower, where the land walls meet the Marmara. Looking out across the Marmara we see the Princes' Isles floating between sea and sky, and beyond them the mountains of Asia; on a clear day we can see the Bithynian Olympus (Uludağ) with its snow-capped summit. In the foreground just below us to the right is the mosque of Sokollu Mehmet Paşa, and straight ahead by the seashore the former church of SS. Sergius and Bacchus with its curiously corrugated dome; these are the next important items on our itinerary. If we look down over the railing, we see the great supporting wall of the Hippodrome. Within this wall, under our feet, are various stone chambers and the long spacious corridor which ran round the whole length of the Hippodrome and from which doors and staircases led to the various blocks of seats. Part of this corridor was converted into a cistern in later Byzantine times and still supplies water to the district below. If we look back in this direction from the seashore beyond SS. Sergius and Bacchus, we will see the whole sweep of the great semicircular wall.

We now return to the street outside and follow it downhill to the second turning on the left, where at the corner we see the remains of an ancient mosque. This is Helvacı Camii, founded in 1546 by one Iskender Ağa: it is too ruinous to be of any interest. Farther down the street to the left is a very odd and interesting tekke, or dervish monastery. This is part of the külliye of Sokollu Mehmet Paşa Camii built by the great Sinan, which is just below it. It is rather oddly designed, but its form is unique because of the steep descent of the hill on which it is built. We enter by a little domed gatehouse and find immediately opposite the large and handsome mescit-zaviye, or room for the dervish ceremonies. On the right is a small porticoed courtyard with the cells of the dervishes; on the left is another courtyard of cells, but in this case it is in two storeys because of the difference in level: one descends to the lower level by a staircase behind the zaviye. Both courtyards are rather low and dark with square pillars instead

SOKOLLU MEHMET PAŞA CAMİİ

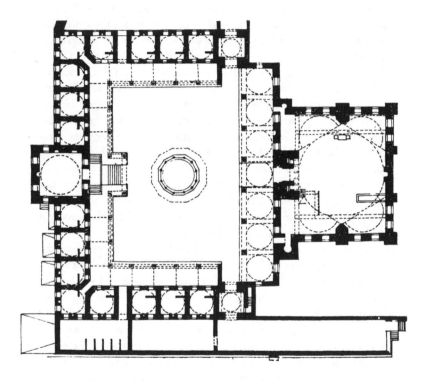

plan no : 8

of columns, which give them a somewhat forbidding appearance; but the arrangement as a whole is ingenious and attractive. The building has recently been rather summarily restored.

THE MOSQUE OF SOKOLLU MEHMET PAŞA

We now return to the street from which we branched off and continue down to the left; presently a gate leads to the garden and courtyard of a great mosque. This is one of the most beautiful of the smaller mosques of Sinan. It was built in A.H. 979 (A.D. 1571–2) for Ismihan Sultan, daughter of Selim II and wife of the Grand Vezir Sokollu Mehmet Paşa after whom the mosque is generally called. This mosque is built on the site of an ancient church, once wrongly identified as that of St. Anastasia, from which doubtless the columns of the courtyard were taken.

The courtyard itself is enchanting in design. It served, as in the case of many mosques, as a medrese; the scholars lived in the little domed cubicles or cells under the portico. Each cell had its own window, its fireplace and its recess for books. Instruction was given in the dershane, the large domed room over the staircase in the west wall, and also in the mosque itself. Notice the charming ogive arches of the portico and the fine şadırvan in the centre. The porch of the mosque forms the fourth side of the court; in the lunettes of the window are some striking and elegant inscriptions in blue and white faience. Entering the building, one is delighted by the harmony of its lines, the lovely soft colour of the stone, the marble decoration and, above all, the tiles. In form, the mosque is a hexagon inscribed in a rectangle (almost square), and the whole is covered by a dome, counter-balanced at the corners by four small semidomes. There are no side aisles, but around three sides runs a low gallery supported on slender marble columns with the typical Ottoman lozenge capitals. The polychrome of the arches, the voussoirs of alternate green and white marble, is characteristic of the classic period.

The tile decoration in the mosque has been used with singularly charming effect. Not the entire wall but only selected areas have been sheathed in tiles: the pendentives of the dome, the exquisite mihrab section of the east wall, and a frieze of floral designs under the galleries. The predominant colour is a cool turquoise, and this has been picked up again here and there in the carpets. The whole effect is extraordinarily harmonious. Above the entrance portal can be seen a small specimen of the wonderful painted decoration of the classical period. It consists of very elaborate arabesque designs in rich and vivid colours. Also above the door, surrounded by a design in gold, is a fragment of black stone from the holy Kaaba in Mecca; other fragments can be seen in the mihrab and mimber, themselves fine work in carved marble and faience.

We leave the mosque by the broad staircase below the west wall of the courtyard (notice the fine inlaid arabesque woodwork of the great doors), and turn left and then right onto Kadirga Liman Caddesi. This picturesque old street soon brings us to a large open square, much of which is now used as a playground. This is the pleasant area known as Kadirga Limanı, which means literally the Galley Port. As its name suggests, this was anciently a seaport, now long since silted up and built over. The port was originally dug and put in shape by the Emperor Julian the Apostate in 362 and called after him. In about 570, Justin II redredged and enlarged it and named it for his wife, Sophia. It had continually to be redredged but remained in use until after the Turkish Conquest. By about 1550, when Gyllius saw it, only a small part of the harbour remained and now even this is gone. Today only bits and pieces of the inner fortifications of the harbour are left, cropping up here and there as parts of houses and garden walls in several of the streets between here and the sea.

In the centre of the square, Kadirga Liman Meydanı, there is a very striking and unique monument. This is the namazgah of Esma Sultan, daughter of Ahmet III, which was built in 1779. It is a great rectangular block of masonry, on the two faces of which are fountains with ornamental inscriptions, the corners having ornamental niches, while the third side is occupied by a staircase which leads to the flat roof. This is the only surviving example in Stamboul of a namazgah, or open-air place of prayer, in which the kible or direction of prayer is indicated but which is otherwise without furniture or decoration. Namazgahs are common enough in Anatolia and the remains of at least two others can be seen in the environs of Istanbul, one in the Okmeydanı overlooking the Golden Horn and the other at Anadolu Hisarı on the Bosphorus; but this is the only one left in the old city.

After leaving the namazgah, we cross to the street at the southern side of the park and turn left. This street soon brings us to a large open field, Cinci Meydanı, which is bordered on the side by the railroad line. Cinci Meydanı, the Square of the Genii, is named after Cinci Hoca, a favourite of Sultan Ibrahim, who once owned land on this site. When Ibrahim first came to the throne there was some doubt as to his sexual potency, and so his mother Kösem sought out Cinci Hoca, who had acquired a considerable reputation as a *büyücü*, that is, a wizard quacksalver. Cinci Hoca would seem to have done his job well, for Ibrahim soon had the Harem swinging with cradles and was performing sexual spectaculars which are still recalled with awe. But when Crazy Ibrahim was deposed in 1648, Cinci Hoca fell too, and he and his friend Pezevenk (the Pimp) were torn to pieces by an angry mob in the At Meydanı. The Square of the Genii is today a football field, which we pass and continue eastward, following a narrow lane parallel to the railroad track.

SS. SERGİUS AND BACCHUS

At the end of this lane, we come to one of the entrances to the courtyard of the beautiful Küçük Aya Sofya Camii, the former Byzantine church of SS. Sergius and Bacchus. The church was begun by Justinian and his Empress Theodora in 527, five years before the commencement of the present church of Haghia Sophia. It thus belongs to that extraordinary period of prolific and fruitful experiment in architectural forms which produced, in this city, buildings so ambitious and so different as the present church, Haghia Sophia itself, and Haghia Eirene – to name only the existing monuments – and in Ravenna, St. Vitale, the Baptistry and St. Apollinare in Classe. It is as if the architects were searching for new modes of expression suitable to a new age. The domes of this period are specially worthy of note: the great dome of Haghia Sophia is of course unique, but the method of transition from the octagon to the dome here is astonishing: the dome is divided into 16 compartments, eight flat

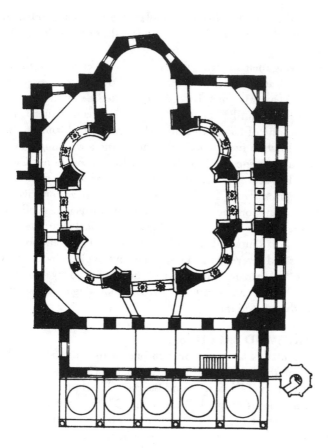

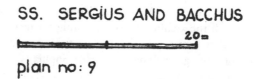

SS. SERGIUS AND BACCHUS

20=

plan no: 9

sections alternating with eight concave ones above the angles of the octagon. This gives the dome the oddly undulatory or corrugated effect we noticed when looking down on it from the *sphendone*. The octagon has eight polygonal piers between which are pairs of columns, alternately of verd antique and red Synnada marble both above and below, arranged straight on the axes but curved out into the exedrae at each corner. The whole forms an arcade that gives an effect almost of choric dancers in some elaborate but formal evolution, as Procopius happily says in another connection. The space between this brightly coloured, moving curtain of columns and the exterior walls of the rectangle becomes an ambulatory below and a spacious gallery above. (One ascends to the gallery by a staircase at the south end of the narthex; don't fail to do so, for the view of the church from above is very impressive.) The capitals and the classic entablature are exquisite specimens of the elaborately carved and deeply undercut style of the sixth century. On the ground floor the capitals are of the "melon" type, in the gallery "pseudo-Ionic", and a few of them still bear the monogram of Justinian and Theodora, though most of these have been effaced. In the gallery the epistyle is arcaded in a way that became habitual in later Byzantine architecture – already in Haghia Sophia, for example; but on the ground floor the entablature is still basically classical, trabeated instead of arched, with the traditional architrave, frieze, and cornice, but how different in effect from anything classical: like lace. The frieze consists of a long and beautifully carved inscription in 12 Greek hexameters in honour of the founders and of St. Sergius; oddly enough St. Bacchus is not mentioned. SS. Sergius and Bacchus were two Roman soldiers martyred for their espousal of Christianity; later they became the patron saints of Christians in the Roman army. These saints were especially dear to Justinian because they saved his life some years before he came to the throne, in the reign of Anastasius. It seems that Justinian had been accused of plotting against the Emperor and was in danger of being executed, but Sergius and Bacchus appeared in a dream to Anastasius and interceded for him. As soon as Justinian himself became Emperor in 527, he expressed his gratitude to the saints by dedicating to them this church, the first of those with which he adorned the city.

In SS. Sergius and Bacchus, as in almost all of the surviving Byzantine churches of the city, we must simply use our imagination in order to recapture the extraordinary beauty of its original condition. The walls, like those of Haghia Sophia, were revetted with veined and variegated marbles; the vaults and domes glittered with mosaics. "By the sheen of its marbles it was more resplendent than the sun," says Procopius, "and everywhere it was filled profusely with gold."

SS. Sergius and Bacchus continued to serve as a church for nearly 1,000 years after its founding, but then in the first decade of the sixteenth century it was converted into a mosque. Its patron at that time was Hüseyin Ağa, who was Kapıağası, or Chief of the White Eunuchs, in the reign of Beyazit II. Hüseyin Ağa's tomb can still be seen in the garden to the north of the church. The building is now called Küçük Aya Sofya Camii, the mosque of Little Haghia Sophia, because of its supposed resemblance to the Great Church.

Just to the north of the church, on Küçük Aya Sofya Caddesi, we find an ancient bath, Çardaklı Hamam. An inscription shows that it was built in 1503 by a Kapıağası under Beyazit II; its date and its proximity to Küçük Aya Sofya Camii suggest that the founder may have been Hüseyin Ağa. The hamam is ruinous and unusable but must have been quite grand.

Returning to the church we pass through the courtyard once again and leave by the gate through which we first entered. Retracing our steps for a short distance, we then turn left to follow a winding lane which passes under the railroad line and eventually leads us out to the Marmara shore. Here we turn left and follow the ancient Byzantine sea walls along the Marmara.

ALONG THE SEA WALLS

The sea walls in the section along which we are walking were originally constructed by Constantine the Great, ending where his land walls met the sea at Samatya. When the Theodosian walls were built in the following century, the Marmara sea walls were extended to meet them. During the ninth century, the Marmara walls were almost completely rebuilt by the Emperor Theophilus, who sought to strengthen the city's maritime defences against the Saracens. The

Marmara defences consisted of a single line of walls 12–15 metres high studded with 188 towers at regular intervals. These walls stretched from the Marble Tower to Saray Point, a total distance of eight kilometres, and were pierced by 13 sea-gates. At Saray Point, the Marmara walls joined up with those along the Golden Horn, thus completing the maritime defence system. Although much of the fortifications along the Marmara have been destroyed in recent years, that which remains is still impressive, particularly the walls and towers along our present itinerary.

Almost immediately in front of SS. Sergius and Bacchus is a small postern gate doubtless for the use of the monastery that was attached to the church. Upon closer inspection, we find that the posts of the gateway are carved with a long inscription in Greek, containing a conflation or cento from Habakkuk and Psalms. It seems to be generally agreed that these inscribed doorposts once formed the base of the celebrated equestrian statue of Justinian which anciently stood in the Augustaeum.

A short distance beyond this gate we come to the ruins of another and grander postern, whose Turkish name is Çatladı Kapı, or the Cracked Gate. The marble sides and archway of the gate are finely carved with acanthus-leaf decorations as well as with a large monogram of Justinian. This postern is probably the one which was called the Imperial Marine Gate, since it appears to have been one of the entrances from the port of Bucoleon, the private harbour of the Great Palace. It was also called the Porta Leonis, from the statues of the two lions which stood on the façade of the Palace of Bucoleon, one of the seaside buildings of the Great Palace. (These are the lions which we saw in the Archaeological Museum.) The main entryway from the port to the palace was by a monumental staircase in the huge tower just beyond the Çatladı Kapı. As we pass this tower we see all that now remains of Bucoleon: the eastern loggia of the palace with its three marble-framed windows and a vaulted room behind them. Below the windows some projecting corbels indicate that a balcony ran along the façade, suspended over a marble quay below. Notice the curious-looking row of large square marble slabs built into the lower part of the wall; if you insert your hand under them you will find that they are Doric capitals of the fifth century B.C., doubtless from some ancient temple that stood nearby.

These ruins are all that now remain above ground of the Great Palace of Byzantium, whose pavilions and gardens covered the Marmara slopes of the First Hill. The palace was first built by Constantine the Great at the time when he founded his new capital. Much of the Palace was destroyed during the Nika rebellion in 532, but it was soon afterwards rebuilt and considerably enlarged by Justinian. Later emperors, particularly Basil the Macedonian in the ninth century, restored and extended the palace and adorned it with works of art. The Great Palace was divided into several different establishments: the Sacred Palace and the Palaces of Daphne and Chalke, which were located near the present site of the Blue Mosque; the Palaces of Magnaura and Mangana, which stood to the south-east of Haghia Sophia, on the slope of the hill leading down the Marmara; and the sea-palace of Bucoleon. In its time, the Great Palace had no equal in the world and medieval travellers have left us awed descriptions of its splendours. The Emperors of Byzantium lived and ruled there for nearly nine centuries, up until the sack of Constantinople by the Crusaders in 1204. After the restoration of the Byzantine Empire in 1261 the Great Palace was found to be in a state of advanced decay and was never afterwards restored. Instead, the later emperors abandoned the palaces by the Marmara and took up their residence in the Palace of Blachernae, in the north-western corner of the city. At the time of the Turkish Conquest, the Great Palace was completely in ruins. Shortly after he entered the city, Sultan Mehmet the Conqueror walked through the ruined halls of the palace and was so saddened as to recite a melancholy distich by the Persian poet Saadi: "The spider is the curtain-holder in the Palace of the Caesars. The owl hoots its night call on the Towers of Aphrasiab."

Passing the Palace of Bucoleon, we continue walking along the sea-walls. The next defence-tower we pass, in the angle just to the east of Bucoleon, was once the Pharos or Lighthouse of Byzantium. In modern times it has been replaced by another lighthouse farther along the sea-walls.

About 400 metres beyond the Bucoleon we come to one of the ancient public gateways in the sea-wall. (The gate is just beyond the

Kalyon Hotel and a little restaurant called Karışma Sen, which means literally Mind Your Own Business.) The Byzantine name of this gateway is unknown, but in Ottoman times it was called Ahır Kapı, or the Stable Gate, because it led to the Sultan's mews nearby. Perhaps it had the same name in Byzantium, for the Emperor Michael III is known to have built some marble stables in this same area in the middle of the ninth century.

The footsore stroller can, at this point, rest in the teahouse beside the Stable Gate, while the more ambitious take a short detour a little farther along the sea-walls.

A short way along in a turn-around, steps lead to a football field behind the sea-walls from where there is a good view of the outer walls of Topkapı Sarayı marching up the hill towards Haghia Sophia, with seven towers in the fortifications visible.

About 500 metres beyond the Stable Gate, past the modern lighthouse, we come to a marble structure called the Incili Köşk, or the Pavilion of the Pearl. An inscription on the fountain which is built into the kiosk attributes its founding to Sinan Paşa and gives the date A.H. 986 (A.D. 1578). This is all that remains of the Sinan Paşa Köşkü, one of the outer pavilions of Topkapı Sarayı. This kiosk was a particular favourite of Murat III. During his last illness in January 1595, the Sultan spent his days in this kiosk, listening sadly to the dirges of his musicians, waiting for death to come. One evening the Ottoman fleet sailed by on its return from the south and, learning that the Sultan was in the kiosk, fired a volley in his honour. But the volley shook loose the plaster ceiling of the kiosk and caused it to come showering down on the Sultan and his musicians. "And so is destroyed the kiosk of my life," said Murat sadly, whereupon he was carried back to his death-bed in the Saray.

A short distance beyond the Incili Köşkü we see the façade of an ancient church built into the sea-walls, with blocked-up doors, windows, niches, and a huge arch rising to the top of the wall. These are the substructures of the church of St. Saviour Philanthropes, built in the first half of the twelfth century by Alexius I Comnenus, one of the greatest of the Byzantine emperors. There is a tradition that the Emperor, himself, was buried in this church, but no trace of his tomb has ever been found. In times past, one could penetrate through one of the openings into a vast crypt with towering vaults and massy walls, obviously of several different periods; but the church has now been sealed off and one can no longer enter its interior.

We now retrace our steps so as to return to the Stable Gate. As we do so we might notice, just beyond the Incili Köşk, the huge vaults which were probably once part of the substructure of the Palace of Mangana. Beyond these substructures we pass a series of small posterns which once gave entrance to the area which in Ottoman times was the lower garden of the Saray. This whole area is filled with subterranean vaults, crypts and complex passages which belonged to the substructure of the various churches, monasteries and palaces which covered this part of the First Hill. Most of these substructures are now almost impossible to access, either for natural causes or because the area is controlled by the military.

We now return to the Stable Gate and pass through the double portal in the sea-walls to re-enter the city. After passing through the gate we immediately turn left on Ahır Kapı Sokağı and then take the first right, Keresteci Hakkı Sokağı, which we follow around a left bend until it comes to Ak Bıyık Meydanı, the Square of the White Moustache. This is the centre of one of the most picturesque neighbourhoods in old Stamboul, and its winding lanes have some of the most marvellous names in town: the Street of the Bushy Beard, the Street of the Sweating Whiskers, the Street of the Shame-Faced, the Street of Ibrahim of Black Hell, and the Avenue of the White Moustache, from which the square and the surrounding neighbourhood are named.

Before leaving the Square of the White Moustache, do not fail to notice the two fountains there, especially the one on the left side of the square, the Ak Bıyık Meydan Çeşmesi. There are more than 400 of these çeşmes in Stamboul alone, ranging in size from the monumental street fountains such as that of Sultan Ahmet III, to simple wall-fountains. For centuries these çeşmes were the only sources of water for the ordinary people of Istanbul, and up until recent years there are many sections of the city which still depend mainly upon them. The Ak Bıyık Meydan Çeşmesi is an attractive example of a Turkish baroque fountain, with its rich decoration of flowers and cypress trees. The chronogram on the fountain reads as follows: "When the mother of Ali Paşa, Vezir in the reign of Sultan Mahmut I, quenched the thirst of the people with the pure and clear water of her charity, Riza of Beşiktaş, a Nakşibendi dervish, uttered the following epigram: 'Come and drink the water of eternal life from this fountain'." The numerical value of the words in the last phrase gives the year of foundation as A.H. 1147 or A.D. 1734.

We leave Ak Bıyık Meydanı by the street opposite the fountain, Ak Bıyık Caddesi. This takes us under the railway line and turns right uphill until it intersects the broad Mimar Mehmet Ağa Caddesi, where we turn left. We then take the first turning on our left, Torun Sokağı, a little street which brings us directly behind the Blue Mosque. A short distance along this street we come to the Mosaic Museum, the next stop on our itinerary. Entering the museum grounds, we first pass through a garden filled with remnants of ancient columns and capitals, uncovered during excavations which began in 1935. These fragments, together with the mosaic pavements inside the museum, were once part of the Great Palace, the colonnaded way known as the Mosaic Peristyle.

What one sees inside the museum is the north-east portico of the Peristyle. There has been considerable disagreement about the date of these mosaics. The arguments are far too technical and complex to be entered into here, but the upshot is that late Roman mosaics of this sort – they belong to the same general type as those at Antioch, at Apamea, at Piazza Armerina in Sicily, in North Africa and else-where – cannot be exactly dated on stylistic grounds alone. But current opinion is that the mosaics date from the reign of Justinian (r. 527–65), probably when he restored the Great Palace after the Nika Revolt in 532.

We leave by the upper gate of the museum, where we turn right on Kabasakal Sokaği, the Street of the Bushy Beard. This is a picturesque seventeenth-century Ottoman arasta, or market street, which was part of the külliye of Sultan Ahmet Camii. The arasta was restored from utter ruin in the 1980s and is now once again serving as a market street, principally for the tourist trade.

At the end of the arasta we turn left on Mimar Mehmet Ağa Caddesi, where we turn left and walk back towards the garden between the Blue Mosque and Haghia Sophia. Here we turn right onto Kabasakal Sokağı, the continuation of the old bazaar street. This passes on its left the Hamam of Roxelana and on its right the seventeenth-century medrese of Cedid Mehmet Efendi and a nineteenth-century mansion known as Yeşil Ev, the Green House. Both of the latter buildings were restored in the 1980s by the Turkish Touring and Automobile Club. The cells of the medrese now house shops where artisans specializing in old Ottoman crafts make and sell their works. Yeşil Ev is now an elegant hotel with an excellent restaurant, which in the summer months spreads out into the very pleasant rear courtyard, a perfect place to restore oneself after a long stroll around the First Hill.

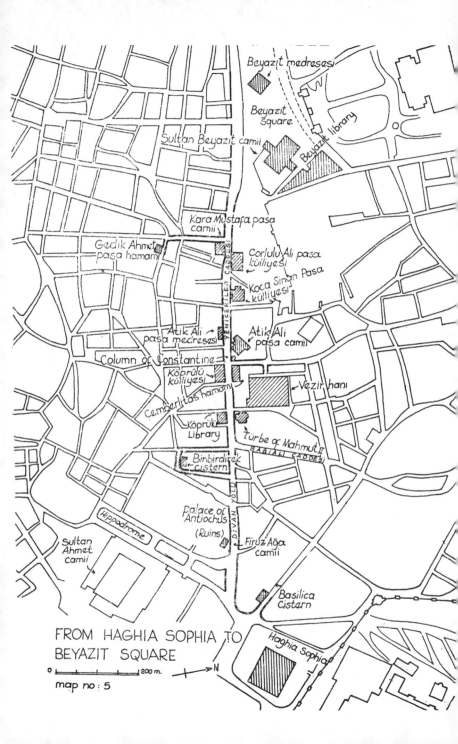

FROM HAGHIA SOPHIA TO
BEYAZIT SQUARE

0 |⎯⎯⎯⎯⎯⎯| 200 m.   ⊢→ N

map no: 5

7

From Haghia Sophia to Beyazit Square

Aya Sofya Meydanı, the square beside Haghia Sophia, occupies a site which was once the heart of Byzantine Constantinople. The square coincides almost exactly with the Augustaeum, the publc forecourt to the Great Palace of Byzantium. On its northern side the Augustaeum gave access to the church of Haghia Sophia and to the Patriarchal Palace, while outside its south-eastern corner stood the Chalke, or Brazen House, the monumental vestibule of the Great Palace. The Hippodrome was located just to the south-west of the Augustaeum and the Baths of Zeuxippus were to its south. A short way to the west of the Augustaeum there was another great communal square, the Stoa Basilica, a porticoed piazza surrounded by the buildings of the University of Constantinople, the central law courts of the empire, the principal public library, and a large outdoor book market. Thus the Augustaeum and its immediate neighbourhood were at the very hub of life in the ancient city. Today the square is no longer a civic centre, but it is still a very central starting point for visting the antiquities on the First and Second Hills of the old city.

At the south-western corner of the Augustaeum, at the beginning of the modern Divan Yolu, there stood a monument called the Miliarum Aureum, the Golden Milestone, known more simply as the Milion. Excavations in 1965 unearthed a fragment of the Milion beside the Ottoman suterazi, or water-control tower, just to the right at the beginning of Divan Yolu. The fragment, a tall marble stele, was part of a four-sided ceremonial archway surmounted by statues of Constantine the Great and his mother Helena, holding between them the True Cross.

The Milion, like its namesake in the Roman Forum, was the point of departure for the great roads which ran out of the city and was the reference point for their milestones. Here began the Mese, or Middle Way, the main thoroughfare of ancient Constantinople, which followed the course of the modern Divan Yolu. The Mese, which was flanked for a good part of its length with marble porticoes, led westward from the Milion along the ridge between the First and Second Hills, atop which it passed through the Forum of Constantine. Continuing westward, along the route of the Modern Yeniçeriler Caddesi, the Avenue of the Janissaries, the Mese then ran along the ridge between the Second and Third Hills and entered the Forum of Theodosius, on the site of the present-day Beyazit Square. Beyond there, the Mese divided into two branches, one of which extended west and the other south-west. The western branch passed through the Gate of Charisius, where it joined the Roman road to Adrianople, now known as Edirne. The other branch passed through the famous Golden Gate and linked up with the Via Egnatia, which marched through Thrace, Macedonia and Epirus to the Adriatic. The main thoroughfares of modern Stamboul follow quite closely the course of these Roman roads built more than 15 centuries ago.

The thoroughfare between Haghia Sophia and Beyazit Square continued to be one of the principal arteries of the town in Ottoman times, for it was the main road from Topkapı Sarayı to the centre of Stamboul. For that reason it is lined with monuments of the imperial Ottoman centuries, as well as some ruined remnants of imperial Byzantium. It is called Divan Yolu, the Road of the Divan, because of the procession of dignitaries that passed along it whenever there were meetings of the Divan, or imperial council, in the Second Court of Topkapı Sarayı.

THE BASİLİCA CISTERN

The first monument on our itinerary is a short way down Yerebatan Caddesi, the street that leads off half-right from Aya Sofya Meydanı at the beginning of Divan Yolu. Almost immediately on the left we come to a small building which is the entrance to an enormous underground cistern, Yerebatan Saray, or the Underground Palace.

Restoration of the cistern began in 1985 and it opened to the public in 1988.

The structure was known in Byzantium as the Basilica Cistern because it lay underneath the Stoa Basilica, the second of the two great squares on the First Hill. The Basilica Cistern was built by Justinian after the Nika Revolt in 532, possibly as an enlargement of an earlier cistern of Constantine. Throughout the Byzantine period the Basilica Cistern was used to store water for the Great Palace and the other buildings on the First Hill, and after the Conquest its waters were used for the gardens of Topkapı Sarayı. Nevertheless, general knowledge of the cistern's existence seems to have been lost in the century after the Conquest, and it was not rediscovered until 1546. In that year Petrus Gyllius, while engaged in his study of the surviving Byzantine antiquities in the city, learned that the people in this neighbourhood obtained water by lowering buckets through holes in their basement floors; some even caught fish from there. Gyllius made a thorough search through the neighbourhood and finally found a house through whose basement he could go down into the cistern, probably at the spot where the modern entrance is located. As Gyllius writes, referring to the Stoa Balica as the Imperial Portico:

The Imperial Portico is not to be seen, though the Cistern remains. Through the inhabitants' carelessness and contempt for everything that is curious it was never discovered except by me, who was a stranger among them, after a long and diligent search for it. The whole area was built over, which made it less suspected that there was a cistern there. The people had not the least suspicion of it, though they daily drew their water out of the wells that were sunk into it. By chance I went into a house where there was a way down to it and went aboard a little skiff. I discovered it after the master of the house lit some torches and rowed me here and there through the pillars, which lay very deep in water. He was very intent on catching his fish, with which the Cistern abounds, and speared some of them by the light of the torches. There is also a small light that descends from the mouth of the well and reflects on the water, where the fish usually come for air.

The Cistern is three hundred and thirty-six feet long, a hundred and eighty two feet broad, and two hundred and twenty-four Roman paces in circumference. The roof, arches and sides are all brickwork covered with terra-cotta, which is not the least impaired by time. The roof is supported by three hundred and thirty six pillars. The space of the intercolumniation is twelve feet. Each pillar is over forty feet, nine inches high. They stand lengthwise in twelve ranges, broadways in twenty-eight... There is an abundance of wells that empty into the Cistern. When it was filling in the winter time I saw a large stream of water filling from a great pipe with mighty noise until the pillars were covered up with water to the middle of the capitals. This Cistern stands west of the Church of St. Sophia a distance of eighty Roman paces.

Ninety of the columns in the south-west corner were walled off in the nineteenth century. The columns are topped by Byzantine Corinthian capitals; these have imposts above them which support little domes of brick in a herringbone pattern. One of the columns on the left side is carved with a curious peacock-eye or lopped branch design. This identifies it as part of the triumphal arch in the Forum of Theodosius I on the Third Hill (see Chapter 9), where fragments of identical columns were excavated in 1965. In the far left corner of the cistern, at a slightly lower level, one of the columns is mounted on ancient classical bases supported by the heads of Gorgons, one of them upside down and the other on its side. (The Gorgons in Greek mythology were three sisters, one of whom, Medusa, was slain by Perseus.) These Gorgon heads and the two we have seen outside the Archaeological Museum were, as we have noted, originally in the Forum of Constantine, whose site we will see later on this itinerary.

FIRUZ AĞA CAMİİ
On leaving Yerebatan Saray, we retrace our steps and return once

again to the beginning of Divan Yolu; 100 metres or so up Divan Yolu and on its left side, we see a tiny mosque, one of the oldest in the city. It was constructed in 1491 for Firuz Ağa, Chief Treasurer in the reign of Sultan Beyazit II. Firuz Ağa Camii is of interest principally because it is one of the few examples in Istanbul of a mosque of the "pre-classical" period, that is, of those built before 1500. This is the architectural style which flourished principally in the city of Bursa when it was the capital of the Ottoman Empire, before the Conquest. In form, Firuz Ağa Camii is quite simple, consisting merely of a square room covered by a windowless dome resting on the walls, the so-called single unit type of mosque. The building is preceded by a little porch of three bays, typical of the single-unit Bursa mosques, while the minaret, unusually, is on the left-hand side. The tomb of the founder, in the form of a marble sarcophagus, is on the terrace beside the mosque. Firuz Ağa Camii is an elegant little building, perhaps the most handsome of the early mosques of its type in the city.

THE PALACES OF ANTİOCHUS AND LAUSUS

Just beyond Firuz Ağa Camii, there is a little park which borders an open area excavated some years ago. The ruins which were exposed in these excavations are so fragmentary that it is difficult to determine their identity. It is thought that what we see here are the ruins of two adjacent palaces, those of Antiochus and Lausus, two noblemen of the early fifth century. The grandest of these is the palace of Antiochus, an hexagonal building with five deep semicircular apses with circular rooms between the apses. In the early seventh century, this palace was converted into a martyrium for the body of St. Euphemia when it was taken from Chalcedon to Constantinople. This lady was a virgin, martyred in Chalcedon in about the year 303. We learn from the Anonymous Englishman, writing in 1190, that St. Euphemia performed an astonishing miracle during the Oecumenical Council at Chalcedon in 451. According to his account, the two opposing parties in the Council, the Orthodox and the Monophysites, decided to resolve their dispute about the nature of Christ by placing their formulas in the saint's casket and letting her decide. A week later they opened the casket and found the Orthodox formula upon her heart and that of the Monophysites lying under her feet, thus bringing victory to the Orthodox party. The martyrium is elaborately decorated with paintings in fresco, representing scenes from the life and especially the gaudy martyrdom of St. Euphemia, and a striking picture of the Forty Martyrs of Sebaste; these are preserved in rather bad condition under a shed beside the Law Courts. They were at first ascribed to the ninth century but the latest study places them in the late thirteenth. Unfortunately, the shed covering the frescoes is closed permanently and the paintings can no longer be seen by the public.

THE BİNBİRDİREK CISTERN

Once past these ruins we take the first left off Divan Yolu, and a short way along on the right we come to the entrance to the ancient cistern known as Binbirdirek, "the Thousand and One Columns". The cistern was restored in the years 1995–2002 and is now open as a tourist attraction. Unfortunately the restoration was badly done and what was once an awesome and romantic site has now lost its historical identity; nevertheless it is still very interesting.

The dimensions of the cistern are 64 by 56.4 metres or 3,610 square metres; thus it is the second largest covered cistern in the city, though with only a third the area of Yerebatan Saray. It is thought that the cistern was originally built in the second quarter of the fourth century by Philoxenus, a Roman senator who came to the city with Constantine the Great, although there is evidence that some of the structure at least dates to the fifth or sixth centuries. During the nineteenth century the cistern was used as a spinning-mill and more recently as a storehouse.

The cistern was originally about 19 metres high from the floor to the top of the little brick domes in herringbone design. The columns are in two tiers bound together by curious stone ties. There were originally 224 double columns in 16 rows of 14 each, but 12 of these were walled in not long after the cistern was completed. The impost capitals are plain except that some of them are inscribed with monograms of the stone masons.

Continuing along the left side of Divan Yolu, on the next block we pass the Galeri Kayseri, the best book shop in the city for works in English on Istanbul and other places in Turkey.

At the next corner we turn left on Piyer Loti Caddesi, named for the French writer Pierre Loti. At the end of the block and on the right we come to the Eminönü Belediye Başbakanlığı building, the Town Hall of the Eminönü district, which has now been merged with the Fatih district, the two together comprising the whole of the old city. A door to the right of the main entrance has a sign indicating the entrance to the Theodosius Cistern, another of the city's late Roman subterranean reservoirs. The cistern measures 42.5 by 25 metres; its roof of brick domes in the usual herringbone design is supported by 32 columns of white marble in four rows of eight each, with some capitals of the the Corinthian order and others Doric, undoubtedly reused from older structures. The cistern is believed to have been built during the reign of Theodosius II (r. 408–50) by his sister Pulcheria, who would later marry her brother's successor Marcian (r. 450–7). The cistern was summarily restored and opened to the public in 1994.

We once again turn to Divan Yolu. Then on the next block we see on the right side of the avenue the rather heavy türbe of Sultan Mahmut II (r. 1808–39) and its long garden wall. Mahmut died in 1839 and his türbe is in the then popular *Empire* style, a little pompous and formal. Here also are buried sultans Abül Aziz (r. 1861–76) and Abdül Hamit II (r. 1876–1909), together with a large number of imperial consorts and princes.

THE KÖPRÜLÜ COMPLEX

Directly opposite the türbe of Mahmut II, on the left side of Divan Yolu, we see an elegant Ottoman library of the seventeenth century. This is one of the buildings of the Köprülü külliyesi, whose other institutions we will presently see in the immediate neighbourhood. These buildings were erected in the years 1659–60 by two members of the illustrious Köprülü family, Mehmet Paşa and his son Fazıl Ahmet Paşa. The Köprülü are generally considered to be the most distinguished family in the whole history of the Ottoman Empire.

During the second half of the seventeenth century and the early years of the eighteenth, no fewer than five members of this family served as Grand Vezir, some of them among the most able who ever held that post. The library of the Köprülü külliyesi is a handsome little building with a columned porch and a domed reading-room, constructed in a mixture of brick and stone. The library contains an important collection of books and manuscripts many of which were the property of its founders, who were known in their time as Mehmet the Cruel and Ahmet the Statist.

One block beyond the library and on the same side of the street, we come to two other institutions of the Köprülü külliyesi, the mosque and the türbe of Mehmet the Cruel. The türbe is of a rather unusual type, in the sense that it is roofed only by a metal grille. This gave rise to the legend that the grave was deliberately left open to the elements, so that the falling rain could cool the shade of the Grand Vezir, who was burning in hell-fire because of the thousands of rebels he had executed while in office. In the graveyard just beside the türbe we see the tombstone of a modern member of this famous family, Mehmet Fuat Köprülü, the distinguished historian and sometimes Minister for Foreign Affairs, who died in 1966. The mosque is a few steps beyond the türbe, projecting out into the sidewalk of Divan Yolu. The mosque, which is octagonal in shape, was once the dershane, or lecture-room, of the Köprülü medresesi, most of which has now disappeared.

THE ÇEMBERLİTAŞ HAMAMI

Directly across the avenue from the Köprülü mosque is the Çemberlitaş Hamamı, one of the finest extant examples of a classical hamam. This hamam was founded by Nurbanu Valide Sultan some time before her death in 1583; she was the wife of Selim II and the mother of Murat III. She was a great builder: her magnificent mosque complex in Üsküdar is described in Chapter 19. Her architect there was Sinan, but he does not appear to have been responsible for the present beautiful structure, for it is not mentioned in the *Tezkere*, the official list of his works. This bath is still fortunately in use, at least the men's section. It was originally double but part of the men's section was destroyed when the avenue was widened. In general it follows the usual plan: a great domed camekân leads to a small three-domed soğukluk, which opens into the hararet. This latter has a rather charming arrangement, seen also at Cağaloğlu and elsewhere; inscribed in a square chamber is a circle of columns supporting an arcade on which rests the dome. In the corners are the little washing-cells, each with its dome and an attractive door; the pavements have geometric designs.

THE COLUMN OF CONSTANTINE

Just across the side street from the hamam we come to one of the most venerable monuments in the city, the Column of Constantine. Ths is known locally as Çemberlitaş, or the Hooped Column, hence the name of the surrounding neighbourhood; in English it was in times past called the Burnt Column because of the marks of a fire that raged around it in the eighteenth century. This column marks the centre of what was once the Forum of Constantine the Great and was erected by him to celebrate the dedication of the city as capital of the Roman Empire on 11 May in the year 330. Constantine's forum with columned porticoes had the unusual shape of an oval. It has been compared to Bernini's superb portico at St. Peter's, though models nearer in time and place are not wanting: for example, the charming elliptical agora at Gerasa (Jerash) in Jordan built 200 years earlier, probably by Hadrian. Around it stood the usual public buildings: a Senate (there was still another Senate House off the Augustaeum), a Praetorium, and several temples and churches. And of course it was adorned with statues both Christian and pagan. The relics of all this grandeur are now buried some three metres beneath the present level of the road, and all that remains visible is the column, itself, much mutilated.

The column now consists of a very ungainly masonry base about ten metres high surmounted by a shaft of six porphyry drums, the joints between them hooped with iron bands; at the summit are ten courses of masonry topped by a marble block; the total height is 34.8 metres. Originally the column had a square pedestal standing on five steps; on the pedestal was a porphyry plinth and column base and seven porphyry drums. (The present masonry casing conceals the lowest of these.) At the summit, instead of the present masonry, there was a large capital, presumably Corinthian, upon which stood a statue of Constantine as Apollo. The iron hoops were an early addition, put on in 416 because the lowest part of the column had a piece knocked out of it and was thought unsafe. The statue of Constantine fell down as the result of a violent wind in 1106, and some 50 years later Manuel I Commenus replaced the capital by the masonry courses we see today, on top of which he placed a large cross. The lower masonry is Turkish work added in 1779 in order to bolster up the column. The column has recently been restored and the iron hoops have been replaced by new ones.

The ceremony of the original dedication of the column was a curious mixture of assorted pagan and Christian rites. Buried under the column or in the statue, itself, was the most incredible collection of relics: the Palladium of Troy, the hatchet of Noah, the stone from which Moses made water flow, the baskets and remains of the loaves with which Christ fed the multitude, the nails of the Passion (intertwined with the rays of Apollo!) and bits of the True Cross discovered by St. Helena at Jerusalem for the occasion. And the Apollo above did not prevent the people from later worshipping the deified Emperor, converted into a Christian saint, in a chapel at the base of the column.

VEZİR HANI

Leaving the main avenue for a moment, we turn to the right on Vezir Han Caddesi, the street which runs downhill beside the Column of Constantine. A short distance down the right side of this street we come to the entrance to Vezir Hanı, another institution of the Köprülü külliyesi. Such hans, or kervansarays, were commercial establishments where a travelling merchant could not only obtain food and lodging for the night but could also sell or store his goods. They are huge and stoutly-built structures of stone, or stone and brick, with two or three storeys around a great courtyard. One enters through a monumental gateway with very strong doors of thick wood, bound with iron, that are locked and barred at night. The vast courtyard is surrounded with porticoes, the one on the ground floor giving access to the windowless storerooms and stables, with staircases on each side leading up to the first floor gallery, more open and brighter, from which the living rooms were reached. In the centre of the courtyard there was generally a small mosque. Today, with the replacement of the horse and camel by the motor-truck, the character of these old hans has changed considerably, and they are now given over to every conceivable form of commerce and industry. Most of them, like Vezir Hanı, are in a shocking state of dilapidation and near ruin. Nevertheless they are still grand and picturesque, evoking something of the now almost vanished Oriental atmosphere of old Stamboul.

Returning once again to Divan Yolu, we continue on past Constantine's column on the same side of the street to an interesting mosque, Atik Ali Paşa Camii. This is one of the oldest mosques in the city, having been built in 1496 by the Hadım (Eunuch) Atik Ali Paşa, Grand Vezir of Sultan Beyazit II. Surrounded by a quiet garden off the busy street, it is an attractive little mosque, especially from the outside. Its plan is somewhat unusual, in that it consists of a rectangular room divided into unequal parts by an arch. The western and larger section is covered by a dome, the eastern by a semidome under which is the mihrab, as if in a sort of great apse. The western section is also flanked to north and south by two rooms with smaller domes. The semidome and the four small domes have stalactite pendentives, a common feature in mosques of early date.

Atik Ali Paşa Camii originally had several dependencies: a tekke, an imaret and a medrese. Of these only a part of the medrese remains; it is across the Divan Yolu from the mosque, the remainder having been destroyed some time ago when the road was widened. This building, though mutilated, is interesting as being one of the very few medreses of the pre-classical period that survive in the city.

THE COMPLEX OF KOCA SİNAN PAŞA

A short distance beyond Atik Ali Paşa Camii, on the same side of the avenue, we come to the külliye of Koca Sinan Paşa, enclosed by a picturesque marble wall with iron grilles. The külliye consists of a medrese, a sebil and the türbe of Koca Sinan Paşa, who died in 1595. Koca Sinan Paşa was Grand Vezir under Murat III and Mehmet III and was the conqueror of the Yemen. Perhaps the most outstanding element in this very attractive complex of buildings is the türbe, a fine structure with 16 sides, built of polychrome stonework, white and rose-coloured, and with a rich cornice of stalactites and handsome window mouldings. The medrese, which we enter by a gate in the alley alongside, has a charming courtyard with a portico in ogive arches. The sebil, too, is an elegant structure with bronze grilles separated by little columns and surmounted by an overhanging roof. The whole complex was built in 1593 by Davut Ağa, the successor to Sinan as Chief Architect.

THE COMPLEX OF ALİ PAŞA OF ÇORLU

On the other side of the alley across from the sebil, a marble wall with grilles encloses another complex of buildings, the külliye of Ali Paşa of Çorlu. This Ali Paşa was a son-in-law of Mustafa II and was Grand Vezir under Ahmet III, on whose orders he was beheaded in 1711 on the island of Mytilene. Ali Paşa's head was afterwards brought back to Istanbul and buried in the cemetery of his külliye, which had been completed three years earlier. This külliye, consisting of a small mosque and a medrese, belongs to the transition period between the classical and the baroque styles. Though attractive, there is nothing especially outstanding about these buildings, although one might notice how essentially classical they still are. The only very obvious baroque features are the capitals of the columns of the porch.

THE COMPLEX OF KARA MUSTAFA PAŞA

Directly across the avenue we see the octagonal mosque of Kara Mustafa Paşa of Merzifon, together with a medrese and a sebil. This unfortunate Grand Vezir also lost his head, which, according to an Ottoman historian, "rolled at the feet of the Sultan (Mehmet IV) at Belgrade" after the unsuccessful second siege of Vienna in 1683, of which Kara Mustafa had been in charge. The buildings were begun in 1669 and finished by the Paşa's son in 1690. This mosque is of the transitional type between classic and baroque and is of interest chiefly as one of the few octagonal buildings to be used as a mosque. This külliye and the other two we have just looked at have recently been well restored; Kara Mustafa's medrese has been converted into an institute commemorating the celebrated poet, Yahya Kemal, who died in 1958.

GEDİK AHMET PAŞA HAMAMI

The street just beyond this little külliye is called Gedik Paşa Caddesi; this leads to a hamam of the same name at the second turning on the left. This is one of the very oldest baths in the city, built in about 1475, and it is still in operation. Its founder was Gedik Ahmet Paşa, one of Mehmet the Conqueror's Grand Vezirs (1470–7), commander of the fleet at the capture of Azof and conqueror of Otranto. This hamam has an unusually spacious and monumental soğukluk consisting of a large domed area flanked by alcoves and cubicles; the one on the right has a very elaborate stalactited vault. The hararet is cruciform except that the lower arm of the cross has been cut off and made part of the soğukluk; the corners of the cross form domed cubicles. The bath has recently been restored and now glistens with bright new marble; it is much patronized by the inhabitants of this picturesque district.

THE BEYAZİDİYE

Returning once again to the main avenue, we continue along to Beyazit Square, a confused and chaotic intersection of no recognizable geometric shape. Crossing to the right-hand side of the avenue, we come to the Beyazidiye, the mosque and associated pious foundations of Sultan Beyazit II. The Beyazidiye was the second great mosque complex to be erected in the city. Founded by Beyazit II, son and successor of Mehmet the Conqueror, it was built between 1501 and 1506, and consists of the great mosque itself, a medrese, a primary school, a public kitchen, a hamam and several türbes. Heretofore, the architect's name has variously been given as Hayrettin or Kemalettin, but a recent study has shown that the külliye is due to a certain Yakub-şah bin Sultanşah, who also built a kervansaray at Bursa. His background is unknown and his origin uncertain, but he may have been a Turk. Whatever his origin, he created a work of the very first

SULTAN BEYAZIT CAMİİ

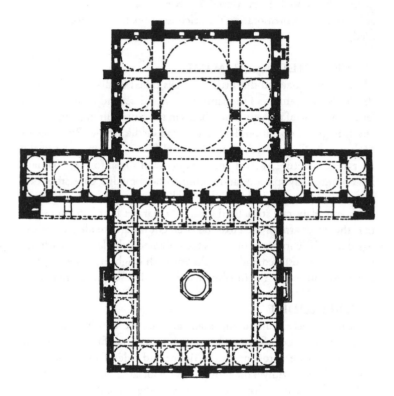

0 ⌊___.___.___.___⌋ 20 m.

plan no: 10

importance, both in its excellence as a building and in its historic importance in the development of Turkish architecture. The mosque marks the beginning of the great classical period which continued for more than 200 years. Before this time, Ottoman architects had been experimenting with various styles of mosques and had often produced buildings of great beauty, as in Yeşil Cami at Bursa or Üç Şerefeli Cami at Edirne; but no definite style had evolved which could produce the vast mosques demanded by the glory of the new capital and the increasing magnificence of the sultans. The original mosque of the Conqueror was indeed a monumental building, but as that was destroyed by an earthquake in the eighteenth century, Beyazit Camii remains the first extant example of what the great imperial mosques of the sixteenth and seventeenth century were to be like.

One enters Beyazit Camii through one of the most charming of all the mosque courtyards. A peristyle of 20 ancient columns – porphyry, verd antique and Syennitic granite – upholds an arcade with red-and-white or black-and-white marble voussoirs. The colonnade is roofed with 24 small domes and three magnificent entrance portals give access to it. The pavement is of polychrome marble and in the centre stands a beautifully decorated şadırvan. (The core of the şadırvan at least is beautiful – the encircling colonnade of stumpy verd antique columns supporting a dome seems to be a clumsy restoration.) Capitals, cornices and niches are elaborately decorated with stalactite mouldings. The harmony of proportions, the rich but restained decoration, the brilliance of the variegated marbles, not to speak of the interesting vendors and crowds which always throng it, give this courtyard a charm of its own.

An exceptionally fine portal leads into the mosque, which in plan is a greatly simplified and much smaller version of Haghia Sophia. As there, the great central dome and the semidomes to east and west form a kind of nave, beyond which to north and south are side aisles. The arches supporting the dome spring from four huge rectangular piers; the dome has smooth pendentives but rests on a cornice of stalactite mouldings. There are no galleries over the aisles, which open wide into the nave, being separated from it only by the piers and by a single antique granite column between them. This is an essential break with the plan of Haghia Sophia: in one way or another the mosques all try to centralize their plan as much as possible, so that the entire area is visible from any point. At the west side a broad corridor divided into domed or vaulted bays and, extending considerably beyond the main body of the mosque, creates the effect of a narthex. This is a transitional feature, retained from an older style of mosque; it appears only rarely later on. At each end of this "narthex" rise the two fine minarets, their shafts picked out with geometric designs in terra-cotta; they stand far beyond the main part of the building in a position which is unique and gives a very grand effect. At the end of the south arm of the narthex, a small library was added in the eighteenth century by the Şeyh-ül Islam Veliyüttin Efendi. An unusual feature of the interior of the mosque is that the sultan's loge is to the right of the mimber instead of the left as is habitual; it is supported on columns of very rich and rare marbles. The central area of the building is approximately 40 metres on a side, and the diameter of the dome about 17 metres.

THE PIOUS FOUNDATIONS OF THE BEYAZİDİYE

Behind the mosque – or, as the Turks say, in front of the mihrab – is the türbe garden; here Beyazit II lies buried in a simple, well-proportioned türbe of limestone picked out in verd antique. Nearby is the even simpler türbe of his daughter, Selçuk Hatun. Beyond these, a third türbe in a highly decorated *Empire* style is that of the Grand Vezir Koca Reşit Paşa, the distinguished leader of the Tanzimat (Reform) movement, who died in 1857. Below the eastern side of the türbe garden facing the street is an arcade of shops originally erected by Sinan in 1580; it had long since almost completely disappeared, but one of the happier ideas in the redesigning of Beyazit Square was to reconstruct it.

Just beside these shops is the large double sibyan mektebi with two domes and a porch; this is undoubtedly the oldest surviving primary school in the city, since that belonging to the külliye of Fatih Mehmet has disappeared. It has recently been handsomely restored and now houses the hakkı tarık us Research Library. (hakkı tarık us was a journalist who, like the poet e.e. cummings, had an aversion to capital letters.) Between this building and the northern minaret is a very pretty courtyard called the Sahaflar Çarşısı, or the Market of the Secondhand Book Sellers, in which we will linger on our next stroll through the city.

Almost opposite the north minaret stands the extremely impressive imaret of the külliye. The imaret, in addition to serving as a public kitchen, seems also to have been used as a kervansaray. The various rooms of the imaret line three sides of the courtyard (now roofed in), with the fourth side containing the monumental entrance-portal. The first room on the right housed an olive-press, the second was a grain storeroom, and the third, in the right-hand corner, was the bakery, equipped with two huge ovens. The large domed chamber at the far end of the courtyard was the kitchen and dining room. The even larger domed structure beside it, forming the left third of the complex, served as a stable for the horses and camels of the travellers who were guests at the imaret, while the chamber between the stable and the courtyard was used as a dormitory. The imaret was converted into a library by Sultan Abdül Hamit II in 1882; it now houses the State Library (Devlet Kütüphanesi). The library is an important one of 120,000 volumes and more than 7,000 manuscripts and the imaret makes a fine home for it.

The medrese of Beyazit's külliye is at the far west end of the square. It is of the standard form; the hücres, or cells, where the students lived and studied, are ranged around four sides of a porticoed courtyard, while the dershane, or lecture-hall, is opposite the entrance portal. This building has also been converted into a library, that of the Municipality (Belediye Kütüphanesi); unfortunately the restoration and conversion were rather badly done, a lot of cement having been used instead of stone and the portico having been very crudely glassed in. Nevertheless, the proportions of the building are so good and the garden in the courtyard so attractive that the general effect is still quite charming.

The medrese is now used to house the Museum of Calligraphic Art. The collections of the museum are organized into various sections; these are: Cufic Kurans, treatises and manuscripts and panels in Indian and Moroccan scripts; Nakshi Kurans and wooden cut-outs; Ta'liq Kurans and Thuluth panels; Ta'liq manuscripts and panels; Thuluth Nakshi collages and calligraphic compositions; the Holy Relics and dar-ül kürsa; Thuluth and mirror writings; Ta'liq panels, compositions, Thuluth and Nakshi Kurans; tuğras and Nakshi Kurans; Hilyes (descriptions of the features and qualities of the Prophet); embroidered inscriptions and works by women calligraphers; calligraphic models and Muhakkak Kurans. There are also examples of calligraphic inscriptions on wood, stone and glass, and other examples of the use of calligraphy, including title deeds, family trees, and even a talismanic shirt. There are also interesting exhibits of calligraphic equipment, and one cell has been set up with wax models showing a calligrapher instructing his students in this quintessentially Islamic art form, wonderfully evoked in this interesting museum.

Beyond the medrese, facing on the wide Ordu Caddesi that leads down into the valley at Aksaray, are the splendid ruins of Beyazit's hamam. This must have been among the most magnificent in the city, and it is now being restored from near ruin; the fabric still seems to be essentially in good condition. It is a double hamam, the two sections being almost identical, the women's a little smaller than the men's. Apart from the monumental façade housing the two camekâns with their great domes, the best view of the hamam may be had from the second floor of the University building just beyond; from here one sees the elaborate series of domes and vaults that cover the soğukluk and the hararet.

ISTANBUL UNIVERSITY AND THE BEYAZIT TOWER

On the north side of Beyazit Square stand the main buildings of the University of Istanbul. Immediately after the Conquest Sultan Mehmet II founded a medrese at the Aya Sofya mosque and a few years later he built the eight great medreses which were attached to his mosque; other such institutions were added by Beyazıt II, Selim I, and above all by Süleyman, who surrounded his own mosque with another seven medreses. In addition to Theology and Philosophy, there were Faculties of Law, Medicine and Science. But the decline of the Empire was accompanied by a corresponding decline of learning.

The first attempt to establish a secular institution of higher learning, known in Turkish as Darülfunun, was begun during the reign of Sultan Abdül Mecit I (r. 1839–61), as part of the reform movement known as the Tanzimat. The Darülfunun, which registered its first students in 1869, was reorganized in 1900 on the model of European universities, including faculties of science, medicine and civil law. After the founding of the Republic of Turkey in 1923 the Darülfunun was reformed and reorganized to become the University of Istanbul. It was then installed in its present building, previously the Seraskerat, or Ministry of War. The main part of the building was constructed by the French architect Bourgeois in 1866 in the sumptuous stylelessness then thought appropriate to ministerial edifices; and during the last two decades or so various wings have been added, equally styleless but not nearly so sumptuous.

The area on which these central buildings of the University stand formed part of the site where Mehmet the Conqueror built the Eski Saray, or Old Seraglio, immediately after the Conquest. Somewhat later he began to build Topkapı Sarayı on the First Hill and the Eski Saray was gradually abandoned as the official residence of the sultans. Some of its various and extensive buildings were used as a place of claustration for the women of defunct sultans, others as private palaces of distinguished vezirs; and a large part of its grounds was appropriated by Süleyman for his great mosque complex. In the end the whole thing disappeared and has left not a trace behind.

In the courtyard of the university stands the Beyazit Tower, a characteristic feature of the Stamboul skyline. There had long been a wooden tower at this point for fire-watchers, but it was not until 1828 that Mahmut II caused the tower to be built. It is some 50 metres high, and its upper platform commands a view of the entire city if one can obtain permission to enter.

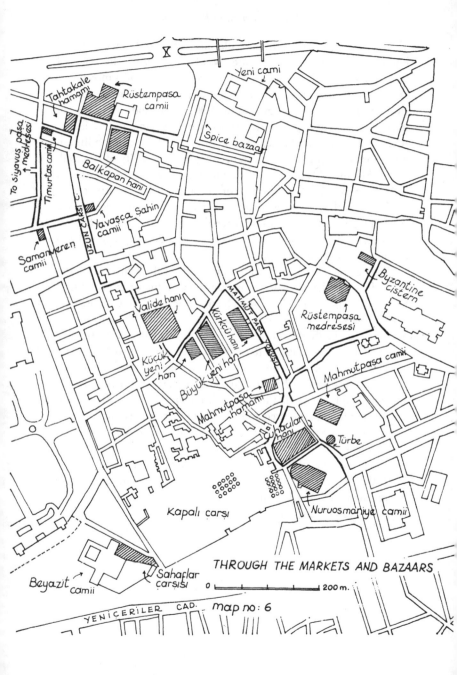

Yeni cami

Rüstempaşa camii

Tahtakale hamami

Spice bazaar

To siyavus paşa medresesi

Timurtas camii

Balkapan hani

UZUN CARSI

Yavaşca Sahin camii

Samankeren camii

Valide hani

MAHMUT PAŞA YOKUŞU

Kürkcü hani

Byzantine cistern

Rüstempaşa medresesi

Küçük yeni han

Büyük yeni han

Mahmutpaşa hamami

Mahmutpaşa camii

Cuhacilar hani

Türbe

Kapali carşi

Nuruosmaniye camii

THROUGH THE MARKETS AND BAZAARS

Saharflar carşisi

Beyazit camii

0   200 m.

map no: 6

YENICERILER CAD.

8

Through the
Markets and Bazaars

The region between Beyazit Square and the Galata Bridge is the principal market district of the city. This is one of the oldest and most picturesque quarters of Stamboul, and the tumultuous streets are full of clamour and commotion, with cars, trucks, carts and porters forcing their way through the milling crowds of shoppers and pavement vendors. Although colourful and fascinating, this neighbourhood can be somewhat wearing for the stroller, for it is often difficult to find one's way in the narrow, winding streets, most of which are not identified by signs, and one is continually fleeing to avoid being knocked down by herculean porters or run down by a lorry. And so, before beginning this tour, one is advised to prepare oneself, as do the Stamboullus, by having a bracing glass of tea in Çınaraltı, the old outdoor çayevi in Beyazit Square.

While sitting in the teahouse one can observe some of the streetside shops and markets which are so characteristic of this district. The street at the far end of the square is called Bakırcılar Caddesi, the Avenue of the Copper-Workers, where most of the coppersmiths of the city make and sell their wares. We will find that many of the streets in this district are named after the tradesmen and artisans who carry on their activies there, as they have for centuries past.

Leaving the teahouse, we pass through the gate beside the mosque (the Gate of the Spoon-Makers) and enter the Sahaflar Çarşısı, the Market of the Secondhand Book Sellers. The Sahaflar Çarşısı is one of the most ancient markets in the city, occupying the site of the Chartoprateia, the book and paper market of Byzantium. After the Conquest this became the market for the turban-makers and metal-engravers, at which time it was called the Hakkaklar Çarşısı, named after the latter of those two guilds. At the beginning of the eighteenth century, during the reign of Sultan Ahmet III, the booksellers set up shop here too, moving from their old quarters inside the Covered Bazaar. In the second half of the eighteenth century, with the legalization of printing in the Ottoman Empire, the booksellers greatly increased their trade and came to dominate the market, which from that time on came to be named after them. During the nineteenth and early twentieth century, the Sahaflar Çarşısı was one of the principal centres in the Ottoman Empire for the sale and distribution of books. In the past half-century, however, the establishment of public libraries and modern bookshops has diminished its importance and it now lives on in honourable old age as a market for secondhand books. It is one of the most picturesque spots in Stamboul; a pleasant, vine-covered, sun-dappled courtyard lined with tome-crammed shops, with stalls and barrows outside piled high with a veritable literary necropolis. The guild of the booksellers in this market is one of the oldest in Istanbul; its origins, like those of many other guilds in the city, go back to the days of Byzantium. In the centre of the square there is a modern bust of Ibrahim Müteferrika, who in 1732 began to print the first works in Turkish.

We pass through the Sahaflar Çarşısı and leave at the other end through an ancient stone portal, Hakkaklar Kapısı, the Gate of the Engrayers. We then turn right, and a few steps farther on we find on our left one of the entrances to the famous Kapalı Çarşı, the Covered Bazaar.

KAPALI ÇARŞI (COVERED BAZAAR)

Most foreigners, and indeed most Stamboullus, find the Covered Bazaar one of the most fascinating and irresistible attractions of Istanbul. No directions need be given for a stroll through the Bazaar, for it is a labyrinth in which one takes delight in getting lost and finding one's way out, after who knows how many purchases and other adventures. As can be seen from the plan, it is a fairly regular structure – which makes it even more maze-like and confusing in practice. It is a small city in itself: according to a survey made in 1880 the Bazaar contained at that time 4,399 shops, 2,195 ateliers, 497 stalls, 12 storehouses, 18 fountains, 12 mescits or small mosques, as well as a larger mosque, a primary school and a türbe. The number of commercial establishments would appear to be about the same now, in addition to which there have been added several new institutions, including half a dozen restaurants (the best is the Havuzlu Lokanta), innumerable teahouses, two banks, plus a toilet and information centre for lost tourists.

The Bazaar was established on its present site and covering almost the same area by Sultan Mehmet II, a few years after the Conquest. Although it has been destroyed several times by fire, the most recent in 1954, the Bazaar is essentially the same in structure and appearance as it was when it was built four centuries ago. The street-names in the Bazaar come from the various guilds that have worked or traded in those same locations now for centuries. Some of these names, such as the Street of the Turban-Makers and the Street of the Ağa's Plumes, commemorate long-vanished trades and remind us that much of the fabled Oriental atmosphere of the Bazaar has vanished in recent decades. A century ago the Bazaar was more quaint and picturesque, and stocked with more unusual and distinctive wares than it is today. But even now, in spite of the intrusion of modern shoddy and mass-made goods, there is still much to be found that is ancient and local and genuine. Shops selling the same kind of things tend to be congregated together in their own streets: thus there is a fine colonnaded street of oriental rug-merchants, whose wares range all the way from magnificent museum-pieces to cheap modern imitations. Here too are sold brocades and damasks, antique costumes, and the little embroidered towels so typically Turkish. There are streets of jewellers, goldsmiths and silversmiths, of furniture-dealers, haberdashers, shoemakers and ironmongers. In short, every taste is catered to; one has but to wander and inspect and bargain. Bargaining is most important; nobody expects to receive the price first asked, and part of the fun consists in making a good bargain. Almost all of the dealers speak half a dozen languages, and there is little difficulty in communication. But time is essential: a good bargain can rarely be struck in a few moments – often it requires a leisurely cup of Turkish coffee, freely supplied by the dealer.

In the centre of the Bazaar is the great domed hall known as the Old Bedesten. This is one of the original structures surviving from

KAPALI ÇARSI

MAHMUT PASA YOKUŞU

TO NURUOSMANIYE CAMii

sandal
bedesteni

old bedesten

0 _____ 100m.

map no : 7

Fatih's time. Then, as now, it was used to house the most precious wares, for it can be securely locked and guarded at night. Some of the most interesting and valuable objects in the Bazaar are sold here: brass and copper of every description, often old and fine; ancient swords and weapons, antique jewellery and costumes, fine glassware, antique coins, and classical and Byzantine pottery and figurines. As we might expect, not all of the antiquities sold in the Bedesten are authentic. Nevertheless, many of the imitations are of excellent workmanship, for the craftsmen who made them often belong to the same guild as those who did the originals, using the same tools and techniques as their predecessors.

If we leave the Bedesten through the Gate of the Goldsmiths we will notice above the outer portal the figure, in low relief, of a single-headed Byzantine eagle. This was the imperial emblem of the Comneni dynasty, which ruled over Byzantium in the eleventh and twelfth centuries. This has suggested to some that the Old Bedesten was originally of Byzantine construction, although most scholars are agreed that it was built in Fatih's time. In his *Seyahatname*, Evliya Çelebi describes this eagle and gives us his own original view of its significance: "Above the Gate of the Goldsmiths there is represented a formidable bird opening its wings. The meaning of the symbol is this: 'Gain and trade are like a wild bird, which if it is to be domesticated by courtesy and politeness, may be done so in the Beclesten'."

The Gate of the Goldsmiths opens onto İnciciler Sokağı, the Street of the Pearl-Merchants. If we follow this street and take the third turning on the right, we will soon come to one of the gateways of the Sandal Bedesteni. This is often called the New Bedesten because it was built some time after Fatih's Bedesten, perhaps early in the sixteenth century, when the great increase in trade and commerce required an additional market and storehouse for valuables. The Sandal Bedesteni is far less colourful in its activities than the Old Bedesten, for it is almost empty most of the time. But for that reason we can examine its splendid structure more easily, with its 12 massive piers, in four rows of three each, supporting 20 brick domes. The best time to visit the Sandal Bedesteni is on Monday and Thursday at one o'clock in the afternoon, when the rug auctions are held. These auctions take place in what looks like a little odeum in the centre of the Bedesten, where rug merchants and spectators, many of them canny Anatolians, sit and bid upon the rugs, carpets and kilims which the sellers exhibit on the floor. At those times one can recapture something of the old Oriental atmosphere of the Covered Bazaar.

We leave the Kapalı Çarşı by the door at the far end of the Bedesten. Turning right on the street outside, we see on our left an arcade of finely built shops which forms the outer courtyard wall of Nuruosmaniye Camii. These shops were originally part of the Nuruosmaniye külliyesi and their revenues were used to help pay for the upkeep of the mosque and its dependencies. These shops have recently been restored in an attractive manner and are now once again performing their original function.

NURUOSMANİYE CAMİİ

At the end of the arcade of shops we come on our left to the gate of the courtyard of Nuruosmaniye Camii, just opposite Çarşı Kapı, one of the main entryways to the Kapalı Çarşı. This is one of the most attractive mosque courtyards in the city, shaded by plane-trees and horse-chestnuts, with the mosque on the left and the various buildings of the külliye – the medrese, library, türbe and sebil – scattered here and there irregularly. The courtyard is a busy one, situated as it is beside one of the main gates of the Bazaar, and is much frequented by beggars and peddlers. Now and then one sees here one of the itinerant folk-musicians called *aşıklar*, who recite and sing their own poetry and songs while playing upon the *saz*. The *aşıklar* follow a tradition which is many centuries old, and are among the last survivors of the wandering bards and minstrels of the medieval world. Their songs and poems are concerned with all aspects of Turkish life, including politics, which is why they are so often in trouble with the police. But in the end the *aşıklar* (their name literally means 'Lover') always sing to their peasant audiences ballads of life and love in Anatolia, and so their songs are generally sad.

Nuruosmaniye Camii was begun by Sultan Mahmut I in 1748 and finished in 1755 by his brother and successor, Osman III, from whom it takes its name, the mosque of the Sacred Light (Nur) of

Osman. It was the first large and ambitious Ottoman building to exemplify the new baroque style introduced from Europe. Like most of the baroque mosques, it consists essentially of a square room covered by a large dome resting on four arches in the walls; the form of these arches is strongly emphasized, especially on the exterior. In plan, the present building has an oddly cruciform appearance because of the two side-chambers at the east end, and it has a semicircular apse for the mihrab. On the west it is preceded by a porch with nine bays, and this is enclosed by an extremely curious courtyard which can only be described as a semicircle with seven sides and nine domed bays! At the north-east corner of the mosque an oddly-shaped ramp, supported on wide arches, leads to the sultan's loge. (Note that a large number of the arches here and elsewhere in the building are semicircular instead of pointed in form, as they are generally in earlier mosques.) The whole structure is erected on a low terrace to which irregularly placed flights of steps give access.

Nuruosmaniye Camii is altogether an astonishing building, not wholly without a certain perverse genius. But its proportions are awkward and ungainly and its oddly-shaped members seem to have no organic unity but to be the result of an arbitrary whim of the architect. (He seems to have been a Greek by the name of Simeon.) Also the stone from which it is built is harsh and steel-like in texture and dull in colour. All things considered, the mosque must be pronounced a failure, but a charming one.

MAHMUT PAŞA CAMİİ

Leaving the mosque courtyard by the gate at the far end, we turn left on the street outside. A little way along, just past the first turning on the left, we veer right into a picturesque little square, one side of which is lined with old wooden houses. This is the outer courtyard of Mahmut Paşa Camii, one of the very oldest mosques in the city. Mahmut Paşa Camii is interesting not only because of its great age, but because it is a very fine example of the typical Bursa style of mosque structure. Built in 1462, only nine years after the Conquest, it was founded by Fatih's famous Grand Vezir, Mahmut Paşa. This distinguished man was of Byzantine origin: his paternal grandfather,

Philaninos, had been ruler of Greece with the rank and title of Caesar. Mahmut Paşa's contemporary, the historian Kritovoulos, gives this attractive picture of him: "This man had so fine a nature that he outshone not only all his contemporaries but also his predecessors in wisdom, bravery, virtue and other good qualities... He was enterprising, a good counselor, bold, courageous, excelling in all lines, as the times and circumstances proved him to be. For from the time he took charge of the affairs of the great Sultan, he gave everything in this great dominion a better prospect by his wonderful zeal and his fine planning as well as by his implicit faith in and good-will toward his sovereign." He was in addition a great patron of learning and the arts, especially poetry. He was put to death by the Conqueror in 1474.

The general plan of the mosque resembles fairly closely that of Sultan Murat I at Bursa. Essentially it consists of a long rectangular room divided in the middle by an arch, thus forming two square chambers each covered by a dome of equal size. On each side of the main hall runs a narrow, barrel-vaulted passage which communicates both with the hall and with three small rooms on each side. To the west a narthex or vestibule with five bays runs the width of the building and is preceded by a porch with five bays.

Let us look at some of the details. The porch is an unfortunate restoration, in which the original columns have been replaced by, or encased in, ungainly octagonal piers. Over and beside the entrance portal are several inscriptions in Arabic and Osmanlı (Old Turkish) verse giving the dates of foundation and of two restorations, one in A.H. 1169 (A.D. 1755) and another in A.H. 1244 (A.D. 1828). The ugly piers are undoubtedly due to this last restoration, since they are characteristically baroque. The entrance portal itself clearly belongs to the same period. On entering one finds oneself in the narthex – a most unusual feature for a mosque, found only once or twice at Bursa and at the Beyazidiye here. The vaults of the narthex are interesting and different from one another. The central bay has a square vault heavily adorned with stalactites. In the first two bays on either side smooth pendentives support domes with 24 ribs; while in the two end ones the domes are not supported by pendentives at all, but by a very curious arrangement of juxtaposed triangles so that the dome rests on a regular 16-sided polygon. Other examples of this odd and not unattractive expedient are found in the west dome of Murat Paşa Camii (see Chapter 16) and in one or two other mosques which belong to the same early period.

The two large domes of the great hall of the mosque have smooth pendentives, rather than the stalactited ones usually found in these early mosques. The mihrab and mimber and in general all the decoration and furniture of the mosque are eighteenth century or later and rather mean in appearance. This is a pity since it gives the mosque a rather unattractive aspect, so that one finds it difficult to recapture its original charm. In the small side-chambers some of the domes have smooth pendentives while others are stalactited. The function of these side-rooms, almost universal in mosques of this type, was for long a puzzle. The solution has been provided by Semavi Eyice, who shows that they were used, here and elsewhere, as a tabhane, or hospice, for travelling dervishes.

Leaving the mosque, we retrace our steps to the intersection outside the courtyard. There, down a short alley on the left, we see a little graveyard in which stands Mahmut Paşa's magnificent and unique türbe. The türbe is dated by an inscription to A.H. 878 (A.D. 1474), the year in which the unfortunate man was executed. It is a tall octagonal building with a blind dome and two tiers of windows. The upper part of the fabric on the outside is entirely encased in a kind of mosaic of tile-work, with blue and turquoise the predominating colours. The tiles make a series of wheel-like patterns of great charm; they are presumably of the first Iznik period (1453–1555), and there is nothing else exactly like them in Istanbul.

Leaving the türbe, we take the narrow street directly opposite, Kılıççılar Sokağı, the Street of the Sword-Makers. This is one of the most fascinating byways in the city, and is one of the very few surviving examples of an old Ottoman bazaar street. The left side of the street is lined with an arcade of ancient shops which were once part of the külliye of Nuruosmaniye Camii. On the right side of the street we pass a number of shops and ateliers which are part of the Çuhacılar Hanı, the Han of the Cloth-Dealers. The Çuhacılar Hanı

MAHMUT PAŞA CAMİİ

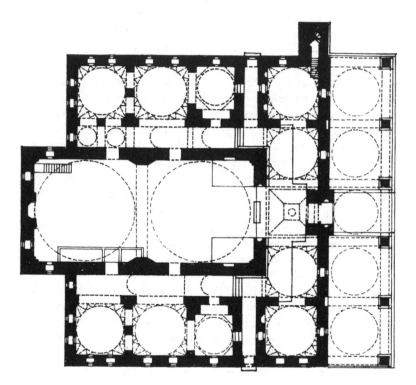

plan no: 11

was built in the first half of the eighteenth century by Damat Ibrahim Paşa, Grand Vezir in the reign of Sultan Ahmet III. It is not as grand as some of the other old hans in this neighbourhood; nonetheless it adds to the distinctively Ottoman character of the surrounding streets. We enter the han through an arched gateway halfway down the street and find ourselves in the cluttered inner courtyard, which is lined with an arcade of shops and ateliers. If we leave the han by the portal in the far left-hand corner, we will find ourselves just opposite one of the gates of the Kapalı Çarşı. We turn right here and after a few steps we pass through an arched gateway over the street and enter Mahmut Paşa Yokuşu, one of the principal market streets of Stamboul.

MAHMUT PAŞA HAMAMI

About 250 metres down Mahmut Paşa Yokuşu, we come to a turning on the left where we see an imposing domed building. This is a part of the Mahmut Paşa Hamamı, one of the two oldest baths in the city, dated by an inscription over the portal to A.H. 871 (A.D. 1476). (The Gedik Ahmet Paşa Hamamı, described in Chapter 7, may possibly be a year or so older, but it is not dated.) This was originally part of the Mahmut Paşa Külliyesi, and, as always in these interdependent pious foundations, its revenues went to the support of the other institutions in the complex. Like most of the great hamams, it was originally double, but the women's section was torn down to make room for the neighbouring han. We enter through a large central hall (17 metres square) with a high dome on stalactited pendentives; the impressive size of the camekân is hardly spoiled by the addition of a modern wooden balcony. The soğukluk is a truly monumental room covered by a dome with spiral ribs and a huge semidome in the form of a scallop shell; on each side are two square cubicles with elaborate vaulting. The hararet is octagonal with five shallow oblong niches, and in the cross-axis there are two domed eyvans, each of which leads to two more private bathing cubicles in the corners. Like all of Mahmut Paşa's buildings, his hamam is a very handsome and well-built structure. For a time it fell into disuse and then served as a storage depot, but it has been restored and now serves as a market hall.

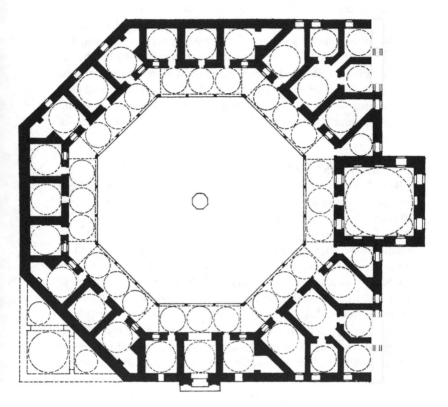

RÜSTEM PAŞA MEDRESESİ

0 |————————————| 5 m.

plan no : 12

RÜSTEM PAŞA MEDRESESİ

On leaving the hamam a somewhat complicated detour leads to an interesting monument. We take Sultan Oda Sokağı, the street which leads off to the right from Mahmut Paşa Yokuşu directly opposite the hamam, and follow it for about 200 metres to its end; then we turn left and then left again at the second turning. This brings us to the medrese of Rüstem Paşa, designed by Sinan and erected, according to an inscription, in 1550. It has a unique plan for a medrese. The courtyard is octagonal with a columned portico of 24 domes and a şadırvan in the centre. Behind this the cells are also arranged in an octagonal plan, but the building is made into a square on the exterior by filling in the corners with auxiliary rooms – baths and lavatories. One side of the octagon is occupied by the lecture hall, a large domed room which projects from the square on the outside like a great apse. This fine and unique medrese has been beautifully restored.

BYZANTINE SUBSTRUCTURE ON
CEMAL NADIR SOKAĞI

From here we can extend our detour to another interesting monument nearby. (This is part of the charm and trouble of strolling through Istanbul: one is continually being diverted by the prospect of another fascinating antiquity around the next corner.) Leaving the medrese, we retrace our way for a few steps and take the first turning on the left. This almost immediately brings us to a step street, Hakkı Tarık Us Sokağı. At the bottom of the steps we turn left on Cemal Nadir Sokağı and immediately to our left we see a massive retaining wall with two iron doors and barred windows. (The doors are locked, but can usually find a local who has the key.) This is perhaps the most astonishing Byzantine substructure in the city, consisting of a congeries of rooms and passages, 12 in all, every size and shape. There is a great central hall, 16 by 10.5 metres in plan and about six metres high, whose roof is supported by two rows of six columns, with simple but massive bases and capitals. From this there opens another great room, 13 by 6.7 metres, that ends in a wide apse. A series of smaller chambers, one of them oval in shape, opens from each of these large rooms and from the passages that lead off in all directions. The whole thing is like an underground palace and must clearly have been the foundation of something very grand indeed. However, all attempts to identify this structure with some building mentioned in Byzantine literature have been inconclusive.

We now retrace our steps back to where our detour began, outside the Mahmut Paşa Hamamı. There we continue downhill along Mahmut Paşa Yokuşu to look at some of the old hans which line the streets of this neighbourhood. There are literally scores of ancient hans in this district. Evliya Çelebi mentions by name more than 25 that already existed by the middle of the seventeenth century, and many others were built during the next 100 years; some go back to the time of the Conquest and many are built on Byzantine foundations.

KÜRKÇÜ HANI

About 100 metres downhill from the Mahmut Paşa Hamamı we see an arched gateway on the left side of the street; this is the entrance to the Kürkçü Hanı, the Han of the Furriers. This, too, is a benefaction of Mahmut Paşa and is the oldest surviving han in the city. Unfortunately, part of it is in ruins or has disappeared and the rest is dilapidated and rather spoiled. Originally it consisted of two large courtyards. The first, nearly square, is 45 by 40 metres, and had about 45 rooms on each of its two floors; in the centre was a small mosque, now replaced by an ugly block of modern flats. The second courtyard to the north was smaller and very irregularly shaped because of the layout of the adjacent streets. It had about 30 rooms on each floor and must have been very attractive in its irregularity; unfortunately it is now almost completely ruined.

BÜYÜK YENİ HAN AND KÜÇÜK YENİ HAN

Leaving the Kürkçü Hanı, we continue down Mahmut Paşa Yokuşu and turn left at the next street, Çakmakçılar Yokuşu. Just beyond the first turning on the left, we come to a massive gateway which leads to another Ottoman han: this is the Büyük Yeni Han, which means literally the Big New Han. It is called new because it was built in 1764, just a youngster in this ancient town, and big because it is: the second largest in the city after the Büyük Valide Han, which we will see presently. Its great courtyard must be over 100 metres in length but very narrow and tall. Unfortunately, it has been divided in the middle by what appears to be a later construction which much diminishes its impressive length. Nevertheless, its three storeys of great round-arched arcades are very picturesque. It was built by Sultan Mustafa III and is one of the best extant examples of the baroque han.

Just beyond the Büyük Yeni Han is a much smaller one of about the same date. This is the Küçük Yeni Han, or the Small New Han, also a construction of Sultan Mustafa III. If you look up at this point you will see the most curiously-situated mosque in the city, perched on the roof of the han. This strange little mosque, which bears Sultan Mustafa's name, has an almost Byzantine-looking dome and a pretty minaret. It is much frequented by the merchants and workers in the market district.

BÜYÜK VALİDE HANI

A little farther up Çakmakçılar Yokuşu and on the opposite side, we come to the entrance to the grandest and most interesting of all the hans in the city, the Büyük Valide Hanı. This han was built by the Valide Sultan Kösem, mother of sultans Murat IV and Ibrahim, shortly before her death in 1651, apparently on the site of an older palace founded by Cerrah Mehmet Paşa. We enter through a great gateway into the first courtyard, small and irregularly shaped because of the alignment of the han relative to the street outside. From there we pass into the main court, a vast area 55 metres square surrounded by a double-tiered arcade, the innumerable chambers of which are now given over to every conceivable form of industry and commerce. Although the entire han is now in a state of appalling squalor and dilapidation, it is nonetheless still impressive and extremely colourful.

A vaulted tunnel leads from a corner of the main court into the inner court, which because of the lay of the land is set at a lower level than the rest of the han. This court now houses a weaving-mill. At the back of this courtyard we see the remains of a Byzantine tower which is built into the structure of the han. This has traditionally been called the Tower of Eirene and is thought to date from the middle Byzantine

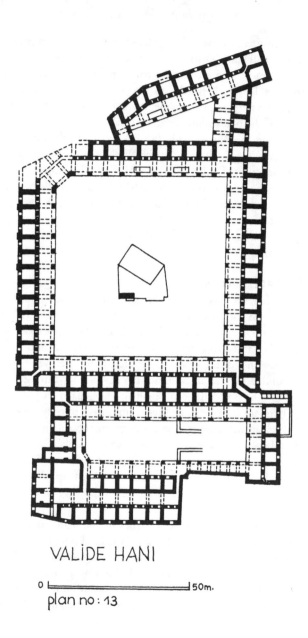

VALİDE HANI

0 ⊢————————————⊣ 50m.

plan no: 13

period, but the evidence for this is very uncertain. This tower appears as a prominent feature of the city skyline in the drawing made by Melchior Lorichs in 1559, where it is shown much taller than it is at present. The lower room of the tower is part of the weaving mill which occupies this part of the han, while the upper room is fitted out as a mosque, with a pretty ribbed dome; the mosque is now disaffected and serves as a storage room.

It was in this han, or rather in the palace which preceded it on the same site, that was established one of the first printing presses in the city. This was set up in 1567 by one Apkar from Sivas, who went to Venice to procure type in the Armenian script. This was not *the* first printing press in the city, however, for the local Jews had a press as early as 1494, the Greeks not till 1624, the Turks only in 1727, although books in Turkish had been printed long before this time in western Europe.

At a corner of the inner courtyard, an archway gives exit to an open area outside the han. Just opposite we see the large mosque of Ibrahim Paşa, one of the most ancient in the city. This mosque was founded in 1478 by Çandarlı Ibrahim Paşa, Grand Vezir under Sultan Beyazit II, who died during the siege of Lepanto in 1499. The mosque was in ruins for many years and was restored in the early 1970s; however, the restoration has wantonly destroyed all that was original in the structure and it is now hardly worth even passing mention.

We now follow the path which leads off to the left between the han and the mosque and soon find ourselves on another bustling market street, Uzun Çarşı Caddesi, or the Avenue of the Long Market. This follows the course of the Byzantine street called Makros Embolos which led from the Forum of Constantine to the Golden Horn, down the valley between the Second and Third Hills. The Greek name means Great Colonnade and the street was indeed lined with columned porticoes on both sides. But today the street is mean and squalid, although always crowded and picturesque. For this is the site of the Secondhand Clothing Bazaar, where the poor of the city sell one another clothes. It is said that, if you are clever enough, you can stroll through this bazaar, sell all the clothes you are wearing, and buy them back farther down the street at a small profit.

As we walk down Uzun Çarşı Caddesi, we might take a short detour along the first street on our right, Riza Paşa Yokuşu. A short way down this street on the right side we come to a handsome nineteenth-century building which houses the Redhouse Press, undoubtedly the oldest established publishing house in Istanbul. Originally founded in Malta by Daniel Temple in 1822, it set up shop in Istanbul 30 years later and moved into its present quarters in 1872. The Press is named after Sir James Redhouse, whose pioneering Turkish-English dictionary was first printed here in the years 1880–90; the most recent edition of this monumental work was published by the Redhouse Press in 1983. The first edition of this guide was published here in 1972.

YAVAŞÇA ŞAHİN CAMİİ

Returning to Uzun Çarşı Caddesi, we continue on downhill. At the first turning on the right we see one of the several insignificant but very ancient mosques which are found in this area, Yavaşça Şahin Camii. Yavaşça Şahin was a captain in the fleet of Sultan Mehmet II at the time of the Conquest; he built this mosque soon afterwards, though the exact date is unknown. It was badly damaged in the fire of 1908 but was well restored in 1950. It is one of a small group of early mosques that form a distinct type, in which the front porch has only two domes, and the entrance portal is consequently shifted off centre under the south dome. Within, a square chamber with a blind dome resting on an octagonal drum is supported by a series of triangles, making a 16-sided base. It is an odd type but not unattractive; unfortunately in this case the porch was not restored because of the impertinent intrusion of a shop.

SAMANVEREN CAMİİ

Just opposite Yavaşça Şahin Camii, a street called Ağızlıkçığı Sokağı leads steeply uphill. At the first corner on the left is a very ruined but ancient mosque called Samanveren Camii which was founded by a certain Sinan Ağa, an inspector of straw (hence the mosque's name) in the time of the Conqueror. Though once in a very advanced state of decay, the mosque has been restored. It is a quaint and interesting building of brick and stone construction; what is left of the original minaret has some curious leaf-like decorations in brick. The mosque itself was on the first floor and it was entered by a staircase which has now disappeared; a little courtyard led to the prayer-room which was covered by a wooden roof.

SIYAVUŞ PAŞA MEDRESESİ

Across from Samanveren Camii, a street with the picturesque name of Devoğlu (Son of the Giant) rambles downhill to the north; if we take the second turning on the left we come to another ancient Ottoman building. This is the medrese of Siyavuş Paşa, wedged in an angle of the hill above and very irregular in structure. Round about are the cells of the medrese, most of them with their domes more or less intact, though the colonnade in front of them, if there ever was one, has wholly disappeared. The dershane, unusually, is in a corner immediately to the right of the once-handsome entrance portal. This medrese was constructed some time before his death in 1601 by Siyavuş Paşa, brother-in-law of Murat III and three times his Grand Vezir. It is incredible to think that his magnificent palace, built by Sinan, was in this immediate neighbourhood, now a run-down market and industrial quarter.

TİMURTAŞ CAMİİ

Returning to the Street of the Giant's Son, we continue on downhill until we come to another ancient mosque. This is Timurtaş Camii, which has now been completely restored. It is very like Samanveren Camii; thus it is built over a vaulted ground floor and is of the same brick and stone construction, with a large wooden porch. Its minaret is unusual; instead of having a balcony, it is entirely enclosed and four small grilled openings are left towards the top through which the müezzin calls to prayer. It is thought that Samanveren Camii originally had the same type of minaret: they seem to be almost twin mosques. The exact date of neither is known, but both belong to the age of Fatih.

TAHTAKALE HAMAMI

If we now turn right along Kantarcilar Caddesi, we immediately see an enormous double bath, Tahtakale Hamamı, which also belongs to the age of Fatih. The hamam was for many years years used as an ice plant and cold storage warehouse, but recently it has been restored and converted into a shopping mall. The camekân, which from its great size must have been very impressive, is almost square in plan, 16.70 by 16.25 metres, covered by a huge dome on a low drum. The hararet is also large and has a high dome.

RÜSTEM PAŞA CAMİİ

We now find ourselves back on Uzun Çarşı Caddesi, where we turn left and continue on downhill for a short distance. Just to the right of the next intersection rises Rüstem Paşa Camii, one of the most beautiful of the smaller mosques of Sinan. This mosque was built in 1561 by Rüstem Paşa, twice Grand Vezir under Süleyman the Magnificent and husband of the Sultan's favourite daughter, the Princess Mihrimah. The rise of Rüstem Paşa began in the autumn of 1539, when he was engaged to marry Mihrimah. At that time he was governor of Diyarbakır, where his enemies tried to prevent him from marrying the princess by spreading the rumour that he had leprosy. But when the palace doctors examined Rüstem they found that he was infested with lice; consequently they declared that he was not leprous, for accepted medical belief was that lice never inhabit a leper. He was allowed to marry Mihrimah and Süleyman appointed him Second Vezir. Five years later he was made Grand Vezir, an office that he held from 1544 to 1553 and again from 1555 to 1561, during which time he became the wealthiest and most powerful of the Sultan's subjects. Thus it was that Rüstem came to be called *Kehle-i-Ikbal*, the Louse of Fortune, from an old Turkish proverb that says: "When a man has his luck in place even a louse can bring him good fortune."

The mosque is built on a high terrace over an interesting complex of vaulted shops, the rent from which went to maintain the foundation. Interior flights of steps lead up from the corners of the platform to a spacious and beautiful courtyard, unique in the city. The mosque is preceded by a curious double porch: first the usual type of porch consisting of five domed bays, and then, projecting from this, a deep and low-slung penthouse roof, its outer edge resting on a row of columns. This arrangement, although unusual, is very pleasant and has a definite architectural unity.

The plan of the mosque consists of an octagon inscribed in a rectangle: the dome rests on four semidomes, not in the axes but in the diagonals of the buildings; the arches of the dome spring from four octagonal pillars, two on the north, two on the south, and from piers projecting from the east and west walls. To north and south are galleries supported by the pillars and by small marble columns between them.

Rüstem Paşa Camii is especially famous for its very fine tiles which almost cover the walls, not only on the interior but also on the façade of the porch. One should also climb to the galleries where the tiles are of a different pattern. Like all the great Turkish tiles, those of Rüstem Paşa came from the kilns of Iznik in its greatest period (c. 1555–1620) and they show the tomato-red or "Armenian bole" which is characteristic of that period. These exquisite tiles, in every conceivable floral and geometric design, cover not only the walls, but also the columns, mihrab and mimber. Altogether they make one of the most beautiful and striking mosque interiors in the city.

Just to the east of Rüstem Paşa Camii, a few steps down Hasırcılar Caddesi, we find a han whose origins may go back to early Byzantine times. This is the Hurmalı Han, the Han for Dates; it has a long, narrow courtyard which one authority ascribes to the sixth or seventh century. There are a great many ancient hans in this neighbourhood, but they are for the most part decayed and cluttered, and almost nothing is known about them but their names.

BALKAPAN HAN

Continuing east along Hasırcılar Caddesi for a few more steps we take the next right and then in the middle of the block turn left into a large courtyard. We are now in the Balkapan Han, the Honey-Store Han. Evliya Çelebi tells us that in his time this was the han of the Egyptian honey-merchants. The han is chiefly interesting for the extensive Byzantine vaults beneath it: these are reached by a staircase leading down from a shed in the middle of the courtyard. Great rectangular pillars of brick support massive brick vaulting in the usual herringbone pattern, covering an area of at least 2,000 square metres. This basement is used today, as it probably was originally, for storage of all kinds of goods. The vaults and superstructures on ground level were doubtless one of the many granaries or storage-depots which are known to have existed in this area from at least the fourth or fifth century.

Returning to Hasırcılar Caddesi, we turn right and continue along until we come to the Spice Bazaar. Once inside we turn left and after passing through the Bazaar we find ourselves in the great square before Yeni Cami. Here, having completed our stroll through the principal markets and bazaars of Stamboul, we might be inclined to stop at the fish or vegetable markets of Eminönü and do a little shopping ourselves.

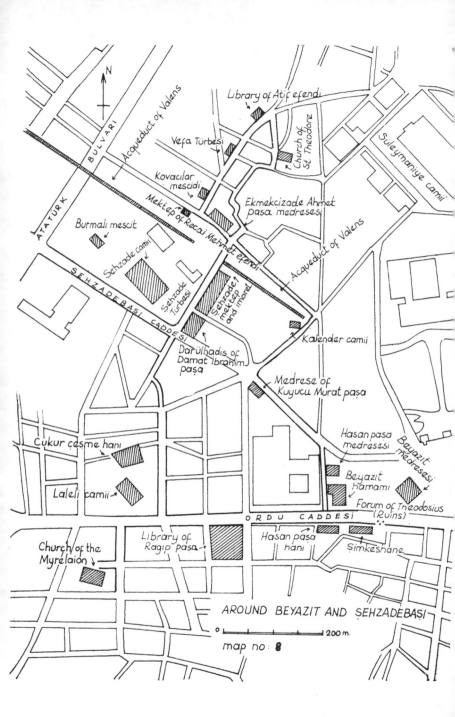

AROUND BEYAZIT AND ŞEHZADEBAŞI

0   200 m.

map no: 8

9

Around Beyazıt and Şehzadebaşı

We will begin this stroll in Beyazıt Square, which may fairly be said to be the centre of modern Stamboul. Indeed this square has been one of the focal points of the city for more than 15 centuries. In late Roman Constantinople this was known originally as the Forum Tauri, named after the colossal statue of a bull that once stood there. In 393 the square was rebuilt by the Emperor Theodosius I, the Great, and thenceforth it was called the Forum of Theodosius. The Forum of Theodosius was the largest of the public squares in Byzantine Constantine. It contained, among other things, a gigantic triumphal arch in the Roman fashion and a commemorative column with reliefs showing the triumphs of Theodosius, like that of Trajan in Rome. Colossal fragments of the triumphal arch and the commemorative column were found during reconstruction of Beyazıt Square in the 1950s, and are now arrayed on both sides of Ordu Caddesi next to the two hans on one side and Beyazıt's hamam on the other. Notice the enormous Corinthian capitals and the columns curiously decorated with the lopped-branch design that we have seen on a column in the Basilica Cistern. Fragments of the commemorative column have also been revealed built into the foundations of the hamam, where they produce a startling effect. There we see the figures of marching Roman soldiers, some of them ingloriously standing on their heads!

ŞİMKEŞHANE AND HASAN PAŞA HANI

At the very beginning of Ordu Caddesi, we see the remains of two enormous hans, each of which lost its front half when the avenue was widened in the 1950s. They were left in ruins, but both of them have since been restored and are once again functioning as commercial buildings. The one to the east is Şimkeşhane, and was originally built as a mint by Mehmet the Conqueror. The mint was later transferred to Topkapı Sarayı and Şimkeşhane was used to house the spinners of silver thread. The han was damaged by fire and then rebuilt in 1707 by Râbia Gülnüş Ümmetullah, wife of Mehmet IV and mother of Mustafa II and Ahmet III. The han to the west was built about 1740 by the Grand Vezir Seyyit Hasan Paşa. Both were handsome and interesting buildings, especially the latter. It is still worthwhile walking round them to see the astonishing and picturesque irregularity of design: great zigzags built out on corbels following the crooked line of the streets.

LIBRARY OF RAGIP PAŞA

Some few hundred metres farther on down Ordu Caddesi, and on the same side of the street, we come to the külliye of Ragıp Paşa. This delightful little complex was founded in 1762 by Ragıp Paşa, Grand Vezir in the reign of Mustafa III. The architect seems to have been Mehmet Tahir Ağa, whose masterpiece, Laleli Camii, is a little farther down Ordu Caddesi and on the opposite side of the avenue. We enter through a gate on top of which is a mektep, or primary school, now used as a children's library. Across the courtyard, surrounded by an attractive garden, is the main library; this has been restored in recent years and is now once again serving its original purpose. From the courtyard a flight of steps leads to a domed lobby which opens into the reading-room. This is square, the central space being covered by a dome supported on four columns; between these, beautiful bronze grilles form a kind of cage in which are kept the books and manuscripts. Round the sides of this vaulted and domed room are chairs and tables for reading. The walls are revetted in blue and white tiles, either of European manufacture or strongly under European influence, but charming nevertheless. In the garden, which is separated from the courtyard by fine bronze grilles, is the pretty open türbe of the founder. Ragıp Paşa, who was Grand Vezir from 1757 until 1763, is considered to have been the last of the great men to hold that office, comparable in stature to men like Sokollu Mehmet Paşa and the Köprülüs. Ragıp Paşa was also the best poet of his time and composed some of the most apt and witty of the chronograms inscribed on the street-fountains of Istanbul. His little külliye, though clearly baroque in detail, has a classic simplicity which recalls that of the Köprülü complex on the Second Hill.

BODRUM CAMİİ (CHURCH OF THE MYRELAION)

We now continue along Ordu Caddesi and take the second turning on the left, just opposite Laleli Camii. We then turn right at the next corner and at the end of this street ascend a flight of steps onto a large marble-paved terrace. Just beyond the far left corner of the terrace we see a former Byzantine church known locally as Bodrum Camii, or the Basement Mosque, because of the crypt that lies beneath it. The building was excavated in 1964–6 by Professor Cecil L. Striker of the University of Pennsylvania, who identified the church as the Myrelaion, "the place of the sacred myrrh", built by the Emperor Romanus I Lecapenus (r. 919–44) at the beginning of his reign along with a monastery of the same name. Beneath the church he built a funerary chapel, where he interred his wife Theodora after she died in 922. Next to the church and monastery Romanus also erected a palace on the substructure of an earlier Roman edifice, known as the Rotunda, beneath the marble terrace we see today. The church was converted into a mosque late in the fifteenth century by Mesih Pasha, a descendant of the Palaeologues who converted to Islam and led the forces of Mehmet II in their first and unsuccessful attack on Rhodes in 1480. The building was several times gutted by fire and was restored in 1965–6, along with the chapel beneath it, and it is once again serving as a mosque, while the Rotunda has been rebuilt as a subterranean shopping mall, with its entrance on the south side of the terrace opposite the mosque.

The most distinctive aspect of the exterior of the Myrelaion is the array of half-cylindrical buttresses that project from the west façade and the sides of the narthex and naos, articulating the internal bay divisions. The dome sits on a high cylindrical drum penetrated by eight round-arched windows. The church and the funerary chapel beneath it are of the same design, namely the four-column type so common in the tenth and eleventh centuries, with a three-bay narthex to the west and to the east the apse flanked by the sacristy and the prothesis, the chapel where the Eucharist was kept.

The funerary chapel can be visited in the company of the imam. A fragmentary fresco can be seen in the bema, the lower part of a panel depicting a female donor kneeling before a standing figure of the Virgin Hodegitria.

The Rotunda was excavated in 1964–5 by R. Nauman and is described by Striker in his book on the Myrelaion. Its external and internal diameters are 41.8 and 29.6 metres, respectively, with walls of finely cut aslar blocks now standing to a maximum height of 3.4 metres. The roof was originlly supported by some 75 columns. The Rotunda seems to have been in ruins when Romanus decided to build his palace on its substructure, erecting his church and funerary chapel just next to it. During the excavations of 1964–6 a fragmentary sculpture in porphyry was discovered in the Rotunda by the Turkish archaeologist Nezih Firatlı. Firatlı showed that this fragment, which we have seen in the Archaeological Museum, was part of a foot of the group of the Tetrarchs that now stands outside the south-west corner of the Basilica of San Marco in Venice.

LALELI CAMİİ

We now return to Ordu Caddesi where we are confronted by the imposing complex of Laleli Camii, built on a high terrace. This is a very frivolous mosque, perhaps the best of all the baroque mosques in the city. It was founded by Mustafa III and built between 1759 and 1763 by Mehmet Tahir Ağa, the greatest and most original of the Turkish baroque architects.

Before we visit the mosque itself we might take a stroll through the galleries below it, a veritable labyrinth of winding passages and vaulted shops. In the centre, directly underneath the mosque, is a great hall supported on eight enormous piers, with a fountain in the centre and a café and shops round about. The whole thing is obviously a *tour de force* of Mehmet Tahir to show that he could support his mosque apparently on nothing!

The mosque itself is constructed of brick and stone, but the superstructure is of stone only; the two parts do not seem to fit together very well. Along the sides run amusing but pointless galleries, the arcades having round arches; a similar arcade covers the ramp leading to the imperial loge. The plan of the interior is an octagon inscribed in a rectangle, all but the western pair of supporting columns being engaged in the walls; the latter support a gallery along the west wall. All the walls are heavily revetted with variegated marbles, yellow, red, blue and other colours, which give a somewhat gaudy effect. In the west wall of the gallery there are panels or medallions of *opus sectile*, in which are used not only rare marbles but even semi-precious stones such as onyx, jasper and lapis lazuli. A rectangular projecting apse contains the mihrab of sumptuous marbles. The mimber is of the same materials, while the kürsü or preacher's chair is a rich work of carved wood heavily inlaid with mother-of-pearl – altogether an extravagant and entertaining decor!

Like all of the other imperial mosques, Laleli Camii was surrounded by the many attendant buildings of a civic centre, some of which have unfortunately succumbed to time. On Ordu Caddesi there still remains the pretty sebil with bronze grilles and the somewhat sombre octagonal türbe in which are buried Sultan Mustafa III and his son, the unfortunate Selim III. On the terrace inside the enclosure is the imaret. This is an attractive little building with a very strange plan indeed, quite impossible to describe: it must be inspected. Unfortunately, the other institutions in the külliye – the medrese and the hamam – have disappeared.

The street just to the east of the mosque, Fethi Bey Caddesi, leads at the second turning on the left to a fascinating han which probably belongs to the Laleli complex. This was formerly known as Çukur Çeşme Hanı, the Han of the Sunken Fountain, but its present residents call it Büyük Taş Han, the Big Stone Han. The plan of this too is almost indescribable. We enter through a very long vaulted passage, with rooms and a small court leading from it, and emerge into a large courtyard, in the middle of which a ramp descends into what were once the stables. Around this porticoed courtyard open rooms of most irregular shape, and other passages lead to two additional small courts with even more irregular rooms! One seems to detect in this the ingenious but perverse mind of Mehmet Tahir Ağa. The han has now been restored and houses a restaurant and shops.

Leaving the han, we turn left and continue along Fethi Bey Caddesi for about 100 metres until it intersects Fevziye Caddesi; there we veer right and continue for another 100 metres until we come to Şehzadebaşı Caddesi, where we turn left. The broad avenue on which we are now strolling follows the course of the ancient Mese, which turned to the north-west after leaving the Forum Tauri. The modern avenue takes its name from Şehzade Camii, the great mosque which we see looming up ahead. Before we visit the mosque, however, let us continue past it for a little way so as to look at two monuments of some minor interest.

THE BELEDİYE AND THE MEDRESE OF ANKARAVI MEHMET EFENDI

Just past Şehzade Camii on the left side of the avenue we see the huge building of the Belediye, or Municipality, the headquarters of the civil government of Istanbul. Erected in 1953, it is of the glass and aluminium variety and not bad of its kind, except for a curious arched excrescence on the lower part of the building which looks like a hangar for airplanes. From the roof of the higher part, one has a fine view of the surrounding district. Behind this building is the little medrese of the Şeyh-ül Islam Ankaravı Mehmet Efendi, founded in 1707. This has recently been restored and is now used as part of the Economics Faculty of the University. It is a small and attractively irregular building, chiefly of red brick, with a long, narrow courtyard, at the far end of which is the lecture-hall reached by a flight of steps.

BURMALİ CAMİ

Crossing now to the opposite side of Şehzadebaşı Caddesi, we find in front of the west wall of the Şehzade precinct a pretty little mosque, recently restored, called Burmali Cami. It was built about 1550 by the Kadı (Judge) of Egypt, Emin Nurettin Osman Efendi. Although of the very simplest kind – a square room with a flat wooden ceiling – it has several peculiarities that give it a *cachet* of its own. Most noticeable is the brick minaret with spiral ribs, from which the mosque gets its name (*burmah* = spiral); this is unique in Istanbul and is a late survival of an older tradition, other examples of which are to be found at

Amasya and elsewhere. Then the porch is also unique: its roof, which is pitched, not domed, is supported by four columns with Byzantine Corinthian capitals. The reuse of ancient capitals also occurred in the earlier architecture of Bursa and among the Selçuks, but it is very rare indeed in Istanbul. (Bayan Cahide Tamer, the architect who so ably restored the mosque, found the original Corinthian capitals so decayed and broken as to be unusable in the restoration, but she was able to find in the Archaeological Museum four others of the same type with which she replaced the originals.) Finally, the entrance portal is not in the middle but on the right-hand side. This is usual in mosques whose porches are supported by three columns only – so as to prevent the door being blocked by the central column – but here there seems no reason for it. The interior of the mosque has no special features.

THE ŞEHZADE COMPLEX

The great mosque of the Şehzade has been looming up before us for some time and we must now visit this magnificent complex systematically. The main entrances are on Şehzadebaşı Caddesi. The complex consists of the mosque, several türbes, a medrese, a tabhane or hospice, a public kitchen and a primary school.

Şehzade Camii, the Mosque of the Prince, was built by Süleyman the Magnificent in memory of his eldest son, Prince Mehmet, who died of smallpox in the 22nd year of his age in 1543. As Evliya Çelebi wrote of Prince Mehmet: "He was a prince of exquisite qualities and possessed of a piercing intellect and a subtle judgement. Süleyman, when laid up with the gout, had fixed on him in his mind to be a successor to his crown; but man proposes and God disposes; death stopped the way of that hopeful youth at Magnesia, from whence his body was brought to Constantinople."

Süleyman was heartbroken at the death of his beloved son and sat beside Mehmet's body for three days before he would permit burial to take place. When Süleyman recovered from his grief he determined to commemorate Prince Mehmet by the erection of a great mosque and pious foundations dedicated to his memory. Sinan was commissioned to design and build it and began work almost

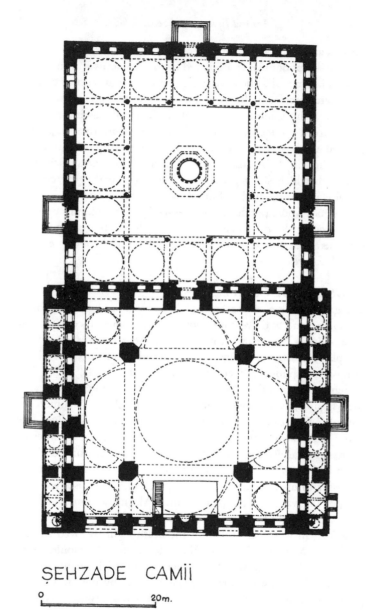

ŞEHZADE CAMİİ

0 _____ 20m.

plan no : 14

immediately, finally completing the project in 1548. Sinan himself called this his "apprentice work", but it was the work of an apprentice of genius, his first imperial mosque on a truly monumental scale.

Sinan, wishing from the very first to centralize his plan, adopted the expedient of extending the area not by two but by four semidomes. Although this is the most obvious and logical way both of increasing the space and of centralizing the plan, the identical symmetry along both axes has a repetitive effect which tends towards dullness. Furthermore, the four great piers that support the dome arches are stranded and isolated in the middle of the vast space and their inevitably large size is thereby unduly emphasized. These drawbacks were obvious to Sinan once he had tried the experiment, and he never repeated it.

The interior, then, is vast and empty; almost alone among the mosques, it has not a single column; nor are there any galleries. Sinan has succeeded in minimizing the size of the great piers by making them very irregular in shape: contrast their not unpleasing appearance with the gross "elephant's feet" columns of Sultan Ahmet. The general effect of the interior is of an austere simplicity that is not without charm: Milton's very un-Horatian "plain in her neatness" might well describe it.

As if to compensate for this interior plainness, Sinan has lavished on the exterior a wealth of decoration such as he uses nowhere else. The handsome courtyard avoids the defect of that of the Süleymaniye (see Chapter 10) by having all four porticoes at the same height, at the expense of sacrificing to some extent the monumentality of the western façade. The şadırvan in the centre is said by Evliya to be a contribution of Murat IV. The two minarets are exceptionally beautiful: notice the elaborate geometrical sculpture in low relief, the intricate tracery of their two şerefes, and the use of occasional terra-cotta inlay. The cluster of domes and semidomes, many of them with fretted cornices and bold ribbing, crowns the building in an arrangement of repetition and contrast that is nowhere surpassed. It was in this mosque, too, that Sinan first adopted the brilliant expedient of placing colonnaded galleries along the entire length of the north and south façades in order to conceal the buttresses, an arrangement which, as we will see, he used with even greater effect at the Süleymaniye: here the porches have but one storey, while at the Süleymaniye they have two. This is certainly one of the very finest exteriors that Sinan ever created; one wonders why he later abandoned, or at least greatly restrained, these decorative effects.

THE ŞEHZADE TÜRBES

Behind the mosque is the usual walled garden of türbes, but the türbes themselves are very unusual indeed, for they provide a veritable historical museum of the two best periods of Turkish tiles, the first extending from the time of the Conquest up until about 1555, and the second and greatest from 1555 up till 1620. The türbes in the precincts of Haghia Sophia are larger and grander, but their tiles, magnificent as they are, are all much of the same date and style, as are those of the Süleymaniye. Here, on the other hand, the buildings are of sufficiently different dates to cover the whole span of the great age of the Iznik kilns, together with a few of those produced at a later period at Tekfur Saray. Unfortunately, these türbes are not open to the public, except for that of Destarı Mustafa Paşa.

The first and largest türbe in the centre of the garden is, of course, that of the Şehzade Mehmet himself. It is octagonal, the faces separated by slender engaged columns; the stonework is polychrome, panels of verd antique with inscriptions being inset here and there in the façades, while the window frames and arches are picked out in terra-cotta. The dome, which is double, on a fluted circular drum, is itself fluted. The small entrance porch has a fine pavement of *opus sectile*. It is a very handsome building in the decorated style of the mosque itself.

The inscription in Persian verse over the entrance portal, which gives the date of the Prince's death, A.H. 950 (A.D. 1543), suggests that the interior is like the garden of paradise. It is indeed – all apple green and vivid lemon yellow – for it is sheathed in tiles from the floor to the cornice of the dome. These are almost the last and by far the most triumphant flowering of the middle period of Iznik tiles, done in the *cuerda seca* technique. Tiles in this technique and in these colours are extremely rare. They were first manufactured at Iznik in about 1514, when Selim I brought back a group of Persian craftsmen after his conquest of Tabriz, while the latest known examples, in the lunettes of the windows of Kara Ahmet Paşa Camii on the Seventh Hill (see Chapter 16), date from 1555. Other examples are in the mosque and türbe of Selim I (see Chapter 13) himself, some here and there in the Saray, and in the porch of the Çinili Köşk, and that is about all. Thus the türbe of the Şehzade contains far and away the most extensive and beautiful collection of tiles of this rare and lovely type.

The tile decoration of the interior was clearly designed as a whole. Panels of floral design separate the lower tier of windows; in the lunettes above them are inscriptions framed in arch-shaped borders; in the spandrels between these appears an occasional boss in faience. Above, a continuous series of large panels, each spanning two windows, contains a long inscription; then comes the upper tier of windows framed in floral panels with a lovely medallion between each pair of windows. The ground is in general apple-green, sometimes dark blue; on this are designs of leaves and flowers in lemon yellow, turquoise, dark blue, white, and a curious unfired pinkish-mauve; the colours are separated by the thin, almost black line of the *cuerda seca*. The whole effect is lyrically beautiful, truly like a garden in paradise, making this türbe a masterpiece unrivalled of its kind.

And the beauty of the türbe is not limited to its ceramics, for the upper row of windows contains some of the most perfect of Turkish stained-glass in rich and brilliant colours. Some of these are, alas, broken and damaged, but several remain entire; only in the Süleymaniye is there so extensive and brilliant a display of Turkish stained-glass of the sixteenth century. The dome, supported on a deep cornice of stalactites with a frieze of *trefles*, preserves its original arabesque painting: a great medallion in the crown with a circle of leaf-like forms in rich brick-red from which a sort of cascade of smaller medallions and lozenges rains down nearly to the cornice. Since one must perforce use superlatives in describing this building, one might venture the view that this is the very best painted dome that survives in the city. Still another unique feature of the türbe is the very curious baldachino over the Şehzade's cenotaph. It is of dark walnut wood, supported on four legs beautifully inlaid with ivory in a style that seems almost Indian; above this is a sort of openwork box of interlacing polygons, made of the same wood without inlay. One wonders if the box-like structure may not be intended to represent the Kaaba at Mecca, so that the effect would be that the Prince had been buried in the most holy place on earth. On his left is buried his daughter Humaşah Sultan; on his right his crippled brother, Prince Cihangir, who died in 1553 from love of his elder half-brother, the unfortunate Prince Mustafa, put to death by their father Süleyman.

Just to the left and behind the türbe of the Şehzade is that of the Grand Vezir Rüstem Paşa. This türbe is also by Sinan and it too is completely sheathed in tiles from floor to dome; but here everything is a little wrong. The building is too high for its diameter and too small to support the overwhelming quantity of tiles; and the tiles themselves, though beautiful, are just too early to display the full perfection of the Armenian bole technique. Rüstem evidently had a passion for tiles since not only his türbe but his mosque is entirely revetted with them; but he was unfortunate in his date, for he died in 1561, just ten years before complete mastery in the new technique was achieved. Here the most gorgeous panels are those between the lower windows; vases with a deep blue mandorla of flowers rising out of them. Between the lower and upper windows is a continuous inscription – white on dark blue – and between the upper windows floral tiles without an overall pattern. The drawing and composition are firm and good and the colours – on a white ground, dark blue, turquoise, a little green and red – are clear and vivid (all but the red, which in many tiles is muddy or brownish). There is no doubt that this türbe suffers greatly by comparison with that of the Şehzade and with that of Ibrahim Paşa nearby.

To this we now proceed – it is just opposite the south-west gate – passing in front of the unadorned türbe of Prince Mahmut, son of Mehmet III. The Grand Vezir Ibrahim Paşa, son-in-law of Murat III, died in 1601 and his türbe was completed in 1603; it is by the architect Dalgıç Mehmet Ağa. This türbe almost equals that of the Şehzade in splendour and perfection. It is octagonal and fairly plain on the exterior, though two marble panels on either side of the entrance portal, carved with elaborate floral and arabesque designs in low relief, are unusual and lovely. Inside, it is another bosk of the paradisical garden, but with a very different colour scheme: white, intense blue, turquoise and scarlet. Here the walls to the top of the lower tier of windows are of marble with a surbase of flower tiles. Between the two rows of windows there are two continuous friezes of calligraphy, white on dark blue, divided by a deep band of interlaced polygons in scarlet on a white ground. The effect is astonishing but beautiful, and there is nothing quite like it in existence. The upper windows are divided by superb floral panels predominantly turquoise picked out in scarlet. All the tiles are absolutely perfect in technique, the Armenian bole standing out boldly in relief and displaying its scarlet colour at its most intense: notice the spots of it in the curliques of the calligraphy, like liquid drops of blood.

This türbe, too, has almost an *embarras de richesses*: between the lower windows are cupboards with carved wooden doors; open these and you will find the interiors also lined with tiles. These were evidently added later, for some of them, one suspects, are from the Tekfur Saray kilns, but very good examples of the work. The two cupboards on either side of the door have tiles with an unusual and attractive Chinese cloud pattern; the other have the more ordinary floral designs. The dome, too, preserves its original painting, with elaborate arabesques and flowers on a terra-cotta ground; it is rather heavy and more cluttered than that of the Şehzade, but far finer than any modern imitation. Ibrahim Paşa's cenotaph is the usual wooden box, but beyond it are two tiny tombs for his son and daughter, of gaily painted marble.

There are two other türbes in the garden, those of Hatice Sultan, daughter of Murat III, and of Fatma Sultan, granddaughter of Prince Mehmet, but these are unadorned. There is, however, one more remarkable türbe to be visited, but it is outside the garden just opposite the south door of the mosque by the entrance to the outer precinct. It is that of Destari Mustafa Paşa, dated by its inscription to A.H. 1020 (A.D. 1611). This has now been restored and is open to the public. It has the unusual form of a rectangle, like two other türbes built by

Sinan: one for Pertev Paşa at Eyüp (see Chapter 18), the other for Ahmet Paşa in the garden of Mihrimah Camii at the Edirne Gate (see Chapter 17). Unlike these, however, this one preserves its roof, a low central dome flanked at each end by a shallow cradle-vault. The effect is very pretty. The walls between the windows are revetted with tiles, still of the best period; they are perhaps not quite so stunning as those of Ibrahim Paşa, but they contain a lot of Armenian bole at its most brilliant.

OTHER INSTITUTIONS OF THE ŞEHZADE COMPLEX

The medrese of the Şehzade foundation is on the far side of the precinct, at the north-west corner. It is a handsome building of the usual form. The south side, facing the mosque precinct, has a portico but no cells. Opposite the entrance, instead of the usual dershane, is an open loggia, the lecture hall itself being in the centre of the east side; opposite, a passage between two cells leads to the lavatories. The building has been well restored and is again in use as a residence for university students.

In line with the medrese but farther east is the kervansaray, which now serves as a science laboratory for the adjacent Vefa Lisesi. This building is probably not by Sinan, though obviously contemporary, or nearly so, with the rest of the complex. It has no door into the mosque precinct but is entered from the other side. It is L-shaped, the bottom stroke of the L consisting of a long, wide hall, its eight domes supported on three columns down its length; perpendicular to this is a block of eight cubicles with two spacious halls giving access to them. This interesting building is in good shape and makes a fine science laboratory.

Between the reservoir tank and the wall of the türbe garden a gate in the east wall of the precinct leads out into a side street, Dede Efendi Caddesi. Opposite, to the left, are the primary school and public kitchen of the complex. The primary school, or mektep, is of the usual type. The public kitchen, or imaret, consists of a spacious courtyard, on one side of which are three double kitchens and a large refectory, its four domes supported on three columns. This is a charmingly proportioned and gracious building. It is now used as a storage place; but the fabric is in good condition and one may hope that a more worthy use can be found for it.

As can be seen even from this necessarily inadequate description, the whole complex of the Şehzade is a triumph, and every one of its component parts has a brilliance and an interest of its own.

DAR-ÜL HADİS OF DAMAT IBRAHİM PAŞA

Turning back towards the main street we find on the left opposite the türbe garden a very pretty medrese, with a grand sebil at the corner. Built by the Grand Vezir Nevşehirli Ibrahim Paşa, son-in-law *(damat)* of Ahmet III, it is dated by its inscription to A.H. 1132 (A.D. 1720) and thus comes just between the end of the classical period and the beginning of the baroque; it has pleasing characteristics of both. At the end of the façade stands a large domed chamber surrounded by an attractive raised portico; the entrance portal is in the centre between them. The chamber to the left served as the library; that to the right was the dershane of the Dar-ül Hadis or School of Tradition, which is what the medrese was. Later the dershane was turned into a mescit, or small mosque, by the addition of a minaret. The far sides of the courtyard are partly lined with porticoes with cells beyond them, but these are irregularly placed after the baroque fashion. The building is in good condition and part of it is now used as a clinic. Outside, at the corner, is an extremely handsome sebil, a favourite with painters and etchers; it was still in use as a fountain up until recent years, but now it is closed. Behind this is a pretty graveyard in which is buried the founder of this fine little külliye. Ibrahim Paşa served as Grand Vezir under Ahmet III from 1718 till 1730, during the golden years of the Tulip Period. That delightful epoch ended on 20 September 1730, when the Tulip King was deposed and his chief minister, Ibrahim Paşa, was strangled by the Janissaries.

LIBRARY OF ŞEHİT ALİ PAŞA

We now walk back down Dede Efendi Caddesi, passing on our right the medrese of Ibrahim Paşa and the mektep and imaret of the Şehzade külliyesi. On our left we see the Vefa Lisesi, built by the architect Kemalettin Bey in the 1920s. In its precincts are two ancient buildings, one of which, the Şehzade tabhane, we have already described. The other is the library of Damat Şehit Ali Paşa, built early in the eighteenth century. The founder, Ali Paşa, was called Damat (son-in-law) because he married Fatma Sultan, daughter of Ahmet III, and Şehit (martyr) because he was killed in the battle of Peterwaredin in 1716. Fatma did not grieve long for Ali, for a few weeks after she heard of his death she married Nevşehirli Ibrahim Paşa, whose külliye we have just seen down the street. Ali Paşa's library is raised on a high substructure and approached by a long flight of steps; it consists of only two rooms, the larger of which is domed. It is not in use at present.

MEDRESE OF EKMEKÇİZADE AHMET PAŞA

At the next corner we turn left on Kovacılar Caddesi and immediately on our right we see another ancient Ottoman building. This is the handsome medrese built some time before his death in 1618 by Ekmekçizade Ahmet Paşa, son of an Edirne baker, who rose to the rank of Defterdar (First Lord of the Treasury) and Vezir, and died one of the richest men in the Empire. Until a few years ago the medrese was a ruin, inhabited by gypsies, but now it has been partially restored. Those who like variations on a theme will be pleased to note some anomalies: the right side of the court is occupied by the usual dershane, next to which, however, is a türbe of the same size, making the courtyard a bit lopsided. Both still preserve remnants of a rather good painted decoration in domes and pendentives, a rich red with deep green meander patterns. Even in its half-restored condition this is an interesting monument and well worth a visit.

PRIMARY SCHOOL OF RECAİ MEHMET EFENDİ

We continue in the same direction along Kovacılar Caddesi past the next intersection and on our left we see a half-ruined Ottoman building. This is the sibyan mektebi, or primary school, of Recai Mehmet Efendi, First Lord of the Treasury and Keeper of the Seal under Abdül Hamit I. The upper floor is built of alternate courses of brick and stone, but the entire ground floor is sheathed in an elaborately decorated marble casing. In the centre is the projecting curve of the sebil with three fine bronze grilles between the columns; on the left is the ornate entrance portal, while balancing this on the right is a çeşme. A long decorative inscription over the sebil gives the date of foundation as A.H. 1189 (A.D. 1775). Unfortunately, the level of the ground has risen considerably since then and this imposing façade has been somewhat swamped and belittled by it. But in spite of this and the poor condition of the fabric, it remains one of the more elaborate and charming of the small Ottoman primary schools.

Returning to the last intersection, we now turn left onto Kâtip Vefa Caddesi. Immediately on our left we pass the famous Vefa Bozahanesi, where the stroller might want to stop for a refreshing glass of boza. (Boza is a drink made from millet, once a great favourite of the Janissaries.) Notice the silver cup in a glass case on the wall; it is preserved there because Atatürk once drank from it.

Just beyond the Vefa Bozahanesi is a little mosque called Mimar Mehmet Ağa Camii. This was built in 1514 by Revani Şuccağ Efendi who was *Sürre Emini*, or official escort, of the annual embassy to Mecca. It is a small square building of brick with a dome; it is of no great interest, but has a pretty fluted minaret. The mosque was well restored in 1960, a little too much perhaps.

TÜRBE OF ŞEYH VEFA

A short way down the street we come to Vefa Camii, the small mosque from which the street and the district took their name. This is a brand new mosque erected on the site of the original Vefa Camii, built in the late fifteenth century. All that is left of the original mosque complex is the türbe of its founder, Şeyh Muslihiddin Vefa, dated A.H. 896 (A.D. 1491). In years past Şeyh Vefa was one of the most popular folk-saints in Istanbul, and even today a few old women occasionally come to pray at his türbe. (Officially there are no saints in Islam, but Istanbul abounds with the tombs and graves of holy men canonized only by the reverence accorded them by the pious poor of the city.) Although Şeyh Vefa was one of the most renowned scholars of his time (we are told that he was well versed in all of the 70 sciences of Islam), he decided quite early in life that he would devote himself entirely to the welfare of the poor. He therefore expended his fortune to build a pious foundation which included a mosque, hamam, primary school, imaret and kervansaray, where the poor could be assured of food and shelter for as long as they were in need. All of these benefactions have now disappeared, although the pious poor of modern Stamboul still come to pay their reverence at Şeyh Vefa's tomb.

LIBRARY OF ATİF EFENDİ

Just beyond Şeyh Vefa's türbe, on the same side of the street, we come to the library of Atif Efendi. Of all the Ottoman public libraries in the city this is the most charming and original. Built in 1741–2 and constructed of stone and brick, it is baroque and consists of two parts, a block of houses for the library staff and the library itself. The former faces the street and its upper storey projects *en cremaillère*, that is in five zigzags supported on corbels. Three small doors lead to the lodgings while a large gate in the middle opens into a courtyard or garden, on the other side of which stands the library. This consists of an entrance lobby, a room for book storage, and a large reading-room of astonishing shape. This oblong area, cradle-vaulted like the other rooms, is surrounded at one end by a series of five deep bays arranged like a fan. A triple arcade supported on two columns divides the two parts of the room; on the exterior this fan-like arrangement presents seven faces. Near the entrance to the reading-room the entire *vakfiye*, or deed of foundation, of the establishment is inscribed on a marble plaque. The library of Atif Efendi is altogether a fantastic and delightful building!

KİLİSE CAMİİ (CHURCH OF ST. THEODORE)

If we take the street just opposite the library entrance, Tirendaz Sokağı (the Street of the Archer), we come immediately to a little Byzantine church with a prettily fluted brick minaret. Converted into a mosque soon after the Conquest, it is called Kilise Camii, literally Church Mosque, a linguistic amalgamation of Christianity and Islam. It was identified by Gyllius as the Church of St. Theodore, but nothing is known of its history. The inner narthex and the church itself, which is of the four-column type, are to be dated some time between the tenth and twelfth century, when this type was predominant. But the most attractive part of the building is the outer narthex with its façade. Constructed of stone, brick and marble, its elaborate design and decoration proclaim it at once as belonging to the last great flowering of Byzantine architecture in the earlier fourteenth century. In the south dome of the outer narthex there were some fine late mosaics of the type of those at St. Saviour in Chora (Kariye Cami, see Chapter 14), but these have now almost vanished. The narthexes contain some handsome columns, capitals and door-frames which appear to be re-used material from an earlier building probably of the sixth century. And if you climb up into the minaret you will see set into the parapet of the şerefe the fine figure in low relief of a peacock, probably taken from a Byzantine fountain that is known to have stood nearby.

Leaving Kilise Camii we turn left and then right onto a street that we follow until we come to the rear of the medrese of Ekmekçizade Ahmet Paşa, which we visited earlier. There we turn left on Kovacılar Caddesi, which we follow for about 200 metres before returning right on the first through street on the right. This leads through a picturesque arched gateway under the Valens Aqueduct and out onto a large open area on the other side. There we see another former Byzantine church, this one of considerable interest.

KALENDERHANE CAMİİ

The church was converted into a mosque by Fatih under the name Kalender Hane, since it was used as a tekke by the Kalender dervishes. It was once identified as the Church of St. Mary Diaconissa, more recently as that of St. Saviour Akataleptos, and now, as the result of an archaeological study and restoration by Cecil L. Striker of Dumbarton Oaks and Doğan Kuban of Istanbul Technical University, as that of the Theotokos (Mother of God) Kyriotissa. The church is cruciform in plan, with deep barrel vaults over the arms of the cross, and a dome with 16 ribs over the centre. It originally had side aisles communicating with the nave, and galleries over the two narthexes. The building has proved to date, not from the ninth century, as was formerly supposed, but to the late twelfth. It still preserves most of its elaborate and beautiful marble revetment, making it one of the most attractive Byzantine buildings in the city, now once again serving as a mosque.

The most sensational discovery made during the archaeological study of the building is a fresco cycle of the life of St. Francis of Assisi in a small side chapel. This was executed during the Latin occupation of the city, probably about 1250, and is the earliest cycle of the life of St. Francis anywhere in the world, painted only about 25 years after his death. It shows the standing figure of the saint with ten scenes from his life and anticipates in many elements the frescoes of Giotto at Assisi. Other discoveries include a mosaic of the "Presentation of the Christ child in the Temple" dating probably to the seventh century, and thus the only pre-iconoclastic icon ever found in the city. Finally a late Byzantine mosaic of the Theotokos Kyriotissa came to light over the main door leading to the inner narthex, thus settling the much disputed dedication of the church. These paintings have been removed from the church and are now on exhibit in the Archaeological Museum, in the gallery devoted to Istanbul Through the Ages.

Excavations under and to the north of the church have revealed a whole series of earlier structures on the site. The earliest is the remains of a Roman bath of the late fourth or early fifth century, including a trilobed room, a circular chamber, and evidence of a hypocaust. This was succeeded by a basilica of the mid-sixth century built up against the Valens Aqueduct and utilizing the arches thereof as its north aisle. Finally, to the south of this, was built in the pre-iconoclastic period another church, part of the sanctuary and apse which were incorporated in the present building. Sections of the *opus sectile* floors of these earlier buildings were found under the floor of the existing apse.

MEDRESE OF KUYUCU MURAT PAŞA

Leaving the church we walk out to Şehzadebaşı Caddesi and turn left. (The last section of the street on which we are walking is called Cüce Çeşmesi Sokağı, the Street of the Dwarf's Fountain.) A short distance along and on the right side of the street we see a small triangular medrese. This elegant little complex was built in 1606 by

Kuyucu Murat Paşa, Grand Vezir in the reign of Ahmet I. Murat Paşa received his nickname *kuyucu,* or the pit-digger, from his favourite occupation of supervising the digging of trenches for the mass burials of the rebels he had slaughtered. The apex of the triangle is formed by the columned sebil, with simple classical lines. Facing the street is an arcade of shops in the middle of which a doorway leads to the courtyard of the medrese. Entering, we find the türbe of the founder in the acute angle behind the sebil, and at the other end the dershane, which, as so often, served also as a small mosque. This building has been taken over and restored by Istanbul University; the courtyard has been roofed in and used as a small museum, while the dershane contains a library.

MEDRESE OF SEYYİT HASAN PAŞA

Continuing along and passing the new University building, we turn right and soon come to another medrese complex, now the Istanbul University Institute of Turkology. This is a baroque building founded in 1745 by the Grand Vezir Seyyit Hasan Paşa, the same who built the han we saw earlier. It is curiously irregular in design and raised on a rather high platform so that on entering one mounts a flight of steps to the courtyard, now roofed in and used as a library and reading-room. In one corner is the dershane-mescit, which has become the office of the Director of the Institute; in another is a room designed as a primary school; this and the cells of the medrese are used for special library collections or as offices. Outside in the street at the corner of the buildings is a fine rococo sebil with a çeşme beside it.

After leaving the medrese we continue walking along the same street, which soon veers left and ends in a flight of steps beside Beyazit's hamam. We descend and find ourselves once more in the chaos of Beyazit Square, back at the point where we began our stroll.

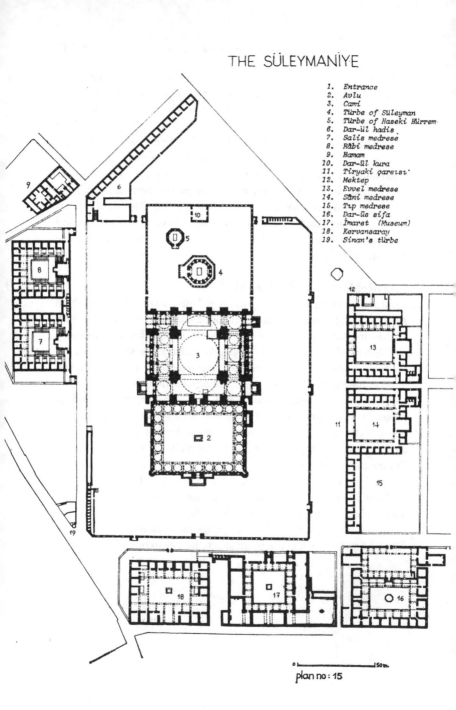

THE SÜLEYMANİYE

1. Entrance
2. Avlu
3. Cami
4. Türbe of Süleyman
5. Türbe of Haseki Hürrem
6. Dar-ül hadis
7. Salis medrese
8. Râbi medrese
9. Hamam
10. Dar-ül kura
11. Tiryaki çarsısı
12. Mektep
13. Evvel medrese
14. Sâni medrese
15. Tıp medrese
16. Dar-üs sifa
17. İmaret (Museum)
18. Kervansaray
19. Sinan's türbe

0 ⊢——————⊣ 50 m.

plan no: 15

10

The Süleymaniye

The Süleymaniye is the second largest but by far the finest and most magnificent of the imperial mosque complexes in the city. It is a fitting monument to its founder, Süleyman the Magnificent, and a masterwork of the greatest of Ottoman architects, the incomparable Sinan. The mosque itself, the largest of Sinan's works, is perhaps inferior in perfection of design to that master's Selimiye at Edirne, but it is incontestably the most important Ottoman building in Istanbul. For four and a half centuries it has attracted the wonder and enthusiasm of all travellers to the city.

The construction of the Süleymaniye began in 1550 and the mosque itself was completed in 1557, but it was some years later before all the buildings of the külliye were finished. The mosque stands in the centre of a vast outer courtyard surrounded on three sides by a wall with grilled windows. On the north side, where the land slopes sharply down towards the Golden Horn, the courtyard is supported by an elaborate vaulted substructure; from the terrace here one has a superb view of the Golden Horn, the hills of Pera on the other side, the Bosphorus, and the hills of Asia beyond. Around this courtyard on three sides are arranged the other buildings of the külliye with as much symmetry as the nature of the site would permit. Nearly all of these pious foundations have been well-restored and some of them are once again serving the people of Istanbul as they did in the days of Süleyman. We will later look at all of those which are presently open to the public, but first let us visit the great mosque itself.

THE MOSQUE

The mosque is preceded by the usual avlu, a porticoed courtyard of exceptional grandeur, with columns of the richest porphyry, marble and granite. The western portal of the court is flanked by a great pylon containing two stories of chambers; these, according to Evliya, were the muvakkithane, the house and workshop of the mosque astronomer. At the four corners of the courtyard rise the four great minarets. These four minarets are traditionally said to represent the fact that Süleyman was the fourth sultan to reign in Istanbul, while the ten şerefes or balconies denote that he was the tenth sultan of the imperial line of Osman.

Entering the mosque we find ourselves in a vast almost square room surmounted by a dome. The interior is approximately 58.5 by 57.5 metres, while the diameter of the dome is 27.5 metres and the height of its crown above the floor is 47 metres. To east and west the dome is supported by semidomes, to north and south by arches with tympana filled with windows. The dome-arches rise from four great irregularly shaped piers. Up to this point the plan follows that of Haghia Sophia, but beyond this – as at the Beyazidive – all is different. Between the piers to north and south, triple arcades on two enormous monolithic columns support the tympana of the arches. There are no galleries here, nor can there properly be said to be aisles, since the great columns are so high and so far apart as not really to form a barrier between the central area and the walls; thus the immense space is not cut up into sections as at Haghia Sophia but is centralized and continuous. The method Sinan used to mask the huge buttresses required to support the four central piers is very ingenious: he has turned what is generally a liability in such a building into an asset, on three sides at least. On the north and south he incorporated the buttresses into the walls of the building, allowing them to project about equally within and without. He then proceeded to mask this projection on both sides by building galleries with arcades of columns between the buttresses. On the outside the gallery is double, with twice the number of columns in its upper storey as in its lower; on the inside there is a single gallery only. In both cases – especially on the outside – the device is extremely successful, and is indeed one of the things which gives the exterior its interesting and beautiful distinction. On the east and west façades the buttresses are smaller, for here the weight of the dome is distributed by the semidomes. On the eastern face, therefore, Sinan merely placed the buttresses wholly outside the building, where their moderate projection gives emphasis and variety to that façade. On the west, in our opinion, he was not so successful. Here, in order to preserve the unity of the courtyard and the grandeur of the western façade, he chose to place the buttresses wholly within the building. Again he masked them with galleries, but in this case the device was inadequate. The great west portal, instead of being impressive as it ought, seems squeezed tight by the deep projection of the buttresses, which moreover not only throw it into impenetrable shadow, but also abut in an unpleasing way on the two small domes on which the western semidome reposes. It can be said that Sinan rarely quite succeeded with the interior of his west walls; in almost every case, even in the smaller mosques, there is a tendency to squeeze the portal. But his solution of the main problem was masterly.

The general effect of the interior is of a severely simple grandeur. The east wall only is enlivened by some touches of colour; here the lovely stained-glass windows are by the glazier known as Sarhoş (the Drunkard) Ibrahim; the tiles, used with great restraint, are the earliest known examples of the new techniques of the Iznik kilns, leaf and flower motifs in turquoise, deep blue and red on a pure white ground. The mihrab and mimber in Proconnesian marble are of great simplicity and distinction, as is also the woodwork, inlaid with ivory and mother-of-pearl, of the doors, window shutters and the kürsü, or preacher's chair. Throughout the building the inscriptions are by the most famous of Ottoman calligraphers, Ahmet Karahisarı, and his pupil Hasan Çelebi.

THE TÜRBES OF SÜLEYMAN AND HASEKİ HÜRREM

Leaving by the north door of the mosque, we find ourselves on the terrace overlooking the Golden Horn. Turning right, we walk around the mosque so as to enter the walled garden behind it, where stand the türbes of Süleyman and Haseki Hürrem. Süleyman's, as is fitting, is the largest and grandest of Sinan's türbes, although not quite the most beautiful. Octagonal in form, it is surrounded by a pretty porch on columns. This türbe, like those at Haghia Sophia and elsewhere, has a double dome, with the inner dome supported by columns in the interior. This inner dome preserves its gorgeous painting in wine-red, black and gold. The walls of the interior are covered with

Iznik tiles, twice as many in this small room as in all the vastness of the mosque itself. However, the grand effect has been marred, for the türbe is dark and overcrowded with cenotaphs; besides that of Süleyman there are also those of his daughter, the Princess Mihrimah, and two later sultans, Süleyman II and Ahmet II. But there is no mistaking the majesty of the magnificent sultan's own cenotaph in the centre of the türbe, surmounted by the huge white turban which he wore in life.

We might pause here for a moment to reflect on the history of this great monarch, under whom the Ottoman Empire reached the pinnacle of its greatness. Süleyman became sultan in 1520, when he was 25 years old, and ruled until his death in 1566, the longest and most illustrious reign in the history of the Empire. As Evliya Çelebi writes of Süleyman: "During the forty-six years of his reign he subdued the world and made eighteen monarchs his tributaries. He established order and justice in his dominions, marched victoriously through the seven quarters of the globe, embellished all the countries which were vanquished with his arms, and was successful in all undertakings."

To the east of Süleyman's türbe is that of Haseki Hürrem, smaller and simpler but decorated with Iznik tiles even finer than his. In this türbe the cylindrical base of the dome, slightly recessed from the octagonal cornice of the building itself, is decorated with a long inscription forming a sort of sculptured frieze. This and the türbe of the princes at the mosque of Selim I are the only ones where this form and these decorations are used. For some reason this türbe is not included in the *Tezkere,* the list of Sinan's works, but it is almost certainly his creation. The türbe is dated 1558, the year of Haseki Hürrem's death. Here, too, we might pause to review the life of the lady who is buried here, one of the most powerful and sinister women in the history of the Ottoman Empire. She is better known to the West as Roxelana, literally the Russian, because of her supposed origin. Süleyman fell in love with Roxelana during the early years of his reign and soon made her his legal wife, putting aside all of the other women in his harem. The Italian Bassano, a page in the Saray at the time, wrote of Süleyman: "He bears her such love and keeps such faith in her that all his subjects marvel and say that she has bewitched him, and they call her Cadi, or the Witch." The power of Roxelana over Süleyman grew so great that she eventually persuaded him to kill his eldest son, Mustafa, on the pretext that the Prince was plotting against his father. In this way Roxelana's own son, Selim the Sot, succeeded to the throne after the death of Süleyman. Historians consider this to be the turning-point in the history of the Ottomans, for with the alcoholic reign of Selim the Sot began the long and almost uninterrupted decline of the Empire.

THE DAR-ÜL HADİS

Farther east along the north terrace and beyond the wall of the türbe garden stands the dar-ül hadis, or school of tradition, which runs off at an angle to the line of the terrace, following the direction of the street below. This is a medrese of most unusual form. It consists of 22 cells arrayed in a long straight line rather than around a courtyard; opposite them is a plain wall with grilled openings enclosing a long narrow garden. At the end of the line of cells nearest the mosque, a staircase leads up to a sort of open loggia above, which appears to have served as the dershane – for summer use, evidently, for it would have been too cold in winter. This unique building has, regrettably, been very badly restored so that an effect which must have been quite charming has been all but ruined.

From the outer edge of the terrace we can look down onto the street which borders the north wall of the outer precinct. This was once an attractive arasta, or market street, with shops built into the retaining wall of the terrace and also opposite. These shops have recently been restored and are once serving the purpose for which they were originally designed.

THE SALİS AND RABİ MEDRESES

Just across the street we see two medreses of the Süleymaniye külliyesi. They are presently closed to the public and can perhaps best be viewed from the terrace. These are by far the most elaborate, original and picturesque of all Sinan's medreses. The one to the west, farther on down the street, is called Salis (Third), while the eastern one is known as Rabi (Fourth). These two medreses form a group with a pair which stand opposite to them on the southern side of the külliye; these are called Evvel (First) and Sani (Second); they were colleges in the four orthodox schools of Islamic law. There is still another medrese, the Mülazimler (Preparatory Students), which lies beneath the Salis and Rabi medreses. These three medreses were built on the steep northern slope of the Third Hill and in order to utilize this almost precipitous site two expedients were necessary. The north side of the courtyard was raised on high superstructures, beneath which lies the Mülazimler medresesi. Even so, the courtyard itself slopes downhill fairly sharply and the hücres, or cells, along the sides are built on five different levels communicating with each other by four flights of six shallow steps under the portico. On each level outside the cells is a *sofa,* in this case a kind of veranda with a low parapet. The dershane occupies most of the upper (southern) side of the courtyard, but since it is at the highest level it is entered from the sides rather than from the façade on the court. Salis and Rabi are absolutely identical; between them is a small court from whose lower level two staircases lead to the courtyard of the Mülazimler medresesi. This medrese consists of 18 cells with barrel-vaults underneath the north side of the upper medreses. As a display of virtuosity, nay of bravura, these medreses surely have no rival. Their effortless charm and simple distinction show that they were no empty vaunting of ingenuity, but a genuine architectural inspiration of a faultless master. They are unique and interesting monuments of Ottoman architecture, and one would hope that they will be opened to the public.

At the end of the street, just below the dar-ül hadis, is the hamam of Süleyman's külliye. This was for many years disaffected and used as a warehouse, and was in a deplorable state. But it has now been restored and is once again being used as a hamam. It is a single hamam and relatively small in size, given the enormous area of the külliye. The hamam is original in design and was once elegant in its decoration. The three-bayed porch has been altered and the camekân has been modified with a timber gallery added in the late Ottoman period. The hararet has an interesting arrangement with four corner cells and four eyvans.

THE DAR-ÜL KURA

The far eastern end of the terrace, the area behind the türbe garden, is a large open area which is triangular in shape because of the direction of the streets below. This was known anciently as the Iron Wrestling Ground, because of the weekly wrestling matches which were once held there. (This has always been an honoured sport in Islam, and the Prophet himself enjoyed wrestling with his companions.) At the western end of this area, set into the middle of the türbe garden wall, we see a handsome building which once served as the dar-ül kura, or school for the various methods of reading and reciting the Kuran. Such schools appear always to have been small buildings, rather like mekteps or the dershanes of medreses. They were sometimes directly attached to a mosque and without accompanying living-quarters for students, for the course in Kuran reading was naturally ancillary to more general studies. This school consists of a large domed chamber of very lovely proportions built over a small Byzantine cistern with four columns.

On the south side of the mosque, outside the precinct walls, stretches a long and broad esplanade lined with institutions belonging to the Süleymaniye külliyesi. This attractive avenue is called Tiryaki Çarşısı, or the Market of the Addicts, because till not very long ago the cafés which line the outer walls of the medreses used to serve opium to their customers in addition to tea, coffee and tobacco. We will start our tour of the outer precincts of the Süleymaniye at the eastern end of the Tiryaki Çarşısı, that is, by turning left after leaving the outer courtyard of the mosque.

THE EVVEL AND SANİ MEDRESES

The first institution which we come to at the eastern end of the esplanade is the former primary school. This little building, whose entrance is around the corner, has been restored and is now in use as a children's library. The next two institutions are the Evvel and Sani medreses, forming a group with the other two schools of Islamic law on the northern side of the mosque. The entrance to these twin medreses is at the far end of the narrow alley which separates them. They now house the celebrated Süleymaniye library, one of the most important in the city, with over 32,000 manuscripts. The buildings are mirror images of one another; and although the arrangement is typical enough – cells around a porticoed courtyard – there are interesting variations. Thus there is no portico on the north side but instead the three hücres are open, forming a kind of loggia, while the portico on the south side is cut by the dershane. All of the porticoes have been glassed in to accommodate the library; this has been well and attractively done and there is a charming garden in the courtyard itself.

THE MEDICAL COLLEGE AND THE HOSPITAL
Just beyond the Sani medrese we come to what was originally the Tip Medresesi, or Medical College, once the foremost in the Empire. Unfortunately, all that remains of it now is the row of cells along the Tiryaki Çarşısı: the other three sides have long since disappeared. In their place has been built a modern concrete structure and the whole now serves, appropriately enough, as a modern maternity clinic.

Across the street from this to the west is the vast dar-üş şifa, or hospital, a large building arrayed around two arcaded courtyards, now closed to the public. Evliya Çelebi gives this description of the Süleymaniye hospital as it was in his time: "The hospital of the Süleymaniye is an establishment so excellent that the sick are generally cured within three days of their admission, since it is provided with the most admirable physicians and surgeons." Like most of the larger hospitals, that of the Süleymaniye had a special section for the care of the insane. Foreign travellers to Istanbul were much impressed by these establishments and praised their number and size, charity and organization. Here, for example, is Evliya's description of one of these Ottoman asylums: "They have excellent food twice a day; even pheasants, partridges and other delicate birds are supplied. There are musicians and singers who are employed to amuse the sick and insane and thus to cure their madness."

THE İMARET
Turning right from Tiryaki Çarşısı onto the street which borders the west end of the mosque courtyard, we come next to the imaret,

or public kitchen, of the külliye. The imaret is enormous, as well it might be, for it had to supply food not only for the poor of the district but for the several thousand people directly dependent on the Süleymaniye: the clergy of the mosque, the teachers and students of the medreses, and the travellers staying at the kervansaray. The courtyard itself is charming with its ancient plane trees and young palms and a lovely fountain in the centre. A few objects from the imaret remain, including an olive press and an enormous stone wheel for grinding grain. The imaret now houses the Darüzziyafe, an excellent restaurant specializing in Ottoman cuisine.

THE KERVANSARAY

Next beyond the imaret is the kervansaray, now closed to the public. The kervansaray included a kitchen, a bakery, an olive press, sleeping quarters for travellers, stables for their horses and camels, and storage rooms for their belongings. According to ancient Turkish tradition, all accredited travellers were given free food and shelter at this and other kervansarays upon their arrival in the city. Evliya Çelebi reports on the hospitality given at these kervansarays in his day: "The kervansaray is a most splendid establishment where all travellers receive twice a day a bowl of rice, a dish of barley soup and bread, every night a candle, and for each horse provender, but the gift to travellers is only for three days."

This, then, is the great külliye of the Süleymaniye. Surely there can be in the world few, if any, civic and religious centres to compare with it in extent, in grandeur of conception, in ingenuity of design, or in the harmony of its parts.

SİNAN'S TÜRBE

Before we take leave of the Süleymaniye, we might stop for a moment at the tomb of the architect, which stands in a little triangular garden at the north-western corner of the complex. Sinan lived on this site for many years and when he died he was buried in his garden, in a türbe which he had designed and built himself. Fom the apex of the triangle radiate the garden walls, enclosing the open marble türbe. An arcade with six ogive arches supports a marble roof which has a tiny dome over the sarcophagus; the latter is of marble with a turbaned tombstone at the head. Outside the türbe are several other graves, presumably of Sinan's wife and children, but unfortunately there are no inscriptions.

On the south wall of the türbe garden there is a long inscription by Sinan's friend, the poet Mustafa Sa'i, which commemorates the architect's accomplishments. Mustafa Sa'i also wrote of Sinan in his *Tezkere-ül Ebniye,* and from this and other sources we can piece together the life-history of this extraordinary genius. Sinan was born of Christian parents, presumably Greek, in the Anatolian district of Karamania in about 1490. When he was about 21 he was caught up in the *devşirme,* the annual levy of Christian youths who were taken into the Sultan's service. As was customary, he became a Muslim and was sent to one of the palace schools in Istanbul. He was then assigned to the Janissaries as a military engineer and served in five of Süleyman's campaigns. In about 1538 he was appointed Chief of the Imperial Architects, and in the following year completed his first large mosque in Istanbul, Haseki Hürrem Camii. In the following half-century he was to adorn Istanbul and the other cities of the Empire with an incredible number of mosques and other structures. In the *Tezkere*, Mustafa Sa'i credits Sinan with 84 mosques, including 42 in Istanbul, as well as 52 mescits, 63 medreses, seven Kuran schools, 22 türbes, 18 imarets, 20 kervansarays, three hospitals, 35 palaces, eight storehouses, 52 hamams, six aqueducts and eight bridges, a total of 378 structures of which 86 still remain standing in Istanbul alone. And although he was in his 50th year when he completed his first mosque in Istanbul, this renaissance man got better as he grew older and was all of 85 when he completed his crowning masterpiece, the Selimiye mosque in Edirne. He did not pause even then and in the years that were left to him he continued his work, building in that period, among other things, a half-dozen of Istanbul's finer mosques. Koca Mimar Sinan, or Great Sinan the Architect, as the Turks call him, died in 1588 when he was 97 years old (100 according to the Muslim calendar). He was the architect of the golden age and his monuments are the magnificent buildings with which he adorned this city.

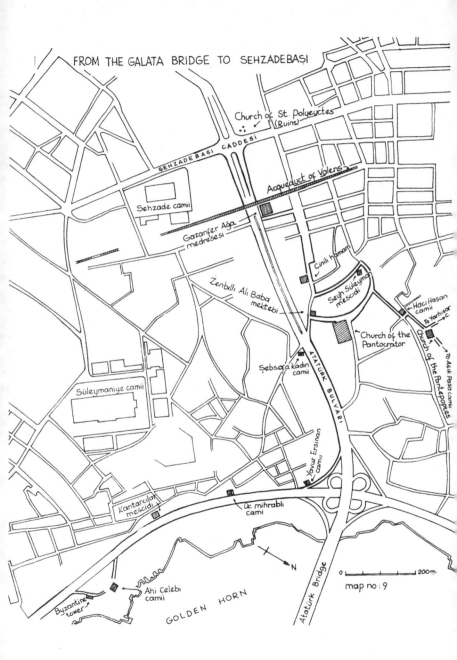

FROM THE GALATA BRIDGE TO SEHZADEBAŞI

Church of St. Polyeuctes
(Ruins)

SEHZADEBAŞI CADDESI

Acqueduct of Valens

Sehzade camii

Gazanfer Ağa
medresesi

Çinili hamam

Zenbilli Ali Baba
mektebi

Şeyh Süleyman
mescidi

Hacı Hasan
camii

To Yarhisar
c.

Church of the
Pantocrator

To Aşık Paşa camii

Church of the Pantepoppes

Şebsefa kadın
camii

Süleymaniye camii

ATATÜRK BULVARI

Yavuz Ersinan
camii

Kantarcılar
mescidi

Üç mihrablı
camii

N

0 _____ 200m.

map no: 9

Ahi Çelebi
camii

Byzantine tower

GOLDEN HORN

Atatürk Bridge

11

From the Galata Bridge to Şehzadebaşı

Once more we begin our stroll at the Galata Bridge, this time to begin walking up the shore of the Golden Horn before heading up hill to the district called Şehzadebaşı, just to the north of the Şehzade mosque. The first part of our stroll takes us through the oldest market area of the city, a rough and colourful quarter that is stubbornly resisting attempts to modernize it.

THE PRISON TOWER

The part of the market district just above the Galata Bridge and between the shore road and the Golden Horn is known as Zindan Kapı, or the Prison Gate. This waterfront quarter was one of the oldest and most picturesque neighbourhoods in Istanbul, but in the early 1970s almost all of its buildings were demolished in a project designed to create parks along the shore of the Golden Horn but which here resulted only in a scabrous parking lot. One of the few surviving monuments is an ancient tower behind a late Ottoman commercial building known as the Zindan Han. This is by far the largest of the few surviving defence towers of the medieval Byzantine sea-walls along the Golden Horn. The tower was for centuries used as a prison (in Turkish, *zindan*) by both the Byzantines and the Ottomans, particularly for galley slaves. Within the tower, known to the Venetians as the Bagno, is buried a certain Cafer Baba, who, according to legend, came to Constantinople as the envoy of Harun al-Rashid to the Empress Eirene (r. 797–802), but was here imprisoned and died; his grave was rediscovered and restored after the Conques and is to this day much venerated. According to Evliya Çelebi: "Cafer Baba was buried in a place within the prison of the infidels, where to this day his name is insulted by all the unbelieving malefactors, debtors, murderers, etc. imprisoned there. But when (God be praised!) Istanbul was taken, the grave of Cafer Baba in the tower of the Bagno became a place of pilgrimage which is visited by those who have been released from prison and who call down blessings in opposition to the curses of the unbelievers." The tower was restored in 1990 and the supposed grave of Cafer Baba on the ground floor of the tower was opened to the public as a Muslim shrine.

Just beyond the Zindan Han are the shattered remnants of an arched gateway from the medieval Byzantine period. The identity of this gate is uncertain, but in early Ottoman times local Greeks referred to it as the Porta Caravion (the Gate of the Caravels), because of the large number of ships which were moored at the pier nearby, the ancient Scala de Drongario. This pier, known as the Yemiş Iskelesi, or Dried Fruit Pier, was still in use up until the mid-1980s, but then it was demolished along with the rest of the Zindan Kapı quarter, which was for many centuries the principal fruit and vegetable market of the old city but is now only a fading memory.

THE MOSQUE OF AHİ ÇELEBİ

Passing the gateway, we soon find ourselves in front of an ancient mosque, Ahi Çelebi Camii. This mosque was founded at an uncertain date by Ahi Çelebi ibni Kemal, who was Chief Physician of the hospital of Fatih Mehmet and who died in 1523 while returning from a pilgrimage to Mecca. The building is of little architectural interest, aside from the fact that it was apparently restored at one point by Sinan. Its principal interest to us is its association with Evliya Çelebi, whose *Seyahatname,* or *Book of Travels,* we have so often quoted in our guide. One night in Ramazan in the year 1631, when Evliya was 20 years old, he fell asleep and dreamt that he was in the mosque of Ahi Çelebi. While praying there, in his dream, he was astonished to find the mosque fill up with what he described as "a refulgent crowd of saints and martyrs," followed by the Prophet, who gave him his blessings and intimated that Evliya would spend his life as a traveller. "When I awoke," writes Evliya, "I was in great doubt whether what I had seen was a dream or reality, and I enjoyed for some time the beatific contemplations which filled my soul. Having afterwards performed my ablutions and offered up the morning prayer, I crossed over from Constantinople to the suburb of Kasım Paşa and consulted the interpreter of dreams, Ibrahim Efendi, about my vision. From him I received the comfortable news that I would become a great traveller, and after making my way through the world, by the intercession of the Prophet, would close my career by being admitted to Paradise. I then retired to my humble abode, applied myself to the study of history, and began a description of my birthplace, Istanbul, that envy of kings, the celestial haven and stronghold of Macedonia." But such beatific visions are denied to the modern traveller, who must now resume his stroll through Stamboul, heading up the main highway that leads along the bank of the Golden Horn between the two bridges.

KANTARCILAR MESCİDİ, KAZANCILAR CAMİİ, AND SAĞRICILAR CAMİİ

As we walk along the left side of the avenue we pass in turn three little mosques which are among the very oldest in Istanbul, all of them built just after the Conquest. The first of these that we come to is Kantarcılar Mescidi, the mescit, or small mosque, of the Scale-Makers, named after the guild whose artisans have had their workshops in this neighbourhood for centuries. This mosque was founded during Fatih's reign by one Sarı Demirci Mevlana Mehmet Muhittin. It has since been reconstructed several times and is of little interest except for its great age.

The second of these ancient mosques which we pass, about 250 metres beyond the first, is called Kazancılar Camii, the mosque of the Cauldron-Makers, here again named for one of the neighbourhood guilds. It is also known as Üç Mihrablı Camii, literally the mosque with three mihrabs. Founded by a certain Hoca Hayreddin Efendi in 1475, it was enlarged first by Fatih himself, then by Hayreddin's daughter-in-law, who added her own house to the mosque, so that it came to have three mihrabs, hence its name. The main body of the building, which seems to be original in form though heavily restored, consists of a square room covered by a dome resting on a high blind drum, worked in the form of a series of triangles so that pendentives or squinches are dispensed with. In the dome are some rather curious arabesque designs, not in the grand manner of the sixteenth or seventeenth centuries nor yet in the degenerate Italian taste of the nineteenth; they are unique in the city and quite attractive both in design and colour. The deep porch has three domes only, the arches being supported at each end by rectangular piers and in the centre by a single marble column. The door is not in the middle but on the right-hand side, so as not to be blocked by the column; this arrangement, too, was common in the preclassical period, but there are only a very few such examples in the city. To the south of the main building is a rectangular annexe with a flat ceiling and two mihrabs; it is through this annexe that we enter the mosque today. According to one authority this section is wholly new; possibly, but as far as form goes, it might well be the dwelling house added by Hayreddin's daughter-in-law.

The third mosque is found about 150 metres farther on, a short distance before the Atatürk Bridge. This is called Sağrıcılar Camii, the mosque of the Leather-Workers, which guild once had its workshops in this area. The building is of the simplest type, a square room covered by a dome, the walls of stone. It was restored in 1960 with only moderate success. But although the mosque is of little interest architecturally, its historical background is rather fascinating. For one thing, this is probably the oldest mosque in the city, founded in 1455 by Yavuz Ersinan, standard-bearer in Fatih's army during the final siege of Constantinople. This gentleman was an ancestor of Evliya Çelebi; his family remained in possession of the mosque for centuries, living in a house just beside it. Evliya was born in this house in about 1611 and there, 20 years later, he had the dream which changed his life (and immeasurably enriched our knowledge of the life of old Stamboul). The founder himself is buried in the little graveyard beside the mosque. Beside him is buried one of his comrades-in-arms, Horoz Dede, one of the fabulous folk-saints of Istanbul. Horoz Dede, or Grandfather Rooster, received his name during the siege of Constantinople, when he made his rounds each morning and woke the troops of Fatih's army with his loud rooster call. Horoz Dede was killed in the final assault and after the city fell he was buried here, with Fatih himself among the mourners at his graveside. The saint's grave is venerated to this day.

ŞEBSAFA KADIN CAMİİ

We now come to Atatürk Bulvarı, the broad highway which leads from the Atatürk Bridge up the valley between the Third and Fourth Hills. We turn left here and about 300 metres along on the left we come to a rather handsome baroque mosque, Şebsafa Kadın Camii. This was built in 1787 by Fatma Şebsafa Kadın, one of the women in the harem of Abdül Hamit I. It is of brick and stone; the porch has an upper storey with a cradle-vault and inside there is a sort of narthex also of two storeys, covered with three small domes. These upper storeys form a deep and attractive gallery overlooking the central area of the mosque, which is covered by a high dome resting on the walls. To the north of the mosque is a long mektep with a pretty cradle-vaulted roof.

Directly across the avenue from the mosque you can see a huge retaining wall whose lower part contains a row of arched niches. This is a huge cistern that was part of the monastery of the Pantocrator, built by the Emperor John II Comnenus in the second quarter of the twelfth century on the Fourth Hill above the present avenue.

The whole area above the mosque on the east side of Atatürk Bulvarı is occupied by the Istanbul Drapers' and Furnishers' Bazaar, a complex of modern shops and offices built in the years 1959–66 by the Municipality. The general conception shows more imagination than one expects to find in a municipal project, but it does not seem quite to come off in detail. Large blank surfaces from place to place are enlivened by panels of mosaics and ceramics in abstract designs done by such leading modern artists of Turkey as Bedri Rahmi Eyüboğlu and the ceramist Füreya.

In the centre of this shopping-centre we come upon an ancient little graveyard which has recently been restored. Among the tombstones there we see one bearing the name of Kâtip Çelebi (1609–58). Kâtip Çelebi, one of the most enlightened scholars of his age, was the author of at least 23 books, along with many shorter treatises and essays. His last and best known work was *The Balance of Truth,* where he writes of the beatific vision in which the Prophet inspired him to go on with his work. This reminds one of Evliya Çelebi and the remarkable vision which he had in the mosque of Ahi Çelebi, some 500 metres removed from Kâtip Çelebi's grave and three decades earlier in time. What a town Ottoman Stamboul must have been in those days, to inspire visions such as theirs.

PRIMARY SCHOOL OF ZENBELLİ ALİ BABA

We now cross Atatürk Bulvarı and take the stepped pathway beside the road which winds uphill directly opposite the mosque. A short distance up the hill, at the second turning, we find a small mektep in a walled garden. The mektep has recently been restored and is now used as a children's library; it is a very pleasing example of the minor architecture of the early sixteenth century. It was built by the Şeyh-ül Islam Ali bin Ahmet Efendi, who died in 1525. The founder is buried beneath a marble sarcophagus which stands in the mektep garden.

THE CHURCH OF THE PANTOCRATOR

Taking the street to the right past the entrance to the mektep, we come almost immediately to a picturesque square lined on three sides with old wooden houses. On the eastern side of the square we see the former monastery church of the Pantocrator, known locally as Zeyrek Camii. The Pantocrator is a composite building consisting of two churches and a chapel between them; the whole complex was built within a period of a few years, between about 1120 and 1136. The church was converted into a mosque soon after the Conquest by Molla Mehmet Zeyrek and came to be called Zeyrek Camii. The mosque is now confined to the south church.

The monastery was founded and the south church built by the Empress Eirene, wife of John II Comnenus, some years before her death in 1124; it was dedicated to St. Saviour Pantocrator, Christ the Almighty. In plan the church is of the four-column type, with a central dome, a triple apse, and a narthex with a gallery overlooking the nave. (The columns have as usual been removed in Ottoman times and replaced by piers.) This church preserves a good deal of its original decoration, including the marble pavement, the handsome door-frames of the narthex, and the almost complete marble revetment of the apse. Work by the Byzantine Institute has brought to light again the magnificent *opus sectile* floor of the church itself, arranged in great squares and circles of coloured marbles with figures in the borders. One of these, which the imam of the mosque will uncover, is a panel tentatively identified as one of the labours of Samson. Notice also the curious Turkish mimber made from fragments of Byzantine sculpture, including the canopy of a ciborium. One of these spolia has been identified as a sculptural fragment from the church of St. Polyeuktos, whose ruins we will see later on this itinerary. The investigations of the Byzantine Institute discovered also fragments of stained glass from the east window, which seem to show that the art of stained glass was a Byzantine rather than a western discovery.

After Eirene's death her husband John decided to erect another church a few metres to the north of hers, dedicated to the Virgin Eleousa, the Merciful or Charitable. It is somewhat smaller but of essentially the same type and plan as Eirene's church, and here again the columns have been replaced by piers. When this church was finished, the idea seems to have struck the Emperor of joining the two churches by a chapel, dedicated to the Archangel Michael. This is a structure without aisles and with but one apse, covered by two domes; it is highly irregular in form to make it fit between the two churches. Parts of the walls of the churches were demolished so that all three sections opened widely into one another. John also added an outer narthex, which must once have extended in front of all three structures, but which now ends awkwardly in front of the mortuary chapel. The middle church was designed to serve as a mortuary chapel for the Comneni dynasty, beginning with the Empress Eirene, who was reburied there after its completion. Her verd antique sarcophagus was opened up and robbed by the knights of the Fourth Crusade when they sacked Constantinople in 1204. Her looted sarcophagus stood outside the Pantocrator up until the middle of the last century, when it was removed to the exonarthex of Haghia Sophia, where it is preserved today.

A programme of restoration and study of the Pantocrator has been undertaken by Professor Robert Osterhaut of the University of

CHURCH OF THE PANTOCRATOR

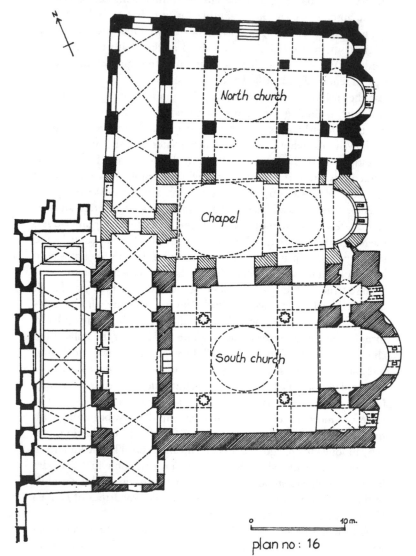

North church

Chapel

South church

0   10 m.

plan no: 16

Pennsylvania and Professors Metin and Zeynep Ahunbey of Istanbul University. The roof and domes have been restored, while a start has been made on restoration of the interior and an archaeological study of the structure.

One of the derelict Ottoman structures behind the Pantocrator has been rebuilt and renovated by Rahmi Koç, and is now a superb restaurant-café known as the Zeyrekhane. The large terrace of the Zeyrekhane, part of which is adorned with ancient architectural fragments, commands a sweeping view of the first three hills of the old city above the Golden Horn, an ideal place to have lunch before continuing to explore the Fourth Hill.

ŞEYH SÜLEYMAN MESCİDİ

What may perhaps be the only surviving part of the monastery of the Pantocrator stands about 150 metres to the south-west of the church. To find it we take the street which leads off from the far left-hand corner of the square and follow it to the first intersection. Following the street which leads around to the left, we come immediately to a tiny, tower-like building known locally as Şeyh Süleyman Mescidi. This may possibly have been one of the buildings of the Pantocrator monastery, perhaps a library or a funerary chapel. The lower part is square on the exterior and octagonal above; within, it is altogether octagonal, with shallow niches in the cross-axes; below is a crypt. This strange building has never been seriously investigated, so that neither its date nor identity are known.

HACI HASAN MESCİDİ

Returning to the last intersection and crossing it, we continue on in the same direction along Hacı Hasan Sokağı. At the end of this street, about 100 metres along, we see on the left a tiny mosque with a quaint and pretty minaret. The people of the district call it Eğri Minare, the Crooked Minaret, for obvious reasons. It has a stone base at the top of which is a curious rope-like moulding. The shaft is of brick and stone arranged to form a criss-cross or chequerboard design, which is most unusual, perhaps unique in Istanbul. The şerefe has an elaborate stalactite corbel and a fine balustrade, partly broken;

but it seems a little too big in scale for the minaret. The mosque itself is rectangular, built of squared stone and with a wooden roof; in its present condition it is without interest. The founder was the Kazasker (Judge) Hacı Hasanzade Mehmet Efendi who died in 1505; the mosque therefore must belong to about this date.

THE CHURCH OF ST. SAVIOUR PANTEPOPTES

If we turn left beyond the mosque and then right at the next corner into Küçük Mektep Sokağı, we see a Byzantine church at the end of the street. This is Eski Imaret Camii, identified with virtual certainty as the church of St. Saviour Pantepoptes, Christ the All-Seeing. This church was founded about 1085 to 1090 by the Empress Anna Delassena, mother of the Emperor Alexius I Comnenus and founder of the illustrious Comneni dynasty which ruled so brilliantly over Byzantium in the eleventh and twelfth centuries. Anna ruled as co-emperor with her son for nearly 20 years and during that time exerted a powerful influence on the affairs of the Byzantine state. In the year 1100 the Empress retired to the convent of the Pantepoptes and spent the remainder of her life in retirement there. She died in 1105 and was buried in the church which she had founded. The church was converted into a mosque almost immediately after the Conquest. For a time it served as the imaret of the nearby Fatih Camii, and thus it came to be known as Eski Imaret Camii.

The building is a quite perfect example of an eleventh-century church of the four-column type, with three apses and a double narthex, many of the doors of which retain their magnificent frames of red marble. Over the inner narthex is a gallery which opens onto the nave by a charming triple arcade on two rose-coloured marble columns. The church itself has retained most of its original characteristics, though the four columns have as usual been replaced by piers, and the windows of the central apse have been altered. The side apses, however, preserve their windows and their beautiful marble cornice. The dome too, with 12 windows between which 12 deep ribs taper out towards the crown, rests on a cornice with a meander pattern of palmettes and flowers. The exterior, though closely hemmed in by the surrounding houses, is very characteristic and charming, with its 12-sided dome and its decorative brickwork in the form of blind niches and bands of Greek-key and swastika motifs and rose-like medallions.

AŞIK PAŞA CAMİİ

The northern slope of the Fourth Hill in this area is rather thickly dotted with small mosques, many of them ancient but few of much interest; some are in a state of ruin or near ruin; others have been restored, often quite badly. We will mention just two in the vicinity of the Pantepoptes; but it should be understood that they are of minor interest and one could be forgiven for passing up these detours.

The first of these mosques is reached by taking Şair Baki Sokağı, the continuation of Küçük Mektep Sokağı, the street which brought us to the Pantepoptes. The mosque is two blocks along on the right, at the corner of Esrar Dede Sokağı. This mosque, constructed of alternate rows of brick and stone, was built in 1564. It is called Aşık Paşa Camii, Aşık Paşa having been a poet of the time of Orhan Gazi, long before the Conquest; it was built for the peace of his soul by one of his descendants, Şeyh Ahmet Efendi. Beside it is a tekke, also called after Aşık Paşa, built somewhat earlier – about 1522 – by a man called Seyyidi-Velâyet Efendi, but in the same general style; and opposite the mosque stands the grand türbe of the founder. Although not exactly planned as a complex, these buildings in their walled garden nevertheless have an attractive unity; a moderate amount of tactful restoration could make them one of the more charming of the minor classical groups.

YARHİSAR CAMİİ

Returning to the Pantepoptes, we turn right off Küçük Mektep Sokağı immediately after the church. If we follow this street past the intersection and two blocks farther along, we will come on our left to an ancient mosque at the corner of Kadı Çeşme and Şebnem Sokaks. This is Yarhisar Camii, the second oldest mosque in the city, apparently pre-dated only by Sağrıcılar Camii, which we saw earlier on our tour. According to the register of pious foundations *(Hayrat Kaydi)* this mosque was built in 1461; its founder Musliheddin

Mustafa Efendi was Judge of Istanbul in Fatih's reign. It was once a handsome edifice, built entirely of ashlar stone, its square chamber covered by a dome on pendentives, preceded by a porch with two domes and three columns. It was burned in the great fire of 1917 which consumed most of this district, but even in its ruined state it was a fine and dignified structure. In 1954–6 the building was restored, with a thin veneer of brick and stone, *à la Byzantine*, covering the original structure, and the interior was redecorated. In our opinion the restoration was unfortunate: it obscures what was still attractive, and is not true to the spirit of the original structure.

Returning to the Pantepoptes, we now retrace our steps to Şeyh Süleyman Mescidi. (Those who don't care to follow the same route back might look for an alternative way through this run-down but picturesque old neighbourhood.) Once arrived at the mescit we continue on past it to the end of the street. There we find ourselves once again on the stepped path which led up from Atatürk Bulvarı, a little way above the mektep of Zenbelli Ali Baba. Here we turn right and continue uphill along Itfaiye Caddesi.

ÇİNİLİ HAMAM

A short distance along on our left we come to an ancient hamam of considerable interest. This is Çinili Hamam, the Tiled Bath, an early work of Sinan: it was built in about 1545 for the great admiral Hayrettin Paşa, known in the West as Barbarossa. It is a double bath, the men's and women's sections lying side by side and the two entrances, rather unusually, being in the same façade: the plans are almost identical. In the centre of the great camekân is an elaborate and beautiful marble fountain with goldfish swimming in it. The narrow soğukluk with two little semidomes at each end leads to the cruciform hararet, where the open arms of the cross are covered with tiny domes, the rooms in the corners each having a larger one. Here and there on the walls are small panels of faience and the floor is of *opus sectile*. In the camekân fragments of a more elaborate wall a revetment of tiles of a later period may be seen. A half-century ago this fine hamam was abandoned and fell into a state of decay, but now it has been restored and is now once again in use.

MEDRESE OF GAZANFER AĞA

Beyond the hamam, Itfaiye Caddesi widens and becomes quite pretty, with a double row of plane trees shading the open stalls of a colourful fruit and vegetable market. We follow this avenue for a few blocks and then turn left just before the aqueduct, taking the street which runs parallel to it.

Just before we come to the intersection with Atatürk Bulvarı we see on our right a small classical külliye built up against the aqueduct. Established by Gazanfer Ağa in 1599, it includes a small medrese, the türbe of the founder, and a charming sebil with handsome grilled windows. Gazanfer Ağa was the younger brother of Cafer Ağa, whose medrese we saw next to Haghia Sophia. He was Chief of the White Eunuchs in the reign of Mehmet III. Gazanfer was the last of the White Eunuchs to control affairs in the Saray, for after his time the Chief Black Eunuch became the dominant figure. He and his brother were born in Chioggia, in the lagoon south of Venice. They were captured by pirates in their youth and, after being castrated, they were sold as eunuchs in the Istanbul slave market, where they were purchased to serve in Topkapı Sarayı, thus beginning their illustrious careers as the last two great Chief White Eunuchs. Gazanfer Ağa was executed in 1603, having involved himself too deeply in the affairs of the Harem.

The külliye was restored in 1945 and originally housed the Municipal Museum; it now serves as the Museum of Cartoons and Humour. Like most city museums, it has a rather provincial and neglected look, though some of the exhibits are not without interest. The cells of the medrese have had doors cut between them to form the galleries of the museum.

THE AQUEDUCT OF VALENS

After leaving the museum we continue along to Atatürk Bulvarı and turn right so as to pass under the aqueduct. We should perhaps pause here for a moment to study this ancient structure, which has been looming on the skyline for much of our stroll. The aqueduct was built by the Emperor Valens in about the year A.D. 375 as part of the water-supply system which he constructed. The water, tapped from various streams and lakes outside the city, appears to have entered through subterranean pipes near the Edirne Gate and to have been led underground along the ridge of the Sixth, Fifth and Fourth Hills to a point near the present site of the Fatih Mosque. From there the water was carried by the aqueduct across the deep valley that divides the Fourth from the Third Hill. On the Third Hill, near the present site of Beyazit Square, the water was received in a large cistern, the *nymphaeum maximum,* from which it was distributed to various parts of the city; this *nymphaeum* seems to have been not far distant from the modern *taksim* which distributes the present water supply from the Terkos Lake. The length of the aqueduct was originally about one kilometre, of which about 900 metres remain, and its maximum height, where it crosses Atatürk Bulvarı, is about 20 metres. The aqueduct was damaged at various times but was kept in repair by the emperors, both Byzantine and Ottoman, the last important restoration being that of Mustafa II in 1697. The long march of the double arches across the valley has a grand and Roman look, and is almost as essential a characteristic of the city's skyline as the great procession of mosques that crowns the ridge along the Golden Horn.

Continuing on along Atatürk Bulvarı under the aqueduct, we soon come to the Şehzadebaşı intersection, which we cross to the south-west corner. This intersection is approximately the site of the ancient Forum Amastrianum, where public executions were held in the days of Byzantium. At the Forum Amastrianum, the Mese divided into two branches, one of which followed much the same course as Şehzadebaşı Caddesi, while the other went along roughly the same route as Atatürk Bulvarı to the Forum Bovis, the modern Aksaray.

THE CHURCH OF ST. POLYEUKTOS

Perhaps the best thing that can be said about the Şehzadebaşı intersection is that it has at least advanced the cause of archaeology. For when the ground was being cleared for the underpass in 1960, there came to light the extensive ruins of an ancient church; we see these just to the right of the underpass road to Aksaray. An excavation was taken in hand by Dumbarton Oaks under the direction of Mr.

Martin Harrison, who identified the ruins as those of the church of St. Polyeuktos, about whom Corneille wrote one of his great tragedies, *Polyeucte*. It was built in the years 524–7 by the Princess Anicia Juliana. The church was an enormous edifice measuring 52 by 58 metres (compare the Süleymaniye, which is about 52 metres square), fronted by an atrium measuring 26 by 52 metres, with a small apsidal building on the north that may have been a martyrium or a baptisry, as well as a structure at the north-west corner of the site that may have been the palace of Anicia Juliana. The church was essentially basilical in form but very probably domed, divided into a nave and two side aisles by an arrangement of piers and columns. The church was already abandoned at the time of the Crusader sack of Constantinople in 1204, and its surviving works of art and architectural members were taken off to adorn churches in western Europe. Two pilasters of the church have been identified in the church of San Marco in Venice; these are the Pilastri Acriani, the Pillars of Acre, so called because they were believed to have come from Acre in Syria. Other fragments, as we have seen, were used in the mimber of Zeyrek Camii, the mosque in the south church of the Pantocrator. Other architectural and sculptural fragments are preserved in the Archaeological Museum, including part of a long and beautifully-written inscription by which the church was identified. But the site itself is now desolate, with only a single column standing amidst the ruins.

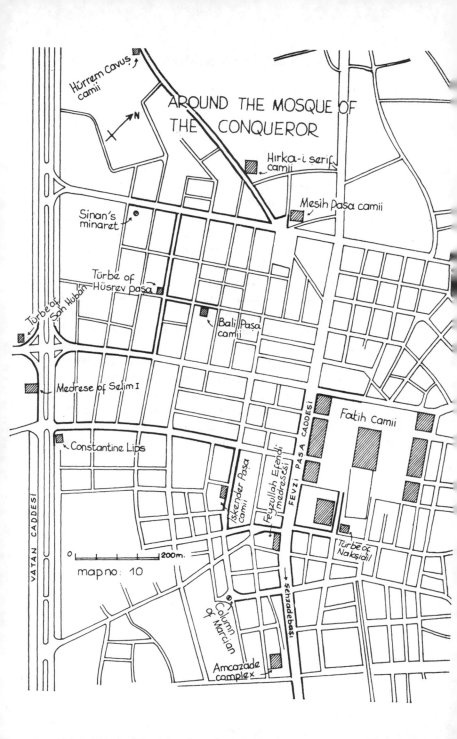

AROUND THE MOSQUE OF THE CONQUEROR

Hürrem Çavuş camii

Hırka-i şerif camii

Mesih Paşa camii

Sinan's minaret

Türbe of Hüsrev paşa

Türbe of Şah Huban

Bali Paşa camii

Medrese of Selim I

Constantine Lips

İskender Paşa camii

Feyzullah Efendi medresesi

FEVZİ PAŞA CADDESİ

Fatih camii

Türbe of Nakşidil

İTFAİYE CADDESİ

VATAN CADDESİ

0   200 m.

map no: 10

Column of Marcian

Amcazade complex

12

Around the Mosque
of the Conqueror

Where one stroll ends another must begin, if we are to see Istanbul in all its detail. And so we return to the south-west corner of the traffic-circle at Şehzadebaşı, to begin our next tour of the city. Once there, we will begin walking westward along the south side of Şehzadebaşı Caddesi. This will bring us into the district called Fatih, named after Fatih Camii, the Mosque of the Conqueror, around which we will be strolling.

THE AMCAZADE COMPLEX

Just to the west of the ruins of the church of St. Polyeuktos, which we examined on our last tour, we come to the fine complex of Amcazade Hüseyin Paşa. This is one of the most elaborate and picturesque of the smaller classical complexes. It was built by Hüseyin Paşa while he was Grand Vezir (1697–1702) under Mustafa II, and thus comes at the very end of the classical period. Hüseyin Paşa was a cousin *(amcazade)* of Fazıl Ahmet Paşa of the able and distinguished Köprülü family. The historian von Hammer says of him: "He was the fourth Köprülü endowed with the highest authority of the Empire and like his relatives he showed himself capable of supporting its weight... After his uncle Mehmet Köprülü the Cruel and his cousins Ahmet the Statist and Mustafa the Virtuous, he well-deserved the surname of the Wise. Unfortunately he remained too short a time on the stage where his high qualities had placed him, fully capable as he was of retarding if not altogether forestalling the decadence of the Empire, from which he disappeared like a meteor after having given rise to the highest hopes."

The complex includes an octagonal dershane or lecture hall, serving also as a mosque; a medrese, a library, a large primary school over a

AMCAZADE HÜSEYİN PAŞA KÜLLİYESİ

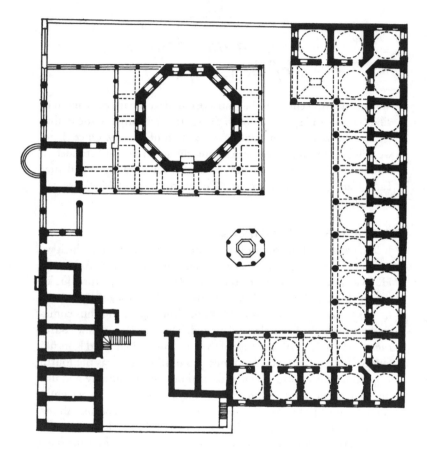

0 |_____| 10 m.

plan no : 17

row of shops, two little cemeteries with open türbes, a şadırvan, a sebil and a çeşme, all arranged with an almost romantic disorder. The street façade consists first of the open walls of the small graveyards, divided by the projecting curve of the sebil. All of these have fine brass grilles, those of the türbe nearest the entrance gate being quite exceptionally beautiful specimens of seventeenth-century grillework. Next comes the entrance gate with an Arabic inscription giving the date 1698. The çeşme just beyond it with its reservoir behind is a somewhat later addition, for its inscription records that it was a benefaction of the Şeyh-ül Islam Mustafa Efendi in 1739. Finally there is a row of four shops with an entrance between them leading to the two large rooms of the mektep on the upper floor. On entering the courtyard, one has on the left the first of the open türbes – the one with the exceptionally handsome grilles – and then the columned portico of the mosque: this portico runs around seven of the eight sides of the mosque and frames it in a rectangle. The mosque itself is without a minaret and its primary object was clearly to serve as a lecture hall for the medrese. It is severely simple, its dome adorned only with some rather pale stencilled designs probably later than the building itself.

The far side of the courtyard is formed by the 17 cells of the medrese with their domed and columned portico. Occupying the main part of the right-hand side is the library building. It is in two storeys, but the lower floor serves chiefly as a water reservoir, the upper being reached by a flight of outside steps around the side and back of the building, leading to a little domed entrance porch on the first floor. The medallion inscription on the front of the library records a restoration in 1755 by Hüseyin Paşa's daughter after the earthquake of 1894 which ruined the complex; the manuscripts it had contained were removed and are now in the Süleymaniye library. The right-hand corner of the courtyard is occupied by the shops and the mektep above them: note the amusing little dovecotes in the form of miniature mosques on the façade overlooking the entrance gate. A columned şadırvan stands in the middle of the courtyard. This charmingly irregular complex is made still more picturesque by the warm red of the brickwork alternating with buff-coloured limestone, by the many marble columns of the portico, and not least by the fine old trees – cypresses, locusts and two enormous terebinths – that grow out of the open türbes and in the courtyard. The külliye now serves as the Museum of Turkish Architectural Works and Construction Elements, including architectural and sculptural fragments, calligraphical inscriptions and old tombstones. One particularly interesting exhibit is the top of one of the minarets of Fatih Camii, toppled by the earthquake in 1894.

DÜLGERZADE CAMİİ

Opposite the Amcazade complex in a pretty little park is an ugly broken-off column, typical of First World War memorials everywhere; it commemorates Turkish aviators killed during the war and is dated 1922. On the north side of the park is the old Fatih Town Hall, built in 1913 in a style known as Ottoman Revivalism. Continuing westward along the main avenue on the same side as the Amcazade complex we pass an ancient but not very interesting little mosque called Dülgerzade Camii; it was built by one of Fatih's officials, Şemsettin Habib Efendi, sometime before his death in 1482.

COLUMN OF MARCİAN

Beyond the mosque we turn left and a short distance down the street we see the second of the four late Roman honorific columns in the city, the Column of Marcian. This column, though known to Evliya, escaped even the penetrating eyes of Gyllius and remained unknown to the West until rediscovered in 1675 by Spon and Wheeler. It continued to be hidden away in a garden behind the houses around it until 1908, when a fire destroyed all the buildings and exposed it to view, and since then it has formed the centre of a little square. It is a monolithic column of Syenitic granite resting on a high marble pedestal; the column is surmounted by a battered Corinthian capital and a plinth with eagles at the corners on which there once must have stood a statue of the Emperor Marcian (r. 450–7). Fragments of sculpture remain on the base, including a Nike, or Winged Victory, in high relief. There is also on the base an elegaic couplet in Latin which says that the column was erected by the prefect Tatianus in honour of the Emperor Marcian. The Turks call the column Kız Taşı, or the Maiden's Column, because of the figure of the Nike on the base. Evliya Çelebi believed the Nike to be the figure of a Byzantine princess, daughter of an apocryphal ruler named King Puzantine (a corruption of Byzantine), and he claimed that the Maiden's Column had talismanic powers: "At the head of the Saddler's Bazaar, on the summit of a column stretching to the skies, there is a chest of white marble in which the unlucky-starred daughter of King Puzantine lies buried; and to preserve her remains from ants and insects was this column made a talisman."

MEDRESE OF FEYZULLAH EFENDI

We now return to the main avenue and continue walking westward on the same side. We soon come to another little külliye built at about the same time as the Amcazade complex; this one is almost as charming though not as extensive. This is the medrese founded in 1700 by the Şeyh-ül Islam Feyzullah Efendi; it now serves as the Millet Kütüphanesi, or People's Library. The cells of the medrese surround two sides of the courtyard in which stands a şadırvan in the midst of a pretty garden. The street side of the courtyard is wholly occupied by a most elaborate and original dershane building: a flight of steps leads up to a sort of porch covered by nine domes of different patterns, the arches of which are supported on four columns. The effect of this porch has been somewhat impaired by glazing in a part of it, but its usefulness has doubtless been increased. To right and left of the porch are the large domed lecture-rooms, now used as library reading-rooms. The medrese, long disaffected and ruinous, was restored and converted into a library by Ali Emiri Efendi, a famous bibliophile who died in 1924 and left the building and his valuable collection of books and manuscripts to the people of Istanbul. The reading-rooms are almost always full of students.

COMPLEX OF FATİH SULTAN MEHMET

We now find ourselves opposite the enormous mosque complex of Mehmet the Conqueror. Let us continue past it along the avenue for a few hundred metres and then turn right on the first through-street,

RESTORED PLAN OF FATİH COMPLEX

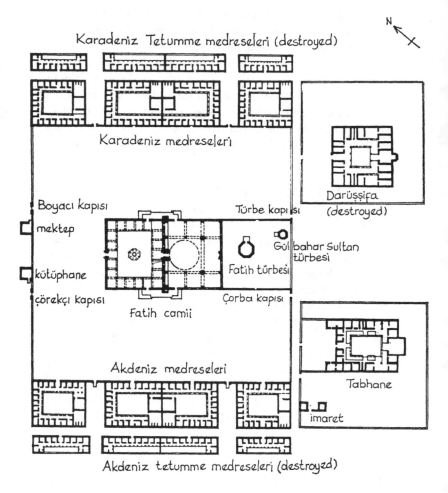

Karadeniz Tetumme medreseleri (destroyed)

Karadeniz medreseleri

Darüşşifa (destroyed)

Boyacı kapısı

mektep

kütüphane

çörekçi kapısı

Türbe kapısı

Gülbahar Sultan türbesi

Fatih türbesi

Çorba kapısı

Fatih camii

Akdeniz medreseleri

Tabhane

imaret

Akdeniz tetumme medreseleri (destroyed)

0 ⊢——┴——┴——┤ 75 m.

PLAN NO: 18

so as to approach the mosque from the western side of the great outer courtyard. The huge mosque complex built by Sultan Mehmet the Conqueror was the most extensive and elaborate in Istanbul, and indeed in the whole of the Ottoman Empire. In addition to the great mosque with its beautiful courtyard and its graveyard with türbes, the külliye consisted of eight medreses and their annexes, a tabhane or hospice, a huge imaret, a hospital, a kervansaray, a primary school, a library and a hamam. It was laid out over a vast, almost square area – about 325 metres on a side – with almost rigid symmetry, and Evliya Çelebi says of it: "When all these buildings, crowded together, are seen from a height above, they alone appear like a town full of lead-covered domes." It occupies approximately the site of the famous Church of the Holy Apostles and its attendant buildings. This church, which was already partially in ruins at the time of the Conquest, was used as a source of building materials for the construction of Fatih's külliye.

The complex is thought to have been built by Sinan the Elder between 1463 and 1470; the dates are given in the great inscription over the entrance portal. There is much controversy but almost no knowledge about who this architect was. He has various sobriquets: Atik, the Elder; Azatlı, the Freedman; or (by Evliya) Abdal, the Holy Idiot. The second of these names suggests that he could not have been a Turk; on the other hand, his identification with an otherwise unknown Byzantine architect named Christodoulos, which is generally accepted by western writers, rests only on the late and suspect authority of Prince Demetrius Cantemir. If he was indeed a Greek, however, he could not possibly have been a "Byzantine architect": one cannot for a moment believe that, in the fifteenth century, there was any Byzantine architect capable of building a dome 26 metres in diameter. He must have been a Greek boy from the European provinces of the Empire taken up in a *devşirme* (annual levy of youths) and trained in an Ottoman school of architecture. His gravestone is extant in the garden of the little mosque he built as his own *vakıf,* or pious foundation, Kumrulu Mescidi (see Chapter 13). But from this we learn only that he was an architect – no mention of the Fatih complex – and, curiously enough, that he was executed in the year after it was completed, 1471. In this connection it is interesting to note the curious tale told by Evliya Çelebi in the *Seyahatname,* in which he says that Fatih ordered both the architect's hands cut off, on the grounds that his mosque did not have as great a height as Haghia Sophia.

Let us now return to the mosque itself. The original mosque built by Atik Sinan was destroyed in the great earthquake of 22 May 1766. Mustafa II immediately undertook its reconstruction and the present building, on a wholly different plan, was completed in 1771. What remains of the original complex is most probably the courtyard, the main entrance portal, the mihrab, the minarets up to the first şerefe, the south wall of the graveyard and the adjoining gate; all the other buildings of the complex were badly damaged but were restored presumably in their original form. What was the original form of the mosque itself? It is of course of the greatest interest and importance to know the original plan, for this was the first large imperial building to be erected after the Conquest. It appears, then, that the mosque had a very large central dome, 26 metres in diameter; that it was supported on the east only by a semidome of the same diameter; that these were supported by two great rectangular piers on the east and by two enormous porphyry columns towards the west, the latter supporting a double arcade below the tympanum walls of the great dome arches; to north and south were side aisles each covered with three small domes. The plan is very similar, on an enormous scale, to that of Atik Ali Paşa Camii at Çemberlitaş, and even more so to that of the Selimiye at Konya, which has been shown to be a small replica of it. This plan was in certain respects a natural development of previous Ottoman buildings. Nevertheless, those who saw and described this mosque before it was destroyed, foreigners and Turks alike, including Sultan Mehmet and his architect, compared Fatih Camii to Haghia Sophia; hence it must already have shown the overpowering influence of the Great Church.

THE MOSQUE COURTYARD

It is time to take a look at what remains of this fascinating külliye. Approaching from the west, one finds that part of the west wall of the precinct has been demolished, together with the small library and mektep that once stood just outside it; trees and wooden houses have intruded, but they make a picturesque enclave in this corner. Opposite is the courtyard of the mosque itself; this, with its monumental portal, is original. In the lunettes of the six western windows are some of the most remarkable inscriptions in the city: the first Surah of the Kuran is written in white marble letters on a ground of verd antique. The effect is extremely lovely and one wonders why this fascinating technique of calligraphy should occur – so far as we know – only here. The calligrapher was Yahya Sofi, and it was his son Ali who wrote the inscriptions over the main portal of the mosque and also over the Bab-ı Hümayün at the Saray. The dignified but simple portal has rather curious engaged columns at the corners. The convex flutes or ribs of their shafts become interlaced at top and bottom to form an intertwined serpentine pattern, while the columns end in a sort of hour-glass shaped capital and base. We shall see this same treatment again in this külliye, but not elsewhere.

In the centre of this picturesque courtyard stands the şadırvan with a witch's cap conical roof resting on eight marble columns and surrounded by tall cypress trees. In essentials it is original even to the cypresses which are constantly mentioned by travellers, though doubtless replanted from time to time. The antique marble columns of the portico have stalactite capitals of fine, bold workmanship. At either end of the mosque porch are two more exquisite lunette inscriptions, this time in faience, showing a vivid yellow combined with blue, green and white in the *cuerda seca* technique typical of this early period. Similar panels are to be seen in the mosque of Selim I, the türbe of the Şehzade Mehmet, and a few other early buildings. The west façade of the mosque itself belongs for the most part to the baroque reconstruction, except for the entrance portal. On the exterior it has the same engaged columns as the gate to the courtyard, and is surmounted by a stalactite canopy enclosed in a series of projecting frames which give depth and emphasis. On the sides and over the door are written in bold calligraphy the historical inscriptions. But the interior side of the portal is even more remarkable; its canopy is a finely carved scallop shell supported on a double cornice of stalactites. However, it is sadly masked by a later baroque balcony built in front of it.

THE MOSQUE

The interior need not detain us long. It is a copy of the type in which the central dome is flanked by four semidomes on the axes, invented by Sinan for the Şehzade and used again for Sultan Ahmet and Yeni Cami. Here the exterior lines are still reasonably classical and pleasing, but the interior is at once weak and heavy. The painted decoration is fussy in detail and dull in colour; the lower part of the wall is sheathed in common white tiles of such inferior make that they have become discoloured with damp! In the right-hand corner is a curious fountain of drinking water (rare inside a mosque) with an old-fashioned bronze pump and silver drinking mugs; the water is cool and delicious. The mihrab, which is from the original building, resembles in style the entrance portal, though one suspects that the gilt-framed panels in the lower part are a baroque addition. Certainly baroque but equally handsome is the mimber, an elaborate structure of polychrome marble. Tea is sometimes served to the happy few who venture into the imperial loge, the antechambers of which are being used as a school for imams. The window shutters in these rooms are fine examples of baroque intarsia work, while the small dome over the loge itself is gaily painted with *trompe l'oeuil* windows.

THE TÜRBES

More interesting than the mosque itself are the magnificent dependencies. In the graveyard behind the mosque are the türbes of Sultan Mehmet and his wife Gülbahar, the mother of Beyazit II. Both of these türbes were completely reconstructed after the earthquake, though on the old foundations. That of Fatih is very baroque and its interior extremely sumptuous in the *Empire* style. During the days of the Ottoman Empire it was the custom for new sultans to visit this türbe immediately after they were girded with the sword of Osman at Eyüp. It was thought that this pilgrimage would endow them with some of the Conqueror's courage and vigour, but it is surely not Fatih's fault that this visit seldom made lions of the new sultans. During the years when the Ottoman armies were victorious in battle, it was customary to deck the walls of Fatih's türbe with captured weapons after a successful campaign. Across the centuries the türbe has been a popular shrine among the common people of the city, and something like a cult of emperor-worship grew up around the memory of the Conqueror and several other great sultans. But then in 1924, after the abolition of the Sultanate, all of the imperial türbes were ordered closed; only in recent years have a very few of them been reopened to the public because of their historical or artistic importance.

The türbe of Gülbahar is simple and classical and must resemble the original quite closely. An old and persistent legend, quite definitely apocryphal, has it that Gülbahar was a daughter of the King of France, sent by him as a bride for the Emperor Constantine Dragases and captured by the Turks when they were besieging the city. The legend goes on to say that Gülbahar, although she was the wife of Fatih and the mother of Beyazit, never embraced Islam and died a Christian. Evliya Çelebi recounts a version of this legend and has this to say of Gülbahar's türbe: "I myself have often observed, at morning prayer, that the readers appointed to chant lessons from the Kuran all turned their backs upon the coffin of this lady, of whom it was so doubtful whether she departed in the faith of Islam. I have often seen Franks come by stealth and give a few aspers to the tomb-keeper to open her türbe for them, as its gate is always kept locked." This story is also repeated by the Italian traveller Cornelio Magni, writing at about the same time as Evliya, who was led by the tomb-keeper to believe that Gülbahar was a Christian princess who lived and died in her faith. "The türbe," he says, "remains always shut, even the windows. I asked the reason for this and was told: 'The sepulcher of her whose soul lives among the shades deserves not a ray of light!'" After much entreaty and the intervention of an Emir who passed by, the tomb-keeper let him in: "I entered with veneration and awe... and silently recited a *De profundis* for the soul of this unfortunate Princess."

The little library in the south corner of the graveyard beside the mosque was built by Mahmut I and dates from 1742.

THE MEDRESES

To north and south of the precinct are the eight great medreses; they are severely symmetrical and almost identical in plan. Each contains 19 cells for students and a dershane. The entrance to the dershane

is from the side, and beside each entrance is a tiny garden planted
with trees – an effect as rare as it is pretty. Beyond each medrese
there was originally an annexe about half as large: these have quite
disappeared, but seem to have consisted of porticoes around three
sides of a terrace. All in all there must have been about 255 hücres,
or students' rooms, each occupied by perhaps four students. Thus
the establishment must have provided for about 1,000 students –
a university on a big scale. These fine buildings have recently been
restored and are now again used as residences by students.

THE HOSPICE
The south-east gate of the precinct, called Çorba Kapısı, or
the Soup Gate, from the proximity of the imaret, is a bit of the
original structure. Notice the elaborate and most unusual designs in
porphyry and verd antique set into the stonework of the canopy, as
well as the "panache" at the top in verd antique. Through this gate
one comes to what is perhaps the finest building of the külliye, the
well restored tabhane, or hospice, for travelling dervishes. It has a
very beautiful courtyard and is in general an astonishing, indeed
unique, building. The 20 domes of the courtyard are supported on
16 exceptionally beautiful antique columns of verd antique and
Syenitic marble, doubtless from the Church of the Holy Apostles.
At the east end a large square room (which has unfortunately lost its
dome) originally served as a mescit-zaviye, or room, for the dervish
ceremonies. On each side of this are two spacious domed rooms
opening onto two open eyvans. These are very interesting: each has
two domes supported on a rectangular pillar that one would swear
at first sight to be baroque. Closer examination, however, shows the
same engaged ribbed columns ending in intertwined designs and an
hour-glass capital and base that we found on the entrance portals of
the mosque itself. The rosettes, too, and even the very eighteenth-
century mouldings, can be paralleled in this and other buildings of
Fatih's time. It is thought that the two open eyvans were used for
meetings and prayers in summer, the two rooms adjoining the mescit-
zaviye for the same purpose in winter, and the two farther rooms in
the corner as depositories for the guests' baggage. The two rooms at

Above: Topkapı Sarayı on the skyline above the Golden Horn

Below: Yeni Cami, with Haghia Sophia above and to the right on the
skyline

Interior of Haghia Sophia from the north-west

Above: Dome and western semidome of Haghia Sophia

Below: Topkapı Sarayı: Throne Room in the Third Court

Above: Mosque of Sultan Ahmet I

Below: Interior of SS. Sergius and Bacchus (Küçük Aya Sofya Camii)

Above: The Süleymaniye on the skyline, Rüstem Paşa Camii below and to the right

Left: Tiles in the mihrab of
Rüstem Paşa Camii

Above: Kariye Camii (St. Saviour in Chora)

Below: Kariye Camii: mosaic of the Virgin and Child in the dome; below are 16 kings of the House of David

Above: Ortaköy Mosque and the first Bosphorus bridge

Below: Fortress of Rumeli Hisarı and the Fatih Mehmet bridge

Above: Köprülü Yalı

Below: Mosque of Şemsi Paşa

the west end of the north and south sides do not communicate with the rest of the building in any way but have their own entrances from the west forecourt; they were used as kitchens and bakehouses and doubtless depended on the adjacent imaret. This leaves only ten, or possibly 12, rooms for guests; for in the middle of the south side a passage leads through a small arched entry to the area where the kervansaray and imaret stood; an adjacent staircase leads to a room with a cradle-dome above. Opposite on the north side a similar area was occupied by lavatories; but here the dome and outer wall have fallen, and a very botched repair make it difficult to see what was the original arrangement. It is altogether an extraordinary building.

THE KERVANSARAY

The great vacant lot to the south, now used as a playing field by the children of the (modern) Fatih school, was the site of the kervansaray, to the east, and the imaret, to the west. Two fragments of the latter – small domed rooms, but ruinous now – remain in the south-west corner. Evliya says it had 70 domes; this would imply that it was a third again as big as the tabhane, which has (or had) 46 domes, and one can believe it. For, when one considers that it had to supply two meals a day to 1,000 students of the medreses, to the vast corps of clergy and professors of the foundation, to the patients and staff of the hospital, to the guests of the tabhane and kervansaray, as well as to the poor of the district, it is clear that the imaret must have been enormous. The kervansaray has wholly disappeared, but it too must have been very big even if one discounts Evliya's statement that its stables could hold 3,000 horses and mules. This whole area to the south should be excavated; it is clear that the ground has risen considerably, presumably with the rubble of the fallen buildings, and it should be possible to determine at least the extent and plan of the imaret and kervansaray. Another building of the külliye which has disappeared is the dar-üş şifa, or hospital. This was placed symmetrically with the tabhane on the north side of the graveyard; a street-name still recalls its site and bits of its wall may be seen built into modern houses.

TÜRBE OF NAKŞİDİL

Opposite Fatih's tabhane is the türbe complex built in 1817–18 for Nakşidil Valide Sultan, wife of Abdül Hamit I and mother of Mahmut II. The legend goes that this lady was Aimèe Dubuc de Rivery, cousin of the Empress Josephine, captured by Algerian pirates and presented to the Sultan by the Bey of Algiers. This legend also holds that it was her influence on her son and others in the Saray which brought about the pro-French policy of the Sublime Porte in the early years of the nineteenth century, and even that she was one of the instigators of the reform movement. A romantic tale has been made of this story by Leslie Blanch in her *Wilder Shores of Love;* unfortunately, there seems to be little or no foundation for the legend. However this may be, Nakşidil's türbe is a very charming one in its baroque-*Empire* way, forming a pleasant contrast to the austerity of the classic structures of the Fatih külliye. At the corner stands the enormous türbe, which has 14 sides; of its two rows of windows the upper ones are oval, a unique and pretty feature. The 14 faces are divided from each other by slender (too slender) columns which bear, on top of their capitals at the first cornice level, tall flame-like acanthus leaves carved almost in the round, giving a fine bravura effect – altogether a very original and entertaining building. The wall stretching along the street opposite the tabhane contains a gate and a grand sebil in the same flamboyant style as the türbe. The gate leads into an attractive courtyard from which one enters the türbe, whose interior decoration is rather elegant and restrained. Diagonally opposite at the far end of the court is another türbe, round and severely plain. In this türbe are interred Gülüstü Valide Sultan, mother of Mehmet VI Vahidettin, the last Sultan of the Ottoman Empire, together with other members of the family of Abdül Mecit. Outside, the wall along the street running north ends in a building at the next corner which was once a sibyan mektebi and is now used as a sewing school. Both wall and mektep building, constructed of brick and stone, seem to belong to an older tradition than the türbe of Nakşidil, but the recurrence here and there of the flame-like acanthus motif shows that they are part of the same complex.

Retracing our steps and passing Nakşidil's türbe, we walk along Aslanhane Sokağı, the Street of the Lion-House, and soon find ourselves back once again on the main avenue, Fevzi Paşa Caddesi. We continue on across the avenue, taking the street which runs down the hill past the west side of the medrese of Feyzullah Efendi; from here we will stroll through the neighbourhood to the south and west of Fatih Camii.

ISKENDER PAŞA CAMİİ

Proceeding downhill, we take the second turning on our right and then one block along on our left we come upon an ancient mosque, Iskender Paşa Camii. It is dated 1505, but it is not certain who the founder was; he is thought to have been one of the vezirs of Beyazit II who was governor of Bosnia. It is a simple dignified building with a blind dome on pendentives resting on the walls; the three small domes of the porch are supported on ancient columns with rather worn Byzantine capitals. The şerefe of the minaret has an elaborately stalactited corbel, but the curious decoration on top of the minaret probably belongs to an eighteenth-century restoration. The mosque has many characteristics in common with Bali Paşa Camii, which we will see a little farther on along our itinerary; both are of about the same date.

MONASTERY OF CONSTANTINE LIPS

Continuing on in the same direction we come at the next turning to Halıcılar Caddesi, where we turn left and stroll downhill for a few blocks. At the corner where it runs into the wide new Vatan Caddesi is a large Byzantine church, called Fenari Isa Camii, or the Monastery of Constantine Lips. The church has been investigated and partially restored by the Byzantine Institute and what follows is a summary of the conclusions reached.

This complicated building, constructed at different dates, consists of two churches, with a double narthex and a side chapel; its original structure had been profoundly altered in Ottoman times when it was converted into a mosque. The first church on the site, the one to the north, was dedicated in 907 to the Theotokos Panachrantos, the Immaculate Mother of God, by Constantine Lips, a high functionary at the courts of Leo the Wise and Constantine Porphyrogenitus. It

CHURCH OF CONSTANTINE LIPS

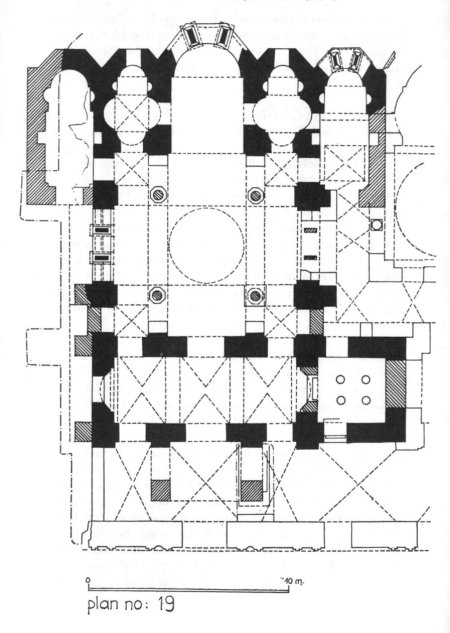

0   ¨10 m.

plan no: 19

was a church of the four-column type (the columns were replaced by arches in the Ottoman period); but quite unusually it had five apses, the extra ones to north and south projecting beyond the rest of the building. The northern one is now demolished, the southern one incorporated into the south church. Another unusual, perhaps unique, feature is that there are four little chapels on the roof, grouped round the main dome. Some 350 years after this northern church was built, the Empress Theodora, wife of Michael VIII Palaeologus (r. 1261–82), refounded the monastery and added another church to the south, an outer narthex for both churches, and a chapel to the south of her new church; the additions were designed to serve as a mortuary for the Palaeologan family. The new church, dedicated to St. John the Baptist, was of the ambulatory type, that is its nave was divided from the aisles by a triple arcade to north, west and south, each arcade supported by two columns. (All this was removed in Ottoman times, but the bases of some of the columns still remain and one can see the narrow arches of the arcades above, embedded in the Turkish masonry.) Of its three apses, the northern one was the southern supernumerary apse of the older church. Thus there were in all seven apses, six of which remain and make the eastern façade on the building exceedingly attractive. On the interior a certain amount of good sculptured decoration survives in cornices and window frames, especially in the north church.

MEDRESE OF SELIM I

Vatan Caddesi runs along the ancient course of the Lycus River through a district called Yeni Bahçe, the New Garden. Until recently this was mostly garden land and a certain number of vegetable gardens still survive, but there is nothing much of interest along the new road except the medrese and türbe immediately to be described. Not far west of Constantine Lips, on the other side of Vatan Caddesi, a large and handsome medrese has recently been restored. This is the medrese of Selim I, the Grim, built in his memory by his son, Süleyman the Magnificent; the architect was Sinan. The 20 cells of the students occupy three sides of the courtyard, while on the fourth stands the large and handsome lecture-hall, which was at one point turned into a mosque. The original entrance, through a small domed porch, is behind the dershane and at an odd angle to it, and the wall that encloses this whole side is irregular in a way that is hard to account for. Nevertheless, the building is very attractive and once inside one does not notice its curious dissymmetry.

TÜRBE OF ŞAH HUBAN

Just west of this medrese across a side street stands a türbe and a mektep in a walled garden. One enters the gaily planted garden by a gate in the north wall and on the left is an octagonal türbe, that of Şah Huban Kadın, a daughter of Selim I who died in 1572. This too is a work of the great Sinan. While there is nothing remarkable about the türbe, the mektep is a grand one. It is double; that is, it consists of two spacious square rooms each covered by a dome and containing an elegant ocak, or fireplace. The wooden roof and column of the porch are modern, part of the recent restoration, but they perhaps replace an equally simple original. The building now serves as an out-patient clinic for mental illnesses.

TÜRBE OF HÜSREV PAŞA

Recrossing Vatan Caddesi, we take the avenue just opposite, Akdeniz Caddesi, and walk uphill once again. We then take the fourth turning on the left into Hüsrev Paşa Sokağı and at the next corner on the left we come to a very handsome and elaborate türbe. It is by Sinan and was built for Hüsrev Paşa, a grandson of Beyazit II. Hüsrev Paşa had been one of the leading generals at the battle of Mohacz in 1526, when the fate of Hungary was decided in less than two hours. He governed Bosnia for many years with great pomp and luxury but also with severe justice. While governor of Syria he founded a mosque at Aleppo in 1536–7 which is the earliest dated building of Sinan and is still in existence. While Beylerbey of Rumelia and Fourth Vezir in 1544, he fell into disgrace because of his complicity in a plot against the Grand Vezir Süleyman Paşa. Despairing because of his fall from power, he took his own life soon afterwards by literally starving himself to death, one of the very rare incidents of suicide among the Ottomans. The türbe of Hüsrev Paşa is octagonal in form, the eight faces being separated from each other by slender columns which run up to the first cornice, elaborately carved with stalactites; the dome is set back a short distance and has another cornice of its own, also carved.

BALİ PAŞA CAMİİ

We now make a short detour on the street which runs uphill directly opposite the türbe. Just past the first intersection and on the right side of the street we see a fine mosque with a ruined porch. An inscription over the portal states that it was built in 1504 by Huma Hatun, daughter of Beyazit II, in memory of her late husband, Bali Paşa, who had died in 1495. Since this mosque appears in the *Tezkere*, the listing of Sinan's works, we conclude that Sinan rebuilt Bali Paşa Camii some time later on, though whether on its old plan or a new one it is impossible to say. The plan of Bali Paşa Camii is simple and to a certain extent resembles that of Iskender Paşa, which we saw earlier on our tour. The chief difference between these two is that in Bali Paşa the dome arches to north, west and south are very deep, being almost barrel vaults; thus room is left, on the north and south, for shallow bays with galleries above. The mosque was severely injured in the earthquake of 1894 and again in the fire of 1917; it was partially restored in 1935 and further work has been done on it in recent years. But the five domes of the porch have never been rebuilt and this gives the façade a somewhat naked look.

SİNAN'S MESCİT

After leaving Bali Paşa Camii we return to Hüsrev Paşa Sokağı and continue on in the same direction. We then take the second turning on the left, on Akşemseddin Caddesi, and walk one block downhill. There, at the corner to our left, we come upon Mimar Sinan Mescidi, part of a vakıf founded by the great architect himself in 1573-4. The present mosque is brand new, except for the minaret, replacing the original mescit, which had long ago disappeared. The original mosque was rather irregular, consisting of two rectangular rooms with a wooden roof. The minaret is of a very rare type, perhaps the only one of its kind that Sinan ever built. It is octagonal and without a balcony; instead, at the top, a decorated window in each of the eight faces allows the müezzin to call to prayer. Although a very minor antiquity indeed, this lonely minaret stands as a monument to the great Sinan – may it be preserved forever from the modern tenements which encroach upon it.

MESİH PAŞA CAMİİ

Retracing our steps, we walk back uphill along Akşemseddin Caddesi for about 250 metres until we come to a square dominated on its left side by a fine classical mosque. This is Mesih Paşa Camii, built by an unknown architect in 1585. (The mosque is popularly attributed to Sinan, but without evidence.) The founder was the eunuch Mesih Mehmet Paşa, infamous for his cruelty as Governor of Egypt, who became Grand Vezir for a short time at the age of 90 in the reign of Murat III. The courtyard of the mosque is attractive but rather sombre. It consists of the usual domed porticoes under which, rather unusually, are the ablution fountains; this is because the place of the şadırvan in the centre of the courtyard has been taken by the picturesque open türbe of the founder. The mosque is preceded by a double porch, but the wooden roof of the second porch has disappeared, leaving the arcades to support nothing; the inner porch has the usual five bays. In plan the building is an octagon inscribed in a square with semidomes as squinches in the diagonals; to north and south are galleries. But the odd feature is that what in most mosques of this form are aisles under the galleries are here turned into porches. That is, where you would expect an arcade of columns, you find a wall with windows opening onto an exterior gallery which, in turn, opens to the outside by enormous arches, now glazed in. The mihrab and mimber are very fine works in marble, as are the grilles above the windows. Tiles of the best period complete the decoration of this interesting building.

HİRKA-İ ŞERİF CAMİİ

If we leave by the south gate of the mosque and follow the winding road uphill, we come in a moment or two to a mosque of a very different style indeed. Hirka-i Şerif Camii, the Mosque of the Holy Mantle, was built in 1851 by Sultan Abdül Mecit to house the second of the two mantles of the Prophet which are among his chief relics in Istanbul. (The other is in its own treasury in the Saray.) The mosque is in the purest *Empire* style and just misses being a great success, as do most buildings in that style; all the same it is very entertaining. A monumental gateway leads to a spacious paved courtyard; the two tall minarets are extremely slender and have balconies in the form of Corinthian capitals. The façade is a little forbidding, more like a palace than a mosque, but the interior is very pleasant; it is in the form of an octagon with an outside gallery. The walls and dome, of a greenish brown, are covered with plaster mouldings of garlands and vines in buff, done with a certain bravura but also with elegance. The mihrab, mimber and kürsü, elaborately carved, are of a deep purple conglomerate marble flecked with grey, green, blue, black and yellow, and highly polished. Part of the decoration consists of elegant inscriptions by the famous calligrapher Mustafa Izzet Efendi, others by Sultan Abdül Mecit, who was himself an able calligrapher. This is a building which should not be missed by anyone who delights in the follies and oddities of architecture as long as they have a certain verve and charm.

HÜRREM ÇAVUŞ CAMİİ

Hirka-i Şerif Camii is built on a high terrace, partly artificial; to the south a long staircase leads down to a lower monumental gateway opening from the street below, Keçeciler Caddesi, the Avenue of the Goat Herder. If we turn right (west) and follow this street, we come after 500 metres or so to a little mosque on the left which is of no interest save that its architect was Sinan. It was built in 1560, as an inscription shows, by a certain Hürrem who was a *çavuş* (messenger) in the Divan. It is of the rectangular type with wooden roof and porch; restorations are recorded in 1844 and 1901. Perhaps because of these, it has lost any charm it may once have had.

Just across the lane from the garden of the mosque there is a pleasant teahouse named after Koca Mimar Sinan, the architect. One might feel inclined to rest here for awhile and have a glass or two of tea before strolling back to the main avenue.

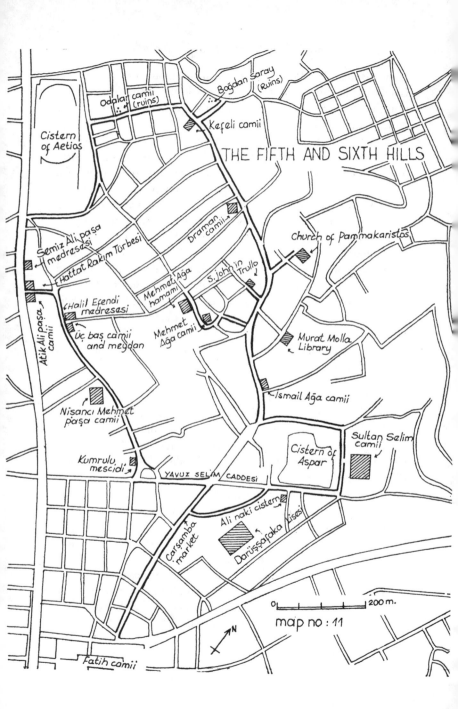

Cistern of Aetios

Odalar camii (ruins)

Boğdan Saray (Ruins)

Kefeli camii

THE FIFTH AND SIXTH HILLS

Semiz Ali paşa medresesi

Hattat Rakım Türbesi

Draman camii

Church of Pammakaristos

Halil Efendi medresesi

Mehmet Ağa hamamı

S. John in Trullo

Atik Ali paşa camii

Üç baş camii and meydan

Mehmet Ağa camii

Murat Molla Library

Nisancı Mehmet paşa camii

İsmail Ağa camii

Kumrulu mescidi

YAVUZ SELIM CADDESI

Cistern of Aspar

Sultan Selim camii

Ali naki cistern

Çarşamba market

Darüşşafaka lisesi

0   200 m.

map no : 11

N

Fatih camii

13

The Fifth and Sixth Hills

Our present tour takes us from the Fatih district on a circuit around the Fifth and Sixth Hills of Stamboul. Here we escape from almost all indications of a modern city and stroll through districts that have changed far less than in the tourist centres of Istanbul. Tourists rarely come here, for with one or two exceptions the monuments, though often interesting historically and architecturally, are not of the first importance. We come upon colourful street-markets, picturesque byways and plane-tree-shaded squares reminiscent of Ottoman Istanbul. An exploration of this out-of-the-way part of the town is rewarding as much for its village-like atmosphere as for the occasional Ottoman mosque or Byzantine church that lies hidden away down its back streets, or perches grandly on some terrace overlooking the Golden Horn.

Our starting-point will be the outer courtyard of Fatih Camii, from where the first part of our stroll will take us along the southern slopes of the Fifth and Sixth Hills, after which we will circle back in a clockwise loop. We leave through the gate to the right at the western end of the courtyard. This brings us to Darüşşafaka Caddesi, which extends north-west towards the Fifth Hill. This avenue takes us through the lively district of Çarşamba, which takes its name from the bustling open market that throngs its streets on that day. This is a travelling market that sets up its stalls and barrows in different parts of the town on different days; thus there are neighbourhoods in Istanbul named after almost all of the days in the week.

A few hundred metres along Darüşşafaka Caddesi we see off on the right the famous institution from which the avenue takes its name, the Darüşşafaka Lisesi. Darüşşafaka, founded in 1855, is an orphanage which has one of the finest secondary schools in Turkey.

The school has moved to another location and its original home in Çarşamba is now empty.

KUMRULU MESCİDİ

Soon after passing Darüşşafaka we reach Yavuz Selim Caddesi and turn left. We walk along this avenue for about 150 metres and then turn right at the first through street. A short way along on the left we come to a little mosque called Kumrulu Mescidi, the Mescit of the Turtle-Dove. The mosque takes its name from a fragment of Byzantine sculpture used in the adjoining çeşme, showing two turtle-doves drinking from the Fountain of Life. This mosque is of interest principally because its founder and builder was Atik Sinan, the Chief Architect of Sultan Mehmet II and the designer of the original Mosque of the Conqueror. Atik Sinan's tombstone is to be seen in the garden of the mosque, with an inscription which tells us that he was executed by Fatih in 1471.

NİŞANCI MEHMET PAŞA CAMİİ

Continuing on the same street we come on our left to the beautiful mosque of Nişancı Mehmet Paşa. This is one of the very best of the classical mosques – and it is *not* by Sinan. (The mosque is, of course, popularly ascribed to Sinan, but is does not appear in the best texts of the *Tezkere,* the list of his works.) The identity of the architect, unfortunately, is not known, but it was built for the Keeper of the Seal (Nişancı) Mehmet Paşa between 1584 and 1588. From a distance one sees the elegance of line and the masterly arrangement of the upper structure: the great dome surrounded by the eight little weight-turrets (the continuation of the columns that support the dome arches), the eight semidomes of two sizes, and the minaret unusually close to the dome base – an excellently proportioned distribution of curves and verticals. One enters through the usual charming courtyard, the arches of which are of the ogive type; under the porch of five bays an inscription with the *tuğra* of Mustafa III records a restoration in 1766, presumably after the very severe earthquake of that year.

The plan of the mosque is an interesting variation of the octagon inscribed in a square. Eight partly-engaged columns support the dome arches; in the axes there are four semidomes, while in the diagonals four smaller semidomes serve as squinches instead of pendentives. The eastern semidome covers a projecting apse for the mihrab, while those to north and south also cover projections from the square. The western corners of the cross so formed are filled with small independent chambers; above on three sides are galleries. The whole arrangement is original and masterly; nor are interesting details wanting. In the corners of the east wall are two charming little kürsüs or platforms, access to which is gained by staircases built into the thickness of the wall from the window recesses. In the voussoirs and balustrades of these platforms, in the window frames, and elsewhere throughout the mosque, an interesting conglomerate marble of pale violet and grey is used; and for the columns which support both platforms and galleries there is another conglomerate marble of tawny brown flecked with yellow, gray, black and green. The arches of the galleries, like those of the courtyard, are of the ogive type. As a whole, the mosque is a masterpiece; it is as if the unknown architect, in the extreme old age of Sinan, had decided to play variations on themes invented by Sinan himself and to show that he could do them as well as the Master. In the little graveyard behind the mosque is the small and unpretentious türbe of Nişancı Mehmet Paşa.

ÜÇ BAŞ CAMİİ, MEDRESE OF HALİL EFENDİ

Leaving Nişancı Mehmet Paşa Camii and continuing along in the same direction we soon come to a small square called Üç Baş Meydanı, literally the Square of the Three Heads. The square takes its name from Üç Baş Camii, the tiny mosque we see to the right of the square. Evliya Çelebi tells us that the mosque received this odd name "because it was built by a barber who shaved three heads for one small piece of money, and, notwithstanding, grew so rich that he was enabled to build this mosque; it is small but particularly sanctified." A more prosaic explanation is given in the *Hadika*, a comprehensive description of the mosques of Istanbul written in 1780; there we learn that the founder, Nureddin Hamza ben Atallah, came from a village in Anatolia called Üç Baş. (But then from where did the village get its name?) An inscription over the gate gives the date of foundation as A.H. 940 (A.D. 1532–3). The mosque is of no interest except for its name.

Opposite the mosque there is a ruined medrese, founded in 1575 by a certain Halil Efendi. In the centre of the square is an old çeşme, the beautifully written inscription on which indicates that it was founded by one Mustafa Ağa in 1681. We have lingered over these oddments because the district is picturesque.

ZİNCİRLİ KUYU CAMİİ

Continuing on in the same direction as before, we take the next turning on the left and find a little mosque called Zincirli Kuyu Camii. This was built around 1500 by Atik Ali Paşa, whose larger and better known mosque is next to Constantine's Column. Zincirli Kuyu is a small rectangular building of brick and stone construction covered by six equal domes in two rows of three supported by two massive rectangular pillars; its original porch of three bays had disappeared but has been poorly reconstructed. The mosque is interesting as being a tiny example of the Ulu Cami type of mosque borrowed from Selçuk architecture and fairly common in the first or Bursa period of Ottoman architecture. The type consists of a square or rectangular space covered by a multiplicity of equal domes supported by pillars or columns; it can be very large and impressive, as in the Ulu Cami of Bursa with its 20 domes. On the small scale of Zincirli Kuyu it is rather heavy and oppressive.

Opposite Zincirli Kuyu is a small baroque türbe dated A.H. 1241 (A.D. 1825). Here is buried the famous calligrapher Hattat Rakkım, who designed the beautiful inscription on the türbe and sebil of Nakşidil Valide Sultan. The interior of the türbe is decorated with photographs of his work.

MEDRESE OF SEMİZ ALİ PAŞA

Beyond the türbe in the main street is an attractive medrese of the classical period, which has been restored and converted into a children's clinic. This medrese, also called Zincirli Kuyu, was founded by another Ali Paşa who was Grand Vezir in the reign of Süleyman the Magnificent. Because of his great girth he was called Semiz Ali, that is

Fat Ali, or sometimes Kalın Ali, Ali the Bear. He was one of the great characters of his time and was known for his wit and conviviality as well as for his honesty, a pleasant contrast to his predecessor Rüstem Paşa. Ali Paşa was a Dalmatian by birth and had been educated in the Palace School at the Saray, later becoming in turn Ağa of the Janissaries, Beylerbey of Rumelia, Second Vezir, and finally Grand Vezir. Since he died in office in 1564, the medrese must have been built before that time. It is a work of Sinan but presents no special features except the two symmetrical entrances on either side of the dershane.

CISTERN OF AETİOS

Continuing along the main avenue for about 100 metres we come to one of the three huge ancient open cisterns. Its attribution was for long in doubt, but it has been identified with great probability as that built by a certain Aetios, a Prefect of the city, in about A.D. 421. Large as it is, it is yet the smallest of the open cisterns in the city, measuring 224 by 85 metres; it was probably about 15 metres deep. Like the others, it was already disused in later Byzantine times and was turned into a kitchen garden. It now serves as a sports arena known as the Vefa Stadium.

PANAGHİA URANON CHURCH

If so inclined, one may now pursue, part way down the valley that divides the Fifth from the Sixth Hill, the traces of some very ruined and insignificant Byzantine churches, scarcely worth the trouble of finding except for the fun of the search. We descend the flight of steps at the south-east end of the stadium and continue ahead on Kelebek Sokağı. At the end of the street we turn left on Kurtağa Çeşme Caddesi, after which we take the third turning on the right on to Dolmuş Kuyu Sokağı. Along this street there were formerly the exigious remains of two Byzantine churches, known locally as Odalar Camii and Kasım Ağa Mescidi, but these have now virtually disappeared. They have been identified as belonging to the Byzantine Monastery of the Theotokos of Petra, but the identification is highly uncertain.

About 150 metres along this street we see on the left the Greek church of the Panaghia Uranon, Our Lady of the Heavens. This church is Byzantine in foundation, but the structure in its present form is due to a complete rebuilding in 1843. Some architectural fragments of the Byzantine church can be seen built into the walls of the church.

KEFELİ MESCİDİ

A little farther along we turn right on Draman Caddesi, where almost immediately on our right we come to a Byzantine building converted into a mosque. This is known as Kefeli Camii or sometimes as Kevevi Camii; it is in fairly good condition and is still in use. It is a long narrow building with two rows of windows and a wooden roof; the entrance is now in the middle of the west wall. As in the cases mentioned above, the identification is much in dispute; it may have belonged to the Monastery of the Prodromos in Petra, and it was probably not a church but a refectory, since it has but one apse and is oriented north instead of east. It has been dated variously from the ninth to the twelfth centuries.

BOĞDAN SARAY

If on leaving Kefeli Camii we turn right and take the first street to the left almost opposite the mosque, and then again the first on the left, we soon come to the ruined crypt of a tiny Byzantine building. It goes by the lordly name of Boğdan Saray, or Moldavian Palace, because from the sixteenth to the eighteenth century it served as the private chapel attached to the palace of the Hospodars of Moldovia. It appears to date from the twelfth or thirteenth century and to have been dedicated to St. Nicholas, but it was probably not originally a church, since it is oriented to the north, but a funerary chapel. And indeed three sarcophagi were found in the crypt during some very clandestine (and unpublished) excavations carried out in 1918. At the beginning of the present century it had an upper storey with a dome, but this has now disappeared. All that remains is a tiny barrel-vaulted room, with a pretty little apse at the end.

DRAĞMAN CAMİİ

We now return to Draman Caddesi and turn left. We will stroll along this avenue, which changes its name several times, for most of the remainder of our tour. The neighbourhood through which we are walking is one of the more picturesque in Istanbul, albeit somewhat broken-down.

About 200 metres beyond Kefeli Camii we see on our right a small mosque on a high terrace reached by a double staircase. This is Drağman Camii, which is a minor work of Sinan. Unfortunately it was very badly restored some years ago and has lost any interest it may have had. It was of the rectangular type covered by a wooden roof and preceded by a wooden porch, now (hideously) rebuilt in concrete. Originally it was the centre of a small complex consisting of a medrese and a mektep, both presumably by Sinan. The medrese has perished but the mektep remains, though in ruins: a fine domed building to the north-east of the mosque. Although the mosque itself is disappointing, the high terrace, the mektep and the wild garden and graveyard are attractive.

Inscriptions show the complex was founded in 1541 by Yunus Bey, the famous interpreter (*drağman*, or dragoman) of Süleyman the Magnificent, of whom Bassano da Zara tells us that he was a Greek from Modon and that he "possessed the Turkish, Greek and Italian languages to perfection." In collaboration with Alviso Gritti, bastard son of the Doge of Venice, he wrote in the Venetian dialect a brief but very important account of the organization of the Ottoman government. He also seems to have served on at least two occasions as the representative of the Grand Vezir Ibrahim Paşa to the Venetian Republic.

CHURCH OF THE THEOTOKOS PAMMAKARİSTOS

We now return to the main avenue, which here changes its name to Fethiye Caddesi, and continue on in the same direction for about 200 metres. Then, just before the road bends sharply right, we turn left and almost immediately come to a Byzantine church standing on a terrace overlooking the Golden Horn. This is the church of the Theotokos Pammakaristos, the Joyous Mother of God. Since the church sits in

▪CHURCH OF THE PAMMAKARISTOS

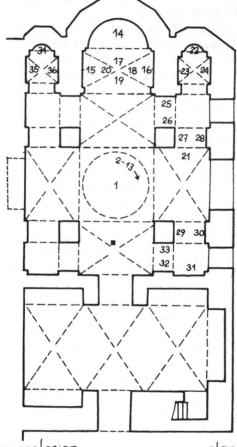

parecclesion   plan no: 20

1. *Pantocrator*	13. *Isaiah*	25. *Gregory Thaumaturgus*
2. *Moses*	14. *Christ Hyperagathos*	26. *Gregory of Agrigentum*
3. *Jeremiah*	15. *The Virgin*	27. *Antipas*
4. *Zephaniah*	16. *John Prodromos*	28. *Blasius*
5. *Micah*	17. *Archangel Michael*	29. *Sabas*
6. *Joel*	18. *Archangel Raphael*	30. *John Climacus*
7. *Zechariah*	19. *Archangel Gabriel*	31. *Euthemius*
8. *Obadiah*	20. *Archangel Uriel*	32. *Chariton*
9. *Habakkuk*	21. *Baptism of Christ*	33. *Arsenius*
10. *Jonah*	22. *Gregory the*	34. *James, Brother of the Lord*
11. *Malachi*	*Theologian*	35. *Clement (?)*
12. *Ezekiel*	23. *Cyril*	36. *Metrophanes of*
	24. *Athanasius*	*Constantinople*

the middle of a large open area, one can walk around it and look at it from all sides, unlike most of the other Byzantine churches in the city. The south and east façades are especially charming with their characteristic ornamental brickwork, the marble cornices beautifully and curiously inscribed, the three little apses of the side chapel, and the multiplicity of domes on high and undulating drums.

The building consists of a central church with a narthex; a small chapel on the south; and a curious "perambulatory" forming a side aisle on the north, an outer narthex on the west, and two bays of an aisle on the south in front of the side chapel. Each of these three sections was radically altered when it was converted into a mosque in 1591. The work of the Byzantine Institute has at last cleared up many of the puzzles arising from the various periods of construction and transformation. It now appears that the main church was built in the twelfth century by an otherwise unknown John Comnenus and his wife Anna Doukaina. In form, the church was on the ambulatory type, a triple arcade on the north, west and south dividing the central domed area from the ambulatory; at the east end were the usual three apses, at the west a single narthex. At the beginning of the fourteenth century a side chapel was added at the south-east as a mortuary for Michael Glabas and his family; this was a tiny example of the four-column type. In the second half of the fourteenth century, the north, west and part of the south sides were surrounded by the "perambulatory", which ran into and partly obliterated the west façade of the side chapel. When the building was converted into a mosque, the chief concern seems to have been to increase the available interior space.

Most of the interior walls were demolished, including the arches of the ambulatory; the three apses were replaced by the present domed triangular projection; and the side chapel was thrown into the mosque by removing the wall and suppressing the two northern columns. All this can scarcely be regarded as an improvement. Indeed, the main area of the church has become a dark, planless cavern of shapeless hulks of masonry joined by low crooked arches. This section has now been divided off from the side chapel and is again being used as a mosque.

The side chapel has been most beautifully restored, its missing columns replaced, and its mosaics uncovered and cleaned. The mosaics of the dome have always been known, for they were never concealed, but they now gleam with their former brilliance: the Pantocrator surrounded by 12 Prophets; in the apse Christ "Hyperagathos" with the Virgin and St. John the Baptist; other surfaces contain angels and full-length figures of saints. Only one scene mosaic survives: the Baptism of Christ. Though much less in extent and variety than the mosaics of Kariye Camii (see Chapter 14), these are nevertheless an enormously precious addition to our knowledge of the art of the last renaissance of Byzantine culture in the early fourteenth century.

The Church of the Pammakaristos remained in the hands of the Greeks for some time after the Conquest; in fact, in 1456 it was made the seat of the Greek Orthodox Patriarchate after the Patriarch Gennadius abandoned the Church of the Holy Apostles. It was in the side-chapel of the Pammakaristos that Mehmet the Conqueror came to discuss questions in religion and politics with Gennadius. The Pammakaristos continued as the site of the Patriarchate until 1568; five years later Murat III converted it into a mosque. He then called it Fethiye Camii, the Mosque of Victory, to commemorate his conquest of Georgia and Azerbaijan.

CHURCH OF ST. JOHN IN TRULLO

Returning to Fethiye Caddesi we follow it in the same direction for a short distance and then take the first turning on the right. We there find ourselves face to face with a charming little Byzantine church which has recently been restored. It is called Ahmet Paşa Mescidi and has been identified with almost virtual certainty as the Church of St. John the Baptist in Trullo. Nothing whatever is known of the history of the church in Byzantine times. Three years after the Conquest, in 1456, when Gennadius transferred the Patriarchate to the Pammakaristos, he turned out the nuns there ensconced and gave them this church instead. Here they seem to have remained until about 1586, when the church was converted into a mosque by Hirami Ahmet Paşa, from whom it takes its Turkish name. The tiny building was a characteristic example of the four-column type of church with a narthex and three semicircular apses, evidently of the eleventh or twelfth century. Until a few years ago it was ruined and dilapidated, but still showed signs of frescoes under its faded and blotched whitewash. The original four columns, long since purloined, have since been replaced with poor columns and awkward capitals, and the restored brickwork is also wrong.

MEHMET AĞA CAMİİ

Returning to the main avenue, we take the next right and at the end of the short street we see a small mosque in its walled garden. Though of modest dimensions, this is a pretty mosque and interesting because it is one of the relatively few that can be confidently attributed to the architect Davut Ağa, Sinan's colleague and successor as Chief Architect to the Sultan. Over one of the gates to the courtyard is an inscription naming Davut as architect and giving the date A.H. 993 (A.D. 1585), at which time Sinan was still alive. The founder Mehmet Ağa was Chief of the Black Eunuchs in the reign of Murat III.

In plan the mosque is of the simplest: a square room covered by a dome, with a projecting apse for the mihrab and an entrance porch with five bays. But unlike most mosques of this simple type, the dome does not rest directly on the walls but on arches supported by pillars and columns engaged in the wall; instead of pendentives there are four semidomes in the diagonals. Thus the effect is of an inscribed octagon, as in several of Sinan's mosques, but in this case without the side aisles; it rather resembles Sinan's mosque of Molla Çelebi at Fındıklı on the Bosphorus (see Chapter 21). The effect is unusual but not unattractive. The interior is adorned with faience inscriptions and other tile panels of the best Iznik period; but the painted decoration is tasteless – fortunately it is growing dim with damp. Mehmet Ağa's türbe is in the garden to the left; it is a rather large square building.

Just to the south outside the precincts stands a handsome double bath, also a benefaction of Mehmet Ağa and presumably built by Davut Ağa. The general plan is standard: a large square camekân, the dome of which is supported on squinches in the form of conches;

a cruciform hararet with cubicles in the corners of the cross, but the lower arm of the cross has been cut off and turned into a small soğukluk which leads through the right-hand cubicle into the hararet; in the cubicles are very small private washrooms separated from each other by low marble partitions – a quite unique disposition. As far as one can judge from the outside, the women's section seems to be a duplicate of the men's.

LIBRARY OF MURAT MOLLA

Returning once again to the avenue, which here changes its name to Manyasizade Caddesi, we continue along in the same direction and take the next left. A short way along to the right we see the fine library of Murat Molla. Damatzade Murat Molla was a judge and scholar of the eighteenth century who founded a tekke, now destroyed, to which he later (1775) added a library that still stands in an extensive and very pretty walled garden. The library is a large square building of brick and stone supported by four columns with re-used Byzantine capitals – the whole edifice indeed is built on Byzantine substructures, fragments of which may be seen in the garden. The corners of the room also have domes with barrel vaults between them. In short, it is a very typical and very attractive example of an eighteenth-century Ottoman library, to be compared with those of Atif Efendi, Ragıp Paşa and others of the same period. Like these, it is constantly in use.

ISMAİL EFENDİ CAMİİ

We now return to Manyasizade Caddesi and at the next corner on the left we come to Ismail Efendi Camii. This is a quaint and entertaining example of a building in a transitional style between the classical and the baroque. It was built by the Şeyh-ül Islam Ismail Efendi in 1724. The vaulted substructure contains shops with the mosque above them, so constructed, according to the *Hadika,* in order to resemble the Kaaba at Mecca! We enter the courtyard through a gate above which is a very characteristic sibyan mektebi of one room. To the right a long double staircase leads up to the mosque, the porch of which has been tastelessly reconstructed in detail (e.g., the capitals of the columns!), but the general effect of which is pleasing except for its glazing. On the interior there is a very pretty – perhaps unique – triple arcade in two storeys of superposed columns repeated on the south, west and north sides and supporting galleries; perhaps because of these arcades the dome seems unusually high. At the back of the courtyard is a small medrese, or more specifically a dar-ül hadis, school of tradition. It has been greatly altered and walled in, but it is again being used for something like its original purpose, a school for reading the Kuran. All-in-all this little complex is quite charming with its warm polychrome of brick and stone masonry; it was on the whole pretty-well restored from near ruin in 1952.

CISTERN OF ASPAR

Returning once again to Manyasizade Caddesi, we continue along for a few paces and then take the next left into Sultan Selim Caddesi. As we walk along we now see on our right a great open cistern, the second of the three ancient Roman reservoirs in the city. This is the Cistern of Aspar, a Gothic general put to death in the year 471 by the Emperor Leo I. This is the largest of the Roman reservoirs; it is square, 152 metres on a side, and was originally ten metres deep. Some years ago one could still see its original construction in courses of stone and brick, with shallow arches on its interior surface. Up until 1985 the cistern was occupied by a very picturesque little farm village whose house-tops barely reach to the level of the surrounding streets, but then the houses were demolished to convert the cistern into a market area. Nevertheless, it is a superb setting for the great mosque of Sultan Selim I that looms ahead at the far end of the cistern.

MOSQUE OF SULTAN SELİM I

The mosque of Sultan Selim I rises on a high terrace overlooking the Golden Horn with an extensive and magnificent view. And the building itself, with its great shallow dome and its cluster of little domes on either side, is impressive and worthy of the site. The courtyard is one of the most charming and vivid in the city, with its columns of various marbles and granites, the polychrome voussoirs of the arches, the very beautiful tiles of the earliest Iznik period in the lunettes above the windows – turquoise, deep blue, and yellow – and the fountain surrounded by tapering cypress trees. The plan is quite simple: a square room, 24.5 metres on a side, covered by a shallow dome, 32.5 metres in height under the crown, which rests directly on the outer walls by means of smooth pendentives. The dome, like that of Haghia Sophia, but unlike that of most Turkish mosques, is significantly less than a hemisphere. This gives a very spacious and grand effect, recalling a little the beautiful shallow dome of the Roman Pantheon. The room itself is vast and empty, but saved from dullness by its perfect proportions and by the exquisite colour of the Iznik tiles in the lunettes. The mosque furniture though sparse is fine, particularly the mihrab, mimber, and sultan's loge. The border of the ceiling under the loge is a quite exceptionally beautiful and rich example of the painted and gilded woodwork of the great age; notice the deep, rich colours and the varieties of floral and leaf motifs in the four or five separate borders, like an Oriental rug, only here picked out in gold. To north and south of the great central room of the mosque there are annexes consisting of a domed cruciform passage giving access to four small domed rooms in the corner. These served, as we have seen elsewhere in the earlier mosques, as tabhanes, or hospices, for travelling dervishes.

The mosque was finished in 1522 under Süleyman the Magnificent, but it may have been begun two or three years earlier by Selim himself, as the Arabic inscription over the entrance portal would seem to imply. Although the mosque is very often ascribed to Sinan, even by otherwise reliable authorities, it is certainly not so, for not only is it too early but it is not listed in the *Tezkere*. Unfortunately the identity of the actual architect has not been established.

In the garden behind the mosque is the grand türbe of Selim I, octagonal and with a dome deeply ribbed on the outside. In the porch on either side of the door are two beautiful panels of tilework, presumably from Iznik but unique in colour and design. The interior has unfortunately lost its original decoration, but it is still impressive in its solitude, with the huge catafalque of the Sultan standing alone in the centre of the tomb, covered with embroidered velvet and with the Sultan's enormous turban at its head. As Evliya Çelebi wrote of this türbe: "There is no royal sepulcher which fills the visitor with so much awe as Selim's. There he lies with the turban called Selimiye on his coffin like a seven-headed dragon. I, the humble Evliya, was for three years the reader of hymns at his türbe."

Selim I, son and successor of Beyazit II, was 42 years old when he became Sultan and ruled for only eight years. (There is a suspicion that Selim ordered the assassination of his father, who died soon after he was forced from the throne.) Nevertheless, during his brief reign he doubled the extent of the Ottoman Empire, conquering western Persia, Syria, Palestine, Arabia and Egypt. After his capture of Cairo in 1517, Selim took for himself the title of Caliph, and thenceforth the Ottoman Sultans assumed the titular leadership of Islam. The Sultan was known to his people as Yavuz Selim, or Selim the Grim, and beheaded his Grand Vezirs at the rate of one a year. The last two years of his reign were spent preparing for a great campaign into Europe, which was cut short by his sudden and premature death in 1520. For long afterwards a cynical Turkish proverb maintained that "Yavuz Selim died of an infected boil and thereby Hungary was spared."

Facing Selim's türbe is another in which are buried four children of Süleyman the Magnificent. This too has a pretty and almost unique feature: the circular drum of the dome, set back a little from the octagon of the building itself, is adorned with a long inscription carved in the stonework. The porch here too has panels of faience, hexagonal tiles with stylized floral motifs set separately on the stone. This türbe was built in 1556, probably by Sinan, although there is a problem here since two of the princelings buried in the türbe died about 40 years before that time.

Standing in the garden near Selim's türbe is the tomb of Sultan Abdül Mecit, who died in 1861; for a building of this late date it is simple and has good lines. Abdül Mecit chose this spot for his türbe because of his admiration for his warrior ancestor. Unlike Selim, Abdül Mecit's conquests were confined to the Harem, where he fathered 42 children with 21 wives. Among the major accomplishments of Abdul Mecit is that he sired the last four Ottoman Sultans, among the worst in the long history of the Empire.

The mosque was formerly surrounded by the usual buildings of the külliye: an imaret, a medrese and a mektep. Of these only the last remains, a little domed building at the south-west corner of the outer courtyard.

CISTERN OF PULCHERİA

Leaving the mosque by the gate through which we entered, we turn left so as to walk along the north side of the Cistern of Aspar. We then turn right at the next corner into Yavuz Selim Caddesi, which borders the eastern side of the cistern. Just opposite the south-eastern corner of the cistern, at the corner of Yavuz Selim Caddesi and Ali Naki Sokağı, we find another ancient cistern, this one covered. Its name and origin are unknown, though it has been identified without any serious evidence as that of the Empress Pulcheria, wife of the Emperor Marcian. In any event, its fine workmanship seems to indicate an early date, perhaps fifth or sixth century. The interior has columns of granite or marble, in four rows of seven, with Corinthian capitals and imposts. The cistern has been restored and is now open to the public.

Continuing on past the cistern we come to Yavuz Selim Caddesi, down which we walked at the beginning of our tour. Turning left here, we walk back to our starting-point at Fatih Camii, strolling once again through the picturesque district known as Wednesday.

ST. SAVIOUR IN CHORA

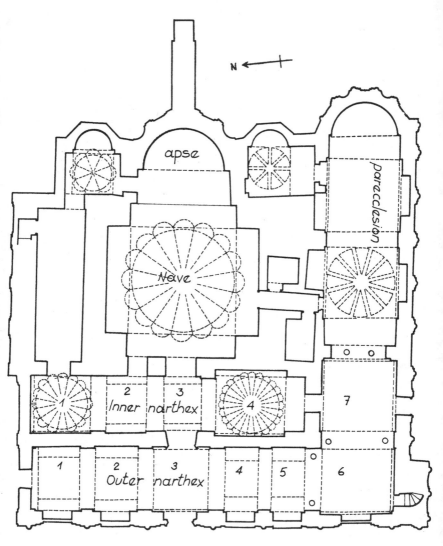

N ←—

apse

parecclesion

Nave

2 3
Inner narthex

1

4

7

1 2 3
Outer narthex

4 5 6

0 ———————— 10 m.

plan no: 21

14

Kariye Camii

The Church of St. Saviour in Chora, called in Turkish Kariye Camii, is after Haghia Sophia the most interesting Byzantine church in the City; not so much for the building itself, pretty as that is, as because of the superb series of mosaics and frescoes which it preserves and which have been magnificently restored and cleaned by the Byzantine Institute of America*. The name of the church "in Chora" means in the country because the very ancient monastery to which it was attached was outside the Constantinian walls; later when it was included within the Theodosian walls, the name remained (compare St. Martin's in the Fields or St. Germain des Près) but was given a symbolic sense: Christ as the "country" or "land" of the Living and the Blessed Virgin as the "dwelling-place" of the Uncontainable, as they are referred to in the mosaics in the church.

No trace remains of the original ancient church, nor is anything certain known about its origin. The present building in its first form dates only from the late eleventh century and was built by Maria Doukaina, mother-in-law of the Emperor Alexius I Comnenus, between the years 1077 and 1081; it was probably of the "four-column" type so popular at that time. But it did not last long in its original form; perhaps because of the slipping of the foundations at the east end, the apses appear to have collapsed, and the opportunity was taken to remodel the building. At the east the present wide central apse with its deep barrel-vault was erected; the walls of the nave were retained, but the piers were added in the corners as supports for the arches of a much larger dome; there was a narrow side chapel to the south, traces of which remain in the passages and gallery between the nave and the present, later, side chapel. This elaborate remodelling was apparently carried out by Maria Doukaina's grandson, the Sebastokrator Isaac Comnenus, third son of Alexius I, early in the twelfth century.

A third period of building activity some 200 years later, after the Latin occupation, gave us the church as it now is. At this time the nave area was left essentially unchanged except for redecoration. But the inner narthex was rebuilt, the outer narthex and the parecclesion or side chapel were added, the small side apses reconstructed, and the northern passage with its gallery was built in its present form. In addition to all these structural alterations, the whole of the present decoration of the church, its marble revetment, its mosaics and its frescoes, is the work of this period, from 1315 to 1321. The man to whom we owe all this was the Grand Logethete Theodore Metochites, whose mosaic portrait we will see over the door from the inner narthex into the nave. The church was converted into a mosque by Atik Ali Paşa in the early sixteenth century. The paintings were never wholly obliterated, though in the course of centuries they were covered with plaster, paint and dirt, and many were shaken down by earthquakes. They have now been brilliantly restored, as far as genuine restoration is possible.

THE MOSAICS

The mosaics and frescoes are far and away the most important and extensive series of Byzantine paintings in the city and among the most interesting in the world. Notice that they are of almost exactly the same date as the work of Giotto in Italy and though quite unlike Giotto's work in detail, they seem to breathe the same spirit of life and reality, so typical of the dawn of the Renaissance; they are a far cry from the formal and stylized painting of the earlier Byzantine tradition. To view them intelligently, as the artist intended them to be seen, one must follow their iconographic order; they fall naturally by position and theme into six groups:

I.   Six large dedicatory or devotional panels in the outer and inner narthexes

II.   The Ancestry of Christ in the two domes of the inner narthex

III.   The Cycle of the Life of the Blessed Virgin in the first three bays of the inner narthex

I.   *Dedicatory and devotional panels*

1.   Christ Pantocrator

In lunette over door to inner narthex

The church was dedicated first to Christ Pantocrator (the Almighty). The inscription reads: "Jesus Christ, the land (country, dwelling-place) of the Living" – with a play on the name of the church and a reference to Psalm 116:9: "I will walk before the Lord in the land of the living."

2.   The Virgin with Angels

Opposite the above, over entrance door to the building

Secondly the church was dedicated to the Blessed Virgin. Here she is praying in an attitude characteristic of the type known as the Theotokos of the Blachernae; Inscription: "The Mother of God, the dwelling-place of the uncontainable" – with the same play on the name of the church and a reference to the mystery of the Incarnation.

3.   Theodore Metochites presenting his Church to Christ

Inner narthex in lunette over door to nave

Theodore offers a model of his church to the enthroned Christ. He is dressed in his official robe: the extraordinary turban-like hat was called a *skiadion*, literally a sunshade! Christ has the same inscription as in the outer narthex; Theodore's reads: "The Founder, Logothete of the Genikon, Theodore Metochites."

4.   St. Peter

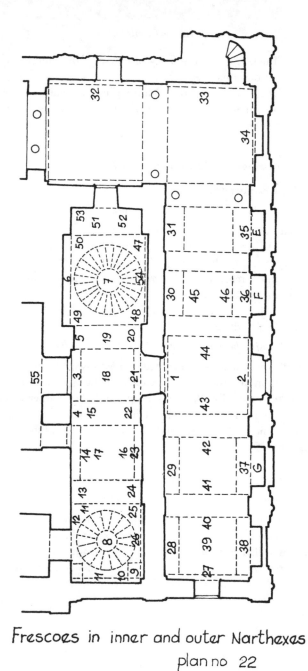

Frescoes in inner and outer Narthexes
plan no 22

5. St. Paul

    To left and right of door to nave

6. The Deesis

    Right of the door in east wall of south bay

    (A Deesis is a representation of Christ with his mother on his right and – usually, though not here – St. John the Baptist on his left.). Here Christ is of the type known as Chalkites from the famous icon over the main gate to the imperial palace. Below are the figures of two donors (very unusual in a deesis). At the Virgin's right stands "The son of the most high Emperor Alexius Comnenus, Isaac Porphyrogenitus": this is Isaac Comnenus, third son of Alexius I, who was probably responsible for the rebuilding of the church in the twelfth century. The inscription of the other figure is partly lost: what remains reads "... of Andronicus Palaeologus, the Lady of the Mongols, Melane the nun." This was either Maria, half-sister of Andronicus II, known as the Despoina of the Mongols, who founded the still extant church of St. Mary of the Mongols (see Chapter 15): or else another Maria, an illegitimate daughter of Andronicus II, who also married a Khan of the Mongols of the Golden Horde: in either case she took the religious name of Melane.

II.   *The Genealogy of Christ*

In the two domes of the inner narthex

7. Southern dome: in the crown a medallion of Christ Pantocrator and in the flutes two rows of his ancestors, from Adam to Jacob in the upper zone, in the lower the 12 sons of Jacob and some others.

8. Northern dome: in the crown a medallion of the Blessed Virgin with the Christ child; below in the upper zone 16 kings of the house of David, in the lower 11 figures representing "other ancestors outside the genealogy".

III.   *Cycle of the Life of the Blessed Virgin*

In the first three bays of the inner narthex

The Cycle of the Life of the Virgin is based mainly on the Apocryphal Gospel of St. James, better known as the *Protoevangelium*, which is at least as old as the second century, and gives an account of her birth and life from the rejection of the offerings of Joachim, her father, to the birth of Jesus. It was very popular in the Middle Ages and is the source of many cycles of pictures both in the East and the West; compare Giotto's cycle in the Arena Chapel at Padua, painted at about the same date as these, and representing many of the same scenes. Here there were 20 scenes, of which 19 are completely or partially preserved.

9.   Joachim's Offerings Rejected

First bay, NW pendentive of dome

Zacharias the High Priest before the altar raises his hands in a gesture of refusal. (The rest of the scene in the NE pendentive is lost: it must have shown Joachim and his wife Anne bearing offerings. Their offerings were rejected because they had borne no children.)

10.   Fragmentary Scene

In lunette of north wall

Probably Joachim and Anne returning home: only a maid looking out of a doorway is preserved.

11.   Joachim in the Wilderness

In SE pendentive

Ashamed at the rejection of his offerings, Joachim goes into the wilderness to pray for offspring.

12.   The Annunciation to St. Anne

In lunette of east wall

(Left half of scene lost.) The right half shows the angel of the Lord announcing to Anne that her prayer for a child has been heard.

13. The Meeting of Joachim and Anne

     In east soffit of arch between first and second bays

     Anne informs Joachim on his return from the wilderness of the annunciation of the angel. The scene is inscribed "The conception of the Theotokos".

14. The Birth of the Blessed Virgin

     In east lunette of second bay

15. The First Seven Steps of the Virgin

     In east soffit of arch between second and third bays

     She took her first seven steps when she was six months old.

16. The Virgin blessed by the Priests (west side)

17. The Virgin caressed by her Parents (east side)

     Two scenes in domical vault of second bay

     Note the pair of magnificent peacocks in the pendentives, representing incorruptibility.

18. The Presentation of the Virgin in the Temple

     In domical vault of third bay

     The scene is inscribed "The Holy of Holies". At the age of three the Virgin was presented as an attendant at the Temple, where she remained until she was about 12.

19. The Virgin receiving Bread from an Angel

     In east soffit of arch between third and fourth bays

     While she remained in the Temple she was miraculously fed by an angel.

20. The Instruction of the Virgin in the Temple

In west soffit of same arch

The central figures of the scene have unfortunately been destroyed.

21. The Virgin receiving the Skein of Purple Wool

In lunette above door from outer narthex

The priests decided to have the attendant maidens weave a veil for the Temple; the royal colours, purple and scarlet, fell to Mary by lot.

22. Zacharias praying before the Rods of the Suitors

In west soffit of arch between second and third bays

When the time came for the Virgin to be married, Zacharias the High Priest called all the widowers together and placed their rods on the altar, praying for a sign showing to whom she should be given.

23. The Virgin entrusted to Joseph

In west lunette of second bay

When the rods were returned to the widowers, Joseph's rod began to sprout with green leaves and the Virgin was awarded to him.

24. Joseph taking the Virgin to his House

In west soffit of arch between first and second bays

Here they are just leaving the Temple; the youth is one of Joseph's sons by his former wife.

25. The Annunciation to the Virgin at the Well

In SW pendentive of dome in first bay

26. Joseph taking leave of the Virgin; Joseph reproaching the Virgin

Two scenes in west lunette of first bay

Joseph had to go away for six months on business; when he returned he found the Virgin pregnant and was angry (until reassured by a dream, as in the first scene of the next cycle).

IV. *The Cycle of the Infancy of Christ*

Each of the 13 extant or partly extant Infancy scenes occupies a lunette of the outer narthex, proceeding clockwise round all seven bays. In the soffits of the arches are saints, while in the domical vaults are the scenes of Christ's Ministry, which will be described later. The Infancy Cycle is largely based on the canonical Gospels and most of the scenes are inscribed with quotations which sufficiently identify them.

27. Joseph Dreaming
    The Virgin With Two Companions
    The Journey to Bethlehem

    Three scenes in north lunette of first bay

    First scene inscribed: "Behold, the angel of the Lord appeared to him in a dream, saying: Joseph, thou son of David, fear not to take unto thee Mary thy wife: for that which is conceived in her is of the Holy Ghost." (Matt. 1:20)
    Second scene uninscribed.
    Third scene inscribed: "And Joseph also went up from Galilee, out of the city of Nazareth, unto the city of David, which is called Bethlehem..." (Luke 2:4)

28. The Enrolment for Taxation

    In east lunette of first bay

    Inscription: "... (because he was of the house and lineage of David) to be taxed with Mary his espoused wife, being great with child." (Luke 2:4–5, continued from above)

29.   The Nativity

   In east lunette of second bay

   Inscription is simply the title *The Birth of Christ.* To the shepherds the angel says: "Fear not: for behold, I bring you good tidings of great joy, which shall be to all people." (Luke 2:10)

30.   The Journey of the Magi
      The Magi before Herod

   Two scenes in east lunette of fourth bay

   Inscription: "And behold, there came wise men from the East to Jerusalem, saying: Where is he that is born King of the Jews?" (Matt. 2:1–2)

31.   Herod enquiring of the Priests and Scribes

   In east lunette of fifth bay

   Partly destroyed. Inscription (mutilated): "And when he had gathered all the priests and scribes together he demanded of them where Christ should be born." (Matt. 2:4)

One now turns the corner, into the seventh bay: the lunette above the door to the inner narthex, now blank, probably contained the Adoration of the Magi. The lunette above the columns and arches that lead to the Pareeclesion retains traces of the Return of the Magi.

32.   The Flight into Egypt

   In south lunette of seventh bay

   Main scene destroyed, only title remaining. On right of window scene of Fall of Idols from the Walls of an Egyptian Town as the Holy Family passes by (from an apocryphal source).

33.   The Massacre of the Innocents

   In west lunette of sixth bay

Inscription: "Then Herod, when he saw that he was mocked of the wise men, was exceeding wroth, and sent forth and slew all the children that were in Bethlehem, and in all the coasts thereof, from two years old and under." (Matt. 2:16)

34. The Massacre continues

In west lunette of sixth bay

Central part and inscription destroyed.

35. Mothers mourning their Children

In west lunette of fifth bay

Inscription: "In Rama was *there* a voice heard, lamentation, and weeping, and great mourning." (Matt. 2:18)

36. The Flight of Elizabeth

In west lunette of fourth bay

Inscription is the title. The scene, from the *Protoevangelium* 22:3, depicts Elizabeth with her baby son, John the Baptist, born about the same time as Christ, seeking refuge from the massacre in the mountains which open to receive her.

37. The Return from Egypt

In west lunette of second bay

Inscription: "Being warned of God in a dream, he (Joseph) turned aside into the parts of Galilee: and he came and dwelt in a city called Nazareth." (Matt. 2:22–3)

38. Christ taken to Jerusalem for the Passover

In west lunette of first bay

Inscription: "Now his parents went to Jerusalem every year at the Passover." (Luke 2:41)

End of the Infancy Cycle.

V. *The Cycle of Christ's Ministry*

This cycle occupies the domical vaults of all seven bays of the outer narthex, as well as parts of the south bay of the inner narthex. Unfortunately, all but one of the vaults in the outer narthex are very badly damaged, many scenes being lost or reduced to mere fragments. The series begins in the vault of the first bay.

39. Christ among the Doctors (north side)

40. John the Baptist bearing witness of Christ (I) (south side)
    In vault of first bay (fragments only)

41. John the Baptist bearing witness of Christ (II) (north side)

42. The Temptation of Christ (south side)
    In vault of second bay

    The first scene is inscribed: "This was he of whom I spake, He that cometh after me is preferred before me: for he was before me." (John 1:15)

    The four scenes of the Temptation are accompanied by a running dialogue between Christ and the Devil (from Matthew 4:3–10): (1) Devil: "If thou be the Son of God, command that these stones be made bread." Christ: "It is written, Man shall not live by bread alone, but by every word that proceedeth out of the mouth of God." (2) Devil: "All these things will I give thee, if thou wilt fall down and worship me." Christ: "Get thee behind me, Satan!" (The Devil has offered "all the kingdoms of the world" represented by six kings in a walled town.) (3) "Then the Devil taketh him up to the holy city (and setteth him on a pinacle of the temple)." (4) Devil: "If thou be the Son of God, cast thyself down." Christ: "It is written, thou shalt not tempt the Lord thy God."

43.   The Miracle at Cana (north side)

44.   The Multiplication of the Loaves (south side)

>   *In vault of third bay*

>   Both badly ruined. The first illustrates John 2:1–11; the second
>   Matthew 14:5–21.

45.   Christ healing a Leper (east side)

46.   Christ walking on the Water (west side)

>   *In vault of fourth bay (fragments only)*

The vaults of the fifth, sixth, and seventh bays have almost
completely lost their mosaics. The fifth vault is entirely empty. In
the sixth can be made out fragments of *Christ healing the Paralytic
at Capernaum* and *Christ healing the Paralytic at the Pool of Bethesda;*
while in the north-east pendentive is the *Paralytic carrying off his Bed,*
and in the north-west pendentive is part of *Christ conversing with the
Samaritan Woman.* In the seventh vault is a fragmentary *Christ calling
Zacchaeus from the Sycamore Tree.*

One now re-enters the inner narthex where the last eight scenes
of Christ's Ministry, almost all well-preserved, are to be found in
the pendentives, vaults and lunettes under the southern dome that
contains the Ancestors of Christ. The inscriptions in this series are
merely the titles of the scenes.

47.   Christ healing the Blind and Dumb Man (Matt. 12:22)

>   *In SW pendentive*

48.   Christ healing the two Blind Men (Matt. 20:29–30)

>   *In NW pendentive*

49.   Christ healing Peter's Mother-in-Law (Matt. 8:14–15)

>   *In NE pendentive*

50.   Christ healing the Women with the Issue of Blood
       (Matt. 9:20–2)

       In SE pendentive

51.   Christ healing the Man with the Withered Hand
       (Matt. 12:10–13)

       In soffit of south arch, east side

52.   Christ healing the Leper (Matt. 8:2–3)

       In soffit of south arch, west side

53.   Christ healing... (inscription and half mosaic lost)

       In southern lunette

54.   Christ healing various Diseases (Matt. 15:30)

       In western lunette

End of the Cycle of Christ's Ministry

VI.   *The panels in the nave*

55.   The Dormition (Koimesis) of the Virgin

       Over the central door from the narthex

The Virgin lies dead on her bier. Behind stands Christ holding her
soul, represented as a babe in swaddling clothes. Over Christ's head
hovers a six-winged seraph. Around stand the apostles, evangelists
and early bishops. The idea is taken from an apocryphal work,
Concerning the Koimesis of the Holy Mother of God, ascribed to St.
John the Divine.

56.   Christ

       In panel at left of bema

Inscription as in outer narthex. Christ holds the Gospels open to
Matthew 11:28: "Come unto me, all ye that labour and are heavy
laden, and I will give you rest."

57.   The Virgin Hodegitria

In panel at right of bema

Inscription as in outer narthex. The type is that of the Hodegitria, the Guide or Teacher, the original of which was supposed to have been painted by St. Luke from life.

THE PARECCLESION: THE FRESCOES

The superb fresco decoration of the parecclesion or side chapel to the south of the church was the last part of Metochite's work of redecoration to be carried out, probably in 1320–1. The great but unknown master artist of these frescoes was probably the same as the one who did the mosaics in the rest of the church. The decoration of the chapel is designed to illustrate its purpose as a place of burial. Above the level of the cornice the paintings represent the Resurrection and the Life, the Last Judgement, Heaven and Hell, and the Mother of God as the Bridge between Earth and Heaven. Below the cornice is a procession of saints and martyrs, interrupted here and there by tombs. We shall deal first with the upper series of frescoes beginning at the east, then list the saints below cornice level, and finally say a few words about the tombs.

I.   *Scenes of Resurrection*

1.   The Anastasis

In the semidome of the apse

This scene, called Anastasis (Resurrection) in Greek, is known in English as the Harrowing of Hell. Christ has broken down the gates of Hell which lie beneath his feet; Satan, bound, lies before him. With his right hand he pulls Adam out of his tomb; behind Adam stand St. John the Baptist, David, Solomon and other righteous kings. With his left hand he pulls Eve out of her tomb; standing in it is Abel and behind him another group of the righteous. This is surely one of the great paintings of the world.

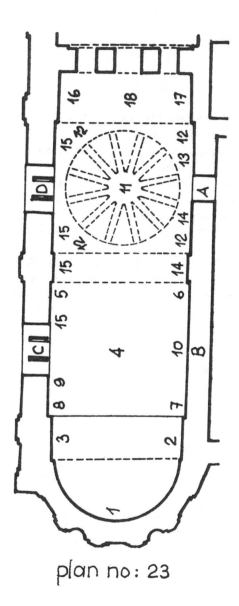

plan no: 23

2. Christ raising the Widow's Son

    North side of bema arch

    The inscription is the title. The story is only told by Luke (7:11–15).

3. Christ raising the Daughter of Jairus

    South side of bema arch

    Inscription illegible but doubtless the title. The story is in all three Synoptic Gospels, perhaps best in Mark (5:22–4, 35–43). In crown of arch the *Archangel Michael* in a medallion.

II. *The Last Judgement: Heaven and Hell*

4. The Second Coming of Christ

    In vault of eastern bay

    This vast scene occupies the whole vault; the title is inscribed at the centre. It represents the Doctrine of the Last Things; death, judgement, immortality in heaven or damnation in hell. In the crown is the Scroll of Heaven (Apocalypse 6:14). In the eastern half sits Christ in Judgement. To the souls of the saved he says: "Come, ye blessed of my Father, inherit the kingdom prepared for you from the foundation of the world." (Matt. 25:34) To the condemned souls on his left he says: "Depart from me, ye cursed, into everlasting fire, prepared for the devil and his angels." (Matt. 25:41) Below to left a River of Fire broadening to a lake in which are the damned. Below Christ the Etimasia or empty throne prepared for the Second Coming: Adam and Eve prostrate before it. Below this the Weighing and Condemnation of Souls. The western half of the vault is occupied by the Choirs of the Elect in clouds.

5. The Land and Sea giving up their Dead

    In SW pendentive

    No inscription; cf. Apocalypse 20:13.

6.   An Angel conducts the Soul of Lazarus to Heaven

7.   Lazarus the Beggar in Abraham's Bosom

8.   The Rich Man in Hell

   In NW, NE and SE pendentives

   The scenes illustrate Luke 16:19–26: the Rich Man had refused alms to Lazarus in this world; he went to hell and appealed to Lazarus in heaven for water but was refused.

9.   The Torments of the Damned

   In lunette of south wall, eastern half

   Four rectangular panels identified as: (upper left) The Gnashing of Teeth; (upper right) The Outer Darkness; (lower left) The Worm that Sleepeth Not; (lower right) The Unquenchable Fire.

10.   The Entry of the Elect into Paradise

   In lunette of north wall

   The Elect are led by St. Peter towards the Gate of Paradise, guarded by a Cherub; the Good Thief welcomes them and points to the enthroned Mother of God.

III.   *The Mother of God and Her Prefigurations*

This cycle, in the western dome and bay, represents the Blessed Virgin and a series of five episodes from the Old Testament which came to be symbolically interpreted as prefigurations or "types" of the Virgin and the Incarnation.

11.   The Virgin and Child with Angels

   In the western dome

   The Virgin and Child in the crown surrounded by the heavenly court of angels in the spaces between the ribs.

12. Four Hymnographers

    In the pendentives of the dome

    These poets were chosen because in their hymns, verses of which are inscribed on their scrolls, they referred to the prefigurations of the Virgin depicted below. (NE) St. John Damascene; (SE) St. Cosmas the Poet; (SW) St Joseph the Poet; (NW) St. Theophanes.

13. Jacob's Ladder; Jacob wrestling with the Angel

    In western half of north lunette

    The ladder or bridge to heaven as a prefiguration of the Virgin. Inscribed: "And Jacob took one of the stones of the place, and put it at his head, and lay down to sleep in that place; and behold, a ladder fixed on the earth, whose top reached to heaven, and the angels of God ascended and descended on it. And the Lord stood upon it." (Genesis 28:11–13). Note that the Lord, here and elsewhere, is represented by the Virgin and Child.

14. Moses and the Burning Bush; Moses hides his Face

    In eastern half of north lunette and on soffit of arch

    The burning bush that was not consumed as a prefiguration of the Virgin. First scene inscribed: "Now Moses came to the mountain of God, even to Choreb. And the angel of the Lord appeared to him in a flame out of the bush ... Put off thy shoes from off thy feet, for the place where upon thy standest is holy ground." (Exodus 3:1–2, 5). Second scene, on adjacent arch, inscribed: "And Moses hid his face; for he was afraid to look upon God." (Exodus 3:6).

15. The Dedication of Solomon's Temple

    Four scenes on south wall

    The Ark of the Covenant as a prefiguration of the Virgin. First scene, in west half of south lunette of east bay, is inscribed:

"And it came to pass when Solomon was finished building the house of the Lord, then he assembled all the elders of Israel in Sion, to bring the Ark of the Covenant to the Lord out of the City of David, that is Sion, and the priests took up the Ark of the Covenant as a prefiguration of the testimony." (I Kings 8:1–4). Second scene, on soffit of arch, inscription lost but probably continuation of verse 4: "and the holy vessels that were in the tabernacle of testimony." Third scene, on east half of south lunette, inscribed: "and the king and all Israel were assembled before the Ark." (v 5). Fourth scene, on west half of south lunette, inscribed: "And the priests bring in the Ark of the Covenant, into the oracle of the house, even into the holy of holies, under the wings of the cherubim." (I Kings 8:6)

16.   Isaiah and the Angel

In south soffit of western arch

The inviolable city as a prefiguration of the Virgin. The inscription on Isaiah's scroll is almost illegible but probably reads: "Thus saith the Lord concerning the king of Assyria: 'He shall not come into this city'." (Isaiah 37:33)

17.   Aaron and his Sons before the Altar

In north soffit of western arch

The altar as a prefiguration of the Virgin. Inscription, practically illegible, is perhaps: "They draw nigh to the altar and offer their sin-offerings and their whole burnt offerings." (Leviticus 9:7)

18.   The Souls of the Righteous in the Hand of God

In crown of western arch

Almost entirely lost, but one can make out part of the Hand of God holding the souls of the righteous, represented as infants in swaddling-bands.

IV. *The Saints and Martyrs*

A long procession of saints and martyrs marches about the lower walls of the parecclesion; in the apse stand six Fathers of the Church (from left to right):

St. Athanasius	St. Gregory the Theologian
St. John Chrysostomos	St. Nicholas of Myra
St. Basil	St. Cyril of Alexandria

The Virgin Eleousa, the Merciful or Compassionate on south wall of bema

South Wall (east to west):	*North Wall* (west to east):
St. George of Cappadocia	St. Eustathius Plakidas
St. Florus (medallion)	St. Samonas of Edessa
St. Laurus (medallion)	St. Gurias of Edessa
St. Demetrius of Thessalonika	St. Artemius or St. Nicetas
St. Theodore Tyro	St. Bacchus (medallion)
St. Theodore Stratelates	St. Sergius (medallion)
St. Mercurius	An unidentified saint
St. Procopius	Medallion of unidentified saint
St. Sabah Stratelates	A stylite saint

West Wall

South pier:	An unidentified saint
North pier:	St. David of Thessalonika (in an almond tree where he lived for three years)

As will be noticed, most of these saints belong to the Eastern Church and are almost unknown in the West. Pictures of many of them appear also in the outer narthex, but since they are chiefly of interest only to the student of Eastern hagiology it has not seemed necessary to name them.

THE TOMBS

There were four tombs in the parecclesion, each in a deep niche which originally held a sarcophagus with mosaics or frescoes above; some fragments of the latter still exist.

Tomb A, the first in the north wall, though it has lost its identifying inscription, is almost certainly that of Theodore Metochites himself; it has an elaborately carved and decorated archivolt above.

Tomb B is entirely bare.

Tomb C has well preserved paintings of a man and woman in princely dress but has lost it inscription.

Tomb D is that of Michael Tornikes, general and friend of Metochites, identified by the long inscription above the archivolt, which is even more elaborately carved than that of Metochites himself; fragments of mosaic and painting still exist.

Tomb E, in the fifth bay of the outer narthex, is that of the princess Eirene Raoulaina Palaeologina, a connection by marriage of Metochites. It preserves a good deal of its fresco painting.

Tomb F, in the fourth bay of the outer narthex, is that of a member of the imperial Palaeologus family but cannot be more definitely identified, though it preserves some vivid painting of clothes.

Tomb G, in the second bay of the outer narthex, is the latest in the church, probably not long before the Turkish Conquest; the painting shows strong influence of the Italian Renaissance, but the owner cannot be identified.

Tomb H, in the north wall of the inner narthex, is that of the Despot Demetrius Doukas Angelus Palaeologus, and has an inscription to the following effect: "Thou art the Fount of Life, Mother of God the Word and I Demetrius am thy slave in love."

Before we leave Kariye Camii, we might pause for a moment before the portrait of Theodore Metochites, the man to whom we owe this church and its magnificent works of art. Seeing him there over the door leading into the nave of his church, proud and at the very peak of his career, we are saddened to learn that Theodore fell from royal favour in his later years. After Andronicus III usurped the throne in 1328, Theodore was stripped of his power and possessions and thrown into prison, along with many other officials of the old regime. Only when his life was drawing to a close was he freed and allowed to retire to the monastery of St. Saviour in Chora. He died there on 13 March 1331 and was buried in the parecclesion of his beloved church. In those last sad days of his life, Theodore was comforted by his friend, the great scholar Nicephorus Gregoras, who was also confined to the monastery. When Nicephorus later recorded the history of those times, he wote this affectionate tribute to Theodore: "From morning to evening he was most wholly and eagerly devoted to public affairs as if scholarship was absolutely indifferent to him; but later in the evening, having left the palace, he became absorbed in science to such a degree as if he were a scholar with absolutely no connection with any other affairs." Theodore was the greatest man of his time, a diplomat and high government official, theologian, philosopher, historian, astronomer, poet and patron of the arts, the leader of the artistic and intellectual renaissance of late Byzantium. But among all his accomplishments, Theodore was proudest of the church that he had built and adorned. Towards the end of his life he wrote of his hope that it would secure for him "a glorious memory among posterity to the end of the world." It has indeed.

* The present description of Kariye Camii is based almost entirely on the great publication of this work by Paul A. Underwood, *The Kariye Djami,* 4 vols; Bollingen Series 70; copyright 1966 by Princeton University Press; excerpts adapted by permission of Princeton University Press. Also on the Preliminary Reports in the *Dumbarton Oaks Papers* (1956–60). These have completely superseded all previous work on the church.

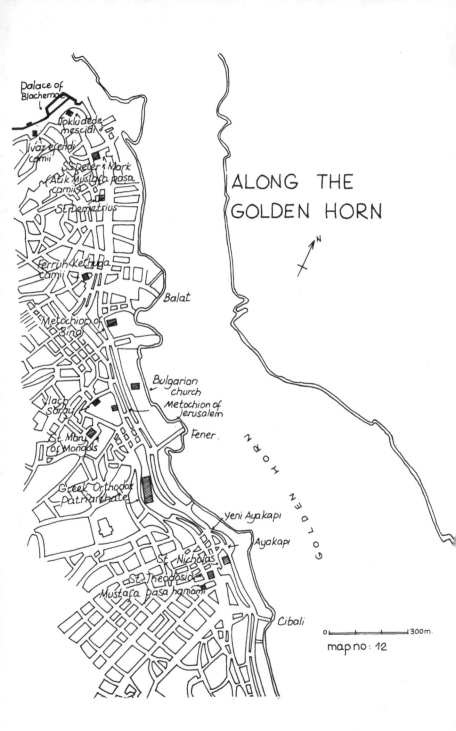

Palace of Blachernae

Toklu dede mescidi

Ivaz efendi camii

SS Peter & Mark

Atik Mustafa paşa camii

St Demetrius

Ferruh kethuda camii

Balat

Metochion of Sina

Bulgarian church

Metochion of Jerusalem

Vlach saray

Fener

St Mary of Mongols

Greek Orthodox Patriarchate

Yeni Ayakapı

Ayakapı

St Nicholas

St Theodosia

Mustafa paşa hamamı

Cibali

ALONG THE GOLDEN HORN

N

GOLDEN HORN

0   300m.

map no: 12

15

Along the Golden Horn

The region along the Stamboul shore of the Golden Horn above the two bridges is one which few tourists ever see, except for one or two of the more famous monuments. This is a pity, for it has a distinctive atmosphere which is quite unlike that of any other part of the city. Some of its quarters, particularly Fener and Balat, are very picturesque and preserves aspects of the life of old Stamboul which have all but vanished elsewhere.

Our tour begins at the Stamboul end of the Atatürk Bridge. This is the place known as Odun Kapısı, the Wood Gate, after a long vanished gateway known in antiquity as the Porta Plarea. The first part of our tour takes us along the shore highway, which is now bordered by a park along the Golden Horn, making our stroll easier and more pleasant than it was in times past.

GOLDEN HORN SEA-WALLS

As we walk along we see on the left side of the avenue stretches of the medieval Byzantine sea-walls that once extended along the shores of the Golden Horn and the Marmara, joining up with the land-walls at both ends. The stretch that we will pass on our present tour, which goes beyond what was once the end-point of Constantine's wall, was originally built by Theodosius II in the fifth century to meet the great land-walls which he constructed at that time. These sea-walls were repaired and reconstructed many times across the centuries, particularly by the Emperor Theophilus in the ninth century. These fortifications consisted for the most part of a single line of walls ten metres in height and five kilometres long, studded by a total of 110 defence towers placed at regular intervals. Considerable stretches of this wall still remain standing, particularly along the route of our present tour, although almost all of it is in ruins. Much of this ruination was brought about in the last great sieges of the city, by the Crusaders in 1203–4 and the Turks in 1453. In both instances the besiegers lined up their warships against the sea-walls along the Golden Horn and repeatedly assaulted them. And the destruction wrought by these sieges and subsequent centuries of decay is now being rapidly completed by the encroachment of modern highways and factories.

The sea-walls along the Golden Horn were pierced by about a score of gates and posterns, many of them famous in the history of the city. Of these only one or two remain, although the location of the others can easily be determined, since the streets of the modern town still converge to where these ancient gates once opened, following the same routes they have for many centuries past. The first of these gates which we pass on our tour is about 450 metres along from the Atatürk Bridge. This is Cibali Kapı, known in Byzantium as the Porta Puteae. A Turkish inscription beside the gate commemorates the fact that it was breached on 29 May 1453, the day on which Constantinople fell to the Turks. This gate also marks the point which stood opposite the extreme left wing of the Venetian fleet in their final assault on 12 April 1204.

The huge building along the side of the avenue before Cibali Kapı is Kadır Has University. This private Turkish university, founded in 2002, is housed in the former Cibali Tobacco and Cigarette Factory, which opened in 1884. The factory was designed by Alexandre Vallaury and built by the architect Hovsep Aznavur. The factory was long disused before it was superbly restored and converted into a university. During the restoration an early Byzantine cistern was discovered beyond the end of the building near Cibali Kapı.

About 250 metres past Cibali Kapı we come on the left to a little pink-walled Greek church dedicated to St. Nicholas. This church dates to about 1720 and was originally the *metochion,* or private property, of the Vathopedi Monastery on Mount Athos. The corbelled stone structure in which the church is housed is typical of the so-called meta-Byzantine buildings we will see along the shore of the Golden Horn, most of them dating from the seventeenth or eighteenth century. The principal treasure of the church is a very rare portative mosaic dating from the eleventh century; it can be seen only during the services on Sunday. Notice also in the lobby the model of an ancient galleon hanging from the ceiling. These are to be found in many of the waterfront churches of the city, placed there by sailors in gratitude for salvation from the perils of the sea.

Just beyond St. Nicholas we come to Aya Kapı, the Holy Gate, a little portal which opens from a tiny square beside the avenue. This was known in Byzantium as the Gate of St. Theodosia, after the nearby church of the same name.

CHURCH OF ST. THEODOSİA

To reach the church we pass through the gate and continue for about 50 metres until we come to the second turning on the left, where we continue for another 50 metres until we come to Gül Camii, somewhat doubtfully identified as the Church of St. Theodosia. Its history is obscure but the foundations recently brought to light date from the late tenth or the eleventh century, as is shown by the "recessed brickwork" typical of this period. Thus the earlier dating of the church to the ninth century appears to be erroneous.

The building is one of the most imposing Byzantine churches in the city and, in spite of a certain amount of Turkish reconstruction, still preserves its original form. It is a cross-domed church with side aisles supporting galleries; the piers supporting the dome are disengaged from the walls, and the corners behind them form alcoves of two storeys. The central dome and the pointed arches which support it are Turkish reconstructions, as are most of the windows. From the exterior the building is rather gaunt and tall: the upper parts have been considerably altered in Turkish times, with the result of making it still more fortress-like. The two side apses, however, are worthy of note, with their three tiers of blind niches and their elaborate brick corbels. Among the more pleasing aspects of the exterior is the minaret, handsomely proportioned and clearly belonging to the classical period when the church was converted into a mosque.

There are two interesting legends associated with the church: one of them perhaps true, the other almost certainly false. The first of these legends (the one which may be true) concerns the Turkish name

CHURCH OF ST THEODOSIA

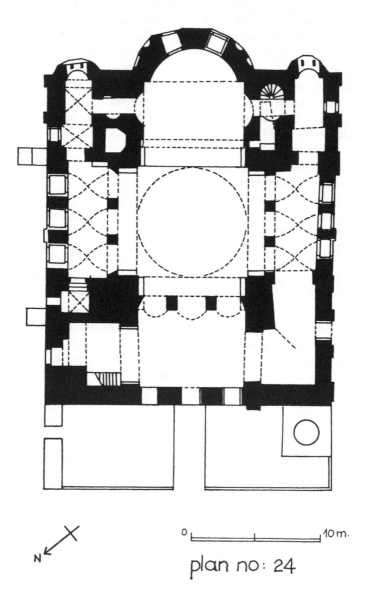

N

0 |___|___|___|___|___| 10 m.

plan no: 24

of the building, Gül Camii, or the Mosque of the Rose. It seems that the saint's feast-day falls on 29 May, and on that day in the year 1453 a great congregation assembled in the church appealing for Theodosia's intercession. The church had been decked with roses in celebration of the feast-day, and when the Turkish soldiers entered the church after the city fell they found the roses still in place: so the romantic story goes, and hence the romantic name.

The second legend, which seems to have originated long after the Conquest, has it that the church of St. Theodosia was the final resting-place of Constantine XI Dragases, the last Emperor of Byzantium. There are several different traditions as to the circumstances of the Emperor's death and the place of his burial, but the one in favour among Greeks of an older generation was that he was interred in a chamber in the south-east pier of St. Theodosia. And indeed there is a burial-chamber there, reached by a staircase leading up inside the pier itself, and within it is a coffin, or sarcophagus, covered by a green shawl. However, an equally persistent Turkish legend has it that this is not the tomb of Constantine but that of a Muslim saint called Gül Baba, the eponymous founder of the mosque! To further complicate the problem, above the lintel of the door leading to the burial-chamber there is a cryptic Turkish inscription which reads: "Tomb of the Apostle, disciple of Christ, peace be to him."

KÜÇÜK MUSTAFA PAŞA HAMAMI

Leaving the church, we turn left and then at the second corner we turn left again. A short distance along on the left side of the street we come to one of the oldest and grandest Turkish baths in the city, now closed for restoration. It is now called Küçük (Little) Mustafa Paşa Hamamı, but it seems actually to have been founded by Koca Mustafa Paşa, Grand Vezir to Beyazit II, who built it sometime before 1512. Its plan and the incredibly varied and intricate structure of its domes would entirely bear out that early date. Its camekân, about 14.5 metres square, is among the largest in the city, so that not even the wooden galleries around it detract much from its impressiveness; in its centre there is a pretty marble basin. The soğukluk, as so often, is merely carved out of the hararet, consisting of its right-hand cubicle and the bottom arm of the cross. The hararet itself is very splendid. The central dome has a deep cornice of elaborately-carved stalactites. Each of the three remaining cross-arms is covered with a vault of utterly different structure, the prettiest being perhaps that on the right which has a semidome in the form of a deeply ribbed shell. The two corner cubicles at the back have domes supported on a cornice of juxtaposed triangles, while the third cubicle has a very beautiful *opus sectile* pavement in a variety of brilliant coloured marbles.

SİNAN PAŞA MESCİDİ

After leaving the hamam we turn right and walk west along Küçük Mustafa Paşa Sokağı for about 100 metres until we come to an intersection with streets winding off in several directions. If we take the street that veers off at about 45° to the right, we soon come to the fragmentary ruins of a small Byzantine church partly concealed by trees and houses. Only a portion of the apse survives, but this is interesting as showing an elaborate decoration in brickwork of meander and zigzag designs. Attempts to identify the building with several churches known to have been in the area lack any serious evidence; it is known locally as Sinan Paşa Mescidi. The church would appear to date from the thirteenth or fourteenth century.

HAVUZLU HAMAM

Once past the church we come quickly to Yeni Aya Kapı, which leads out to the main road along the Golden Horn. This portal is not one of the original gateways in the Byzantine sea-walls, but was constructed in 1582 by Sinan. The local residents had petitioned the government to open a gate there so that they could more easily make their way to the new bath which Sinan had constructed outside the walls at that point. This bath, the Havuzlu Hamam, or Bath with a Pool, was built by Sinan in 1582 for the Valide Sultan Nurbanu, mother of Murat III. Unfortunately the hamam is now disaffected and in a state of advanced decay.

THE PETRİON

About 100 metres beyond Yeni Aya Kapı, we come to a point where a second road, Sadrazam Ali Paşa Caddesi, branches off to the left at a slight angle to the main road along the Golden Horn. This was the site of the Gate of the Petrion, one of the portals in the Byzantine sea-walls. The Petrion itself was a walled enclave on the lower slope of the Fifth Hill; the portal here being its eastern sea-gate. The Petrion figured prominently in the assaults upon the sea-walls by the Crusaders and the Turks. On 13 July 1203, the Venetian galleys under Doge Dandolo pushed their prows up against the sea-walls of the Petrion and captured 25 defence towers. The French knight Villehardouin describes Dandolo in action at that time: "The Doge of Venice, though an old man [he was nearly ninety] and totally blind, stood at the bow of his galley with the banner of St. Mark unfurled before him. He cried out to his men to put him on shore or he would deal with them as they deserved. They obeyed him promptly, for the galley touched ground and the men in it leapt ashore, carrying the banner of St. Mark to land before the Doge." In the final Crusader assault upon the city on 12 April 1204, the Petrion was once again the centre of the action. It was here that two brave knights jumped from the flying-bridge of the galleon Pelerine onto a defence tower, and from there led the charge that breached the walls and brought about the capture of the city. On 29 May 1453, the Petrion withstood a sustained attack by the Turkish fleet and the defenders surrendered only when they heard that the land-walls were breached and that the city had fallen. Since it had been surrendered rather than being taken by assault, Fatih decreed that the houses and churches in the Petrion be spared in the general sack of the city. Evliya Çelebi tells us that as a result of their prudent surrender the fishermen of the Petrion "are even now free from all kinds of duties and give no tithe to the Inspector of the Fisheries."

THE GREEK ORTHODOX PATRİARCHATE
Leaving the main road and veering left along Sadrazam Ali Paşa Caddesi, we soon come to the entrance to the Greek Orthodox Patriarchate. On entering, we notice that the main gate is permanently welded shut and painted black. This is the famous Orta Kapı, the Central Gate, which has become almost a symbol of Greek-Turkish intransigence. For it was here that Gregory V, Patriarch of Constantinople, was hanged for treason on 22 April 1821.

The Greek Orthodox Patriarchate has been on this site since about 1601, having moved around for a number of years after leaving the Pammakaristos in 1586. The present patriarchal church of St. George, however, dates only from 1720. Like almost all the post-Conquest churches in the city, it is a small basilica. This form was adopted partly because of its simplicity, but largely because the Christians were forbidden to build churches with domes or masonry roofs, so that the basilica with its timbered roof, a traditional Christian edifice, was the obvious solution. The earlier church seems to have had the same form, for an Italian traveller who saw it in 1615 describes it as "of moderate size, long in form and with several aisles." Among the many relics in the church are the remains of St. Omonia, St. Theophano and St. Euphemia of Chalcedon, whose martyrium we have seen near the Hippodrome; their coffins are in the south aisle. On the right side of the central aisle is the Partriarchal Throne, which is thought to date from the late Byzantine period, although the pious claim that it is the original throne of St. John Chrysostomos, who was Patriarch at the beginning of the fifth century. The church also contains a very lovely portative mosaic of the Blessed Virgin, of the same type and date as the one at St. Nicholas.

Across the courtyard from the church are the other buildings of the Patriarchate. With the exception of the library, a pleasing old building, these are all modern structures erected after the disastrous fire of 1941 which gutted most of the buildings on this side of the courtyard. It is hard to believe that this modest establishment was the centre of the entire Orthodox Church, or that in its great days the Ecumenical Patriarch of Constantinople dominated the religious affairs of the entire Eastern Christian world. Today, although the present Patriarch, Bartholomeos, is still the spiritual leader of Orthodox Christianity, his actual flock in Turkey consists of only the few thousand Greeks still resident in Istanbul and the Aegean islands of Imbros and Tenedos.

THE FENER

After leaving the Patriarchate we continue on along Sadrazam Ali Paşa Caddesi for a few paces to the next intersection. Just to the right at this point is the site of the former Fener Kapısı, the ancient Porta Phanari, or the Gate of the Lighthouse. This gate, now vanished, long ago gave its name to the adjacent quarter, the Fener, so famous in the history of Istanbul in past centuries. Beginning in the sixteenth century, Greeks of this neighbourhood, the Feneriotes, amassed considerable wealth in trade and commerce under the protective mantle of the Ottoman Empire. Many Feneriotes achieved positions of great eminence in the Empire and several families between them even gained control of the trans-Danubian principalities of Moldavia and Wallachia, client states of the Ottomans. The Feneriotes ruled as Hospodars, or Princes, and much of the wealth which they thus acquired was funnelled back into the Fener, where they built magnificent mansions and palaces. The palaces of the Feneriotes have now vanished, but a few of their mansions still survive, reminding us of that colourful period in the city's past.

Continuing along in the same direction for a few steps past Fener Kapısı, we take the first left and then almost immediately turn right into the next street, Vodina Caddesi. About 100 metres along this street on the left side we see a high wall which encloses a large open area extending up the side of the hill. This area is the property of the Greek Orthodox Patriarchate and within it are two churches of some interest. (Those wishing to see these churches should make enquiries at the Greek Orthodox Patriarchate.) The first of these is the church of St. George Metochi, just inside the walls along Vodina Caddesi. It is entered through the gate we see halfway down the block. Since the middle of the seventeenth century this has been the Metochion of the Patriarchate of Jerusalem. The church, which has been rebuilt several times since then, was originally given to the Patriarch of Jerusalem by Michael Cantacuzenus, one of the first Feneriote plutocrats, whose palace stood within the walled enclosure where we find the church today. Michael Cantacuzenus, whom the Turks called Şeytanoğlu, the Son of Satan, used his wealth to good advantage, acquiring a vast library which included a collection of most of the extant ancient manuscripts in the city. Among the manuscripts in St. George there was discovered in 1906 a lost work of Archimedes. This manuscript, a tenth-century copy in palimpsest, was a perfect and complete text of *Archimedes' Method of Treating Mechanical Problems, Dedicated to*

Eratosthenes. This is perhaps the single most important work of the greatest mathematical physicist of antiquity, and constitutes a very great addition to our knowledge of ancient science.

Passing St. George's and continuing along Vodina Caddesi to the next corner, we turn left and follow the walled enclosure along a steep cobbled street leading uphill. A little way up the hill we see another iron gate which leads to the second of the two churches in this enclave. This is the church of the Panaghia Paramithias (St. Mary the Consoler), which served as the Patriarchal church from 1586 till 1596, in the years just after the Patriarchate was moved from the Pammakaristos. Notice the double eagle carved on the marble flagstone at the entrance to the church; this is the symbol of the imperial Palaeologan dynasty and of the Greek Orthodox Patriarchate. This church is more commonly called Vlach Saray, or the Palace of the Wallachians, because it was attached to the adjacent palace of the Cantacuzenus family, who were Hospodars of Wallachia as well as of Moldavia. Unfortunately, Vlach Saray was destroyed by a fire in 1976, and only charred ruins remain to be seen today.

ST. MARY OF THE MONGOLS

Continuing up the hill we turn left at the corner and then take the second right. We then see ahead a rose-red Byzantine church, deformed in shape and with an unusually high drum. This is the church dedicated to the Theotokos Panaghiotissa, the All-Holy Mother of God, but it is more generally called the Mouchliotissa, or St. Mary of the Mongols. This church was founded, or rebuilt, in about 1282 by the Princess Maria Palaeologina, an illegitimate daughter of the Emperor Michael VIII Palaeologus. In the year 1265 Maria was sent by her father as a bride to Hulagu, the Great Khan of the Mongols. Hulagu died before Maria arrived at the Mongol court, however, so she was married instead to his son and successor Abagu. Maria lived at the Mongol court in Persia for about 15 years, and through her influence the Khan and many of his court became Christians. But then, in 1281, Abagu was assassinated by his brother Ahmet and Maria was forced to return to Constantinople. After Maria's return her father offered her as a bride to still another Khan of the Mongols, Charabanda, but this time she refused; perhaps she had had enough of Khans. At about this time Maria founded the church which we see today, together with a convent, and dedicated it to the Mouchliotissa, Our Lady of the Mongols. Maria, the Despoina of the Mongols, as she was known, then became a nun and spent her last years in retirement in her convent: This romantic tale appears to be only partially true, for the church seems actually to have been founded by Isaac Dukas, uncle of Michael VIII, about 1261.The Despoina of the Mongols perhaps merely added to it and gave it further adornments. After the Conquest, Sultan Mehmet II, at the request of his Greek architect Christodoulos (who may be Atik Sinan, the architect of the original Fatih Camii), issued a decree confirming the right of the local Greeks to keep this church. The Greeks remain in possession of the church to this day, and what is claimed to be Fatih's *ferman*, or decree, is still displayed there. This is the only Byzantine church which has been continuously in the hands of the Greeks since before the Turkish Conquest.

The church was originally quatrefoil in plan internally and trefoil externally. That is, the small central dome on a high drum was surrounded by four semidomes along the axes, all but the western one resting on the outer walls of the building, which thus formed exedrae; the whole was preceded by a narthex of three bays. But the entire southern side of the church was swept away in modern times and replaced by a squarish narthex which is in every direction out of line with the original building. The effect is most disconcerting. The church is still adorned with one art treasure from its Byzantine period, a very beautiful portative mosaic of the Theotokos Pammakaristos, the All-Joyous Mother of God. The obvious similarity of this icon to those we have seen at St. Nicholas and at the patriarchal church of St. George strongly suggests that they were all done by the same artist, working in the eleventh century. These are the only three such portative mosaics remaining in the city, and there are only about ten others still known to exist elsewhere.

MEGALİ SCHOLİO

As we leave the church we see off to our right the huge structure which dominates the skyline of this part of the city; it houses a very old and illustrious institution, the Greek Lycee of the Fener, known in Greek as the Megali Scholio, or the Great School. The present red brick building was built in 1881. But the original Megali Scholio, by tradition, was founded before the Turkish Conquest and remained the principal Greek institution of secular education throughout the course of Ottoman history. Here were educated many of the Greek voivodes (governors) and hospodars of Moldavia and Wallachia, and many of the chief interpreters who often wielded such great influence at the Sublime Porte – men with the resounding names of the Byzantine aristocracy, Palaeologus, Cantacuzenus, Cantemir, Mavrocordato and Ypsilanti.

FROM FENER TO BALAT

We now retrace our steps back to the last turning before the church and there take the street to the right. This almost immediately brings us to a steep step-street which bounds the walled enclosure containing the churches of St. George Metochi and Vlach Saray. Halfway down the steps we come to another of the gateways to the enclosure. Beside the gate is a plaque honouring Demetrius Cantemir, a Feneriote Greek who became Prince of Moldavia. Cantemir wrote a history of the Ottoman Empire covering the years 1688–1710 and he also wrote an important treatise on Turkish musicology.

At the bottom of the steps we turn left and then right at the next corner, bringing us back to Vodina Caddesi. We retrace our steps to Fener Kapısı, after which we continue walking up the shore of the Golden Horn.

About 100 metres beyond Fener Kapısı we come to a restored meta-Byzantine building that now houses the Women's Library and Cultural Centre. The library, which opened in 1990, is the first institution of its kind in Turkey. Its collection includes works by and about women in Turkish and other languages, including a complete collection of all the women's magazines and periodicals published in Turkey in the late Ottoman era and in the early years of the Turkish Republic. It is also a research centre for women's studies.

About 150 metres farther along, we see on our right a very astonishing church indeed, that of St. Stephen of the Bulgars. This and the building opposite, the former Exarchate, were erected in 1871, at a time when the Bulgarian Church was asserting its independence from the Greek Orthodox Patriarchate of Constantinople. The church of St. Stephen is a Gothic building entirely constructed of cast iron! The church was prefabricated in Vienna and shipped down the Danube in sections, and then erected here on the shore of the Golden Horn. Not only the outside but the interior as well is of cast iron; even what appear to be panels of marble revetment prove on one's knocking them to be iron, likewise the seemingly sculptured ornamentation! Nevertheless, the church is rather handsome, both its interior and exterior, and it is kept in excellent repair for the small community of Bulgarians who still worship there. The church is surrounded by a pretty and well-tended garden in which are buried several metropolitans of the Bulgarian Church.

Continuing along in the same direction, we come after about 250 metres to the Metochion of Mount Sinai, the oldest and grandest of the meta-Byzantine mansions of the Fener. This house is typical of the few remaining Feneriote mansions, chiefly of the seventeenth century, erected apparently in a continuation or modification of the old Byzantine style. They are constructed of alternate courses of stone and brick; each storey projects over the street, corbelled out on elaborate consoles; the cornice under the roof consists of courses of brick in saw-tooth design. They are very stoutly built, with massive walls and iron doors and window-shutters, more like fortresses than ordinary houses. The house which we are now looking at is of particular interest because it was for nearly three centuries the Metochion of the Monastery of St. Catherine on Mount Sinai. The Monastery of St. Catherine, first founded by Justinian, was for long a semi-autonomous church under the control of the Patriarchate of Alexandria. The Monastery, like many others, has always been represented in Constantinople by one of its archimandrites, who first took up residence in this mansion in 1686. The Metochion is now abandoned and is rapidly falling into ruins.

Just beyond the Archimandrite's mansion, a gateway leads us into the courtyard of the church of St. John the Baptist, the chapel of the monastery which was once part of the Metochion. The church is probably of Byzantine foundation, but it has been burned down and reconstructed several times and the present structure dates only from 1830. It is of no interest except for its connection with the Metochion of Mount Sinai.

BALAT

About 150 metres beyond the church we come to Balat Kapısı, the site of another of the Byzantine sea-gates along the Golden Horn, of which nothing now remains. This has been identified variously as the Gate of the Kynegos (Hunter) or that of the Prodromos (St. John the Baptist). The Turkish name Balat is a corruption of the Greek Palation, or Palace, so called because of the Byzantine Palace of Blachernae which stood nearby. Although the gate has now disappeared, its name survives in that of the surrounding quarter, the picturesque and venerable Balat. Balat has been for many centuries one of the principal Jewish quarters of the city. Many of these were Greek-speaking Jews who lived here in Byzantine times, but these were later absorbed by the Sephardic Jews who emigrated from Spain in 1492 and took up residence in the Ottoman Empire on the invitation of Beyazit II. There are still half a dozen ancient synagogues in the quarter, one of them dating in foundation from Byzantine times, although most of the present structures date from no earlier than the first half of the nineteenth century. Although much of the Jewish community has now moved to more modern neighbourhoods of Istanbul or emigrated to Israel, some still remain in their old quarter in Balat, continuing to speak the medieval Ladino which they brought with them from Spain more than five centuries ago.

There are a few monuments of some minor interest in the immediate neighbourhood of Balat Kapısı. The first of these monuments is found in the second street in from the highway along the Golden Horn and somewhat to the left of the gate. (Although the gate no longer exists, there is no mistaking its former location, for all the local streets converge on it.) After a few twists and turns through the tortuous streets, we come to the rather handsome church of Surp Reşdagabet (Holy Archangels), which has been in the possession of the Armenian community since 1629. It appears to have taken the place of a church of the thirteenth or fourteenth century dedicated to the Taxiarch Saints, that is, the Archangels Michael and Gabriel as chiefs *(taxiarchoi)* of the celestial militia. The present church dates from a complete rebuilding in 1835.

FERRUH KETHÜDA CAMİİ

To the right of Balat Kapısı and on the same street as the church we come to a small mosque which is a minor work of the great Sinan. A long and handsomely written inscription in Arabic over the fine entrance portal of red conglomerate marble informs those who can read it that the mosque was built in A.H. 970 (A.D. 1562–3) by Ferruh Ağa, Kethüda (Steward) of the Grand Vezir Semiz Ali Paşa. The building is of the simple rectangular type; it most probably once had a wooden ceiling with a little dome, but this has been replaced in a recent restoration by a flat concrete ceiling. The building is very long and shallow, with a long and shallow apse for the mihrab, which is adorned with tiles of the Tekfur Saray period. A wooden balcony runs along the west wall, but this is clearly not like the original, for it obstructs the windows in an awkward way. A deep porch precedes the mosque; it must have been rather impressive, supported, as it would appear, on eight columns, the plinths for which remain; but it has been very summarily restored and glazed in. All the same, it is attractive with its grand marble portal, two handsome niches with pretty conch tops, and at each end a curious sort of "anta" or projection of the mosque wall with windows above and below. This is the handsomest and most interesting of Sinan's many mosques of this simple type and it deserves a more sympathetic restoration.

There is an ancient hamam just to the east of the mosque. This has been attributed to Sinan, but wrongly; it is not in the *Tezkere* and it appears much earlier in a *vakfiye* (deed of a pious foundation) of Fatih himself. It is not very impressive and is hardly worth a visit.

The oldest and most historic synagogue in Balat is a short way to the south on Kürkçü Çeşme Sokağı. This is the recently restored Ahrida Synagogue, which dates back to the first half of the fifteenth century, the only synagogue in Istanbul remaining from the Byzantine era. (Permission to visit the synagogue can be obtained from the office of the Chief Rabbinate in Beyoğlu.)

BALAT TO AYVANSARAY

We now retrace our steps to Ferruh Kethüda Camii and continue walking northwards. About 150 metres beyond the mosque we see on the left side of the street the gateway of a little Greek church, interesting only because of its great age. This is the church of the Panaghia Balinu, which is known to have stood on this site as early as 1597, although the present structure dates only from 1730, with later alterations. There are a great many so-called "modern" Greek churches in Istanbul of comparable antiquity, although few of their present structures predate the nineteenth century. The earliest list of post-Conquest Greek churches is that by Tryphon Karabeinikoff, who was sent to Istanbul in 1583 and again in 1593 by the Czar to distribute money to the Christian churches there. Tryphon listed seven monasteries and convents and 47 churches which were functioning in Istanbul at that time, including the Panaghia Balinu.

About 100 metres farther along we see on the right another of the churches mentioned by Tryphon, that of St. Demetrius Kanabu. Although the present church dates only to 1730 at the earliest, its origins go back to Byzantine times, for a church of that name is known to have existed on this site as early as 1334. It is suggested that the church may have been founded by the family of Nicholas Kanabu, who became emperor for a few days in April 1204, in the brief interval between the deposition of the co-emperors Alexius IV and Isaac II and the later usurpation by Alexius V. St. Demetrius served as the Patriarchal church from 1597 until 1601, when the Patriarchate moved to its present site.

ATİK MUSTAFA PAŞA CAMİİ

About 150 metres farther along on Mustafa Paşa Bostanı Sokağı we turn right on a short street that leads out to the Golden Horn. Near the end of the street we see on the right a pretty little Byzantine church converted into a mosque known as Atik Mustafa Paşa Camii. This has been identified tentatively as the Church of SS. Peter and Mark.

The building appears to be the only cross-domed Byzantine church of the ninth century remaining in the city. The wooden porch, the dome and its drum, and probably some of the roofs and many of the windows are Turkish restorations. For the rest, the church preserves its original plan which is simple and, for a Byzantine structure, regular. A dome, doubtless originally on a fairly high drum with windows, covers the centre of the cross; the arms are barrel-vaulted, as are the four small rooms beyond the dome piers which fill up the corners of the cross; they are entered through high, narrow arches. The three apses, semicircular within, have three faces on the exterior. It must have been an attractive little church and it still has a decayed charm.

BLACHERNAE AYAZMA

We now return to Mustafa Paşa Bostanı Sokağı and continue on in the same direction as before. At the next corner on the left we come to the entrance of the famous *ayazma*, or holy spring, of Blachernae. This *ayazma*, like countless others in the city and elsewhere in the Greek world, has been venerated since pre-Christian times, and its waters are believed to possess miraculous powers. The *ayazma* at Blachernae was one of the most popular in the city and even the Emperor and Empress came here to partake of the life-giving waters. In 451 a great church was built over the spring by Pulcheria, wife of the Emperor Marcian. A few years later the church served to house the celebrated robe and mantle of the Virgin. These garments, which had been stolen from a Jewess in Jerusalem by two Byzantine pilgrims, were considered to be the most sacred relics in Constantinople, "the palladium of the city and the disperser of all warlike foes." Thus Blachernae became the most important shrine in the city and remained so throughout the history of Byzantium. The ancient church of the Blachernae was destroyed by fire in 1434, but its site is still occupied by a modern Greek chapel above the sacred spring.

IVAZ EFENDİ CAMİİ

After leaving the *ayazma* we turn left and then right at the next corner onto Dervişzade Sokağı, the Street of the Dervish's Son. At the northern end of the terrace, built almost up against the towers of the Byzantine city-walls, we see Ivaz Efendi Camii. This is a very attractive mosque and while of no great size it is the only monumental building in the whole district. Some scholars have attributed it to Sinan, but it does not appear in his *Tezkere* and there seems to be no definite evidence to identify the architect. There is no historical inscription and the date of construction is given variously as 1581 or 1585, the latter being the year when Ivaz Efendi died. The mosque is almost square, its dome resting on four semidomes with stalactite cornices; the mihrab is in a projecting apse and is decorated with Iznik tiles of the best period. The centre of the west wall is occupied by a gallery in two stories supported on slender marble columns. There are also wooden galleries to north and south, but these are probably not original – certainly not in their present form. The interior is very elegant and gives a great sense of light, illuminated as it is by many windows in all its walls. The west façade is most unusual: instead of a central entrance-portal there are double doors at each end of the façade, the rest of it being filled with windows; the effect is very pretty. Another odd, indeed unique, feature is that the minaret is at the south-east corner. Originally there was a porch, evidently with a sloping roof supported by columns, which ran round three sides of the building.

THE PALACE OF BLACHERNAE

The terrace on which Ivaz Efendi Camii stands is the site of the famous Palace of Blachernae, of which now only a few ruined towers and some substructures remain. The first palace on this site was built by the Emperor Anastasius in about the year 500. The palace was thenceforth used by the imperial family whenever they came to visit the nearby shrine of Blachernae. Over the centuries the Palace of Blachernae was rebuilt and enlarged several times, particularly during the reign of the Comneni dynasty during the eleventh and twelfth centuries. From that time on Blachernae became the favourite residence of the imperial family, gradually supplanting the Great Palace on the First Hill. The splendours and magnificence of the Palace of Blachernae particularly impressed the Crusaders, some of whom have left glowing accounts of it. This may have heightened their desire to take the city for themselves. After the restoration of the Empire in 1261 the Great Palace on the Marmara was abandoned altogether, and for the remainder of the Byzantine period the imperial family lived exclusively at Blachernae; they were still in residence there when the city fell to the Turks on 29 May 1453.

The two towers which we see just behind Ivaz Efendi Camii are a part of the palace. The one to the left is traditionally called the Tower of Isaac Angelus and that to the right the Prison of Anemas, although there are scholars who would identify the latter with one of the towers closer to the Golden Horn. The Prison of Anemas appears frequently in the history of the last centuries of Byzantium. A half-dozen emperors were at one time or another imprisoned, tortured and mutilated in this tower, and two of them were murdered there. The Tower of Isaac Angelus is so-called because it was most probably built by that emperor, in about 1188, perhaps as a private apartment with its upper level serving as a belvedere. Certainly the upper storey of the tower, on a level with the terrace, commands a superb view of the Golden Horn and of the surrounding countryside; notice outside the windows the shafts of columns which once supported a balcony. Seven years after he completed his tower, Isaac Angelus was incarcerated in the Prison of Anemas and blinded – the traditional Byzantine disfiguration of deposed emperors. He was restored briefly in 1213, ruling as co-emperor with his son, Alexius IV, but the two were deposed early in the following year. Isaac and Alexius were then confined to the Prison of Anemas and were strangled there shortly afterwards.

A modern concrete stairway in the terrace leads down to the substructures of the palace. These are quite impressive, but to visit them one must be equipped with a flashlight. The penetralia consist of two nearly parallel walls some 60 metres long, the space between which varies from 8 to 12 metres in width, being divided by arched cross-walls into three storeys of compartments – 42 in all. Since the wooden floors have long since decayed, these vast dungeons give an impression of immense height. From this passage one can enter the towers of Isaac Angelus and Anemas, where a ramp leads down to a small entrance at the foot of the wall; here one gets a good view of the enormous towers from the outside and notices the curious "counterfort" by which they were surrounded at the bottom.

TOKLU DEDE MESCİDİ

Leaving the Palace of Blachernae, we retrace our steps for a short way down the Street of the Dervish's Son; then we take the first left along a winding lane that leads us downhill towards the Golden Horn. A little way along, at a bend in the road to the right, there were once visible the fragmentary remains of a tiny Byzantine church. Not many years ago the apse and two walls of the church were still standing and traces of frescoes could still be discerned within. But since then one wall and the apse have disappeared and all that remains is the south wall, which now forms part of a house. The church was converted into a mosque after the Conquest and called Toklu Dede Mescidi, in honour of Toklu Ibrahim Dede, a companion of the Prophet who died in the first Arab siege of the city in 673. We mention this now almost unidentifiable wall because a lot has been written about it by the Byzantinists – but to no great purpose. It used to be identified as the church of St. Thecla, founded by a daughter of Theophilus the Unfortunate in the ninth century, but this ascription has now become unfashionable; the arguments both for and against it, or any other identification, are exceedingly tenuous. Undoubtedly the remaining wall of the church will soon disappear as well; then the tedious arguments can at last be laid to rest.

A few feet farther on, the lane comes to an end and we find ourselves once more on the main coast road. We are now on the site of the last sea-gate in the walls along the Horn, the Porta Kiliomene, of which not a trace remains. To our left on the avenue, we see the last stretch of the maritime fortifications, a massive wall and the impressive ruins of three defence-towers. Here the land-walls ended their long march and joined the sea-walls along the Golden Horn.

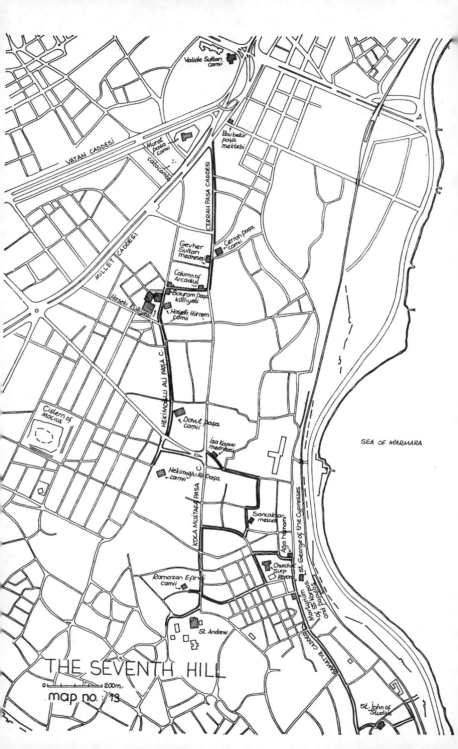

Valide Sultan camii

Murat Paşa camii

catacombs

Ebu bekir paşa mektebi

VATAN CADDESI

CERRAH PAŞA CADDESI

MILLET CADDESI

Gevher Sultan medresesi

Cerrah Paşa camii

Column of Arcadius

Bayram Paşa külliyesi

Haseki Külliyesi

Haseki Hürrem Camii

HEKIMOĞLU ALI PAŞA C.

Cistern of Mocius

Davut Paşa camii

Isa Kapısı medresesi

SEA OF MARMARA

Hekimoğlu Ali Paşa camii

KOCA MUSTAFA PAŞA C.

Sancaktar mescidi

Ağa Hamam

Martyrium of SS Karpos and Papylos

St. George of the Cypresses

Ramazan Efendi camii

Church of Surp Kevork

SAMATYA CADDESI

St. Andrew

St. John of Studius

THE SEVENTH HILL

0   200m.

map no. 19

16

The Seventh Hill

The first six hills of the city march in an almost straight line along the Stamboul shore of the Golden Horn. The Seventh Hill stands by itself towards the Marmara shore, covering most of the south-western part of Stamboul. Its highest point is at the Gate of Romanus (Topkapı), whence it slopes down to the north towards the valley of the Lycus, which divides it from the Sixth, Fifth and Fourth Hills, while to the south it approaches the sea, leaving sometimes a wide, sometimes a narrow plain along the shore. Our present tour will take us along the Marmara slopes of the Seventh Hill, through one of the most pleasant and picturesque parts of the city. This region, like the slopes of the Fifth and Sixth Hills above the Golden Horn, preserves much of the flavour of Ottoman Stamboul, with its winding cobbled streets lined with old wooden houses, its vine-covered teahouses sitting under venerable plane-trees, and its ancient mosque courtyards still serving as communal centres as they did in centuries past. This lovely old district is one of the most enchanting quarters of Stamboul, and nowhere else in the city can one enjoy more pleasurable strolls than there.

AKSARAY AND VALİDE SULTAN CAMİİ
We will start our tour at the crossroads in Aksaray, the second of the two great squares in modern Stamboul. Like Beyazit Square, Aksaray occupies approximately the site of an ancient Roman forum, in this case the Forum Bovis. At the Forum Bovis the Mese once again divided into two branches, one leading off to the north-west along the route of the modern Millet Caddesi, the other south-west following approximately the course of Cerrah Paşa Caddesi. Up until a few years ago Aksaray was a lively, bustling crossroads and market square, but now it has been utterly destroyed by a massive clover-leaf intersection. We will begin our stroll at this point, where stand

almost cheek-by-jowl examples of the first interesting beginnings of Ottoman architecture and of its bitter end. The latter, Valide Sultan Camii, can be seen just to the north of the overpass. It combines elements from Moorish and Turkish, Gothic, Renaissance and *Empire* styles in a garish rococo hodgepodge. The mosque was built in 1871 for Pertevniyal Valide Sultan, the mother of Sultan Abdül Aziz. It used to be ascribed to the Italian architect Montani, but it seems actually to be by the Armenians Hagop and Sarkis Balyan, who built some of the late Ottoman palaces we will see along the Bosphorus.

At the west of the overpass and to the left down the first cross street, we come to a handsome sibyan mektebi. This was founded by Ebu Bekir Paşa in A.H. 1136 (A.D. 1723–4); it has recently been restored and is now in use as a children's library, like so many others of its type.

Beyond the western end of the overpass the two new highways meet in an acute angle; the southern one, Millet Caddesi, runs up along the back of the Seventh Hill to Top Kapı and is a very busy and important thoroughfare; the northern one, Vatan Caddesi, follows the course of the Lycus River which is canalized beneath it.

MURAT PAŞA CAMİİ

In the angle between these two avenues stands the attractive and ancient mosque of Murat Paşa, the second of the two mosques of the "Bursa type" that still exist in Istanbul. It is smaller and less elaborate than Mahmut Paşa Camii but resembles it in general plan: a long rectangular room divided by an arch into two squares each covered by a dome, with two small side-chambers to north and south forming a tabhane for travellers. Of the two large domes, the eastern one rests on pendentives with bold and deeply cut stalactites, but the western one has that curious arrangement of triangles which we have seen on the smaller domes at Mahmut Paşa. The porch has five domed bays with six very handsome ancient columns: two of Syenitic granite, four of verd antique. The capitals are of three different kinds, arranged symmetrically, two types of stalactites and the lozenge capital. The construction of the building is in courses of brick and stone. The pious foundation originally included a medrese and a large double hamam; but these have unfortunately perished in the widening of the adjacent streets.

The founder, Murat Paşa, was a convert from the imperial family of the Palaeologues; he became a vezir of Fatih and died in battle as a relatively young man. The date of construction of his mosque is given in an intricate inscription in Arabic over the main door – A.H. 874 (A.D. 1469) – later than Mahmut Paşa Camii by only seven years. The calligraphy in this inscription is exceptionally beautiful and is probably by Ali Sofi, who did the fine inscription over the Imperial Gate to the Saray.

Behind Murat Paşa Camii a large catacomb was discovered in 1972 during excavations for a sewer. Eight vaulted chambers were found extending over an area roughly 30 metres square. It is thought that there is a second storey of comparable size beneath the first, but this has not yet been explored. The catacomb is believed to date from the sixth century A.D. The catacomb was closed off soon after its discovery and now there is no trace of it visible.

A little farther up Millet Caddesi, on the same side of the avenue, we find a newly removed and reconstructed mosque of some interest. It was founded by Selçuk Hatun, daughter of Sultan Mehmet I and an aunt of Mehmet the Conqueror. Selçuk Hatun died in 1485 and so her mosque must be from about that date. In the seventeenth century the mosque was partly burned and then was reconstructed by the Chief Black Eunuch, Abbas Ağa. In 1956, when Millet Caddesi was widened, the mosque was demolished and re-erected not far from its old site. How far the reconstructed building follows the old plan is not clear; at all events the mosque is rather attractive and the reconstruction at least adequate.

We now cross Millet Caddesi and continue south for a short distance until we come to Cerrah Paşa Caddesi, where we turn right and begin walking along the Marmara slope of the Seventh Hill. Here we leave the modern city behind, for the most part, and stroll through a more serene and old-fashioned quarter of Stamboul.

CERRAH PAŞA CAMİİ
A short way along the left side of the avenue we come to an imposing

mosque in its walled garden. This is Cerrah Paşa Camii, after which the avenue and the surrounding neighbourhood are named. Cerrah Mehmet Paşa, who founded it, had been a barber and therefore a surgeon (*cerrah*), having gotten this official title by performing the circumcision of the future Sultan Mehmet III. The latter in 1598 appointed him Grand Vezir and wrote him a letter warning him that he would be drawn and quartered if he did not do his duty. But he was only required to do his duty for six months or so, for he was dismissed – without being drawn and quartered – in consequence of the ill success of the war against Hungary.

An Arabic inscription over the door gives the date as A.H. 1002 (A.D. 1593); the architect was Davut Ağa, Sinan's successor as Chief Architect. One might rank Cerrah Paşa Camii among the half-dozen most successful of the vezirial mosques. Its plan presents an interesting modification of the hexagon-in-rectangle type. The four domes which flank the central dome at the corners, instead of being oriented along the diagonals of the rectangle, are parallel with the cross axis. This plan has the advantage that, for any hexagon, the width of the building can be increased without limit. Such a plan was never used by Sinan and is seen again only in Hekimoğlu Ali Paşa Camii, which is a little farther west on this same hill. The mihrab is in a rectangular apse which projects from the east wall. The galleries, which run around three sides of the building, are supported by pretty ogive arches with polychrome voussoirs of white stone and red conglomerate marble; in some of the spandrels there are very charming rosettes. In short, the interior is elegant in detail and gives a sense of spaciousness and light. The exterior, too, is impressive by its proportions, in spite of the ruined state of the porch and the unfortunate restoration job that was done on the domes and semidomes. The porch originally had seven bays and its eight handsome antique columns are still standing, four of Proconnesian marble, two of Theban granite, and two of Syenitic granite. The türbe of the founder, a simple octagonal building, is in front of the mosque beside the entrance gate. Nearby is a ruined şadırvan and outside in the corner of the precinct wall is a pretty çeşme. The complex originally included an interesting hamam which unfortunately has been destroyed.

MEDRESE OF GEVHER HATUN

Immediately across the street is an interesting medrese which is not part of Cerrah Mehmet Paşa's foundation. This was built in the second half of the sixteenth century by Gevher Sultan, daughter of Selim II and wife of the great admiral Piyale Paşa. This medrese, which has been restored, has the standard form of a rectangular porticoed courtyard with cells beyond.

COLUMN OF ARCADİUS

We now continue along Cerrah Paşa Caddesi for another 100 metres and take the second turning on the right, Haseki Kadın Sokağı. A short distance up the street on the right we find the shapeless remains of the Column of Arcadius, wedged tightly between two houses and as tall as they are; its marble surface is rent and pitted and it is overgrown with a mantle of ivy. Erected in 402 by the Emperor Arcadius, the column was decorated with spiral bands of sculpture in bas relief representing the triumphs of the emperor, like Trajan's column in Rome. It stood in the centre of an imperial forum called after Arcadius. At the top of the column, which was more than 50 metres high, there was an enormous Corinthian capital surmounted by an equestrian statue of Arcadius, placed there in 421 by his son, Theodosius II. This statue was eventually toppled from the column and destroyed during an earthquake in 704. The column itself remained standing for another 1,000 years until it was deliberately demolished in 1715, when it appeared to be in immanent danger of collapsing on the neighbouring houses. Now all that remains are the mutilated base and some fragments of sculpture from the column which are on display in the Archaeological Museum. It is possible to enter the interior of the base through a side door in the house to the left. Once inside the base, we can climb up an interior stairway to the top of the ruin, where there is still visible a short length of the column with barely discernible remnants of the sculptured decoration.

COMPLEX OF BAYRAM PAŞA

Leaving the column, we continue on along Haseki Kadın Sokağı to the end of the street. There we come to the külliye of Bayram Paşa, which is divided by the street itself; on the right are the medrese and mektep, and on the left the mescit, tekke, türbe, and sebil. An inscription on the sebil gives the date of construction as A.H. 1044 (A.D. 1634). At that time Bayram Paşa was Kaymakam, or Mayor, of the city; two years later he became Grand Vezir and soon after died on Murat IV's expedition against Baghdad. At the corner to the left is the handsome sebil with five grilled openings; behind it is the really palatial türbe of the founder, looking rather like a small mosque. (It is said to have fine and original tiles; unfortunately it is shut up and inaccessible.) At the far end of the enclosed garden and graveyard stands the mescit surrounded on two sides by the porticoed cells of the dervish tekke. The mescit, is a large octagonal building which served also as the room where the dervishes performed their music and dance ceremonies. The whole complex is finely built of ashlar stone in the high classical manner and the very irregularity of its design makes it singularly attractive.

COMPLEX OF HASEKİ HÜRREM

Turning left at the corner and passing the külliye of Bayram Paşa, we come immediately to that of Haseki Hürrem, which is contiguous with it to the west. This külliye was built by Haseki Hürrem, the famous Roxelana, and is the third largest and most magnificent complex in the old city, ranking only after those of Fatih and Süleyman. The mosque and its dependencies were built by Sinan and completed in 1539, making these the earliest known works by him in the city. The mosque is disappointing: originally it consisted of a small square room covered by a dome on stalactited pendentives, preceded by a rather pretentious porch of five bays which overlapped the building at both ends. It may perhaps have had a certain elegance of proportion and detail. But in 1612 a second and identical room was added on the north, the north wall being removed and its place taken by a great arch supported on two columns. The mihrab was then moved to the middle of the new extended east wall so that it stands squeezed behind one of the columns. The result is distinctly unpleasing.

Not so the other buildings of the külliye which are magnificent: a medrese, a primary school, a public kitchen and a hospital. Moreover, most of the complex has been well restored. The medrese is immediately across the street from the mosque. It is of the usual type – a porticoed courtyard surrounded by the student's cubicles and the dershane; but apart from its truly imperial size, it is singularly well-proportioned and excellent in detail. Its 20 columns are of granite, Proconnesian marble, and vend antique; their lozenge capitals are decorated with small rosettes and medallions of various elegant designs and here and there with a sort of serpentine garland motif, a quite unique design. Also unique are the two pairs of lotus flower capitals, their leaves spreading out at the top to support a sort of abacus; though soft and featureless, they make a not unattractive variation from the almost characterless lozenge. Two carved hemispherical bosses in the spandrels of the arcade call attention to the dershane, a monumental square room with a dome. The great charm of the courtyard must have been still greater when the faience panels with inscriptions were still in place in the lunettes of the windows; many years ago when the building was dilapidated they were removed to the museum and are now on display in the Çinili Köşk. Next to the medrese is the large and very oddly-shaped sibyan mektebi in two storeys with widely-projecting eaves.

The imaret, which was still in use up until the early 1970s, is beyond the mektep, entered through a monumental portal which leads to an alleyway. At the end of this, one enters the long rectangular courtyard of the imaret, shaded with trees. Vast kitchens with large domes and enormous chimneys (better seen from inside at the back) line three sides of the courtyard.

The hospital is behind the medrese, entered from the street behind the külliye to the north. It is a building of most unusual form: the court is octagonal but without a columned portico. The two large corner rooms at the back, whose great domes have stalactited pendentives coming far down the walls, originally opened to the courtyard through huge arches, now glassed-in; with these open rooms or eyvans all the other wards and chambers of the hospital communicated. Opposite the eyvans on one side is the entrance portal, approached through an irregular vestibule, like that so often found in Persian mosques. On the other side are the lavatories, also

HASEKİ HÜRREM KÜLLİYESİ

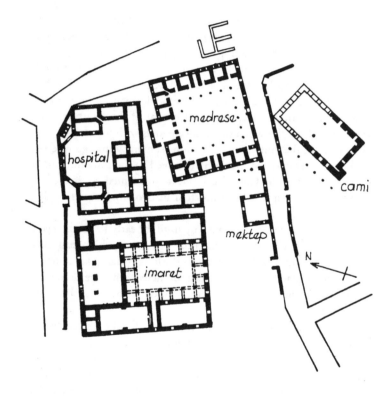

0 ⊢——┴——┴——┴——┘30m.

plan no: 25

irregular in shape; while the eighth side of the courtyard forms the façade on the street with grilled windows. This building too has been well restored and is once again in use as a hospital.

DAVUT PAŞA CAMİİ

Returning to the street outside Haseki Hürrem Camii, we continue on in the same direction for about 400 metres. Then to our left, set back from the road and partly concealed by trees and houses, we see a fine but dilapidated old mosque. This is Davut Paşa Camii, dated by an inscription over the door to A.H. 890 (A.D. 1485). Davut Paşa, the founder, was Grand Vezir under Sultan Beyazit II. In plan the mosque belongs to the simple type of the square chamber covered by a large blind dome; but the mihrab is in a five-sided apse projecting from the east wall and to north and south are small rooms, two on each side, once used as tabhanes for travelling dervishes. What gives the building its distinction and harmony, however, is the beautiful shallow dome, quite obviously less than half a hemisphere. The pendentives of the dome are an unusually magnificent example of the stalactite form, here boldly incised and brought far down the corners of the walls. Unfortunately they are in very bad condition, as is the interior in general. A small amount of very careful restoration is called for, for this mosque is one of the half-dozen of the earliest period which are most worthy of preservation. In fact, the five-domed porch, which was partially in ruins, has now been well restored; let us hope the interior will soon be too.

Behind the mosque a delightfully topsy-turvy graveyard surrounds the founder's türbe, octagonal in form and with an odd dome in eight triangular segments. Across the narrow street to the north stands the medrese of the külliye, almost completely surrounded and concealed by houses. The courtyard must have been extremely handsome – indeed it still is – with its re-used Byzantine columns and capitals, but it is in an advanced state of ruin. Here immediate restoration is urgently needed to save it before it is too late, for this is the only one of the fifteenth-century vezirial medreses which survives in something like its original form. The külliye once also had an imaret and a mektep, but these have completely disappeared.

HEKİMOĞLU ALİ PAŞA CAMİİ

Some 200 metres beyond Davut Paşa Camii and on the same side of the street, we come to a grand and interesting complex, that of Hekimoğlu Ali Paşa. This nobleman was the son *(oglu)* of the court physician *(hekim)* and was himself Grand Vezir for 15 years under Sultan Mahmut I. A long inscription in Turkish verse over the door gives the date of construction as A.H. 1147 (A.D. 1734–5); the architect was Ömer Ağa. One can consider this complex either the last of the great classical buildings or the first of the new baroque style, for it has characteristics of both. At the corner of the precinct wall beside the north entrance is a very beautiful sebil of marble with five bronze grilles; above runs an elaborate frieze with a long inscription and fine carvings of vines, flowers and rosettes in the new rococo style that had recently been introduced from France. The façade of the türbe along the street is faced in marble, corbelled out towards the top and with a çeşme at the far end. It is a large rectangular building with two domes dividing it into two equal square areas. This form was not unknown in the classical period – compare Sinan's Pertev Paşa türbe at Eyüp (see Chapter 18); but it was rare and the use of it here seems to indicate a willingness to experiment with new forms. Farther along the precinct wall stands the monumental gateway with a domed chamber above; this was the library of the foundation. Though the manuscripts have been transferred elsewhere, it still contains the painted wooden cages with grilles in which they were stored; an elegant floral frieze runs round the top of the walls and floral medallions adorn the dome. From the columned porch at the top of the steps leading to the library, one commands a good view of the whole complex, with its singularly attractive garden full of tall cypresses and aged plane trees, and opposite the stately porch and very slender minaret of the mosque.

The mosque itself, raised on a substructure containing a cistern, is purely classical in form. Indeed its plan is almost an exact replica of that at Cerrah Paşa, which we saw earlier on this tour. In contrast to that, the present building is perhaps a little weak and effeminate; there is a certain blurring of forms and enervating of structural distinctions, an effect not mitigated by the pale colour of the tile revetment. The tiles are still Turkish, not manufactured at Iznik as formerly, but at the recently established kilns at Tekfur Saray. All the same, the general impression of the interior is charming if not exactly powerful. There is a further hint of the new baroque style in one of its less pleasing traits in some of the capitals of the columns both in the porch and beneath the sultan's loge. The traditional stalactite and lozenge capitals have been abandoned there in favour of a very weak and characterless form, such as an impost capital which seems quite out of scale and out of place. The whole complex within the precinct wall has been very completely and very well restored. Outside the precinct, across the street to the north-east, stands the tekke of the foundation, but little is left of it save a very ruinous zaviye, or rooms for the dervish ceremonies.

CHURCH OF THE PANAGHİA GORGOEPİKOOS, MEDRESE OF NİŞANCI MEHMET BEY

We now walk back to the intersection we passed just before we reached the mosque. There we turn left into Yaprağı Sokağı, which after the first intersection becomes Sırrı Paşa Sokağı. Just before the first turning on the left we come to a Greek church surrounded by a walled garden. This is the church of the Panaghia Gorgoepikoos, the Virgin Who Answers Requests Quickly. The church is referred to as early as 1343, and it is mentioned in Tryphon's list of 1583. The present building dates from the early nineteenth century.

We turn left at the corner beyond the church, and then after the next intersection we see on our right the ruins of a once handsome medrese. It was built by Sinan for Nişancı Mehmet Bey, who served as Keeper of the Royal Seal (Nişancı) for Süleyman the Magnificent. The medrese was built before 1566 when Mehmet Bey died on hearing the news of Süleyman's death.

At the corner beyond the medrese we turn right on Köprülüzade Sokağı, which after three blocks brings us to the south-west corner of an enormous open cistern on the summit of the Seventh Hill. This is the third and largest of the extant Roman reservoirs in the city, that of St. Mocius, so called from a famous church dedicated to that saint, a local martyr under Diocletian. It is a rectangle 170 by 147 metres, or just under 25,000 square metres in area. Constructed under the Emperor Anastasius (r. 491–518), it fell into disuse in Byzantine times; like the other two Roman reservoirs it served as a vegetable garden and orchard, with a few wooden houses at the eastern end. In 1993 it was converted into the Fatih Educational Park.

Returning to Hekimoğlu Ali Paşa Camii, we take the street that runs past the northern side of the mosque precinct. We follow this to its intersection with Koca Mustafa Paşa Caddesi; then we take the street opposite and slightly to our left; this immediately brings us to a pathetic ruin which is of interest only because of its association with the great Sinan.

ISA KAPI MESCİDİ

This complex consists of two walls of a Byzantine church and the wreck of a medrese by Sinan. Of the church only the south and east walls remain. It was of the simplest kind; an oblong room without aisles ending at the east in a large projecting apse and two tiny side apses. In the southern side apse there could be seen till recently the traces of frescoes; these have now almost entirely disappeared. The building is probably to be dated to the beginning of the fourteenth century, but nothing is known of its history nor even the name of the saint to whom it is dedicated. About 1560 the church was turned into a mosque by the eunuch Ibrahim Paşa, who added to it a handsome medrese designed by Sinan. Both church and medrese were destroyed by the great earthquake of 1894 and have remained abandoned ever since. The ruins of the medrese, which is unusual in plan, are rather fine; its large dershane still bears traces of plaster decoration around the dome, and the narrow courtyard beyond must have been very attractive. The medrese, known as Isa Kapı Mescidi, is now under restoration. The name Isa Kapısı means the Gate of Christ and the theory is that it preserves the memory of one of the gates in the city walls of Constantine the Great which are thought to have passed close by. This is possible, but the arguments of the authorities are contradictory and inconclusive.

Following the alley that leads round behind the medrese, we pass a little square and find ourselves at the top of a steep hill leading down to the Marmara, of which one has an extensive view. Below on the left the great new building of the Istanbul Hospital – the usual block of concrete and glass – makes a curious contrast with the ancient cobbled streets and the decrepit but picturesque wooden houses among which we have been wandering.

SANCAKTAR MESCİDİ

At the top of the hill we turn right into Sancaktar Tekke Sokağı, which leads after several zigzags to an octagonal Byzantine building called Sancaktar Mescidi. This has been identified, on *very* slender evidence, as one of the buildings of the Monastery of Gastria. The legend is that this monastery was founded in the fourth century by St. Helena, mother of Constantine the Great, and that it derives its name of Gastria, which means vases, from the vases of flowers she brought back from Calvary where she had luckily discovered the True Cross! This story has been refuted by the French scholar Janin, who shows that there is no trace of the existence of the monastery before the ninth century. The present little building has the form of an octagon on the exterior with a projecting apse at the east end; within, it has the form of a domed cross. It is thought that it was once a funerary chapel; it has been dated variously from the eleventh to the fourteenth century. The building was for long an abandoned ruin, but it has now been restored and is once again serving as a mosque.

Leaving Sancaktar Mescidi, we walk straight ahead for a few paces to the next intersection and then turn right on Marmara Caddesi. This brings us back to Koca Mustafa Paşa Caddesi, where we turn left and stroll through the pleasant district of Samatya.

RAMAZAN EFENDİ CAMİİ

Continuing along the avenue, we take the second right onto Ramazan Efendi Caddesi, where a short way along on the right we come to a small but charming mosque with a pretty garden courtyard in front. The official name of the mosque is Hoca Hüsrev Camii, for the court official who originally founded it, but it is more usually called Ramazan Efendi Camii, after the first şeyh of the dervish tekke which was part of the original foundation. The building is by Sinan, and a long inscription over the inner door by his friend the poet Mustafa Sa'i, gives the date as A.H. 994 (A.D. 1586); thus, this is undoubtedly the last mosque built by the great architect, completed in his 97th year. It is a building of the simplest type: a small rectangular room with a wooden roof and porch. It is thought that it was originally covered with a wooden dome and that it had a porch with three domed bays supported by four marble columns; the present wooden porch and flat wooden ceiling are botched restorations after an earthquake. The minaret is an elegant structure both in proportion and in detail, while the small şadırvan in the courtyard is exquisitely carved. But the great fame of the mosque comes from the magnificent panels of faience with which it is adorned. These are from the Iznik kilns at the height of their artistic production and are thus some of the finest tiles in existence: the borders of "tomato-red" or Armenian bole are especially celebrated.

After leaving the mosque we return to Koca Mustafa Paşa Caddesi and continue on in the same direction as before. A short distance along, the avenue forks to the right, and we soon come to a picturesque square shaded with trees and lined with teahouses and cafés. On the left side of the square is the entrance to the mosque complex of Koca Mustafa Paşa, after whom the avenue and the surrounding neighbourhood are named.

CHURCH OF ST. ANDREW IN KRİSEİ (KOCA MUSTAFA PAŞA CAMİİ)

The central building of this picturesque complex is Koca Mustafa Paşa Camii, anciently a church known as St. Andrew in Krisei. The identification and history of the church are very obscure and much disputed. One may summarize the discussions of the learned in a series of subjunctive statements: that Koca Mustafa Paşa Camii may have been one of the churches in the region dedicated to a St. Andrew; that if it is, it is probably that dedicated by the Princess Theodora Raoulina about 1264 to St. Andrew of Crete; that the present building was fairly certainly of the ambulatory type; that it may have been built on the foundations of an earlier church dedicated to St. Andrew the Apostle; and that it certainly re-used sixth-century materials, especially capitals.

The mosque has been reoriented by 90° so that the mihrab and mimber are under the semidome against the south wall; the entrance is in the north wall, in front of which a modern porch has been added. One enters through a door at the west end of the north aisle and should proceed at once to the central bay of the narthex. This bay has a small dome supported by columns with beautiful sixth-century capitals of the pseudo-Ionic type. From here one enters through the central portal into a sort of inner narthex, or aisle, separated from the church by two verd antique columns; this aisle is regrettably obstructed by a large wooden gallery. But from this point the whole church is visible; it now has a trefoil shape but was probably originally ambulatory; that is, there would have been a triple arcade supported by two columns to north and south, like the one which still exists on the west. To the east the conch of the apse is preceded by a deep barrel vault; to north and south open out the two later Ottoman semidomes. Even in its greatly altered form it is an extremely attractive building.

The dependencies of the mosque include a medrese, a tekke, a mektep and two türbes; what survives of these are of a much later date than the conversion of the church into a mosque. The mosque is one of the most popular religious shrines in the city, for in one of the türbes is buried the famous folk-saint Sümbül (Hyacinth) Efendi. Sümbül Efendi was the first şeyh of the dervish tekke which was established here in the sixteenth century, and since then he has been prayed to by the common people of Istanbul for help in solving their problems. In the other türbe beside that of Sümbül Efendi is buried his daughter Rahine, who is generally prayed to by young women looking for a suitable husband. The ancient plane tree tottering above her türbe is said to possess talismanic powers.

We now retrace our steps for a short way back along Koca Mustafa Paşa Caddesi and then take the first right after the fork in the road. This street, Mudafaai Milliye Caddesi, takes us down the slope of the Seventh Hill towards the Marmara shore. About 250 metres along we turn left on Marmara Caddesi, a wide and pleasant avenue that runs along the heights parallel to the sea. As we begin walking along this avenue we see on our right the large Armenian church of Surp

Kevork (St. George), called in Turkish Sulu Manastir, built in the precincts of the ancient Byzantine monastery of St. Mary Peribleptos. Of the latter nothing but substructures remain. It was founded in the eleventh century by Romanus III Argyros and has remained a Christian church ever since. The tradition heretofore generally accepted is that the church remained in the hands of the Greeks until 1643, when it was given to the Armenians by Sultan Ibrahim under the influence of a favourite Armenian concubine. (This lady's name was Şeker Parça, or Piece of Sugar; she is said to have weighed more than 300 pounds.) This story, however, appears to be fictitious, for we read in the recently published work of the Armenian traveller Simeon of Zamosc in Poland, who visited the city in 1608, that it was already at that date in the hands of the Armenians and was the cathedral church of the Armenian Patriarch.

Apparently Surp Kevork had been the Armenian cathedral church since 1461, when Sultan Mehmet the Conqueror recognized the Armenian Patriarchate of Istanbul. The first Armenian Patriarch was Bishop Hovakim of Bursa. The Patriarchate remained in Samatya until 1641, when it was moved to its present location in Kumkapı. The Patriarchal church in Kumkapı, Surp Astvadzadzin, was originally built in 1645, but the building which we see there today dates only from 1913.

AĞA HAMAMI

Once past the church we turn right and take the road which leads down towards the sea. As we do so we are confronted almost immediately with an interesting view of a vast double hamam. It is astonishing how many domes of all sizes and arranged apparently at random these hamams have, and it is not often that one can get a good view of them from above. This one is called Ağa Hamamı and is a work of Sinan. It is unfortunately disaffected and ruinous, used for commercial purposes. The workshop is installed in what was once the hararet of the bath, a typical cruciform room with cubicles in the corners.

After passing the hamam we turn right on Samatya Caddesi, which skirts the foot of the Seventh Hill not far from the sea. As we walk along we soon pass on our left the courtyard wall of a very venerable Greek church, St. George of the Cypresses. This church was originally founded in the ninth century and has remained in the hands of the Greeks ever since. The present building, however, dates only from 1830.

MARTYRIUM OF SS. KARPOS AND PAPYLOS

A little farther along the avenue on the right side we see on the height above the tall tower of the modern Greek church of St. Menas. The church itself is of no interest, but beneath it, though in no way structurally connected with it, are some very important and ancient substructures. They are entered from Samatya Caddesi and are presently used as a workshop. These substructures, discovered only in 1935, have been identified as the crypt of the Martryium of SS. Karpos and Papylos, who perished in the Decian persecutions in 250–1. The crypt is a large circular domed chamber which reminds one of the beehive tombs at Mycenae, only constructed not of stone but of brick, in the excellent technique of the fourth or fifth century A.D. At the east is a deep apse, while completely round the chamber runs a vaulted passage, also of brick. (This passage can be entered through a door in the teahouse just beyond the workshop.) Since this appears to be one of the oldest surviving places of Christian worship in the city and since it is unique in form, it is much to be hoped that it will be rescued from its base uses, and thoroughly investigated and restored.

Some 500 metres farther along the avenue we see on the left a modern Greek church, that of SS. Constantine and Helena. This church has only very recently been rebuilt, but its foundation goes back at least as far as 1563, the date of the earliest recorded reference to it.

CHURCH OF ST. JOHN THE BAPTIST OF STUDIUS

We turn left at the second street beyond SS. Constantine and Helen and come to the walled courtyard of a very ancient and interesting Byzantine church. This is the church of St. John the Baptist of Studius, known in Turkish as Imrahor Camii. It was founded by a Roman named Studius in 450, and is thus the oldest surviving church in the city. In form it is a pure basilica with a single apse at the east end; it is preceded by a narthex and an atrium. The narthex is divided into three bays, of which the wider central one has a very beautiful portal consisting of four columns *in antis*, with magnificent Corinthian capitals supporting an elaborate entablature with richly sculptured architrave, frieze and cornice. Two of the marble door-frames still stand between the columns. From the narthex five doors lead into the church, which is divided, in the traditional basilican style, into a nave and side aisles by two rows of seven columns. Six of those on the north side still stand; they are of verd antique, with capitals and entablature as in the narthex. The nave ends in a single semicircular apse where once rose the tiers of seats for the clergy and in front of them the altar. Above the aisles and narthex ran galleries, the columns of which supported a trussed timber roof. The interior was revetted with marble and the upper parts decorated with mosaics. The floor was also of mosaic or *opus sectile*, and of this some portions may still be seen, although they are fast disappearing.

Nothing now remains of the monastery of the church, the Studion, once the most famous and powerful institution of its kind in the Byzantine Empire. This monastery first came into prominence in the year 799, when the great abbot Theodore assumed direction of its affairs. Inspired by Theodore's spiritual and intellectual leadership, the Studion became a centre for the first renaissance of Byzantine culture in the ninth century. Many monks of the Studion won renown as composers of sacred hymns, painters of icons, and illuminators of manuscripts. The Studion was particularly noted for its scholarship and was active in the preservation and copying of ancient manuscripts. The Emperor Isaac I Comnenus, who had studied there as a youth, referred to it as "that glorious and illustrious school of virtue." The Studion continued as one of the spiritual and intellectual centres of the Empire right up to the time of the Conquest. During the first half of the fifteenth century the University of Constantinople was located at the Studion, and during that period some of the greatest scholars in the history of Byzantium taught and studied there. The Studion survived the fall of Byzantium and continued to function for nearly half a century after the Conquest, having celebrated its millennium in 1450. But then at the close of the fifteenth century the church of St. John was converted into a mosque and the few monks who were still resident were forced to seek shelter elsewhere. What was left of the monastery in modern times was utterly destroyed in the earthquake of 1894 and now not a trace remains.

Before we leave St. John's, we might read what one of the monks of the Studion wrote in praise of it some centuries ago, apparently in a moment of great happiness: "No barbarian looks upon my face, no woman hears my voice. For a thousand years no useless man has entered the monastery of the Studion, none of the female sex has trodden its court. I dwell in a cell that is like a palace; a garden, an olive grove and a vineyard surround me. Before me there are graceful and luxuriant cypress trees. On one hand is the great city with its market places and on the other the mother of churches and the empire of the world."

Leaving the church we turn left and follow the winding path which leads us around to the south-eastern corner of its outer precincts. Here, at the edge of a vacant field, we find a small shed which gives access to a covered cistern which was once part of the Studion. It is quite impressive, containing 23 granite columns with handsome Corinthian capitals. Beside it is an ayazma, or holy well, with two columns.

After leaving the cistern we continue on in the same direction until we arrive at the railway line. There we turn left and follow the railway as far as the first underpass, from which a path leads us out to the sea-walls. There we turn right and in a few steps come to a portal called Narlı Kapı, the ancient Pomegranate Gate, whence a path takes us out to the Marmara road. Here we can stroll back towards town along the shore, enjoying a splendid view of the Stamboul skyline.

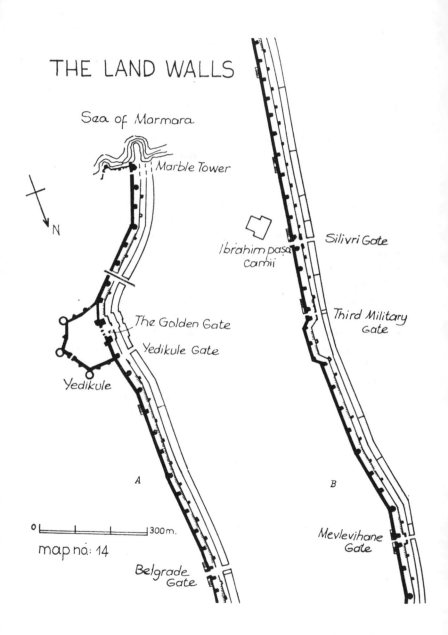

THE LAND WALLS

Sea of Marmara

Marble Tower

N

Ibrahim paşa camii

Silivri Gate

The Golden Gate

Yedikule Gate

Third Military Gate

Yedikule

0   300 m.

map no: 14

A

B

Belgrade Gate

Mevlevihane Gate

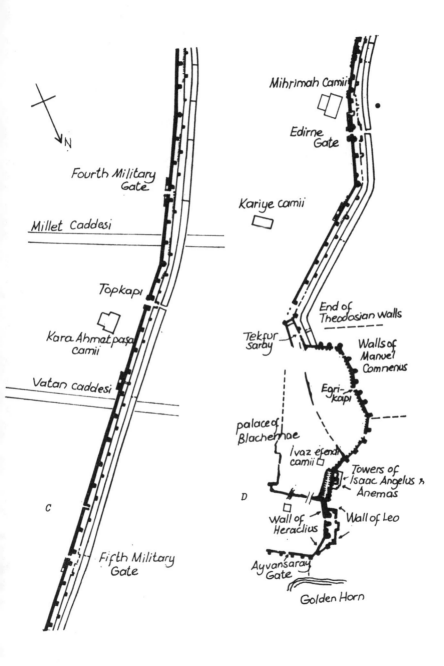

N

Mihrimah Camii

Edirne Gate

Fourth Military Gate

Millet Caddesi

Kariye camii

End of Theodosian walls

Topkapı

Tekfur Saray

Walls of Manuel Comnenus

Kara Ahmatpaşa camii

Egri-kapı

Vatan caddesi

palace of Blachernae

Ivaz efendi camii

Towers of Isaac Angelus & Anemas

D

Wall of Heraclius

Wall of Leo

C

Fifth Military Gate

Ayvansaray Gate

Golden Horn

17

Along the Land Walls

The Byzantine land-walls extend from the Sea of Marmara to the Golden Horn, a total distance of about 6.5 kilometres. These walls protected Byzantium from its enemies for more than 1,000 years, and in that way profoundly influenced the history of medieval Europe. Although they are now in ruins, the walls of Byzantium are still a splendid and impressive sight, with towers and battlements marching across the hills and valleys of Thrace. Although a hike along the land-walls can be somewhat arduous, it is nevertheless quite rewarding, for on and around them we discover aspects of Stamboul which are not evident within the town itself. And in springtime this stroll can be extremely pleasant, when the walls and towers are covered with ivy, the terraces carpeted with fresh grass, and the moat colourful with wild flowers and blossoming trees.

The land-walls were, for the most part, constructed during the reign of Theodosius II in the first half of the fifth century. The first phase of the Theodosian wall was completed in 413 under the direction of Anthemius, Prefect of the East. This consisted of a single wall studded with defence towers at regular intervals. However, in 447 a violent earthquake destroyed much of the wall, throwing down 57 defence towers. This happened at a very critical time, for Atilla the Hun was then advancing on Constantinople with his Golden Horde. Reconstruction of the wall began immediately under the direction of the new Prefect of the East, Constantine. The circus factions of the Hippodrome all worked together in one of their rare periods of cooperation, and within two months the walls had been rebuilt and were far stronger than before. For in addition to restoring and strengthening the original wall, Constantine added an outer wall and a moat. This stupendous achievement is commemorated by inscriptions in Latin and Greek on the Mevlevihane Gate, anciently known as the Gate of Rhegium. The Greek inscription merely gives the facts, the Latin one is more boastful; it reads: "By the command of Theodosius, Constantine erected these strong walls in less than two months. Scarcely could Pallas herself have built so strong a citadel in so short a span." The pride is understandable, for the new defence walls saved the city from Atilla, the Scourge of God, who withdrew his forces and, instead, ravaged the western regions of the Roman Empire.

Even though they are in ruins, enough remains of the Theodosian walls to reconstruct their original plan. The main element in the defence system was the inner wall, which was about five metres thick at the base and rose to a height of 12 metres. This wall was guarded by 96 towers, 18 to 20 metres high, at an average interval of 55 metres; these were mostly square but some were polygonal. Each tower is generally divided into two floors which do not communicate with one another. The lower stories were used either for storage or for guardhouses; the upper rooms were entered from the parapet walk, which communicated by staircases with the ground and with the tops of the towers, where were placed engines for hurling missiles and Greek fire at the enemy. Between the inner and outer walls there was a terrace called the peribolos, which varied from 15 to 20 metres in breadth, and whose level was about five metres above that of the inner city. The outer wall, which was about two metres thick and 8.5 metres in height, also had 96 towers, alternating in position with those of the inner wall; in general these were either square or crescent-shaped in turn. Beyond this was an outer terrace called the parateichion, bounded on the outside by the counter-scarp of the moat which was a battlement nearly two metres high. The moat itself was originally about ten metres deep and 20 metres wide, and may have been flooded whenever the city was threatened. All-in-all it was a most formidable system of fortification – perhaps the most elaborate and unassailable ever devised. Had it not been for the invention of gunpowder and cannons these walls might never have been breached.

Most of the inner defence-wall and nearly all of its huge towers are still standing, although sieges, earthquakes and the ravages of time have left their scars. Although a few of the towers are relatively intact, most of them are split and shattered or have half-tumbled to the ground. The outer walls have been almost completely obliterated and the fragmentary remains of only about half of its towers can still be seen. Grass, bushes, vines and trees have everywhere overgrown the ruins and softened their outlines. There are little kitchen gardens and orchards flourishing in the moat and along the parateichion and the peribolos.

FROM THE MARBLE TOWER TO YEDİKULE

We will begin our tour in the south-western corner of the city, just beyond where we ended our last stroll in Samatya. Here the sea-walls along the Marmara joined the land-walls, anchored to them by the Marble Tower, the handsome structure which we see standing on a little promontory by the sea. This tower, 13 metres square at its base and 30 metres high, its lower half faced in marble, is unlike any other structure in the whole defence-system, and may have been part of an imperial sea-pavilion. Indeed the ruins beside it seem to indicate that it was part of a small castle. Beyond the tower there are the sunken remains of a mole which must have been part of the castle harbour.

A short way in from the shore highway, immediately to the north of the first tower of the inner wall, we see one of the ancient gateways of the city. This is called the Gate of Christ because of the laureate monogram XP above it. In the long stretch of the Theodosian walls there were only ten gates and a few small posterns. Five of the ten gates were public entryways and five were used by the military, such as the one which we see here (it was sometimes called the First Military Gate). The distinction was not so much in their structure as in the fact that while the public gates had bridges over the moat leading to the country beyond, the military gates did not, but gave access only to the fortifications. Until the end of the last century Stamboul was still a walled town and these gates were the only entryways to the city from Thrace, but in recent times the walls have been breached to permit the passage of the railway and of several modern highways. Nevertheless, nearly all the ancient city gates continue in use, as they have now for more than 15 centuries.

CROSS - SECTION OF THE THEODOSIAN WALLS

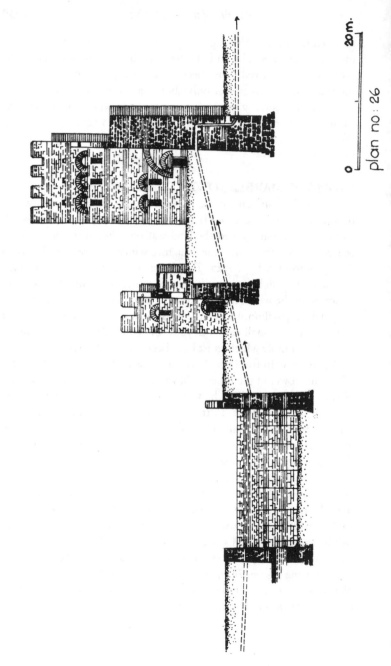

0   20 m.

plan no : 26

The first stretch of the Theodosian walls is rather difficult to inspect because of the obstacles presented by the railway and the various industries that are located here. But the stroll here is more pleasant than it was in times past, because in recent years the authorities have removed the noxious tannery that reeked here since early Ottoman times. As Evliya describes this malodorous tannery as it smelt in his time: "The overpowering reek prevents people of quality from taking up their abode here, but the residents are so used to the stench, that should they happen to meet any musk-perfumed dandy, the scent quite upsets them."

The best route on the first part of this stroll is to walk along inside the walls from the Marmara highway as far as the railway; then, after crossing the tracks cautiously, one can walk along the highway outside the walls as far as the gate at Yedikule, where one can enter the city again.

YEDİKULE AND THE GOLDEN GATE

Yedikule, the Castle of the Seven Towers, is a curious structure, partly Byzantine and partly Turkish. The seven eponymous towers consist of four in the Theodosian wall itself, plus three additional towers built inside the walls by Mehmet the Conqueror. The three inner towers are connected together and joined to the Theodosian walls by four heavy curtain-walls, forming a five-sided enclosure. The two central towers in the Theodosian wall are marble pylons flanking the famous Golden Gate of Byzantium. The structure was never used as a castle in the usual sense, but two of the towers were used in Ottoman times as prisons; the others were used as storage places for a part of the State treasure.

To visit Yedikule we must first enter the city through a little gate just north of the castle. Though it was somewhat reconstructed in Turkish times, the Byzantine eagle above the arch on the inside proclaims its origins. This must always have been the public entrance to the city in this vicinity, as indeed it is today, for the Golden Gate itself seems to have been reserved for the emperor and for distinguished visitors and processions.

We enter Yedikule itself by a gate near the east tower; once inside the grounds we turn left to enter the tower. This is sometimes called the Tower of the Ambassadors, since in Ottoman times foreign envoys were often imprisoned there. Many of these unfortunates have carved their names and dates and tales of woe upon the walls of the tower in half a dozen languages. An inscription in French gives this advice in verse: "Prisoners, who in your misery groan in this sad place, offer your sorrows with a good heart to God and you will find them lightened." The floors of the tower have fallen, but one climbs up by a staircase in the thickness of the wall. When at the top it is worthwhile walking around the *chemin de ronde* as far as the Golden Gate, for there is a fine view of the castle and the walls down to the sea, and, if it is spring, one finds a profusion of orchids, hyacinths and Roman anemones growing in the turf.

We then return to the courtyard, in the middle of which there was once a small mosque for the garrison; the remains of its minaret are still standing. We next enter the pylon to the left of the Golden Gate; this too was used as a prison and place of execution in Ottoman times. One is shown the instruments of torture and the infamous "well of blood", a pool said to communicate with the sea, down which were supposed to have been thrown the heads of those executed here. (We do not guarantee the truth of this story.) Sultan Osman II was one of those executed here, on 22 May 1622, when he was only 17 years old. Evliya Çelebi gives this account of the execution of Young Osman, as he was called: "They carried him in a cart to Yedikule where he was barbarously treated and at last most cruelly put to death by Pehlivan (the Wrestler). Whilst his body was exposed upon a mat, Kafir Ağa cut off his right ear and a Janissary one of his fingers for the sake of a ring upon it."

The much celebrated Golden Gate between the pylons was originally a Roman triumphal arch erected in about 390 by Theodosius I the Great. At that time the present city walls had not yet been built and the triumphal arch, as was customary, stood by itself on the Via Egnatia, about a mile outside the walls of Constantine. The arch was of the usual Roman type with a triple arcade containing a large central archway flanked by two smaller ones. The outlines of the arches can still be seen clearly although the openings were bricked up in later Byzantine times. The gates themselves were covered with gold plate –

hence the name – and the façade was decorated with sculptures, the most famous of which was a bronze group of four elephants, placed there to commemorate the triumphal entry of Theodosius after his victory over Maxentius. When Theodosius II decided to extend the city two decades later, he incorporated the Golden Gate within his new land-walls. It was presumably in connection with this new wall that he built the small marble gate outside the triumphal arch; the arch itself, of course, could have had no gates, except for ornamental iron or bronze grilles, and would have been indefensible. The outer gateway is part of the general system of defence and forms, with the curtain wall which joins it to the city walls near the polygonal towers, a small courtyard in front of the Golden Gate.

After the time of Theodosius I, the Golden Gate was several times the scene of triumphal entries by victorious emperors: Heraclius in 629 after his defeat of the Persians; Constantine V, Basil I, and Basil II after their victories over the Bulgars; John I Tzimisces after his defeat of the Russians; Theophilus and his son Michael III after their victories over the Saracens. Perhaps the most emotional of all the triumphal entries was the one that occurred on 15 August 1261, when Michael VIII Palaeologus rode through the Golden Gate on a white charger after Constantinople was recaptured from the Latins. But that was the last time an Emperor of Byzantium was to ride in triumph through the Golden Gate, for the history of the Empire in its last two centuries was one of continuing defeat, and by then the gateway had been walled up for good.

YEDİKULE TO BELGRAD KAPISI

From Yedikule to the next gate, Belgrad Kapısı, it is possible to walk either on top of the great wall or on the terrace below, for the walls here are in quite good condition. All of the 11 towers which guard the inner wall in this stretch are in quite good condition, as are all but one of those in the outer wall. An inscription on the eighth tower in the inner wall records repairs by Leo III and his son Constantine V in the period 720–41, and one on the tenth tower of the outer wall notes that it was restored by John VIII Palaeologus in 1434.

We now come to Belgrad Kapısı, known in Byzantium as the Second Military Gate. This is the largest of all the military gates and in Byzantium it may have been used as a public gate, as indeed it has ever since the Conquest. The gate took its Turkish name from the fact that Süleyman the Magnificent settled in its vicinity many of the artisans he brought back with him from Belgrade after his capture of that city in 1521.

BELGRAD KAPISI TO SİLİVRİ KAPISI

The stretch of walls from Belgrad Kapısı to the next gate, Silivri Kapısı, is also in good condition, with all 13 towers still standing along the inner wall and only one missing in the outer. These towers also have inscriptions recording repairs by Leo II, Constantine V and John VIII. Silivri Kapısı is the first of the large public gates we come to when walking from the Marmara. Like all of the public gates it is double, that is with gateways through both the inner and outer walls. The most memorable day in the history of the Silivri Gate was 25 July 1261. On that day a small body of Greek troops led by Alexius Strategopoulos overpowered the Latin guards at the gate and forced their way inside, thus opening the way for the recapture of Constantinople and the restoration of the Byzantine Empire.

THE SACRED SPRING OF BALIKLI

Silivri Kapısı was known in Byzantium as the Gate of the Pege because it led to the famous shrine of the Zoodochus Pege, or the Life-Giving Spring. The shrine, known in Turkish as Balıklı Kilise, or the Church with Fish, is so called because of the fish that swim in its sacred spring; it is reached by walking out from the gate along Seyitnizam Caddesi for a short distance and veering right along Silivrikapı Balıklı Caddesi. The shrine has been popular since the early days of Byzantium, and several emperors built churches on the site; the present one dating only from 1833. The outer courtyard is particularly interesting because it is paved with old tombstones in the curious Karamanlı script, that is, Turkish written in the Greek alphabet. The inner courtyard is filled with the elaborate tombs of bishops and patriarchs of the Greek Orthodox Church. The entrance to the shrine is in the corner between the two courtyards. We descend down a long flight of steps and find ourselves in a small chapel at the west end of which is the *ayazma,* or sacred spring. The spring is said to be inhabited by a species of fabulous fish which are brown on one side by virtue of their ancestors having leaped from a monk's frying-pan into the water five centuries ago, on hearing the news that Byzantium had fallen. However, closer inspection will reveal that the fish in the sacred spring have since reverted to a uniform gold.

IBRAHİM PAŞA CAMİİ

Returning to the Silivri Gate and entering the city there, we find immediately inside a fairly large and charming mosque by Sinan. This was built in 1551 for Hadım (the Eunuch) Ibrahim Paşa, the second of the two Grand Vezirs of that name under Süleyman the Magnificent. The mosque has a fine porch with five domed bays and a portal surmounted by an elaborate stalactited baldachino. In form it is an octagon inscribed in a rectangle with galleries on each side; it has no columns but in the angles of the octagon, pretty pendentives in the form of shells support the dome. The marble mimber and sultan's loge are of admirable workmanship, as are the panels of the doors, inlaid with ivory. Over the mihrab are tiles with inscriptions; these must be a subsequent addition, for they appear to be from the very latest Iznik period or even perhaps from the eighteenth-century potteries of Tekfur Saray. In the mosque garden is the attractive open türbe of the founder with a marble sarcophagus. The pious foundation, whose date is given in inscriptions over the garden gates, originally included a mektep and a hamam, but these have perished.

SİLİVRİ KAPISI TO MEVLEVİHANE KAPISI

Returning to the Silivri Gate we proceed along the walls, which are here not as well preserved as in the previous sections. Less than midway along there is a curious jog, or indentation, in the wall known as the Sigma from its resemblance to the uncial form of that letter – like the letter C. Just beside the Sigma is the Third Military Gate, now walled up. Over this little gate there once stood a statue of the

Emperor Theodosius II, builder of these walls; it did not disappear until the fourteenth century.

Mevlevihane Kapısı takes its name from the tekke of Mevlevi dervishes which once stood outside the gate. This tekke was founded in the sixteenth century by Merkez Efendi, the son-in-law of the Sümbül Efendi whose türbe we have seen in the courtyard of Koca Mustafa Paşa Camii. In Byzantium this entryway was called the Gate of Rhegium, or sometimes the Gate of the Reds, after one of the four factions of the Hippodrome. On the south corbel of the outer gate is the inscription which we have already mentioned, recording the construction of the walls by Theodosius and the Prefect Constantine. There is also an inscription on the lintel of the outer gate which reads in part: "This tower of the Theodosian wall was restored under Justin and Sophia, our most pious sovereigns, and by Narses, the most glorius Spatharius and Sacellarius..." The emperor referred to here is Justin II, nephew and successor of Justinian the Great, who ruled from 565 till 578. The strain of his imperial duties must have been too much for poor Justin, for he ended his days in total madness, being pulled through the halls of the Great Palace in a toy cart. Narses, who succeeded Belisarius as commander of Justinian's army, conquered Totila, King of the Goths, and so saved for a time the Western Empire. Narses later became the Byzantine ruler of Italy, the last before the peninsula fell to the Lombards. He was perhaps the greatest of all the eunuchs who served Byzantium.

MEVLEVİHANE KAPISI TO TOPKAPI

The line of walls extending from Mevlevihane Kapısı to Topkapı, the next public gate, forms the centre of the long arc of walls between the Marmara and the Golden Horn. On the seventh tower along, where the walls extend farthest into Thrace, there is this inscription: "Oh Christ, God, preserve thy city undisturbed and free from war. Conquer the wrath of our enemies."

Before reaching Topkapı we come to the Fourth Military Gate, now walled up, and then to the wide new breach in the walls made for the passage of Millet Caddesi. If we turn into Millet Caddesi and walk about 300 metres we come on the right to a vast bus depot. Just inside the gate of the depot there is a tiny Byzantine building known by its Turkish name, Manastir Mescidi. Its Byzantine name and its history are unknown; various identifications have been proposed, none of them with any conviction or probability. It is of the very simplest form: a long rectangular chamber ending at the east with the usual three projecting apses and preceded at the west by a small narthex with two columns. It is most probably to be dated to the thirteenth or fourteenth century.

Opposite this on the north side of Millet Caddesi is an equally insignificant little mosque called Kürekçibaşı Camii, founded by one Ahmet Bey in the reign of Süleyman the Magnificent. It is rectangular in form and with a wooden roof. It once had a fine porch of which only the columns now remain; they arc Byzantine with crosses on the shaft and interesting Byzantine capitals.

We now stroll up the side street, Topkapı Caddesi, past this little mosque, and at the end of it on the left we find still another but even older mosque. This is Beyazit Ağa Camii and dates from the age of Fatih. It is of the same type as Kürekçibaşı Camii, that is, rectangular with a wooden roof, and appears to be built on top of an ancient cistern. Like the other buildings we have seen on this little detour, this is worth only a passing glance.

KARA AHMET PAŞA CAMİİ

Opposite the end of the street on which we have been walking we come to a great mosque complex which is one of the loveliest and most masterful of the works of Sinan. It was built in 1554 for Kara Ahmet Paşa, one of Süleyman's Grand Vezirs. We enter by a gate in the south wall into a spacious and charming courtyard shaded by plane trees. The court is formed by the cells of the medrese; to the left stands the large dershane with pretty shell-shaped pendentives under the dome; beside it a passage leads to the lavatories. The porch of the mosque has unusually wide and attractive arches supporting its five domes. Over the embrasures or niches of the porch are some rather exceptional tiles, predominantly apple-green and vivid yellow, done in the old *cuerda seca* technique. They are the latest recorded examples of the second period of the Iznik potteries, the only other important examples being those in the türbe of the Şehzade and the fine series of panels in the mosque of Sultan Selim. A few more such panels, but with blue and white inscriptions, will be found inside the mosque on the east wall. The marble revetment around the entrance portal evidently belongs to a restoration carried out in 1896; fortunately, though very *Empire* in style, it is restrained and does not clash badly with the rest.

On entering we find that the plan of the mosque is a hexagon inscribed in a rectangle. The four semidomes lie along the diagonals of the building and each rests on two small conches; six great columns support the arches, and there are galleries on three sides. The proportions of the building are unusually fine, as are many of the details; for example, the polychrome voussoirs of the arches and the elegant mihrab and mimber. But what is rarer are the wooden ceilings under the western galleries, painted with elaborate arabesques in rich reds, dark blue, gold and black. This is perhaps the most extensive and best preserved example of this kind of painting in the city; it is singularly rich and beautiful. Unfortunately, the ceiling on the left has recently been spoiled by an attempt at restoration, but the one on the right still retains its sombre brilliance.

Outside the precinct wall, towards the west, is the türbe of the founder, a simple octagonal building, unfortunately ruined inside. Beyond it stands the large mektep, double and of very interesting design, a long rectangular building with a wooden roof; it is still used as a primary school.

We now find ourselves in the large, irregular and picturesque square in front of Topkapı, the Cannon Gate. Until a few years ago, when the new breaches in the walls were made, this was one of the two main entrances to the city and, like the other one, Edirnekapı, hopelessly narrow and impossible for traffic. One pleasant result of the new breaches for the modern highways is that the districts around the ancient gates have become backwaters, to some extent, and are no longer so congested with traffic. Topkapı was anciently known as the Gate of St. Romanus, from a nearby church of that name. Its Turkish name, the Cannon Gate, comes from the fact that outside it in 1453 Sultan Mehmet placed his largest cannon, the famous Urban. Here too the Conqueror pitched his tent to direct the siege operations, which were chiefly concentrated against the stretch of walls between the Seventh and Sixth Hills. Inside the gate are suspended some of the stone cannon balls fired by Urban during the last siege.

TAKKECİ IBRAHİM AĞA CAMİİ

Before we stroll along the next stretch of walls we might take a short detour along the road that faces Topkapı and leads into the Thracian downs. After about 500 metres we see on our left an extremely picturesque mosque, Takkeci Ibrahim Ağa Camii. This is the only wooden mosque in Istanbul that appears to preserve essentially its original appearance. It is rectangular in form, with a wooden roof and porch. This is the simplest and cheapest to build and is therefore the commonest of all mosque types; but in almost all surviving examples the wooden roof and porch have succumbed to fire and have been reconstructed even more cheaply, losing thereby their charm and distinction. Doubtless because of its isolation in the country outside the walls, Takkeci Ibrahim Ağa Camii seems to have escaped the fires and has preserved its original porch and roof. It was founded in 1592 by a certain Ibrahim who was a maker of the felt hats called *takke* or *arakiye*, especially the long conical kind worn by the dervishes.

A stone wall with grilles and the remains of a fine sebil at the corner surrounds the mosque courtyard-garden. The deeply projecting wooden tiled roof of the porch is supported by a double row of wooden pillars. Since the porch extends halfway round both sides of the mosque, the pillars give the effect of a little copse of trees, the more so since the paint has long since worn off. The roof itself has three dashing gables along the façade; a very quaint and pretty arrangement. On the right rises the fine minaret with a beautiful stalactited şerefe. Handsome but rather heavy inscriptions adorn the spaces over the door and windows. Within, a wooden balcony runs round the west wall and half of the side walls; it has a cornice which preserves the original arabesque painting, such as we have just seen at Kara Ahmet Paşa Camii. The ceiling is of wood painted dark green and in the centre is a wooden dome on an octagonal cornice; one sees how greatly the dome adds to the charm of the interior and what a disaster it is when these ceilings are reconstructed flat. Two rows of windows admit light; the tiny one over the mihrab preserves some ancient, brilliant stained glass. Beneath the upper row of windows the walls are entirely revetted with tiles of the greatest period of Iznik in great panels with vases of leaves and flowers. These are celebrated and are as fine as those we have seen at Ramazan Efendi Camii.

TOPKAPI TO EDİRNEKAPI

We now return to Topkapı and resume our stroll along the walls toward Edirnekapı, the next of the Byzantine public gates. This section of the walls, anciently known as the Mesoteichion, was the most vulnerable in the whole defence system, since here the walls descend into the valley of the Lycus, which entered the city midway between the two gates. During the last siege the defenders on the Mesoteichion were at a serious disadvantage, being below the level of the Turkish guns on either side. For that reason the walls in the Lycus valley are the most badly damaged in the whole length of the fortifications: and most of the defence towers are mere piles of rubble or great shapeless hulks of masonry. It was this section of the wall which was finally breached by the Turks on the morning of 29 May 1453. The final charge was led by a giant Janissary named Hasan, who fought his way up onto one of the towers of the outer wall. Hasan himself was slain, but his companions then forced their way across the peribolos and over the inner wall into the city, and within hours Constantinople had fallen.

The course of the ancient river Lycus is today marked by the brash new Vatan Caddesi, which breaches the walls midway between Topkapı and Edirnekapı. Just inside the walls between here and the Fifth Military Gate, about 400 metres beyond, is the little neighbourhood called Sulukule, the site of a gypsy village which has been here since the fourteenth century but is now being demolished. This section of walls was anciently called the Murus Bacchatureus: according to tradition this is where the Emperor Constantine Dragases had his command post during the last siege. He was last seen there just before the walls were breached, fighting valiantly beside his cousins Theophilus Palaeologus and Don Francisco of Toledo and his faithful comrade John Dalmata. The Fifth Military Gate is known in Turkish as Hücum Kapısı, the Gate of the Assault, preserving the memory of that last battle. On the outer lintel of the gate there is an inscription recording a repair by one Pusaeus, presumably in the fifth century.

The Edirne Gate stands at the peak of the Sixth Hill and is at the highest point in the city, 77 metres above sea-level. This gate has preserved in Turkish form one of its ancient names, Porta Adrianople, for from here started the main road to Adrianople, the modern Edirne. It was also known in Byzantium as the Gate of Charisius or sometimes as the Porta Polyandrium, the Gate of the Cemetery. This latter name undoubtedly came from the fact that there was a large necropolis outside the walls at this point. Several ancient funerary steles from this necropolis can still be seen set into the courtyard wall of the Greek church of St. George, which stands just inside the walls near the gate.

It was through the Edirne Gate that Sultan Mehmet II made his triumphal entry into the city on 29 May 1453, and a modern plaque beside the gate commemorates this event. Evliya Çelebi, whose ancestor Yavuz Ersinan was present at the time, gives this vivid description of that historic moment: "The Sultan then having the pontifical turban on his head and sky-blue boots on his feet, mounted on a mule and bearing the sword of Mohammed in his hand, marched in at the head of seventy or eighty thousand Moslem heroes, crying out 'Halt not conquerors! God be praised! Ye are the conquerors of Constantinople!' "

MİHRİMAH CAMİİ

Just inside the Edirne Gate to the south stands the magnificent mosque of Mihrimah Sultan, which dominates the Sixth Hill and can be seen for miles about in all directions. It is one of the architectural masterpieces of the great Sinan, built by him for the Princess Mihrimah, the favourite daughter of Süleyman the Magnificent. The külliye was built between 1562 and 1565 and includes, besides the mosque, a medrese, a mektep, a türbe, a double hamam, and a long row of shops in the substructure of the terrace on which it is built. Unfortunately the complex has been very severely damaged by earthquakes at least twice, in 1766 and 1894. Each time the mosque itself was restored but the attendant buildings were for the most part neglected; in recent years some not altogether satisfactory reconstruction has been carried out.

We enter from the main street through a gate giving access to a short flight of steps leading up to the terrace. On the right is the great courtyard, around three sides of which are the porticoes and cells of the medrese. The west side, which stands just opposite the Theodosian walls with only a narrow road between, has only had its portico restored, and it is difficult to be sure how many cells there were along this side and whether the dershane stood here as one might expect. In the centre of the courtyard is an attractive şadırvan. The mosque is preceded by an imposing porch of seven domed bays supported by eight marble and granite columns. This porch was originally preceded by another, doubtless with a sloping wooden roof supported on 12 columns, traces of which may be seen on the ground. This double porch was a favourite device of Sinan's, found again at Mihrimah's other mosque at Üsküdar and in many others.

The central area of the interior is square, covered by a great dome 20 metres in diameter and 37 metres high under the crown, resting on smooth pendentives. The tympana of all four dome arches are filled with three rows of windows. To north and south high triple arcades, each supported on two great granite columns, open into side aisles with galleries above, each of three domed bays; but these galleries reach only to the springing of the dome arches. The plan thus gives a sense of enormous space and light. Altogether Mihrimah Camii is one of the very finest mosques in the city and must be counted as one of Sinan's masterpieces. It is curious that this mosque, although imperial, has but one minaret, while Mihrimah's other mosque in Üsküdar has two.

The interior stencil decoration is modern, insipid in colour and characterless in design. The mimber, however, is a fine original work of white marble with a beautiful medallion perforated like an iron grille. The voussoirs of the gallery arches are fretted polychrome of verd antique and Proconnesian marble.

From the exterior the building is strong and dominant as befits its position at the highest point of the city. The square of the dome base with its multi-windowed tympana, identical on all sides, is given solidity and boldness by the four great, weight-towers at the corners, prolongations of the piers that support the dome arches. Above this square rises the dome itself on a circular drum pierced by windows.

If we walk around to the south side of the mosque, we find a small graveyard at the end of which stands an unusually large sibyan mektebi with a central dome flanked by two cradle-vaults. Beyond this and entered through it is the türbe of the Grand Vezir Güzelce Ahmet Paşa, Mihrimah's son-in-law. (Mihrimah herself is buried in her father's türbe at the Süleymaniye.) Ahmet Paşa's türbe is like only one other built by Sinan, that of Pertev Paşa at Eyüp. It is rectangular, more than twice as long as it is wide, covered by a large dome and two cradle-vaults. A third example of a classical türbe of this form is that of Destari Mustafa Paşa at the Şehzade. Ahmet Paşa's türbe contains a large number of sarcophagi of members of the family of Princess Mihrimah, many of them children.

On the north-east side of the mosque, entered from the main street, we see the double hamam of the foundation which has recently been restored. There is nothing unusual about the plan of this hamam: the eyvans of the hararet have semidomes, the hücre domes are on simple pendentives, and the entrance is, as often, off-centre through one of the hücres. At the corner of the hamam is a simple but attractive çeşme.

EDİRNEKAPI TO TEKFUR SARAY

The Theodosian walls continue for about 600 metres beyond the Edirne Gate; the inner wall in this stretch is well preserved and has nine towers which are more or less intact. (The remaining stretch of walls leading down to the Golden Horn was built in later times, from about the seventh to the twelfth century.) At the very end of the existing Theodosian wall, just next to the last tower in the inner wall, is the site of a small portal which played a fateful role in the last siege. This is the Porta Xylokerkou, the Gate of the Wooden Circus, named after a hippodrome which once stood outside the walls in this area. It was through here that the Janissaries first made their way into the city. And it was from the tower beside the Porta Xylokerkou, the very last bastion on the long line of the Theodosian walls, that the Turkish ensign first waved over this city.

TEKFUR SARAY

Just beyond the site of this gate there stands one of the most remarkable buildings remaining from the days of Byzantium. It is known in Turkish as Tekfur Saray, or the Palace of the Sovereign, though it is sometimes called the Palace of the Porphyrogenitus. The palace was probably built in the latter part of the thirteenth or early in the fourteenth century, and served as one of the imperial residences during the last two centuries of the Empire: it was perhaps an annexe of the nearby Palace of Blachernae. It is a large three-storeyed building wedged in between the inner and outer walls of the last stretch of the Theodosian fortifications. On the ground floor an arcade with four wide arches opens onto the courtyard, which is overlooked on the first floor by five large windows. The top floor, which projects above the walls, has windows on all sides, seven overlooking the courtyard, a curious bow-like apse on the opposite side, and a window with the remains of a balcony to the east. The roof and all the floors have disappeared. The whole palace, but especially the façade on the court, is elaborately decorated with geometrical designs in red brick and white marble so typical of the later period of Byzantine architecture; compare the façades of St. Saviour in Chora and of St. Theodore, both of the fourteenth century.

After the Conquest the palace was used for a variety of purposes. During the sixteenth and seventeenth centuries it was used as a menagerie, particularly for larger and tamer animals such as elephants and giraffes. (The latter animal particularly amazed European travellers, for they had never seen one before. In 1597, Fynes Moryson describes it thus: "a beaste newly brought out of Affricke, (the Mother of Monsters) which beaste is altogether unknowne in our parts, he many times put his nose in my necke, when I thought my selfe furthest distant from him, which familiarity I liked not; and howsoever his Keepers assured me he would not hurt me, yet I avoided those his familiar kisses as much as I could.") Before the end of the seventeenth century the animals were moved elsewhere and the palace served for a while as a brothel. But it was soon redeemed from this misuse; for in 1719 there was set up here the famous Tekfur Saray pottery. This works produced a new kind of Turkish tile, the so-called Tekfur Saray type, inferior indeed to those of Iznik and beginning to show European influence, but nevertheless quite charming. The project, however, was short-lived and by the second half of the eighteenth century the palace was in full decline and finally lost its roof and floors. During the first half of the nineteenth century Tekfur Saray served as a poorhouse for the indigent Jews of Stamboul. About 1860, the American missionary Cyrus Hamlin, searching for a site for the future Robert College, seriously considered purchasing the palace and restoring it for use as an educational institution; perhaps fortunately, the idea was abandoned in favour of the present site of the College (now Boğaziçi University) on the Bosphorus. In recent years the palace has served as a bottle works and storehouse – the lamentable history of a palace down on its luck. The building is now a mere shell; but in recent years the surviving structure has been well restored.

Just beyond Tekfur Saray the Theodosian wall comes to an abrupt end, and from there the fortifications are continued by walls of later construction. There has been much discussion about the original course of the Theodosian walls from Tekfur Saray down to the Golden Horn. It would appear that they turned almost due north at Tekfur Saray and from there followed a more or less straight line down to the Horn, whereas the present walls are bent in an arc farther out into Thrace. Stretches of what are undoubtedly the original Theodosian wall can be seen at Tekfur Saray and also along Mumhane Caddesi, which we reach by turning right in the little square beyond the palace and then taking the first left. The ruined walls along this street are quite impressive and picturesque.

The present stretch of walls from Tekfur Saray to the Golden Horn is quite different from the Theodosian fortifications. It is a single bulwark without a moat; to make up for this deficiency it is thicker and more massive than the main Theodosian wall and its towers are stronger, higher and closer together. The part of the wall that encloses the western bulge between Tekfur Saray and the Blachernae terrace

can be fairly well inspected if we follow the street closest to the wall
and walk through the gardens of the intervening houses.

WALL OF MANUEL COMNENUS

The first part of this section of the walls was built by the Emperor
Manuel Comnenus (r. 1143–80). This wall begins just beyond
Tekfur Saray, where it starts westward almost at right angles to the
last fragment of the Theodosian wall, then turning north at the third
tower. The wall of Manuel is an admirably constructed fortification
consisting of high arches closed on the outer face and containing nine
towers and one public gate, now called Eğri Kapı. Most authorities
identify Eğri Kapı with the ancient Gate of the Kaligaria. It was here
that Constantine Dragases was last seen alive by his friend, George
Phrantzes, who would later write a history of the fall of Byzantium. On
the night of 28 May 1453 the Emperor, accompanied by Phrantzes,
had stopped briefly at the Palace of Blachernae after returning from
his last visit to Haghia Sophia.

According to Phrantzes, Constantine assembled the members
of his household and said goodbye to each of them in turn, asking
their forgiveness for any unkindness he might ever have shown them.
"Who could describe the tears and groans in the palace?" Phrantzes
wrote, "Even a man of wood or stone could not help weeping." The
Emperor then left the Palace and rode with Phrantzes down to the
Gate of the Kaligaria. They dismounted there and Phrantzes waited
while Constantine ascended one of the towers nearby, whence he
could hear the sounds of the Turkish army preparing for the final
assault. After about an hour he returned and mounted his horse once
again. George Phrantzes then said goodbye to Constantine for the
last time and then watched as the Emperor rode off to his post on the
Murus Bacchatureus, where he met his death the following morning
in defence of his doomed city.

Eğri Kapı, the Crooked Gate, is so-called because the narrow
lane which enters the city there must detour around a türbe which
stands almost directly in front of the gate. This is the supposed tomb
of Hazret Hafız, a companion of the Prophet, who, according to
tradition, was killed on this spot during the first Arab assault on

the city. Several sainted Arab heroes of that campaign are buried in the vicinity, all having been violently dispatched to paradise by the defenders on the walls of Byzantium. The burial place of Hazret Hafız was only 'discovered' in the eighteenth century by the Chief Eunuch Beşir Ağa, who thereupon built this türbe, thus blocking the road.

From Eğri Kapı we continue along the path just inside the walls to see the remainder of the wall of Manuel Comnenus, which ends at the third tower past the gate. The rest of this section of wall, from the third tower to where it joins the retaining wall of the Blachernae terrace, appears to be of later construction. The workmanship here is much inferior to that of Manuel's section, as can clearly be seen where the two join, without being bonded together, just beyond the third tower from Eğri Kapı. This section contains four towers, all square and also much inferior to those built by Manuel. Manuel's wall bears no dated inscription; the northern and later one has three: one dated 1188 (Isaac II Angelus), another 1317 (Andronicus II Palaeologus), and the third 1441 (John VIII Palaeologus). There is also in this northern section a postern, now walled up, which is thought to be the ancient Gyrolimne Gate. This was an entryway to the Palace of Blachernae, whose outer retaining wall and two towers continue the line of fortifications in this area.

WALLS OF LEO AND HERACLİUS

The fortification from the north corner of the Blachernae terrace to the Golden Horn consists of two parallel walls joined at their two ends to form a kind of citadel. The inner wall was built by the Emperor Heraclius in 627 apparently in an attempt to strengthen the defences in this area, which the year before had been breached by the Avars. The three hexagonal defence towers in this short stretch of wall are perhaps the finest in the whole defence system. In 813 the Emperor Leo V decided that this wall by itself was inadequate and therefore added to it the outer wall, protected by four small towers. (The city was then being threatened by Krum of the Bulgars.) However, Leo's wall is thin and much inferior to the older one behind it. These walls were pierced by a single entryway, the Gate of the Blachernae; that part of the gate which passed through the wall of

Leo has now collapsed but it is still open through the Heraclian wall, passing between the first and second towers.

The citadel between the walls of Leo and Heraclius is in its own peculiar way quite fascinating. At one end of the citadel there is a small Muslim graveyard which contains the graves of Ebu Şeybet ül-Hudri and Hamd ül-Ensari, two other martyred Companions of the Prophet. We find here also the türbe of Toklu Dade, the Muslim saint who would seem to be the reincarnation of St. Theca, whose church just outside the citadel became Toklu Dede Mescidi when it was converted into a mosque.

At the northern corner of the citadel the walls of Leo and Heraclius come together and there link up with the sea-walls along the Golden Horn. This, then, is the end of our tour. We leave the citadel through the Gate of the Blachernae and turn left on the street outside, Toklu Dede Sokağı, down which we walked on a previous tour. This brings us out to the main road along the Golden Horn, where we finish our long stroll along the land-walls.

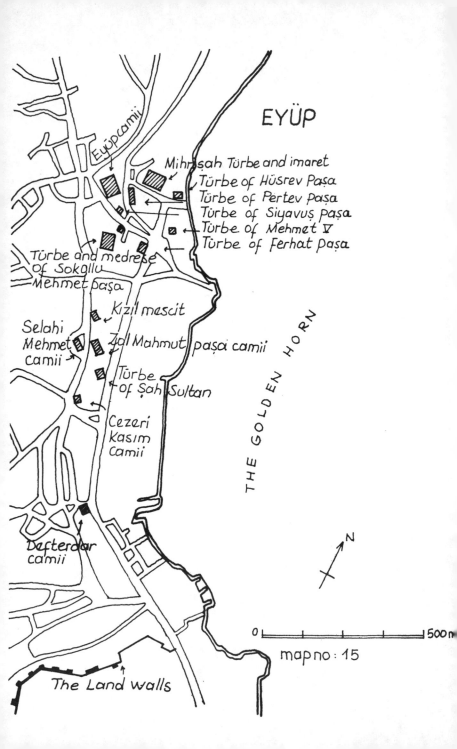

EYÜP

Mihrişah Türbe and imaret
Türbe of Hüsrev Paşa
Türbe of Pertev Paşa
Türbe of Siyavuş paşa
Türbe of Mehmet V
Türbe of Ferhat Paşa

Türbe and medrese
of Sokollu
Mehmet paşa

Kızıl mescit

Selahi
Mehmet
camii

Zal Mahmut paşa camii

Türbe
of Şah Sultan

Cezeri
Kasım
Camii

THE GOLDEN HORN

Defterdar
camii

N

0 _____ 500m

map no : 15

The Land walls

18

Up the
Golden Horn to Eyüp

Eyüp, a village far up the Golden Horn, had in the nineteenth century the reputation of being wildly romantic and picturesque. Surrounded on two sides by high hills covered with groves of cypress trees and turbaned tombstones, commanding magnificent views of both shores of the Golden Horn, it was a peaceful backwater devoted to death and religion. The modern world in its most dreary form of shabby factories and warehouses and cheap housing developments has unfortunately caught up with it and is investing it on all sides, though the view down the Golden Horn is still romantic at sunset.

Nevertheless, Eyüp itself has so far resisted the worst encroachments of the modern world and it contains some of the most interesting as well as some of the most sacred relics of Ottoman piety; of all the suburbs of Istanbul it is the one which most repays a visit. The best way of reaching Eyüp is by ferry from the Galata Bridge, particularly now that new and more comfortable ferries have been put into service. The journey is pleasant and affords an opportunity of viewing from a distance the villages and districts on the way. Alternatively one can take a taxi, stopping en route at a number of the interesting monuments on the north shore of the Golden Horn above the Atatürk Bridge, which we will visit on this itinerary.

The Golden Horn (Haliç or Estuary in Turkish) has become badly polluted in the past century, although a vigorous effort is now being made to clean up the Horn and its shores. The Golden Horn is an inlet of the Bosphorus, stretching north-west for some 11 kilometres from Saray Point, with an average width of about 400 metres. At its northern end two little streams flow into the Horn, Alibey Suyu on the west and Kâğıthane Suyu on the east; they were once known to Europeans as the Sweet Waters of Europe. For centuries the charming meadows between them were the site of royal gardens, palaces and pavilions, and were a favourite holiday resort for city-dwellers, as they are once again becoming today.

PİYALE PAŞA CAMİİ

The first stop of the ferry is on the north shore of the Golden Horn at Kasım Paşa, a short way above the Atatürk Bridge. Here one might make an excursion by taxi in order to visit one of the most interesting and enigmatic of the classical mosques, that of Piyale Paşa, about a mile straight up the valley from the landing stage. Constructed in 1573, the mosque is unique in the classical period in more than one respect. In the first place it is the only classical mosque to revert in plan to the Ulu Cami or multidomed type, common in the Selçuk and early Ottoman periods. Its six ample and equal domes in two rows of three are supported by two great red granite columns. Thus far it follows the earlier type, but all else is different. In the centre of the west wall opposite the mihrab is a small balcony supported on six columns, and behind this rises very unusually the single minaret, which is thus in the middle of the west façade. The entrance portals are to the right and left of the balcony, and there are narrow galleries along the sides of the building. The room is lighted by numerous windows, many of the upper ones being round, *oeils-de-boeuf;* between the second and third tier a wide frieze of faience has inscriptions from the Kuran in white on a blue ground, from the hand of the famous *hattat* (calligrapher) Karahisarı, who wrote the inscriptions in the Süleymaniye. The mihrab also is a very beautiful work of Iznik tiles of the best period. The whole interior is not merely unusual but exceptionally charming. The exterior is even more unusual. Around three sides of the building runs a deep porch whose vaults are supported by stout rectangular pillars; above the side porches were galleries with sloping roofs supported on innumerable small columns, while in front of the main western porch was another lower one with 22 columns. The roofs of this and the upper galleries on the sides have unfortunately disappeared, but from old pictures one can see how fascinating this unique arrangement was. The founder's türbe behind the mosque also had a columned porch, and it is said that the total number of columns was 118; evidently Piyale had a passion for them. Piyale Paşa, son of a Croatian shoemaker, was brought up in the Palace School and married a daughter of Selim II; he was Lord High Admiral and conquered the island of Chios as well as repeatedly harrying the coasts of Italy.

At Kasım Paşa is the famous naval Arsenal *(Tershane)*, originally built by Mehmet the Conqueror. During the sixteenth and seventeenth centuries it made a great impression on foreign travellers, for it could accommodate 120 ships in drydock and there was nothing like it in Europe. Now its activities are more modest. At the water's edge not far beyond the landing stage is a pretty little nineteenth-century palace for the commandant in charge of the Taşkızak Naval Arsenal.

Farther up the north shore of the Golden Horn, opposite Balat, we see the former imperial residence known as Aynalı Kavak Kasr, the Pavilion of the Mirroring Poplars. This handsome building was probably constructed during the reign of Ahmet III (r. 1703–30), restored by Selim III (r. 1789–1807), and given its present form with alterations by Mahmut II (r. 1808–39). Aynalı Kavak figures in Turkish history as the site of the peace conference which in 1779 ended a war between Russia and the Ottoman Empire. The palace was restored and reopened in 1993 as a museum, housing a fascinating collection of Turkish musical instruments.

After Kasım Paşa the next ferry stop is at Fener on the south shore of the Golden Horn. The ferry then crosses over to stop at Hasköy on the north shore before going on to its last stop at Eyüp. At Hasköy one might want to break the journey by visiting the very interesting Rahmi M. Koç Industrial Museum. Part of the museum is housed in a beautifully restored Ottoman lengerhane, a forge for making ship's chains and anchors, a structure dating from the reign of Ahmet III. One of the buildings of the lengerhane has been converted into a very attractive restaurant called the Café du Levant.

THE MOSQUE AND TÜRBE OF EYÜP

The mosque of Eyüp is the holiest in Istanbul; indeed after Mecca and Jerusalem it is perhaps the third most sacred place of pilgrimage in the Islamic world. This is because it is the reputed burial place of Eyüp (Job) Ensari, the friend and standard-bearer of the Prophet Muhammed. Long after the Prophet's death, Eyüp is said to have been one of the leaders of the first Arab siege of Constantinople from 674 to 678 and to have been killed and buried somewhere outside the walls. When some eight centuries later Fatih Mehmet besieged the city, he and his advisors, as Evliya Çelebi writes,

> spent seven whole days searching for the tomb. At last Akşemsettin (the Şeyh-ül Islam) exclaimed, "Good news, my Prince, of Eyüp's tomb!" Thus saying he began to pray and then fell asleep. Some interpreted this sleep as a veil cast by shame over his ignorance of the tomb; but after some time he raised his head, his eyes became bloodshot, the sweat ran from his forehead, and he said to the Sultan, "Eyüp's tomb is on the very spot where I spread the carpet for prayer." Upon this, three of his attendants together with the Şeyh and the Sultan began to dig up the ground, when at a depth of three yards they found a square stone of verd antique on which was written in Cufic letters: "This is the tomb of Eba Eyüp." They lifted the stone and found below it the body of Eyüp wrapped up in a saffron-coloured shroud, with a brazen play-ball in his hand, fresh and well-preserved. They replaced the stone, formed a little mound of the earth they had dug up, and laid the foundations of the mausoleum amidst the prayers of the whole army.

This pleasant story, though still current and recounted in one form or another by the guides and guidebooks, seems rather unlikely – apart from its supernatural elements – because it appears that the tomb had always been known and respected even by the Byzantines. Various Arab historians note that it was made a condition of peace, after the first Arab siege, that the tomb should be preserved. An Arab traveller during the reign of Manuel I Comnenus (r. 1143–80) mentions it as still existing in his day, while another traveller, Zakariya al-Kazwini (ca. 1203–83), relates that "this tomb is now venerated among them (the Byzantines) and they open it when they pray for rain in times of drought; and rain is granted them." If the tomb was still extant in early Palaeologan times, it seems improbable that it should so completely have disappeared before the Turkish Conquest. Probably, Fatih restored or rebuilt it on a grander scale.

The külliye as a whole, originally including the türbe, mosque, medrese, han, hamam, imaret and market, was built by Fatih Mehmet in 1458, five years after the Conquest. Here on their accession to the throne the Ottoman sultans were girded with the sword of Osman, a ceremony equivalent to coronation. By the end of the eighteenth century the mosque had fallen into ruin, perhaps a victim of the great earthquake of 1766 which had destroyed Fatih's own mosque. At all events, in 1798 under Sultan Selim III, what remained of the building was torn down and the present mosque erected in its place and finished in 1800; only the minarets, the gift of Ahmet III, remain from the older building.

One approaches through an outer courtyard of irregular shape but great picturesqueness. The two great gateways with their undulating baroque forms, the staircase and gallery to the imperial loge, the huge and aged plane trees in whose hollows live lame storks and in whose branches beautiful grey herons build their nests in spring, the flocks of pampered pigeons – all this makes the courtyard the most delightful in Istanbul. From here one enters the inner court, surrounded on three sides by an unusually tall and stately colonnade and also shaded by venerable plane trees. The mosque itself in plan is an octagon inscribed in a rectangle and closely resembles Sinan's Azap Kapı Camii, though on a rather larger scale and with many baroque details of decoration. But in spite of its late date the mosque is singularly attractive with its pale honey-coloured stone, the decorations picked out in gold, and the elegant chandelier hanging from the centre of the dome.

The side of the building opposite the mosque is a blank wall, most of it covered with panels of tiles without an overall pattern and of many different periods, some of them of great individual beauty. A door in the wall leads to the vestibule of the türbe of Eyüp, an octagonal building three sides of which project into the vestibule. The latter is itself sheathed in tiles, many of them of the best Iznik period.

The türbe is sumptuously decorated, though with work largely of the baroque period.

Of the other buildings of the külliye the medrese, which according to Evliya formed the courtyard of the mosque, was evidently swept away when the latter was rebuilt; the imaret is a ruin. But of the hamam the soğukluk and hararet still remain and are in use; they have the elaborate and attractive dome structure typical of the early period, and handsome marble floors. The original camekân has completely disappeared and been replaced by a rather make-shift one largely of wood. In the Victoria and Albert Museum there is a very fine panel of 24 Iznik tiles of about 1570 from this hamam, very probably from the demolished camekân.

THE KÜLLİYE OF MİHRİŞAH SULTAN

Leaving Eyüp Camii by the north gate, one finds oneself in a narrow street that leads down to the Golden Horn. Most of the left side of this street is occupied by the enormous külliye built in 1794 by Mihrişah Valide Sultan, mother of Selim III. This is one of the largest and most elaborate of all the baroque complexes and includes the türbe of the foundress together with a mektep, an imaret, and a splendid sebil and çeşmes. The türbe is round, but the façade undulates turning it into a polygon, the various faces being separated by slender columns of red or dark grey marble; in general it recalls the türbe of Nakşidil at Fatih, though it is not quite so flamboyant. The entrance is in a little courtyard filled with tombstones and trees, along one side of which runs the columned portico of the mektep or primary school. Farther along the street another monumental gateway leads into the vast courtyard with more and tombstones and surrounded on three sides by the porticoes of the huge imaret or public kitchen. This is one of the very few imarets in Istanbul which still fulfil their function as food kitchens for the poor of the district; some 500 people are served daily at 11 o'clock with food to take away. In leaving you should notice the magnificent sebil at the end of the garden wall on the street side.

Continuing towards the water, one passes on the right the türbe and on the left the library of Hüsref Paşa, dated 1839 and both in heavy *Empire* style; but the domes of the library reading-rooms contain a good example of that horrendous Italianate comic opera painted decoration of garlands, draperies and columns, which is so distressing when it occurs in classical buildings but is quite appropriate here. At the end of the street at the water's edge one gets a good view of the neo-classical türbe of the Sultan Mehmet V Reşat who died in 1918, oddly enough the only one of all the sultans to be buried in the holy precincts of Eyüp and the last to be buried in his own country. It is a rather heavy building, the interior revetted in modern Kütahya tiles predominantly of a vivid (too vivid) green.

Taking the street parallel to the Golden Horn, one soon comes to a crossroads where stand several classical türbes. The finest and most elaborate of these is that of Ferhat Paşa, octagonal in structure with a richly decorated cornice and polychrome voussoirs and window-frames.

THE TÜRBE COMPLEX OF SOKOLLU MEHMET PAŞA

Further up the street that leads back towards Eyüp Camii two classical türbes of great simplicity face one another. The one on the left is that of Sokollu Mehmet Paşa, built by Sinan in about 1572; it forms part of a small külliye. Elegant and well-proportioned, it is severely plain, but the interior contains some interesting stained glass, partly ancient and partly a modern imitation but very well done; alternate windows are predominantly blue and green. A little colonnade attaches the türbe to the dershane of the very fine medrese of the complex. Notice the handsome identical doorways of the two buildings, differing only in that the rich polychrome work of the türbe is in verd antique, that of the dershane in red conglomerate marble. The dershane also has stained glass windows, but they are modern and not so good as those in the türbe. Its dome is supported on squinches of very bold stalactites. The opposite door leads into the medrese courtyard, long and narrow, its colonnade having ten domes on the long sides, only three on the ends. The building has been well restored and is used as a children's clinic: it is so pretty and charming, with a delightfully well-kept garden, that it must almost be a pleasure to be a patient! In the little garden of the türbe are buried the family and descendants of Sokollu Mehmet, and just beyond the graveyard is a building in the same style as the dershane: this is the dar-ül kura or school for the various methods of reading the Kuran. This little complex as a whole is certainly one of Sinan's most attractive.

Sokollu Mehmet Paşa was perhaps the greatest and most capable of the long line of able grand vezirs of the sixteenth century. He was the son of a Bosnian priest and was born in the castle of Sokol, "the falcon's nest", in Bosnia. But he was taken in the devşirme and brought up in the Palace School at the Saray. He married the princess Ismihan Sultan, daughter of Sultan Selim the Sot. His outstanding genius brought him early preferment and he successively held the posts of Lord High Treasurer, Grand Admiral, Beylerbey of Rumelia, Vezir, and finally Grand Vezir, a position which he held continuously for 15 years under three sultans, Süleyman, Selim II and Murat III, from 1564 to 1579, in which year he was murdered in the Divan itself by a mad soldier. Posterity owes him three of the most beautiful architectural monuments in Istanbul: the present complex, the mosque at Azap Kapı, and – most beautiful of all – the mosque at Kadirga Liman under the Hippodrome; all were the work of Sinan.

The türbe across the street from Sokollu's is that of Siyavuş Paşa, austere like the other but adorned within by inscriptions and pendentives in excellent Iznik tiles. It is also by Sinan; Siyavuş outlived Sinan by a dozen years and died in 1601, but he seems to have had Sinan build this türbe originally for some of his children who died young, and then was finally buried there himself. Still another türbe by Sinan is to be found half-way up a narrow and picturesque little alleyway beside the türbe of Siyavuş that leads back towards the mosque of Eyüp through a forest of tombstones. This is the tomb of Pertev Paşa, of a very unusual design, rectangular and more like a house than a tomb. It was originally divided into two equal areas each covered by a dome of wood exquisitely painted; this survived until 1927 when it fell victim to neglect. Inside are still to be seen some charming marble sarcophagi of Pertev and his family.

One has now come full circle back to the north gate of the courtyard of Eyüp Camii. If one crosses the court and takes the inner of the two roads parallel with the Golden Horn, one soon comes to the second group of buildings that make Eyüp illustrious. The first, Kızıl Mescit, is perhaps hardly worth a visit though it has been reasonably well restored. Built in 1581 by Kiremitçi Süleyman Çelebi, it is of the simplest type, a rectangular room of stone and brick with a tiled roof and a brick minaret. A little farther on, on the opposite side of the street stands the mosque of Silahi Mehmet Bey, also of the simplest type but nearly a century older than the other and with a fascinating minaret. This is hexagonal in shape, built of stone and brick and without a balcony, but instead a sort of lantern with six windows and a tall conical cap. There are in the city three or four other minarets with this lantern arrangement, but this is much the most striking and pretty.

THE COMPLEX OF ZAL MAHMUT PAŞA

Opposite Silahi is the grandest and most interesting mosque in Eyüp, that of Zal Mahmut Paşa, a mature but unique work of Sinan. Its date of construction is unknown; that usually given, 1551, is at least 20 years too early, and a date in the mid 1570s seems most probable. Zal was a rather unsavoury character: when in 1553 Süleyman had his son Mustafa put to death, it was Mahmut (who got his forename Zal from that of a Persian hero famous for his Herculean strength) who finally overcame the young prince's resistance and strangled him. Later he married the Princess Şah Sultan, sister of Selim the Sot, as a reward, it is said, for having smoothed that prince's path to the throne by the elimination of his brother. In 1580, Zal and his wife died in a single night.

A fine view of the south façade of the building may be had from the garden of Silahi Camii which is a little higher. With its four tiers of windows and its great height and squareness it looks more like a palace than a mosque. The north façade is even more towering, for the mosque is built on a slope and supported on vaulted substructures in which rooms for the lower medrese have been made. The mosque is constructed of alternate courses of stone and brick. A handsome porch of five bays gives access to the interior. This is a vast rectangular room; the massive dome arches spring on the east from supports in the wall itself, on the west from thick and rather stubby pillars some distance in from the west wall; galleries supported on a rather heavy arcade, some of whose arches are of the ogive type, run round three sides. The walls, which rise in a rectangle to the full height of the dome drum, are pierced with many windows and in spite of the width of the galleries provide plenty of light. The general effect of the interior is perhaps a little heavy but nonetheless grand and impressive: and it is quite different from that of any other mosque.

The leaves of the main entrance door are fine inlaid work in wood, as are the mimber and mahfil in carved marble. The only other remaining decoration is some excellent faience in the mihrab; perhaps there was once more tile work which has perished, for Evliya tells us that "architectural ornaments and decorations are nowhere lavished in so prodigal a way as here"; and he calls it "the finest of all the mosques in the Ottoman empire built by vezirs," and adds: "the architect Sinan in this building displayed his utmost art." The mosque was for many years in a state of near ruin but has now been very well restored.

The complex includes two medreses, like the mosque itself built of stone and brick, one round three sides of the main courtyard, the other on a lower level to the north, enclosing two sides of the türbe garden. They are both extremely picturesque and irregular in design. In the upper medrese most of the south side consists of a building without a portico, which looks rather like an imaret and may perhaps have served as one. The dershane is not in the centre of the west wall but has been shifted to near the north end, and the last arches of the portico on this side are smaller than the others. There is no obvious reason for any of these abnormalities but they have a certain charm, enhanced by the ogive arches of the arcade. At the north-east corner a long flight of steps leads down to the garden of the türbe. The lower medrese partly encloses two sides of it. It is an octagonal building of the usual type in which are buried Zal and his wife.

A door in the east wall of the türbe garden leads to another külliye of a very different type, one of the most delightful of the smaller baroque complexes. It consists of an elaborate türbe and mektep with a sebil on the street and a çeşme in the garden. It was built at the end of the eighteenth century by Şah Sultan, a sister of Selim III.

The undulating façades of the türbe and the amusing turned back staircase of the mektep are very charming.

One now returns to the inner street along which there are two or three buildings that are worth at least a glance. One comes first to the small mosque of Cezari Kasım Paşa, erected in 1515. It has a pretty porch with four handsome antique columns of red granite, and the balcony of the minaret is supported on an unusual zigzag corbel. A little further down the street is the mosque of the Defterdar (Lord High Treasurer) Mahmut Efendi; it is also ancient in foundation, but wholly rebuilt in the eighteenth century and of little interest in itself. In the garden is the founder's curious open türbe with a dome supported on arches with scalloped soffits.

This completes our stroll to Eyüp, after which we walk back to the iskele to take a ferry back along the Golden Horn to the Galata Bridge.

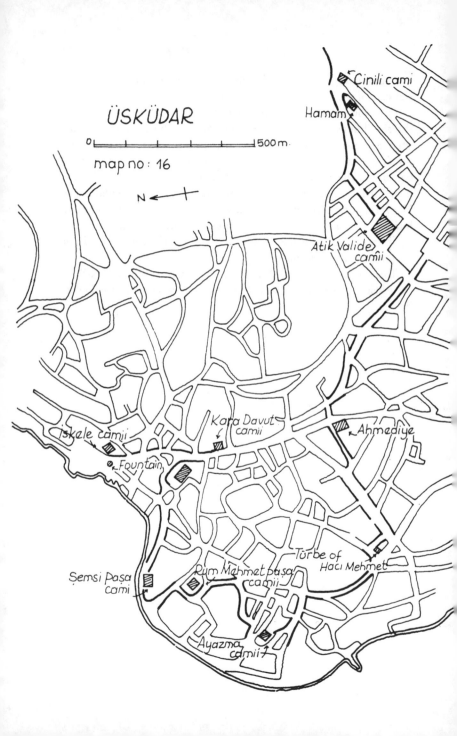

ÜSKÜDAR

0 |——|——|——|——| 500 m.

map no: 16

N ←—+

Çinili cami

Hamam

Atik Valide camii

Kara Davut camii

Ahmediye

İskele camii

Fountain

Türbe of Hacı Mehmet

Şemsi Paşa cami

Rum Mehmet paşa camii

Ayazma camii

19

Üsküdar and the Princes' Islands

Visitors to Istanbul sometimes forget that an important part of the city is located in another continent, across the way in Asia. The most interesting of these Anatolian suburbs from the point of view of historical monuments is Üsküdar, which lies directly opposite the mouth of the Golden Horn.

Üsküdar was anciently known as Chrysopolis, the City of Gold, founded by the Athenians under Alcibiades in 409 B.C. Chrysopolis was in antiquity a suburb of the neighbouring and more important town of Chalcedon, the modern Kadıköy, now itself a suburb of the great city across the strait. According to tradition, Chalcedon was founded in about 687 B.C., two decades before the original settlement of Byzantium. Chrysopolis, because of its fine natural harbour and its strategic location at the head of the strait, began to develop rapidly and later surpassed Chalcedon in size and importance. Chrysopolis became the starting place for the great Roman roads which led from Byzantium into Asia and was a convenient jumping-off place for military and commercial expeditions into Anatolia. Throughout the Byzantine period it was a suburb of Constantinople and thus had much the same history as the capital. Its site was not well-suited for defence, however, and it was on several occasions occupied and destroyed by invading armies while Constantinople remained safe behind its great walls. For this reason there are no monuments from the Byzantine period remaining there. The town was taken by the Turks in the middle of the fourteenth century, more than 100 years before the fall of Constantinople. (The Byzantine name Scutari, of which the modern Turkish Üsküdar is merely a corruption, dates from the twelfth century and derives from the imperial palace of Scutarion, which was at the point of land near Leander's

Tower. This has vanished, as have all other traces of Byzantine Chrysopolis.)

During the Ottoman Empire several members of the royal family, particularly the Sultan Valides, adorned Üsküdar with splendid mosques and pious foundations, most of which are still to be seen there today. Many great and wealthy Osmanlıs built their mosques, palaces and konaks there too, preferring the quieter and more serene environment of Üsküdar to the tumult of Stamboul. Time was, and not so long ago either, when Üsküdar had a charmingly rustic and rural atmosphere reminiscent of Ottoman days. Traces of this still remain, although modern progress is fast destroying old Üsküdar, as it is so much else in this lovely city.

We can reach Üsküdar either by passenger ferry from the Galata Bridge or by the smaller boats from Kabataş on the European shore of the lower Bosphorus. Either way we land at the iskele beside Iskele Meydanı, the great seaside square of Üsküdar, much of which occupies the site of the ancient harbour of Chrysopolis. In Ottoman days it was known as the Square of the Falconers and was the rallying place for the Sürre-i-Hümayun, the Sacred Caravan that departed for Mecca and Medina each year with its long train of pilgrims and its sacred white camel bearing gifts from the Sultan to the Şerif of Mecca.

ISKELE CAMİİ

The ferry-landing is dominated on the left by a stately mosque on a high terrace; it takes its name, Iskele Camii, from the ferry-landing itself. The mosque was built in 1547–8 by Sinan for Mihrimah Sultan, daughter of Süleyman the Magnificent and wife of the Grand Vezir Rüstem Paşa. The exterior is very imposing because of its dominant position high above the square and its great double porch, a curious projection from which covers a charming fountain. The interior is perhaps less satisfactory, for the central dome is supported by three instead of the usual two or four semidomes; this gives a rather truncated appearance which is not improved by the universal gloom. Perhaps it was the gloominess of this building which made Mihrimah insist on floods of light when, much later, she got Sinan to build her another mosque at the Edirne Gate. Of the other buildings of the külliye the medrese is to the north, a pretty building of the rectangular type, now used as a clinic; the primary school is behind the mosque built on sharply rising ground so that it has very picturesque supporting arches; it is now a children's library. On leaving the mosque terrace one finds at the foot of the steps the very handsome baroque fountain of Ahmet III, dated 1726.

Passing the fountain and entering the main street of Üsküdar we soon come on the left to a supermarket housed in the remains of an ancient hamam. The owner calls it Sinan Hamam Çarşısı, thus ascribing the bath to Sinan; this is probably not so though it certainly belongs to his time. It was a double hamam, but the main entrance chambers were destroyed when the street was widened.

A little farther on is an ancient and curious mosque built by Nişancı Kara Davut Paşa towards the end of the fifteenth century. It is a broad, shallow room divided into three sections by arches, each section having a dome, an arrangement unique in Istanbul.

YENİ VALİDE CAMİİ

Across the street and opening into the square is the large complex of Yeni Valide Camii, built between 1708 and 1710 by Ahmet III and dedicated to his mother the Valide Rabia Gülnüş Ümmetullah. At the corner is the Valide's charming open türbe like a large aviary, and next to it a grand sebil. On entering by the gate from the square one sees a very attractive wooden façade, a later addition, which is the entrance to the imperial loge. The mosque itself is in the classical style at its very last gasp and before the baroque influence had come to liven it up; it is a variation of the octagon-in-square theme; the tiles are late and insipid. Walking through the outer courtyard one comes to the main gate, over which is the mektep, and outside the gate stands the large imaret with a later, fully baroque, çeşme at the corner.

ŞEMSİ PAŞA CAMİİ

Taking the street opposite the main gate and turning left, then right, one reaches the precincts of one of Sinan's most delightful smaller külliyes, that of Şemsi Paşa, which attracts the attention as one approaches Üsküdar by boat because of its picturesqueness and the whiteness of its stone, just at the water's edge. Built by Sinan for the Vezir Şemsi Paşa in 1580, the mosque is of the simplest type: a square room covered by a dome with conches as squinches. Şemsi's türbe opens into the mosque itself, from which it is divided merely by a green grille, a most unusual and pretty feature. The well proportioned medrese forms two sides of the courtyard, while the third side consists of a wall with grilled windows opening directly onto the quay and the Bosphorus. The külliye has been beautifully restored in recent years.

RUM MEHMET PAŞA CAMİİ

The walk along this quay to the south is very pleasant and brings one in a short time to an ancient mosque halfway up a low hill to the left. This is the mosque of Rum Mehmet Paşa, built in 1471. In its present state, part of it badly restored, it is not a very attractive building, but it has some interesting and unusual features. Of all the early mosques it is the most Byzantine in external appearance: the high cylindrical drum of the dome; the exterior cornice following the curve of the round-arched windows; the square dome base broken by the projection of the great dome arches; and several other features suggest a strong Byzantine influence, perhaps connected with the fact that Mehmet Paşa was a Greek who became one of Fatih's vezirs. Internally the mosque has a central dome with smooth pendentives and one semidome to the east like Atik Ali Paşa Camii, but here the side chambers are completely cut off from the central area. Behind the mosque is Mehmet Paşa's gaunt türbe.

AYAZMA CAMİİ

If one leaves the mosque precinct by the back gate and follows the winding street outside, keeping firmly to the right, one comes before long to an imposing baroque mosque known as Ayazma Camii. Built in 1760–1 by Sultan Mustafa III and dedicated to his mother, the Valide Sultan Mihrişah Emine, it is one of the more successful of the baroque mosques, especially on the exterior. A handsome entrance portal opens onto a courtyard from which a pretty flight of semicircular steps leads up to the mosque porch; on the left is a large cistern and beyond an elaborate two-storeyed colonnade gives access to the imperial loge. The upper structure is also diversified with little domes and turrets, and many windows give light to the interior. The interior, as generally in baroque mosques, is less successful, though the grey marble gallery along the entrance wall, supported by slender columns, is effective.

Leaving by the south gate and following the street to the east, one comes to a wider street, Doğancılar Caddesi, with two pretty baroque çeşmes at the intersection; turning right one finds at the end of this street a severely plain türbe built by Sinan for Hacı Mehmet Paşa, who died in 1559. It stands on an octagonal terrace bristling with tombstones and overshadowed by a dying terebinth tree.

AHMEDİYE COMPLEX

The wide street just ahead leads downhill past a little park; the third turning on the right followed immediately by one on the left leads to an elaborate and delightful külliye, the Ahmediye mosque and medrese. Built in 1722 by Eminzade Hacı Ahmet Paşa, comptroller of the Arsenal under Ahmet III, it is perhaps the last ambitious building complex in the classical style, though verging towards the baroque. Roughly square in layout, it has the porticoes and cells of the medrese along two sides; the library, one entrance portal, and the mosque occupy a third side, while the fourth has the main gate complex with the dershane above and a graveyard alongside; but the whole plan is very irregular because of the alignment of streets and the rising ground. The dome of the little mosque is supported by scallop-shell squinches and has a finely carved marble mimber and kürsü. But the library and the dershane over the two gates are the most attractive features of the complex and show great ingenuity of design. The whole külliye ranks with those of Bayram Paşa and Amcazade Hüseyin Paşa as among the most charming and inventive in the city.

We leave the Ahmediye by the main gate at the south-east corner of the courtyard, where a stairway under the dershane takes us to the street below. A short, narrow street opposite the outer gate soon leads to a wider avenue, Toptaşı Caddesi, where we turn right. We follow

ATİK VALİDE KÜLLİYESİ

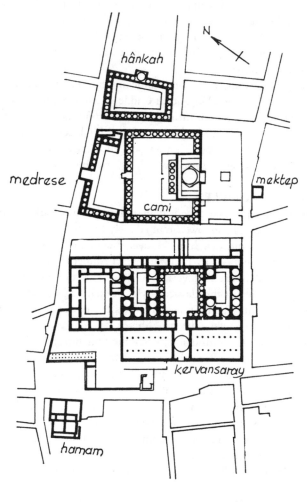

hânkah

medrese

mektep

cami

kervansaray

hamam

0 ⊦⊦⊦⊦⊦ 40m.

plan no: 27

this avenue for about 600 metres as it winds its way uphill. Then, towards the top of the hill and somewhat to the left we see the great mosque which dominates the skyline of Üsküdar, Atik Valide Camii.

ATİK VALİDE COMPLEX

The great külliye of Atik Valide Camii was built by Sinan in 1583 for Nurbanu Sultan, wife of Selim II and mother of Murat III. This is the most splendid and extensive of all Sinan's constructions in Istanbul with the sole exception of the Süleymaniye. In addition to the mosque itself, the külliye consists of a medrese, a hospital, an imaret, a tabhane a dar-ül hadis, a dar-ül kura, a mektep, a kervansaray, a hamam and a hânkah, or dervish hospice; all these buildings are still in existence, though some have not been restored and are not open to the public.

We enter the precinct by an alley beside the graveyard behind the mosque and find ourselves in one of the most beautiful of all the mosque courtyards, a grandly proportioned cloister with domed porticoes supported on marble columns; in the centre are the şadırvan and many ancient plane trees and cypresses. The mosque is entered through an elaborate double porch, the outer one with a penthouse roof, the inner domed and with handsome tiled inscriptions over the windows. Inside one finds a wide rectangular room with a central dome supported by a hexagonal arrangement of pillars and columns; to north and south are side aisles each with two domed bays; the aisles were added at a later date and although on a close examination the arrangement leads to certain anomalies, the general impression is very attractive. There are galleries round three sides of the room and the wooden ceilings under some of them preserve that rich painting typical of the period: floral and arabesque designs in black, red and gold. The mihrab is in a square projecting apse entirely revetted in magnificent tiles of the best Iznik period; note also the window-frames of deep red conglomerate marble with shutters richly inlaid with mother-of-pearl. The mihrab and mimber are fine works in carved marble.

The medrese of the complex stands at a lower level than the mosque and is entered by a staircase in the west wall of the courtyard.

Its own courtyard is almost as pretty as that of the mosque itself and is oddly irregular, having five domed bays to the south but only three to the north. The dershane is in the centre of the west side in the axis of the mosque though at an obtuse angle to it, and it projects over the street below which passes under it through an archway. If one leaves the medrese by the gate in the south side, one can walk round the building and pass under this picturesque arch. At the next corner beyond it stands the large hânkah, or dervish hospice, also highly irregular in plan but quite as attractive as the other buildings. These various irregularities are partly due to the alignment of pre-existing streets and the varying level of the terrain, but were perhaps courted by Sinan to give variety and liveliness to his design, for he could quite easily have avoided them if he had chosen.

The mektep is across the street to the south of the mosque. Across the street to the west of the mosque are the imaret, tabhane, dar-ül hadis, dar-ül kurra and kervansaray, none of which are open to the public. The hamam, which has been restored and is once again in use, is two blocks west of the medrese and on the same street. One hopes that all of the buildings of that Atik Valide külliye will be restored and opened to the public, for it is certainly one of the half-dozen most impressive monuments of Ottoman architecture not only in the city but anywhere in the country.

ÇİNİLİ CAMİİ

The street to the east of Atik Valide leads after a walk of about one kilometre to Çinili Camii, a small complex by another Valide Sultan, Kösem, mother of Murat IV and the mad Ibrahim, built at the beginning of the latter's reign in 1640. The mosque, in a pretty garden filled with flowers and trees, is small and simple: a square room covered by a dome, but it has both on the façade and in the interior a revetment of tiles (hence its name, *çinili* = tiled) just after the best period, but still quite fine, chiefly pale blue and turquoise on a white ground. The mimber of white marble has its carving very prettily picked out in gold, red and green, and its conical roof is tiled. The porch of the mosque is a baroque addition, as is the minaret, of which the şerefe has a corbel of very pretty folded-back acanthus leaves, such as we have seen nowhere else. In the precinct is a very fine şadırvan with a huge witch's cap for a roof, and a tiny medrese triangular in shape sloping headlong down hill. Just outside the precinct is a handsome mektep, and not far off a large hamam also belongs to the foundation.

The street outside the mosque, Çavuş Dere Caddesi, winds downhill and in about a mile leads one back to Iskele Meydanı.

There are many interesting and pleasant excursions to be made in the environs of Üsküdar, for, as Evliya Çelebi informs us: "Üsküdar is surrounded on all sides with delightful walks." These places can easily be reached by bus or taxi from the Iskele Meydanı, or, if one is feeling really energetic, one could stroll to them through the town none of them is at any great distance.

CEMETERY OF KARACA AHMET

One walk for which Üsküdar is famous is that to the vast Turkish cemetery of Karaca Ahmet which covers the hills to the south-west towards Kadıköy. This rivals in extent and picturesqueness the cemeteries outside the walls of Stamboul and in Eyüp. Acre after acre is thick with cypress trees and with serried but topsy-turvy ranks of tombstones; here and there an old suterazi or water-control tower rivals the trees in height and gauntness. Many of the older tomb-stones are beautifully designed and carved, usually bearing elaborate obituary inscriptions, some of which are quite poetic and touching and others even irreverent and amusing. The stones are topped with representations of the headdresses of the deceased, from which we learn their sex and station. The tombstones of the men are surmounted with large stone turbans, whose variety exhibit the full range of the Ottoman civil, military and religious hierarchies; here and there we see the turban of a paşa, a dervish, a sipahi or a eunuch. Those of the women are decorated with floral designs in low relief and are crowned with archaic oriental hats or draped with simple shawls, feminine even though in stone. One could stroll for hours in this serene suburb of the dead.

BARRACKS AND MOSQUE OF SELİM III

At no great distance from the cemetery are the gargantuan barracks of Selim III. The barracks, a huge rectangle with very characteristic towers at the corners, are now chiefly famous as the scene of Florence Nightingale's ministrations during the Crimean War. They were originally erected in wood by Selim III to house the new troops he hoped would quell and take the place of the Janissaries. Later they were partly rebuilt in stone by Mahmut II after he had in fact liquidated that rebellious corps; and later still the rest was done in stone by Abdül Mecit. They are still used by the military; the general public can visit the little museum in the tower where Florence Nightingale lived when she was running the hospital.

Opposite the main entrance to the barracks is the mosque that Selim III built for his new corps of soldiers. Built in A.H. 1209 (A.D. 1803–4), it is the last and one of the handsomest of the pure baroque mosques. Not only are its proportions and details most attractive, but it is placed in an exceptionally lovely garden with three of the finest plane trees in the city. The interior as usual is a little stark, though of impressive proportions. The western gallery, the mihrab and the mimber are all of highly polished (too highly polished) grey marble and give the place a certain charm. A short distance to the south of the Selimiye barracks we find the British Crimean cemetery.

ÇAMLICA

In describing the excursions in the neighbourhood of Üsküdar, Evliya tells us that "the most celebrated walk of all is that of Great Camlıca, where a kiosk was built by the present monarch (Mehmet IV), the chronograph of which was composed by me, poor Evliya." The Great Çamlıca stands about four kilometres east of Iskele Meydanı and can be reached by the main highway leaving Üsküdar in that direction. It is the taller of the twin peaks of Mount Bulgurlu, the highest point in the vicinity of Istanbul (267 metres above sea level). There is no trace of the imperial kiosk mentioned by poor Evliya, its place being taken by a large teahouse and café in the midst of the pine grove which gives the peak its name (*cam* = pine). From here there is an absolutely magnificent view, which makes it well worth the climb. In the morning when the sun is still easterly one has a clear panoramic view of the whole city: the Bosphorus almost as far as the Black Sea, the Marmara with the Princes' Islands, and behind that the great snow-covered peak of Ulu Dağ, the Bithynian Olympos. Towards evening the sun sets almost directly behind Stamboul and its domes and minarets are silhouetted against the flaming western sky.

KIZ KULESİ

One of the most familiar sights in Istanbul is perhaps the one least visited. This is Kız Kulesi, the Maiden's Tower, which stands on a tiny islet a few hundred metres off Üsküdar. Its Turkish name is derived from the legend concerning a princess who was confined there by her father to protect her from the fate foretold by a dire prophecy: that she would die from the bite of a serpent. Needless to say, the princess was eventually bitten by the serpent, smuggled out to the islet in a basket of grapes. In English the place is usually called Leander's Tower, in the mistaken notion that Leander drowned there in his attempt to swim the strait to see his lover Hero, which legendary tragedy actually occurred near Abydos in the Dardanelles. According to Nicetas Choniates, the Emperor Manuel I Comnenus in the twelfth century built a small fortress here to which he attached one end of the chain with which he closed the strait, the other end being attached to the Tower of Mangana below the acropolis. Since then it has been used as a lighthouse, semaphore station, quarantine, customs control point and home for retired naval officers. The present building dates from the eighteenth century. It has recently been rebuilt and now houses a restaurant and café.

THE PRINCES' ISLANDS

The most famous of all the beauty spots in the vicinity of Istanbul are the Princes' Islands, the little suburban archipelago just off the Asian coast of the Marmara. The isles are about an hour's sail by ferry from the Galata Bridge, though in spirit they seem at a far greater remove than that, so different are they from the rest of the city in atmosphere and appearance.

During Byzantine times the islands were inhabited only by fishermen and by the monks and nuns in the monasteries and convents that had been founded there, most of which at one time or another housed emperors, empresses and patriarchs who had been exiled to the islands. It is only since the latter half of the nineteenth century that the Princes' Islands have become fashionable as resorts and places to bathe and picnic. Before that they were sparsely inhabited and rarely visited. But their picturesqueness and their rather grim historical associations appealed to the romantic imagination of the nineteenth century. This aspect of the islands is well preserved in a purple passage at the beginning of Gustave Schlumberger's charming book *Les Isles des Princes:*

> Naples has its Capri and its Ischia; Constantinople has its Princes' Islands. The Neapolitan is not more proud of the jewels which adorn his bay than is the Greek of Pera of his charming islands, places of repose and pleasure, that raise their enchanting silhouettes at the entrance to the Sea of Marmara. Just as the crimes of Tiberius almost as much as the splendours of nature have made Capri famous, so the gloomy adventures of emperors, empresses, and all the exiles of high rank, relegated to the convents of Proti, Antigone, and Prinkipo as a result of the revolutions with which the history of Byzantium bristles, have made these radiant islands one of the most tragic sites of the ancient world... Add to these moving souvenirs the fact that this archipelago in miniature possesses beauties designed to ravish an eye sated with the marvels of Italy and Sicily; that nowhere does the delighted eye repose on coasts more lovely, on a bay more gracious, on mountainous distances more grandiose; that nowhere is the verdure fresher or more varied; that nowhere in short do bluer waters bathe more gently a thousand shady coves, a thousand poetic cliffs; you will then understand why the Princes' Islands, bedewed of yore with so many tears, vaunted today with so much praise, are a favourite place of pilgrimage for all those who are attracted by the study of a dramatic past or the charm of a smiling present.

Unfortunately, the souvenirs of the past so poetically evoked by Schlumberger must be supplied by the imagination – or by that scholar's fascinating essay – for the islands preserve almost no relics of antiquity: the convent cells bedewed with tears have vanished without a trace or survive only in a crumbling wall, a half-buried cistern. The beauties of nature, however, remain, though they are fast being encroached upon by summer villas and camping sites, especially in Prinkipo; but the smaller islands and the more outlying parts of that one are still as lovely as Schlumberger describes them.

The little archipelago consists of nine islands, four of them of a certain size, the rest tiny. Ferries stop in turn at the four principal isles, the closest of which is Kınalı, known to the Greeks as Proti, followed by Burgaz (Antigoni), Heybeliada (Halki) and finally Büyükada (Prinkipo), the largest and most populous of the isles. During the summer months there is a ferry from Büyükada to Sedef. There are a few summer residents on Kaşıkadası (Pita), but Tavşanadası (Neandros), Yassıada (Plati) and Sivriada (Oxia) are uninhabited. Except for a few municipal vehicles, only faytons, or horse-drawn carriages, are used on Büyükada, Heybeliada and Burgaz, while not even those are allowed on Kınalı.

The nearest of the large islands is some 15 kilometres from the city; it is appropriately called Proti (First) by the Greeks. Its Turkish name is Kınalı, Dyed-with-Henna, because of the reddish colour of its cliffs along the shore. It is a rather barren island, but the village is very pretty and next to it there is a pebble beach. The house at #23 Fazıl Ahmet Aykaç Caddesi was the home of the famous Armenian composer Gomidas during the years 1909–13. The island has always had an Armenian community, though here and on the other three large islands the great majority of the year-round residents are Muslim Turks, with small Greek communities on Burgaz, Heybeliada and Büyükada, where there is also a Jewish community. In times past the islands were predominately Greek. The Armenian church, dedicated to St. Gregory the Illuminator, was founded in 1857; the present building is the result of a complete reconstruction in 1998. The Greek church, dedicated to the Birth of the All Holy Mother of God, was founded in 1886. When the foundations of the present church were being built a number of ancient architectural fragments were unearthed, and two of these are now arrayed in the forecourt, including a sixth-century capital similar to those in Haghia Sophia. It is possible that these belonged to a Byzantine monastery that stood on this site.

There is a Greek monastery dedicated to the Transfiguration of Christ on the peak of one of the island's three hills, Manastir Tepesi. This was built in the Ottoman period on the site of a Byzantine monastery of the same name. Three Byzantine emperors spent their last days in exile in this monastery after they were deposed: Michael I Rhangabe (r. 811–13), Romanus I Lecapenus (r. 919–44) and Romanus IV Diogenes (r. 1067–71).

The second large island is called Burgaz by the Turks (from the Greek *pyrgos* = tower), on account of an ancient watchtower on its summit that is mentioned by travellers as late as the beginning of the eighteenth century. The Byzantines called it Panormos or later – and still today – Antigone. It is about the same size as Kınalı but much more fertile and well-wooded, and thus more pleasant to wander about on.

The village is quite pretty and there are a number of fine houses of the late Ottoman and early Republican eras. The house at #15 Çayır Aralığı Sokağı was in the years 1934–54 the house of the famous writer Sait Faik Abasıyanık, and it is now open as a museum dedicated to his memory.

The most prominent monument in the village is the Greek church of St. John the Baptist, built in 1899. The church is believed to stand on the site of a Byzantine monastery of the same name. This was the monastery where St. Methodius Confessor, Patriarch of Constantinople (r. 842–6), was exiled by Michael II in the years 822–9 because of his opposition to the emperor's policy of iconoclasm. The crypt beneath the present church of St. John is dedicated to St. Methodius, for this is where he is believed to have been imprisoned during his exile on the island.

The Greek monastery of St. George Karyptis is on the northern shore of the island, approached along Gönüllü Caddesi. Although the monastery is believed to have been founded in the Byzantine era, the earliest reference to it is in the second half of the seventeeenth century. This was when the Greek innkeepers of Istanbul decided to restore and maintain the monastery, which apparently had fallen into ruins. The present dormitory was erected in 1858–9, while the church was erected in 1897. There are ancient architectural fragments which would appear to have been part of the original monastery, including a capital in the courtyard and part of an architrave set into the entryway of the enclosure.

The site of the Byzantine monastery of the Transfiguration of Christ is on the summit of Hristos Tepesi, the Hill of Christ. Greek tradition has it that the monastery was founded by Basil I the Macedonian (r. 867–76), and there is evidence of a decree by Manuel I Comnenus granting its rights as a monastery in 1158. The earliest reference to the monastery after the Conquest is by Petrus Gyllius in 1547. All that remains today is an abandoned church built in 1869 and a two-storey building erected in the eighteenth century, along with the ruins of earlier structures. Inside the entrance to the enclosure there are a number of ancient architectural fragments, including four beautifully carved Byzantine capitals.

Just opposite the landing-stage at Burgaz is a tiny island called Kaşık, or Spoon, because of its shape. Its Greek name is Pita, or Piece of Bread. It is the smallest isle of the Princes' Islands and its highest point is a mere 18 metres above sea level. It has no known history, and it was the only isle in the archipelago that did not have a monastery in Byzantine times. It was virtually uninhabited up until recent times, but now a number of summer houses have been built on it.

Some little distance off to the west of Burgaz lie the two small outlying islands of the group, Sivriada, known in Greek as Oxya, and Yassıada, Plate in Greek. The Turkish and Greek names are descriptive and mean the same thing in each case – the Pointed and the Flat. Both islands are uninhabited; they can be reached by hiring a boat on Burgaz.

Sivri is nothing but a tall craggy reef rising to a height of 90 metres, taller than any of the Seven Hills of Constantinople. The south-eastern part of the island was used as a quarry to provide stone for the new Kadıköy pier and breakwater, and as a result that side of the hill has been gouged away. Beside the landing-stage you can see the substantial remains of a Byzantine monastery. This is mentioned in the list of monasteries compiled in 1158 by Manuel I Comnenus. The monastery had two churches: a katholikon of the Archangel Michael and a chapel dedicated to a number of martyr saints. The island's chief fame in more recent times stems from the fact that on several occasions all the wild dogs of Istanbul were rounded up and exiled there where they soon ate each other up.

Yassıada, as its name implies, is relatively flat, with a maximum elevation of 40 metres. It too had a monastery, founded, according to tradition, in the mid-ninth century by St. Ignatius, twice Patriarch of Constantinople. The monastery is mentioned in the list compiled in 1158 by Manuel I Comnenus, who noted that it had a katholikon dedicated to the Forty Martyrs and also a chapel of the Virgin. Ernest Mamboury, in his 1943 guide to the Princes' Islands, reports that he found remnants of one of these churches, whose ruins now seem to have vanished. Directly above the landing stage we see the folly that Murray's *Handbook* of 1892 quaintly describes as "a dilapidated Anglo-Saxon castle", built by Sir Henry Bulwer, English ambassador to the Sublime Porte and brother of the novelist Bulwer-Lytton; here he is popularly supposed to have indulged in nameless orgies. To the right of this we see one of the buildings erected for the trial of the deposed Turkish Prime Minister Adnan Menderes and several of his associates. After a lengthy trial they were convicted, whereupon on the night of 16–17 September 1961 Menderes and two of his ministers were hanged on Imralı, an island off to the south-west in the Sea of Marmara. Other abandoned buildings on Yassıada were structures erected in the 1960s for a short-lived military school.

The third of the large islands is nowadays called Heybeliada, Saddle-Bag Island, from its shape; anciently it was known as Chalkitis or Halki, from the famous copper mines mentioned by Aristotle. The island has (or had) two important schools of rather different sorts. The elder, which was closed by the government in 1971, was the principal theological seminary of the Greek Orthodox Church, housed in modern buildings among the remnants of the Monastery of the Holy Trinity, of Byzantine foundation, on an incomparable site in the saddle between the two summits of the northern hill. The younger, the Turkish Naval College, is chiefly at the water's edge near the landing stage, but also occupies the site of another Byzantine monastery on a hill to the west. This site preserves the only surviving Byzantine church in the Islands, and a very interesting one. Dedicated to the Blessed Virgin Kamariotissa, it is a tiny chapel of the quatrefoil or tetraconch variety, that is, with a central dome surrounded by four semidomes over exedrae, three of which project on the outside, the fourth being contained within the narthex. The other church of this plan in the city, that of St. Mary of the Mongols, has been completely wrecked by subsequent rebuilding, so that the present little chapel is the only example of its kind that more or less preserves its original plan. The chapel is attributed to Maria Comnena, third wife of John VIII Palaeologus and the last Empress of Byzantium. It was built some time between 1427 and 1439 and is thus the last known church to be erected in the city before the Turkish Conquest. The church remained in the possession of the Greek community up until 1942, when it was confiscated by the government. It is not generally open to the public, but permission to visit it may be obtained from the Commandant of the Naval School.

On the shore south of the village, just beyond the grounds of the Naval School, we see the monastery of Haghios Georgios tou Kremnou (St. George on the Cliff). The setting is quite beautiful, with pines, cypresses and other trees embowering the picturesque buildings of the monastery above the blue Marmara. The monastery is believed to have been founded in the years 1586–93; it is still functioning, though with only one or two monks in residence.

There is another monastery on the south-west coast of the island, that of St. Spyridon. This little monastery was founded in 1868 and restored in 1968 by the then Patriarch, Athenagoras. The katholikon of the monastery remains in use, though services are held there only occasionally. There are the remnants of still another monastery, that of the Metamorphosis of Christ the Saviour, on the peak known as Baltacıoğlu Tepesi at the south-eastern end of the island. This was founded in 1835; all that remains today is a small chapel and an attached house, both embowered in a picturesque setting on the hilltop.

The Greek church of St. Nicholas dominates the main square in the village. It was erected in 1857 on the ruins of a Byzantine church dedicated to St. Nicholas, the patron of mariners, appropriate for an island where in times past virtually all of the men were seafarers or fishermen.

The house at #7 Refah Şehitler Caddesi is now a museum dedicated to the memory of Ismet Inönü, the first prime minister of the Turkish Republic and later president of Turkey. The house at #19 Demirtaş Sokağı is a house museum honouring Hüseyin Rahmi Gürpınar, the renowned journalist, essayist and novelist.

We come at last to the largest of the islands, Büyükada, the Greek Prinkipo. This is the only one most people visit and is the summer resort *par excellence*. Its rapidly expanding village has a large number of attractive residences surrounded by well-kept gardens, several good hotels and a very posh country-club, the Anadolu Club. Some of the grandest of the mansions are along Çankaya Caddesi, including the Fabiato Köşkü, built in 1878 and restored in 1997 by Çelik Gülersoy of the Turkish Touring and Automobile as the Büyükada Cultural Centre, with a café-restaurant. The Iliasko Yalı Köşkü at the foot of Hamlacı Sokağı was during the years 1929–33 the home of Leon Trotsky when he was living in exile on Büyükada, and it was here that he wrote his autobiography and began his *History of the Russian Revolution*.

There are two Greek churches in the village. The church of the Dormition of the Mother of God was first erected on its present site in 1735 and was renovated in 1871. The church of St. Dimitrios was built in 1856–60. When the foundations were being laid workers found a relief monogram of the emperor Justin II (r. 565–78), who built a palace and monastery on the island in 569. It is from Justin that the island took its name Prinkipo, the Isle of the Prince.

Once you get out of the built-up area you find lovely pine groves and other forests, wild cliffs plunging down to the sea, and sandy coves for bathing. But in summer the island is really too crowded; the best time for a visit is early spring or late autumn, or on those magical warm and sunny days that occur here from time to time in the depth of winter: then the island is really perfect, for you have the amenities of civilization without the people.

The island consists of two large hills separated in the middle by a broad valley, so that the road around it makes a figure eight. You can make the tour by fayton, the Büyük, or Grand Tour, going all the way round the island and the Küçük, or Short Tour, going around the northern half. From the road that crosses the island between the hills, foot paths lead up on either side to the monasteries which crown each. The Monastery of the Transfiguration on the north hill, Isa Tepesi, or the Hill of Christ, is in the depths of a pine forest. The original monastery is mentioned in the list compiled in 1159 by Manuel I Comnenus, and the first mention of it after the Conquest is in 1597; the katholikon of the present monastery is due to a complete rebuilding in 1869.

On the southern hill, Yiice Tepe, is the more famous monastery of St. George Koudonas; situated at almost the highest point of the island, 202 metres above the sea. According to tradition, the monastery was founded during the reign of Nicephorus II Phocas (r. 963–9), and it is mentioned in the list compiled in 1158 by Manuel I Comnenus. The present complex includes, besides the monastery itself, six separate churches and chapels on different levels, the older ones being on the lowest levels. The monastery celebrates the feast-day of St. George on 23 April, when many thousands of pilgrims make their way to the hilltop, some of them walking barefoot, tying talismans to the branches of the bushes and trees along the way. Many of them have lunch at the little outdoor restaurant beside the monastery drinking the rough red wine made by the monks, in a setting reminiscent of the Aegean isles.

The great block of monastic buildings on the western side has a pretty courtyard with galleries along one side; at the back it plunges dramatically into the valley below and looks from there like a fortress. From here one can look out across the sea to the remaining islands of the group. To the west is tiny Sedef Adası, the Island of the Pearl, known in Byzantium as Antherovitos. To the south we see the uninhabited little crag called Tavşan Adası, Rabbit Island, known anciently as Neandros. Both of these islets once had their monasteries, of which now only a few scattered stones remain. A number of summer villas have in recent years been built on Sedef, but Neandros is inhabited only by sea-birds, who can be seen in their thouands perched on the cliffs on the southern end of the island.

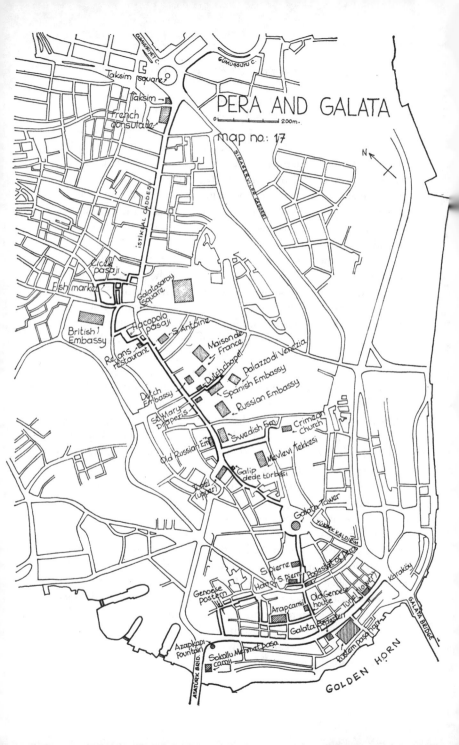

20

Pera and Galata

The historic origins of Pera and Galata are as remote in time as that of Constantinople itself.

From very early times there had been settlements and communities along the northern shores of the Golden Horn; Byzas himself is said to have erected a temple there to the hero Amphiaraus. The most important of these communities, Sykai, the Figtrees, where Galata now stands, was already in the fifth century A.D. included as the VIIIth Region, Regio Sycaena, of the city of Constantinople itself: it had churches, a forum, baths, a theatre, a harbour and a protecting wall. In 528 Justinian restored its theatre and wall and called it grandiloquently after himself Justinianae, a name which was soon forgotten. Towards the end of the same century, Tiberius II (r. 578–82) is said to have built a fortress to guard the entrance to the Golden Horn, from which a chain could be stretched to the opposite shore to close its mouth against enemy shipping; some substructures of this still exist at Yer Altı Camii near the Galata Bridge (see Chapter 21). The name, Sykai, continued in use until, in the ninth century, the name Galata began to supplant it, at first for a small district only, later for the whole region. The derivation of the name Galata is unknown, though that of the other apellation, Pera, is quite straightforward. In Greek *pera* means "beyond", at first in the general sense of "on the other side of the Golden Horn", later restricted to medieval Galata, and still later to the heights above. In the past generation these old Greek names have been supplanted by new Turkish ones; Pera is now known officially as Beyoğlu and Galata as Karaköy, but old residents of the town still refer to these quarters by their ancient names.

The town of Galata took its present form chiefly under the Genoese. After the reconquest of Constantinople from the Latins in 1261, the Byzantine emperors granted the district to the Genoese as a semi-independent colony with its own *podesta* or governor, appointed by the senate of Genoa. Although they were expressly forbidden to fortify the colony, they almost immediately did so and went on expanding its area and fortifications for more than 100 years. Sections of these walls with some towers and gates still exist and will be described later. After the Ottoman Conquest of 1453 the walls were partially destroyed and the district became the general European quarter of the city. Here the foreign merchants had their houses and their shops and here the ambassadors of the European powers built sumptuous embassies. For the rest, as Evliya Çelebi tells us, the inhabitants of Galata "are either sailors, merchants, or handicraftsmen, such as joiners and caulkers. They dress for the most part in the Algerine style, because a great number of them are Arabs and Moors. The Greeks keep the taverns; the Armenians are merchants and bankers; the Jews are negotiators in love matters and their youths are the worst of all the devotees of debauchery... The taverns are celebrated for the wine from Ancona, Sargossa, Mudanya, and Tenedos. When I passed through here, I saw many hundreds barefooted and bareheaded lying drunk in the streets." Even now, there are evenings in the back streets of Beyoğlu when the scene is much the same as Evliya described it three centuries ago.

As time went on the confines of Galata became too narrow and crowded and the embassies and the richer merchants began to move out beyond the walls to the hills and vineyards above. Here the foreign powers built palatial mansions surrounded by gardens, all of them standing along the road which would later be known as the Grand Rue de Pera. Nevertheless, the region must have remained to a large extent rural till well on into the eighteenth century; in that period one often sees reference to "les vignes de Pera". But as Pera became more and more built up, it fell a prey like the rest of the city to the endemic fires that ravage it periodically. Two especially devastating ones, in 1831 and 1871, destroyed nearly everything built before those dates. Hence the dearth of anything of much historic or architectural interest in Beyoğlu.

TAKSİM SQUARE

Taksim Square is the centre of Beyoğlu and thus the hub of the modern town. The square takes its name from the taksim, or water-distribution centre, which is housed in the handsome octagonal structure at the south-west corner of the area; this was built in 1732 by Sultan Mahmut I, and is the collection-point for the water that is brought into the city from the reservoirs in the Belgrade Forest. The statue group in the centre of the square commemorates the founding of the Turkish Republic in 1923; this was done in 1928 by the Italian sculptor Canonica. At the north-east corner of the square is the Atatürk Cultural Centre, one of the principal sites for cultural events produced during the annual International Istanbul Festival. The avenue that leaves the square from its south-east corner is Gümüşsuyu Caddesi, which leads downhill to the Bosphorus at Dolmabahçe, passing on its right side the stolid edifice of the German Embassy. (We shall continue to call these great buildings embassies, though, since the removal of the capital to Ankara they are used largely as consulates only; for they are really too grandiose to be described as consulates.)

CUMHURİYET CADDESİ AND THE MODERN CITY

The northern side of Taksim Square is bordered by the Public Gardens, on whose western side runs Cumhuriyet Caddesi, the avenue that leads to the various quarters of the modern city. The first of these is Harbiye, where a branch of the avenue passes the Military Museum, housed in the old Military School. Arrayed outside the museum are a splendid collection of ancient cannon, most of them captured by the Turks during the days when the Ottoman armies swept victoriously through southern Europe and the Middle East. Inside the museum there is an extraordinary collection of arms and other military objects from both Europe and Islam ranging in date from the early Ottoman period up to modern times, as well as other objects of considerable historic interest. At the Military Museum there are also performances of military music by the famous Mehtar Band, dressed in Ottoman costumes and playing old Turkish instruments, a very stirring spectacle.

An avenue branching off Cumhuriyet Caddesi to the right brings one to the Spor ve Sergi Sarayi (the Sport and Exhibition Palace), the Açık Hava Tiyatrosu (the Open-Air Theatre) and the Muhsin Ertuğrul Şehir Tiyatrosu (the City Theatre) which, together with the Opera House, form the centre of the city's cultural life.

ISTİKLAL CADDESİ

The avenue that leads off from the south-west corner of Taksim Square from the taksim itself is Istiklal Caddesi. This was formerly known as the Grand Rue de Pera, of which the Austrian historian Josef von Hammer once said: "It is as narrow as the comprehension of its inhabitants and as long as the tapeworm of their intrigues." The avenue has now been conveted into a pedestrian mall. The old trolley line has been re-established, running the full length of the avenue between Taksim and Tünel, with a stop halfway along at Galatasaray Meydanı.

Just beyond the taksim building and on the same side of the street is the old French Consulate (consulate, not embassy, which is farther on down the avenue); it is a building with a rather quaint courtyard originally constructed by the French in 1719 as a hospital for those suffering from the plague.

The streets leading off on either side from Istiklal Caddesi between Taksim and Galatasaray are lined with restaurants, cafés, bars and night clubs, for this district is the centre of Istanbul's night life, which has tremendously expanded in recent years, attracting celebrants from all over the world. Many of the buildings along the avenue date from the last-half-century of the Ottoman era, such as the Tokatlian Han, Cercle d'Orient, Atlas Cinema and Cité Roumelie. Halfway between Taksim and Galatasaray we see on the right the only mosque on the avenue, Ağa Camii. The first mosque on this site was founded in 1594–5 by Hüseyin Ağa, commander of the Janissary detachment at Galatasaray; this was rebuilt in 1834 and restored in 1936.

After a ten or 15 minute stroll from Taksim we come to Galatasaray Meydanı. The square takes its name from the Galatasaray Lisesi, whose ornate entrance we see on the left side of the avenue. Although the buildings of the lycée are modern (1908), Galatasaray is a venerable and distinguished institution. It was founded by Sultan Beyazit II around the end of the fifteenth century as a school for the imperial pages, anciliary to the one in Topkapı Sarayı. The school was reorganized in 1868 under Sultan Abdül Aziz as a modern lycée on the French model, with the instruction partly Turkish, partly in French. It is the oldest Turkish institution of learning in the city with a more or less continuous history; and for the past 100 years it has been the best as well as the most famous of Turkish lycées. A large proportion of the statesmen and intellectuals of Turkey have pursued their studies there and it has undoubtedly played a major role in the modernization of the country. It now has a university as well, situated on the Bosphorus near Beşiktaş.

On the opposite side of the avenue from the Lycée, a short distance before the square, we find a famous institution of quite another sort. One might easily pass it by, for it is just a little alley that leads off to the right from Istiklal Caddesi. This is the famous Çiçek Pasajı, the Passage of Flowers. The Passage goes through an edifice known as the Cité de Pera, a rococo structure erected in 1876 with a line of shops on the ground floor and luxury apartments above; notice the two splendid entrance portals, one on the main avenue and one on the side street. The Pasaj is lined with meyhanes, old-fashioned taverns where one can enjoy a tasty snack washed down with draft beer or rakı, the anise-flavoured intellect-deadenings national drink. At its inner end the Pasai opens into Şahne Şokağı, a street that leads from Istiklal Caddesi down through the Galatasaray Fish Market, one of the most colourful street-markets in the city.

Returning to Istiklal, we now turn off to the right at Galatasaray Meydanı and at the end of the first block we turn left on Meşrutiye Caddesi, passing on our right the old British Embassy. This is a handsome building in the Italian Renaissance style. It was originally designed by Sir Charles Barry, architect of the Houses of Parliament. But it was completed in 1845 by W. S. Smith along somewhat different lines. At the rear of the Embassy there is a magnificent and very English garden.

We continue along Meşrutiye Caddesi, which at the next corner turns half-left to bring us to the neighbourhood known as Tepebaşı

(Top of the Hill), where we have a sweeping view out over the Golden Horn to the old city. Along the crescent-shaped avenue we pass in turn two of the city's oldest hotels, both of them handsome neo-classical buildings of the late nineteenth century, first the Büyük Londra and then the Bristol. The Bristol Hotel has been superbly restored and is now the Pera Museum, celebrated for its collection of Orientalist paintings and other works of art. At the far end of the crescent we see on the right side of the avenue the famous Pera Palas Hotel, completed in 1893 by the French architect Alexandre Vallaury. The hotel is currently closed for renovation.

We now return to Galatasaray Meydanı and resume our stroll down the avenue. At the first corner on the right we see the Hacopulo Pasajı, a narrow alleyway that opens into a picturesque arcade surrounded by buildings of the mid-nineteenth century. Off the left side of the arcade we see the Greek church of the Presentation of the Virgin, dedicated in 1807 and rebuilt in 1855.

Returning to Istiklal, we turn right at the next corner into another little alleyway, Olivio Pasajı, which at its end brings us to the famous Rejans Lokantası. This is a Russian restaurant founded in the 1930s, famous for its borsch, chicken kievsky and lemon-flavoured vodka.

On the left side of the avenue we see a handsome Catholic church at the back of a large courtyard. This is the Franciscan church of St. Anthony of Padua, the largest Catholic church in the city. It was established on this site in 1725; the present building, a good example of Italian neo-Gothic in red brick, was designed by the architect Giulio Mongeri and completed in 1912. The impressive Art Nouveau building to the left of the church, the Mısır Apartman, or Egyptian Apartment, was built in 1910 for Abbas Halim Pasha of Egypt.

St. Anthony's is one of the churches that was built along the old Grand Rue de Pera along with the embassies of the European powers. The embassies in this part of old Pera, on or near the Grand Rue, belong to those powers which have had legations here since the early centuries of the Ottoman Empire. Though most of these buildings are relatively modern, the embassies themselves, especially those of Venice, France, England, Holland, Sweden and Russia, are of some historical interest. They were established more or less where they are now in the course of the sixteenth, seventeenth and eighteenth centuries, generally by grants of land bestowed by the sultans, and each formed the centre of its "Nation", as it was called, that is, of the community of resident merchants and officials of the various countries. These embassies came to play a greater and greater role in the destiny of the Ottoman Empire as its powers declined, and collectively they dominated the life of Pera until the establishment of the Turkish Republic. Near the embassies, various churches were established, more or less under their protection, and some of these survive in a modern form.

Taking the second turning on the left after St. Anthony's, we see on the right the Maison de France; it is situated in a fine French garden with views of the Bosphorus and the Marmara. Though one of the earliest embassies to be established in Pera towards the end of the sixteenth century, the present building dates only from soon after the fire of 1831. (It was on this site that the great Turkish astronomer, Takiuddin, built his observatory in the 1570s.)

The chapel connected with the embassy, that of St. Louis of the French, is the oldest in foundation of the Latin Churches in Pera, dating from 1581; though the present structure dates only from about 1831. Among the masses celebrated there every Sunday is one in the Chaldean rite. St. Louis is the local house of worship for the Chaldean Church, an eighteenth-century offshoot of the ancient Nestorian Church which is now in union with Rome. The members of this Church in Istanbul are all from the Hakkari section in the far south-east of Turkey and are descendants of the ancient Chaldean and Assyrian peoples; parts of the mass are still sung in Aramaic, the language which Christ would have spoken.

Continuing along Istiklal Caddesi on the same side of the street we come next to the Dutch Embassy, a very pretty building looking rather like a small French chateau. The present building was designed by the Fossati brothers and completed in 1855; the lower structure, visible from the garden, goes back two centuries or more in time. The original Embassy, built in 1612, was burned twice, but parts of the substructure of the earlier buildings were preserved and incorporated into the present Embassy.

The first turning on the left beyond the Embassy brings us to the Dutch Chapel, whose entrance is a short way down along the left. Since 1857 this building has housed the Union Church of Istanbul, an English-speaking congregation from many lands. The chapel dates from the late seventeenth or early eighteenth century, although the original chapel must go back to the founding of the Dutch Embassy. The basement rooms of the chapel, now used as a Sunday school, have in the past served as a prison. The building is basically a single massive barrel vault of heavy masonry; the brickwork of the façade, newly exposed to view, is especially fine.

A frequent visitor to the original Dutch Chapel in the early years of its existence was Cyril Lucaris, six times Patriarch of Constantinople and once of Alexandria. Influenced by his conversations with theologians connected with the Dutch Chapel, Lucaris in 1629 published his *Declaration of Faith,* in which he proclaimed his belief in the basic principles of Calvinism. This caused a scandal in the Greek Orthodox Church which eventually led to the Patriarch being denounced to Murat IV as a Russian spy. On 25 June 1638, Lucaris was executed by the Janissaries and his body thrown into the Marmara, thus bringing to an end the remarkable career of the man whom Pope Urban had called "the son of darkness and the athlete of hell."

A little farther down the street we pass on our right the former Spanish Embassy, now no longer functioning, with only the embassy chapel remaining in use. This chapel, dedicated to Our Lady of the Seven Sorrows, was originally founded in 1670; the present church dates from 1871.

Still farther down the street we come to the handsome Palazzo di Venezia, now the Italian Embassy. The present building dates from about 1695, though the Embassy itself was established here long before that. In the great old days this was the residence of the Venetian bailo, the ambassador of the Serene Republic of Venice and one of the most powerful of the foreign legates in the city. The Palazzo is large and imposing, its garden as typically Italian as that of the English Embassy is English. We learn from his *Memoirs* that Giacomo Casanova was a guest here in the summer of 1744; in his three months in the city this great lover made not a single conquest and was himself seduced by one Ismail Efendi.

Returning to Istiklal Caddesi we come next to the Franciscan church of St. Mary Draperis, down a flight of steps from the street level. The first church on this site was built in 1678 and the present structure dates from 1789. The parish itself, however, is a very ancient one, dating to the beginning of the year 1453 when the Franciscans built a church near the present site of Sirkeci Station. After the Conquest the Franciscans were forced to leave Constantinople, settling first in Galata and then later here in Pera. The Franciscans still preserve a miraculous icon of the Virgin which they claim to have taken with them from their first church in Constantinople.

Just past the church we come to the Russian Embassy; this was built in 1837 by the Fossati brothers who, a decade later, were to restore Haghia Sophia. The Fossati brothers had been for several years in Moscow as official architects to the Tsar, who sent them to Istanbul to build his new embassy; here they remained for 20 years or so as official architects to the Sultan.

Down a steep street to the left beyond the Russian Embassy and around a corner to the left we come to the Crimean Memorial Church, by far the largest and most handsome of the few Protestant churches in the city. This was built between 1858 and 1868 under the aegis of Lord Stratford de Redcliffe and was designed by C.E. Street, the architect of the London Law Courts. It is a very Streetian Gothic building with a cavernous porch, like the Law Courts themselves.

Returning once again to Istiklal Caddesi, we come next to the last of the old embassies on the avenue. This is the Embassy of Sweden, which was established here towards the end of the seventeenth century. Directly across the street from the Swedish Embassy is the Narmanlı Han, a huge old building which housed the Russian Embassy till they moved to their new quarters down the street in 1837. This building, which appears to date from the early eighteenth century, is now a congeries of shops, storerooms, offices and ateliers.

We are now at the end of Istiklal Caddesi. Just ahead, where the avenue forks to the right, is the entrance to Tünel, the underground funicular railway which in one minute and 20 seconds takes one to the bottom of the hill near the Galata Bridge. Tünel was built in 1875 and is thus one of the oldest subways in Europe and probably also the shortest; Periotes used to refer to it affectionately as "The Mouse's Hole".

GALATA MEVLEVİ TEKKE

Rather than taking Tünel, we will stroll down the steep street called Galip Dede Caddesi. Up until recent years this was a step street, like so many others in Galata, but now it has been paved in the interest of the automobile. A short way down this street on the left side we see a sebil founded in 1819 by one Halet Efendi. Just beside the sebil we come to the gateway of the Galata Mevlevi Tekke.

Entering, we find ourselves in a large and pleasant courtyard in front of the tekke with a garden on the right side and a picturesque graveyard on the other. The tekke was founded in 1491 by Şeyh Muhammed Semai Sultan Divanı, a descendant of Mevlana Celaleddin Rumi, the great divine and mystic poet who in the thirteenth century founded the religious brotherhood known as the Mevlevi, famous in the West as the "Whirling Dervishes". The most famous şeyh of the Galata tekke was the seventeenth-century poet Galip Dede, whose ornate türbe is on the left of the path leading into the courtyard.

At the rear of the courtyard we come to the heart of the tekke, the semahane, or dancing room, a beautiful octagonal chamber that was splendidly restored in the early 1970s. The semahane and its adjacent chamber now house the Divan Edibiyatı Museum of Turkish Court Poetry, a form inspired by the mystical verses of Mevlana. The collection includes manuscripts of the works of Galip Dede and other poets, as well as examples of Ottoman calligraphy and memorabilia of the Mevlevi dervishes who lived here until the mid-1920s, when all of the dervish orders in Turkey were banned and their tekkes closed. Performances of the ethereal Mevlevi dance and the hauntingly beautiful music that accompanies it are occasionally performed in the tekke.

The graveyard beside the tekke has some very interesting old tombstones, most of them in the form of the characteristic truncated conical headdresses of the Mevlevi. One of these marks the grave of the famous Count Bonneval, known in Turkish as Kumbaracı Ahmet Paşa. Bonneval was a French officer who enrolled in the Ottoman army in the reign of Sultan Mahmut I (r. 1730–54) and was made Commandant of the Corps of Artillery. He became a Muslim, changed his name to Kumbaracı (the Bombardier) Osman Ahmet, and spent the remainder of his life in the Ottoman service, dying in Istanbul in 1747. A contemporary of Bonneval wrote of him that he was "a man of great talent for war, intelligent, eloquent with turn and grace, very proud, a lavish spender, extremely debauched and a great plunderer."

THE GALATA TOWER

We now continue on down Galip Dede Caddesi for about 250 metres until we see on our right the huge Galata Tower. This tower was the apex of the Genoese fortifications of medieval Galata. Originally known as the Tower of Christ, it was built in 1348 in connection with the first expansion of the Genoese colony. The first fortified area, built as early as 1304, was a long narrow rectangle along the Golden Horn between where the two bridges now stand. In order to defend themselves more adequately on the side of the heights above Galata, the Genoese then added a triangular wedge with the Tower of Christ at its highest point. Later still, in 1387 and 1397, they took in successive areas to the north-west, and finally in 1446 they enclosed the eastern slope of the hill leading down to the Bosphorus. The final defence system consisted of six walled encientes, with the outer wall bordered by a moat, a short stretch of which can still be seen beside the Tower. Bits and pieces of the defence walls and towers still exist here and there around Galata, but none of them amounts to very much. The Galata Tower has been restored and there is now a modern restaurant and café on its upper levels. From the observation deck on the uppermost level one has a magnificent view out over the entire city and its surrounding waters.

In the little square beside the Tower, fixed against the remnants of the barbican, is a famous street fountain. In its present form it dates from 1732, but it was originally constructed by Bereketzade

Hacı Ali Ağa, first Turkish governor of the citadel of Galata; it still bears his patronymic. It was moved to its present position in 1950 from Bereketzade's mosque a short distance away when the latter was destroyed. Unfortunately, this charming rococo fountain has suffered badly from being painted.

Behind the tower a steep and winding street, Galata Kulesi Sokağı, leads downhill towards the Golden Horn. Not far down on the left we see the queer folly-like tower that looks so extraordinary when viewed from the two bridges; it is merely an example of Art Nouveau and belongs to the Istanbul Hospital.

CHURCH OF SS. PETER AND PAUL

Farther down on the right is the extensive domain of the Dominician church and monastery of SS. Peter and Paul, founded in the late fifteenth century by the Genoese. Later it was taken under the protection of France and became the French parochial church in Galata. During the nineteenth century it became the parish church of the local Maltese community, several of whose tombstones are built into the courtyard wall along with an ancient Greek funerary relief. The present church dates from a rebuilding in 1841 by the Fossati brothers. At the rear of the monastery there is a fairly well preserved stretch of the medieval Genoese wall that led up from the Golden Horn to the Galata Tower, with two defence towers still standing.

At the next corner we come to a cross street, which on the left side is called Kart Çınar Sokağı. The two buildings facing one another to the left across the side street are Genoese, the one above dated 1314 and the other 1316. The latter is the former Palazzo Communale, also known as the Podestat, the official residence and headquarters of the Podesta, the Genoese governor of Galata. The Podesta retained its original appearance until the late nineteenth century, when its façade was rebuilt during the widening of the avenue below.

Turning right on the side street, which on this side is called Eski Banka Sokağı, we see on the right a huge old building known as the Han of Saint Pierre. This was built in 1771 by the Compte de Saint Priest as the "lodging-place and bank of the French Nation", as recorded in his bequest. The French poet Andre Chènier was born in an earlier house on this site on 30 October 1762, as noted in a plaque on the façade: next to it are the arms of the Compte de Saint Priest and of the Bourbons.

We retrace our steps to Galata Kulesi Sokağı, which after a few steps brings us to Bankalar Caddesi, formerly known as Voyvoda Caddesi. The present name of the avenue comes from the several banks that were built along it in the latter half of the nineteenth century. The most famous of these is the Osmanlı Bankası, the Ottoman Bank, the huge building that dominates the south side of the avenue to our left, founded in 1856.

PERŞEMBE PAZAR SOKAĞI

We now cross the avenue and continue straight ahead on Perşembe Pazar Sokağı, the Street of the Thursday Market. On the right side of the street we see two ancient stone houses, and beyond an alley we see two more of them. These were in times past referred to as Genoese houses, but they are actually Ottoman structures of the eighteenth century, one of them inscribed with the date A.H. 1148, or A.D. 1735–6. And indeed the masonry in alternate stone and brick, the pointed arches of the windows, and the general structure could not be more characteristic of Turkish building of the period. The dated building has three storeys, the upper ones projecting in zigzags held up by corbels, two zigzags in Perşembe Pazar Sokağı but four in the tiny alley to the right. This is a fine old building and one hopes that it will be preserved, for at present it and the others on this street are roughly used and are deteriorating.

ARAP CAMİİ

We take the next turning on the right and soon come to a very unusual edifice ending in a tall square tower with a pyramidal roof; this is known in Turkish as Arap Camii, the Mosque of the Arabs, one of the former Latin churches of Genoese Galata. There are many baseless legends concerning the origin and history of this church, but the evidence indicates that it was constructed by the Dominicans during the years 1323–37 and dedicated to St. Domenic. It seems to have taken the place of, or included, a chapel dedicated to St. Paul, by whose name it was also called. It seems to have been converted into a mosque in the last decade of the fifteenth century, probably for the Moors who were resettled in Galata after their expulsion from Spain, and hence the name Arap Camii. The building has been partially burned and restored several times, and in the process it was considerably widened by moving the north wall outwards several metres. Nevertheless it continues to look like a rather typical Latin church, originally Gothic, a long hall ending in three rectangular apses and with a belfry (now the minaret) at the east end. The flat wooden roof and the rather pretty wooden galleries date only from a restoration during the years 1913–19. At that time also the original floor was uncovered and large quantities of Genoese tombstones came to light; these are now in the Archaeological Museum. Fragments of a fourteenth-century fresco were recently discovered in the central apse. On the north side is a large, unkempt but not unattractive courtyard with a şadırvan.

We now return to the street by which we arrived at Arap Camii and continue on till the second turning on the right; from this we take the second turning on the left. This brings us onto Yanık Kapı Sokağı, the Street of the Burnt Gate, which takes its name from the ancient portal which we come to about 100 metres along. This is the only surviving gate of the medieval Genoese town; it once led from the fourth enceinte to the fifth. Above the archway we see a bronze tablet upon which is emblazoned the cross of St. George, symbol of Genoa the Superb, between a pair of escutcheons bearing the heraldic arms of the noble houses of Doria and De Merude.

AZAP KAPI CAMİİ

After passing through the archway we take the next left; this soon brings us out to the main highway paralleling the Golden Horn. A short distance off to the right, just beside the Atatürk Bridge, we see the handsome mosque known as Azap Kapı Camii, taking its name from the Marine Gate, or Azap Kapı, of the Tershane, or Ottoman shipyard, on the other side of the bridge highway. Founded by the Grand Vezir Sokollu Mehmet Paşa, the mosque was built in A.H. 985 (A.D. 1577–8) and its architect was Sinan. While it hardly equals Sokollu Mehmet's slightly earlier mosque near the Hippodrome, it is nevertheless a fine and interesting building. Like the mosque of Rüstem Paşa on the other side of the Golden Horn, it is raised on a high basement in which there were once vaulted shops; the entrance, now rather squeezed by the approach to the bridge, is by staircases under the enclosed porch. The minaret is unusual both in position and structure. First of all, it is on the left or north side instead of the south, doubtless because the sea at that time came up very close to the south wall and the ground would not have been firm enough for so heavy a structure as a minaret. Furthermore, it is detached from the building and placed on a solid foundation of its own, and is connected with the mosque above porch level by a picturesque arch containing a communicating passage so that it can be entered from the porch. Internally the arrangement is an octagon inscribed in a rectangle (nearly square). The dome is supported by eight small semidomes, those in the axes slightly larger than those in the diagonals, while the eastern semidome covers a rectangular projecting apse for the mihrab, with narrow galleries surrounding three sides. The mihrab and mimber are very fine work in carved marble. It appears that the interior was once decorated with fine Iznik tiles, like that of Sokollu's other mosque, but these have disappeared and been replaced by modern Kütahya tiles. Seventy years ago the mosque was in a ruinous condition and the municipality actually proposed to demolish it to make way for the newly planned Atatürk Bridge. A public protest succeeded in saving the mosque and finally getting it restored. This was indeed fortunate, for it is certainly among the more interesting and important of Sinan's buildings.

Just to the north of the mosque stands the famous baroque, or rococo fountain, of Azap Kapı. Built in A.H. 1145 (A.D. 1732–3) by Saliha Valide Hatun, mother of Mahmut I, it consists of a projecting sebil with three grilled windows flanked by two large and magnificent çeşmes. The façades of the çeşmes and sebil are entirely covered with floral decorations in low relief and with a little dome. For many years in almost total ruin, it has recently been fairly well restored, though unfortunately the fluted drum of the dome has been done in concrete. It is one of the most attractive of the early eighteenth-century fountains.

We now turn back and stroll in the direction of the Galata Bridge, passing a stretch of the medieval Genoese walls that was exposed when the buildings around them were demolished in the 1990s.

GALATA BEDESTEN, HAN OF RÜSTEM PAŞA

A little more than halfway along the avenue between the two bridges we come to an ancient and imposing building with nine domes. This is the Galata Bedesten, or covered market, built by Fatih Mehmet. A nearly square structure, its nine equal domes are supported by four great rectangular piers, and around the outside are a series of vaulted shops. Several authorities have claimed that this building is seventeenth or eighteenth century; however, both the form of the building and the masonry in brick and rubble are obviously typical products of the fifteenth century. One has only to compare it to the Old Bedesten in the Kapalı Çarşı, a construction of Fatih, to be convinced that it too is from that period.

Beside the Bedesten but entered from the next turning to the east is a handsome and unusual han. This was built by Sinan for the Grand Vezir Rüstem Paşa shortly before 1550. The date is fixed by Gyllius, who says that it was built on the foundations of the Latin church of St. Michael, which still existed when he arrived in 1544, but had been pulled down before he left to make way for the new han. It is in two storeys with a long narrow courtyard, from the centre of which rises a staircase leading to the upper floor, in an arrangement as picturesque as it is unique. The lower arcade of the courtyard has round arches, while those of the gallery above are of the ogive type. This building has been very badly treated and is in a sad state of dilapidation and squalor.

Leaving the han, we continue on towards the Galata Bridge; here we might find the streets closer to the Golden Horn somewhat more interesting than the main avenue. (Along the shore at this point there is a ferry service of small motor-boats across the Golden Horn. This is a very pleasant way to pass back and forth between Galata and Stamboul and has been in use for centuries.)

We now arrive at the great square in Karaköy, where all the streets of Galata converge chaotically towards the bridge. There is more of Galata yet to see, along the European shore of the lower Bosphorus, but perhaps we should pause here and leave the rest for our next tour. And besides, whenever one is in this area one is always tempted to relax at a café or restaurant on the lower level of the bridge. From there one can observe how the sometimes golden light of late afternoon gives even Galata a brief and spurious beauty. Then, as the sun sets behind Stamboul, silhouetting the domes and minarets of the imperial mosques on the skyline of the old city, the polluted waters of the Golden Horn do indeed look like molten gold.

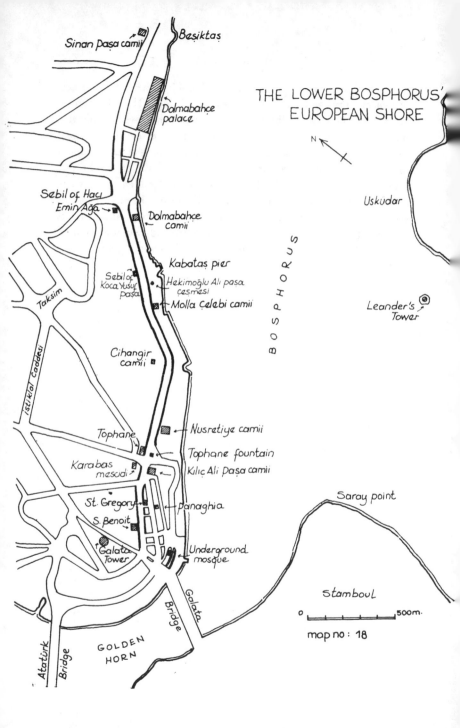

THE LOWER BOSPHORUS'
EUROPEAN SHORE

N

Beşiktaş

Sinan Paşa camii

Dolmabahçe
palace

Üsküdar

Sebil of Hacı
Emin Ağa

Dolmabahçe
camii

B O S P H O R U S

Kabataş pier

Sebil of
Koca Yusuf
Paşa

Hekimoğlu Ali paşa
çeşmesi

Molla Çelebi camii

Leander's
Tower

Taksim

Cihangir
camii

İstiklal Caddesi

Tophane

Nusretiye camii

Tophane fountain

Karabaş
mescidi

Kılıç Ali Paşa camii

Saray point

St. Gregory

Panaghia

S. Benoit

Galata
Tower

Underground
mosque

Stamboul

Galata Bridge

0   500m.

map no : 18

Atatürk Bridge

GOLDEN
HORN

21

The Lower Bosphorus'
European Shore

We will begin this tour where the last one ended, at the Karaköy end of the Galata Bridge. There are few monuments of great importance along this stretch; nevertheless it makes a pleasant and interesting stroll.

Before we begin, we might say a word or two about the Galata Bridge, where we have begun or ended so many of our strolls through Istanbul. The present bridge was completed in 1992, replacing an earlier bridge dating from 1910, which now rests unused between Ayvansaray and Hasköy. The central section of the bridge opens at four o'clock each morning to permit the passage of shipping to that part of the Golden Horn between the two bridges. (It is also opened occasionally at times of civic disturbance to isolate Stamboul from the rest of the city.) The first bridge at this point was built in 1845 by Bezmialem Valide Sultan, mother of Sultan Abdül Mecit; it was of wooden construction and quite pretty, as we see from the old prints.

YERALTI CAMİ
Leaving Karaköy we begin walking along the seaside road, which is always bustling with pedestrians rushing to and from the ferry station. About 200 metres along, past the ferry pier, we turn left and then left again at the next street. A short way along on our right we come to the obscure entrance to Yeraltı Cami, the Underground Mosque. This is a strange and sinister place. The mosque is housed in the low, vaulted cellar or keep of a Byzantine tower or castle which is probably to be identified with the Castle of Galata. This was the place where was fastened one end of the chain which closed the mouth of the Golden Horn in times of siege. Descending into the mosque, we find ourselves in a maze of dark, narrow passages between a forest of

squat passages supporting low vaults, six rows of nine or 54 in all. Towards the rear of the mosque we find the tombs of two sainted martyrs, Abu Sufyan and Amiri Wahabi, both of whom are supposed to have died in the first Arab siege of the city in the seventh century. Their graves were revealed to a Nakşibendi dervish in a dream in 1640, whereupon Sultan Murat IV constructed a shrine on the site. Then in 1757 the whole dungeon was converted into a mosque by the Grand Vezir Köşe Mustafa Paşa.

CHURCH AND LİSE OF ST. BENOİT

Walking northward to Kemeraltı Caddesi, we see on the far side of the avenue a tall medieval tower. This is all that remains of the fifteenth-century church of St. Benoit. This church was founded by the Benedictines in 1427 and later became the chapel of the French ambassadors to the Sublime Porte, several of whom are buried there. After being occupied by the Jesuits for several centuries, it was given on the temporary dissolution of that order in 1773 to the Lazarists, to whom it still belongs. In 1804 they established a school here which is still ones of the best of the foreign lises in the city. Apart from its original tower, the present church dates partly from 1732 (the nave and south aisle) and partly from 1871 (the north aisle).

CHURCH OF ST. GREGORY

Somewhat farther along the avenue and on the opposite side of the avenue stands the Armenian church of St. Gregory the Illuminator (Surp Kirkor Lusavoriç). This was erected in 1958 after the original church nearby had been demolished when the avenue was widened. The new building is interesting as a replica of the famous church at Echmiadzin, built in the seventh century and one of the masterpieces of ancient Armenian architecture. The older church which was pulled down was an early nineteenth-century structure of no great architectural interest, but it contained some unusual tiles from the Tekfur Saray kilns; these have been transferred to the crypt of the present church.

Galata is a town of surprises and in particular shelters a large number of Christian and other sects. For instance, if you go down the alley in front of Surp Kirkor and wander about in the rather mean streets between it and the sea, you will find three churches that originally belonged to the Greek Orthodox Patriarchate but which are now the property of the so-called Turkish Orthodox Church. The latter was founded in 1924 by a dissident priest from Anatolia named Papa Eftim, who took control of the three churches in Galata and set up his own church for his parishioners, in which the mass is said in Turkish rather than Greek. Papa Eftim, who styled himself Patriarch Efthemios I, engaged in a running battle with the Greek Orthodox Patriarchate that at one point reached the League of Nations. After his death he was succeeded as patriarch by his two sons in turn, but by now the congregation is virtually non-existent, though the three churches in Galata – St. John, St. Nicholas and the Panaghia (Virgin) Kafatiani – still belong to the Turkish Orthodox Patriarchate such as it is. The Panaghia Kafatiani, the oldest of the three churches, founded in 1475 by Greeks from Kaffa in the Crimea, though the present church dates only from 1840, is the patriarchate of the Turkish Orthodox Church; it preserves a sacred icon of the Virgin Hodegitria brought from the Crimea by the original parishioners.

We now come to the district of Tophane, just outside the old walls of Galata; it takes its name from the cannon foundry which still dominates the road on the left-hand side. There was once a small but busy and picturesque port here; this has now been largely filled in, but there are still several Ottoman buildings of some interest in the immediate vicinity.

KILIÇ ALİ PAŞA CAMİİ

The first monument one comes to, on the right, is the mosque complex which Sinan built in 1580 for Kılıç Ali Paşa. This Ali was an Italian from Calabria called Ochiali who had become a Muslim and risen high in the Ottoman navy, being among the few officers who distinguished himself at the disastrous battle of Lepanto in 1571. As a reward for his outstanding service Selim II appointed him Kaptan Paşa, that is, Lord High Admiral, and conferred upon him the name Kılıç, the Sword. He twice captured Tunis from the Spaniards, the second time permanently. When he died in 1587, his fortune was estimated at 500,000 ducats. "Although ninety years of age," says von Hammer, "he had not been able to renounce the pleasures of the harem, and he died in the arms of a concubine."

To return to the mosque. Profoundly as Sinan had been impressed and inspired by Haghia Sophia, he had always avoided any kind of direct imitation of that great building. Now in his old age – he was over 90 when he designed this mosque – whether for his own amusement or on instructions from Kılıç Ali Paşa cannot be known – he deliberately planned a structure which is practically a small replica of the Great Church. It is one of his least successful buildings. One does not know quite why this is; it must have something to do with the greatly reduced proportions. But the fact is that the building seems heavy, squat and dark; it is not improved by the plethora of lamps, but this, of course, is not Sinan's fault. His main departures from the plan of Haghia Sophia are: the provision of only two columns instead of four between each of the piers to north and south, and the suppression of the exedrae at the east and west ends; both seem to have been dictated by the reduced scale, and indeed to have retained the original disposition would clearly have made the building even heavier and darker. Nevertheless, the absence of the exedrae deprives the mosque of what in Haghia Sophia is one of its main beauties. The mihrab is in a square projecting apse, where there are some Iznik tiles of the best period. At the west there is a kind of pseudo-narthex of five cross-vaulted bays separated from the prayer area by four rectangular pillars.

The mosque is preceded by a very picturesque double porch. The inner one is of the usual type, five domed bays supported by columns with stalactited capitals; over the entrance portal is the historical inscription giving the date A.H. 988 (A.D. 1580), and above this a Kuranic text in a fascinating calligraphy and set in a curious projecting marble frame, triangular in shape and adorned with stalactites. The outer porch has a steeply sloping penthouse roof, supported by 12 columns on the west façade and three on each side, all with lozenge capitals; in the centre is a monumental portal of marble, and there are bronze grilles between the columns; the whole effect being quite charming.

The külliye of Kılıç Ali Paşa is extensive, including a türbe, a medrese and a hamam. The türbe is in the pretty graveyard behind the mosque; it is a plain but elegant octagonal building with alternately one and two windows in each façade, in two tiers. The medrese, opposite the south-east corner of the mosque, is almost square and like the mosque itself a little squat and shut in; it may well not be by Sinan since it does not appear in the *Tezkeret-ül Ebniye*. It is now used as a clinic. The hamam just in front of the medrese is single; unfortunately it is no longer in use. The plan is unique among the extant hamams of Sinan. The vast camekân doors lead into two separate soğukluks lying not between the camekân and the hararet, as is habitual, but on either side of the latter; each consists of three domed rooms of different sizes. From that on the right a passage leads off to the lavatories; the rooms on the opposite side were used as semi-private bathing cubicles. The hararet itself, instead of having the usual cruciform plan, is hexagonal with open bathing places in four of its six arched recesses, the other two giving access from the two soğukluks. The plan is an interesting variation on the standard, and it has been pointed out that broadly similar plans may be found in one or two of the older hamams at Bursa.

Across the street north of Kılıç Ali Paşa Camii is one of the most famous of the baroque fountains, known as Tophane Çeşmesi. Built in 1732 by Mahmut I, it has marble walls completely covered with floral designs and arabesques carved in low relief and originally painted and gilded. Its charming domed and widely overhanging roof was lacking for many years but has recently been restored. The fountain with the mosque beside it and the busy and picturesque throngs around the port used to be a favourite subject with etchers of the eighteenth and nineteenth century.

On the west side of the wide street in front of Kılıç Ali Paşa Camii, at the bottom of the hill coming down from Galatasaray, is a little mosque recently rather well-restored. It is not very interesting except it is ancient and well exemplifies the simple rectangular plan with a hipped wooden roof. It was founded by the Chief Black Eunuch Karabaş Mustafa who died, according to the *Hadika,* in 1530. Long a ruin, it was rebuilt in 1962; the interior is without interest.

TOPHANE

Opposite, on an eminence, is the cannon foundry from which the district takes its name, Tophane. A foundry was established here by Fatih himself and was extended and improved by Beyazit II. However, according to Evliya, Süleyman the Magnificent "pulled down the gun foundry built by his ancestors and built a new one, which no one who has not seen it is able to judge of what may be accomplished by human strength and understanding." This he did, Evliya explains, because he was constantly at war with the Emperor of Germany: "These Germans are strong, warlike, cunning, devilish, coarse infidels whom, excelling in artillery, Sultan Süleyman endeavoured to equal by assembling gunners and artillerymen by rich presents from all countries," and by improving the gun foundry. He goes on to give a detailed description of the methods used in casting the cannon. Süleyman's foundry has long since disappeared and the present structure was built by Selim III in 1803, doubtless in connection with his own attempt to reform and modernize the army. It is a large rectangular building of brick and stone with eight great domes supported by three lofty piers. Beyond the foundry itself, along the height overlooking the street, a series of ruined substructures, walls and domes once formed part of the general complex, which included extensive barracks for the artillerymen. The foundry has now been restored and is open to the public as an exhibition hall. Across the street beside the Nusretiye mosque a small kiosk in the *Empire* style, built by Abdül Aziz, was a review pavilion where the sultan came to inspect his artillery troops.

NUSRETİYE CAMİİ

Nusretiye Camii was built between 1822 and 1826 by Mahmut II, its architect being Kirkor Balyan, the founder of that large family of Armenian architects who served the sultans throughout most of the nineteenth century and built so many of whose mosques and palaces we shall encounter along the shores of the Bosphorus. Kirkor Balyan (1764–1831) had studied in Paris and his mosque shows a curious blend of baroque and *Empire* motifs, highly un-Turkish, but not without a certain charm. This mosque abandons the traditional arrangement of a monumental courtyard and substitutes for it, as it were, an elaborate series of palace-like apartments in two storeys which forms the western façade of the building; such a plan had first been tried some 30 years earlier by Mehmet Tahir for the Hamidiye at Beylerbey, but it became a regular feature of all the Balyan mosques – for example, those at Dolmabahçe, Yıldız, Ortaköy and Aksaray. Notice the bulbous weight towers, the dome arches like jutting cheekbones, the over-slender minarets, so thin that they fell down soon after construction and had to be re-erected, the ornate bronze grilles here and there, or look at the interior dripping with marble and *Empire* garlands, and the mimber, a marvellous baroque changeling. The architect may have been perverse but he certainly had verve. The founder, Mahmut II the Reformer, called his mosque Nusretiye, Victory, because it was finished in 1826 just after his triumph over the Janissaries whom he had succeeded in liquidating.

Along the docks between Kılıç Ali Paşa Camii and Nusretiye Camii one of the warehouses has been converted into an art museum called Istanbul Modern, which opened in 2004. The collections include outstanding works of Turkish artists of the late Ottoman and early Republic eras, displayed in a very interesting and attractive setting.

Not far beyond Nusretiye Camii, on the heights above, can be seen the dome and minarets of the mosque of Cihangir, which gives its name to this upper district. Unfortunately the present building is of no interest whatever, having been built in 1890 by Abdül Hamit II. It occupies the site, however, of a mosque by Sinan which was founded by Süleyman the Magnificent in memory of his hunchback son Cihangir, who died in 1553 from sorrow, it is said, for his half-brother, the unfortunate Prince Mustafa, whom their father had just executed; Prince Cihangir was buried in the türbe of his other brother Mehmet at the Şehzade. Sinan's mosque was burned down in 1720 and several times thereafter reconstructed and burned down, until the present rather exceptionally ugly mosque was built, "bigger and better than the old ones," as Abdül Hamit boasts in his inscription over the portal.

On the Bosphorus side of the shore highway in Fındıklı one comes to the Güzel Sanatlar Akademisi, or Fine Arts Academy, which is now part of Mimar Sinan Universitesi, the University of Sinan the Architect. The academy has an exhibition hall on the Bosphorus where art exhibits are held periodically.

MOLLA ÇELEBİ CAMİİ

At Fındıklı there is a little mosque of Sinan's called Molla Çelebi Camii. This Molla was the Kadıasker (Chief Justice) Mehmet Efendi, a savant and poet; he built here also a hamam, but this was demolished when the street was widened. Erected in A.H. 969 (A.D. 1561–2), the building is of the hexagonal type, but here the pillars are actually engaged in the walls; between them to north and south are four small semidomes, and another covers the rectangular projecting apse in which stands the mihrab. The mosque is at the water's edge and its position as well as its graceful lines make it very picturesque.

Between here and Dolmabahçe there are three fountains of considerable interest, all of which were moved from their original places when the street was widened and have been re-erected on their present sites. Between the mosque and the Kabataş ferry landing, beside the Bosphorus, stands the square çeşme of Hekimoğlu Ali Paşa erected in 1732; it is of marble, beautifully carved; it had lost its overhanging roof but this has now been replaced. There are çeşmes on two faces of the fountain. Nearly opposite this çeşme, across the road, is one of the most pleasing of the baroque or rococo sebils, built by Koca Yusuf Paşa, Grand Vezir to Abdül Hamit I, in 1787. It has a magnificent çeşme in the centre, flanked on each side by two grilled windows of the sebil, and a door beyond; it is elaborately carved and has incrustations of various marbles, while its long inscription forms a frieze above the windows of the sebil. It is pleasantly embowered in trees and is once more in use as a sebil, with the tables of a little café in front of it. Finally, just opposite the Dolmabahçe mosque is a little külliye with a sebil as its dominant feature. This was built in 1741 by the sipahi Hacı Mehmet Emin Ağa. Halil Ethem says rightly that it is "perhaps the most interesting eighteenth-century sebil in Istanbul." The five-windowed sebil is flanked symmetrically on one side by a door, on the other by a çeşme; there follow three grilled windows opening into a small graveyard for the members of the sipahi's family, his own tomb being, most unusually, in the sebil itself; beyond the graveyard there was once a small mektep which has not been restored. The whole is handsomely carved and decorated with various marbles. This poor little complex has been several times demolished and re-erected in slightly different places; it still remains incompletely restored.

We now come to Dolmabahçe, where Gümüşsuyu Caddesi passes the main football stadium in the city and joins the Bosphorus road. Just before this intersection one comes to a baroque mosque on the seaside, with a clock-tower of similar style at the far end of a terrace to the north, beyond which is Dolmabahçe Palace. Dolmabahçe Camii, begun by Bezmialem Valide Sultan, was finished in 1853 by her son Abdül Mecit. Like the neighbouring palace, it was designed by Nikoğos Balyan, a grandson of the Kirkor whom we have already met as architect of the Nusretiye. He came at a bad period and it is only with difficulty that one can admire any of his buildings. The great cartwheel-like arches of this mosque seem particularly disagreeable; but the two very slender Corinthian minarets, one at each end of the little palace-like structure that precedes the mosque, have a certain charm. The baroque clock-tower to the north of the mosque was erected by Nikoğos Balyan in 1854; it is made of cut stone and has a height of 27 metres, making it one of the most prominent landmarks on the European shore of the lower Bosphorus.

DOLMABAHÇE PALACE

We now come to Dolmabahçe Sarayı, the largest and grandest by far of the imperial palaces on the Bosphorus. The name means filled-in garden, for this was once an inlet of the Bosphorus and a harbour before it was filled in to create a royal park, a process begun by Ahmet I and completed by Osman II. A series of kiosks and seaside pavilions were later built in the park by the royal family, eventually evolving into a palace with a great Hall of the Divan for meetings of the state council. Mahmut II was the first sultan to make Dolmabahçe his principal residence, finding the palace on the Bosphorus more comfortable and agreeably situated than the crowded confines of Topkapı Sarayı. Abdül Mecit decided to build a much larger and more luxurious palace at Dolmabahçe, appointing as his chief architect Nikoğos Balyan, who worked in collaboration with his father, Karabet. The Balyans were from a distinguished Armenian family of architects who built several palaces and mosques for the sultans during the second half of the nineteenth century. The present palace of Dolmabahçe was completed in 1854, although Sultan Abdül Mecit and the royal family did not move in till 1856, finally abandoning the palace at Topkapı Sarayı that had been the imperial residence for nearly four centuries. Dolmabahçe was used as the principal imperial residence by all of the latter sultans except Abdül Hamit II, who preferred his own more sequestered palace at Yıldız. After the end of the Empire, Dolmabahçe served for a time as a state residence and was used to entertain visiting royalty and other distinguished visitors. Atatürk used it as the presidential residence when he was in Istanbul, and he died here on 10 November 1938. In recent years Dolmabahçe has been completely restored and is now open as a museum, one of the most popular attractions in the city. Tours of the palace begin at the ornate entryway to the south of the palace, passing from there through the royal gardens to the south wing of the palace.

The most impressive aspect of the palace is its seaside façade of white marble, with the edifice itself 284 metres in length along the seaside and fronting on a walled quay 600 metres long. The central part of the palace is a great imperial state hall flanked by the two main wings containing the state rooms and the royal apartments, the selamlık on one side and the harem on the other, with the apartment of the Sultan Valide in a separate wing linked to the harem through the apartment of the Crown Prince, and with an additional harem for his women and those of the other princes, and then still another residence at the north-west corner of the palace for the Kızlar Ağası, the Chief Black Eunuch. The palace complex also included rooms for those of the palace staff who lived within Dolmabahçe, as well as kitchens, an imaret to feed the staff, a pharmacy, stables, carriage houses, and barracks for the halberdiers who guarded the imperial residence. All in all, there are a total of 285 rooms, 43 large salons, six balconies, and six hamams on three storeys, with the Sultan's private bath equipped with an alabaster bath tub.

The palace interior was the work of the French decorator Sechan, who designed the Paris Opera, and thus the decor and furniture of Dolmabahçe are strongly reminiscent of those of French palaces and mansions of the period. A number of European artists were commissioned to adorn the palace with paintings, murals and ceiling frescoes, and outstanding examples of their work, most notably works of Zonaro, Fromentin, and Aivazovkski, can be seen *in situ* and also in the Exhibition Hall, which has a separate entrance approached by the ornate entryway on the main road. The opulent furnishings of the palace includ 4,455 square metres of hand-woven Hereke carpets; fireplaces and chandeliers of Bohemian and Baccarat crystal, with the chandeliers numbering 36 in all, the biggest being the 4.5-tonne giant that hangs over the State Room, the largest chandelier in the world. Other furnishings include some 280 Chinese, Japanese, European and Turkish porcelains, the latter produced in the workshops of Yıldız Palace, along with 156 clocks, more than 500 silver and crystal candelabras, a dozen silver braziers, and innumerable sets of crystal and silverware. A great showpiece is the ornate stairway that leads up from the Salon of the Ambassadors, its balusters made of crystal and its upper level framed with a colonnade of monoliths of variegated marble, the grandest of seven stairways in the palace.

The palace is built on a site famous in history as that from which began the astonishing journey overland of some 70 ships of Fatih Mehmet's fleet on 22 April 1453; up the hill to Pera they were drawn on wheeled platforms and down the valley of Kasım Paşa to the Golden Horn, thus bypassing the insuperable obstacle of the chain which barred its mouth. After Fatih's time the area became a royal garden; Evliya says that Selim I built a kiosk here, and in Gyllius' time it was known as the Little Valley of the Royal Garden *(Vallicula Regii Horti)*. It was Ahmet I who began to fill in the small harbour in order to extend his gardens, and the filling-in process was continued by his son Osman II. As Evliya writes: "By order of Sultan Osman II all ships of the fleet, and all merchant ships at that time in the harbour of Constantinople, were obliged to load with stones, which were thrown into the sea before Dolmabahçe, so that a space of 400 yards was filled up with stones where the sea formed a bay, and the place was called 'the filled-up garden,' or Dolmabahçe."

Evliya goes on to tell one of his astonishing stories about his unpredictable friend, Murat IV: "Sultan Murat IV happened once to be reading at Dolmabahçe the satirical work *Sohami* of Nefii Efendi, when the lightning struck the ground near him; being terrified he threw the book into the sea, and then gave orders to Bayram Paşa to strangle the author Nefii Efendi."

And on that mad note we will end our tour. We might then retrace our steps to the square before Dolmabahçe; from there we can return to Taksim along the Ayazpaşa road, which winds uphill to the left of the football stadium.

THE LOWER BOSPHORUS

0 ⊢————————⊣ 4 km.

map no. 19 a

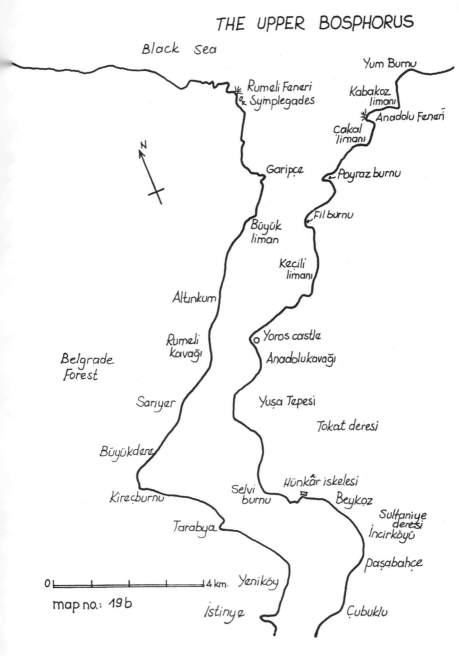

THE UPPER BOSPHORUS

Black Sea

Yum Burnu

Rumeli Feneri
Symplegades

Kabakoz
limanı

Anadolu Feneri

Çakal
limanı

Garipçe

Poyraz burnu

Fil burnu

Büyük
liman

Keçili
limanı

Altınkum

Yoros castle

Rumeli
kavağı

Anadolukavağı

Belgrade
Forest

Yuşa Tepesi

Sarıyer

Tokat deresi

Büyükdere

Hünkâr iskelesi

Selvi
burnu

Beykoz

Kireçburnu

Sultaniye
deresi
İncirköyü

Tarabya

Paşabahçe

0 ⊢———————⊣ 4 km.

Yeniköy

map no.: 19 b

İstinye

Çubuklu

22

The Bosphorus

We will begin our final tour of Istanbul where we began our first, at the Galata Bridge, where we will board a ferry to sail up the Bosphorus. Here we have saved the best for last, for the Bosphorus and its shores are by far the most beautiful part of Istanbul.

The history of the Bosphorus begins with the "Inachean daughter, beloved of Zeus" Io, who was turned into a heifer to conceal her from Hera. Pursued by the jealous Hera's gadfly, Io plunged into the waters that separate Europe from Asia and bequeathed them the name by which they have ever since been known, Bosphorus, or Ford of the Cow. The next event in Bosphoric history is the passage of the Argonauts on their way to seek the Golden Fleece in Colchis at the far end of the Black Sea. On our own journey up the Bosphorus we will stop at several places which ancient and local tradition associated with Jason and his fabulous crew.

The first fully historic event connected with the Bosphorus is the passage across it in 512 B.C. of the huge army which Darius led against the Scythians. From that time onward it played an important and even decisive role in the history of the city erected at its southern extremity in 667 B.C.; for, as Gyllius eloquently points out, the Bosphorus is "the first creator of Byzantium greater and more important than Byzas, the founder of the City." And he later sums up the predominant importance of this "Strait that Purpasses all straits" by the epigram: "The Bosphorus with one key opens and closes two worlds, two seas."

The Bosphorus is a strait some 30 kilometres long, running in the general direction north-north-east to south-south-west, and varying greatly in width from about 700 metres at its narrowest to over 3.5 kilometres at its widest. Its average depth at the centre of the channel is between 50 and 75 metres, but at one point it reaches a depth of over 100 metres. The predominant surface current flows at a rate of three to five kilometres per hour from the Black Sea to the Marmara, but, because of the sinuosity of the channel, eddies producing strong reverse currents occupy most of the indentations of the shore. A very strong wind may reverse the main surface current and make it flow north, in which case the counter eddies also change their direction. At a depth of about 40 metres there is a subsurface current, called *kanal* in Turkish, which flows from the Marmara north towards the Black Sea. Its waters, however, are for the most part prevented from entering the Black Sea by a threshold just beyond the mouth of the Bosphorus; these lower waters, denser and more saline than the upper, are turned back by the threshold, mingle with the upper waters, and are driven back towards the Marmara with the surface current. The lower current is strong enough so that under certain conditions, if fishing nets are lowered into it, it may pull the boats northward against the southerly surface current.

The casual visitor to Istanbul, especially if one comes in summer, might find it difficult to believe that the Bosphorus can be a perverse and dangerous body of water. Seen from the hills along its shore as it curves and widens and narrows, it often looks like a great lake or series of lakes; while its rapid flow from the Black Sea to the Marmara gives it something of the character of a river. Yet anyone who has observed its erratic currents and counter-currents, the various winds that encourage or hinder navigation, the impenetrable fogs that envelop it, even occasionally the icebergs that choke it, will realize that it is indeed a part of the ungovernable sea. Here Belisarius fought the invincible whale Poryphyry, that Moby Dick that wrecked all shipping; here Gyllius observed the largest shark he had ever seen; while even now one still sees schools of dolphins sporting in its waves. Since it is an international waterway, the Bosphorus is busy day and night with a traffic of cargo ships, oil-tankers and ocean-liners, as well as with the local and more colourful ferries and fishing boats. The frequent sharp and unexpected bends in the straits, the tricky currents and occasional storms and dense fogs can make the passage quite difficult at times. Nearly every year large ships collide with one another on the Bosphorus or run aground on its banks, smashing into the houses along its shores. Old Bosphorus-dwellers will regale you with tales of having been awakened from their slumbers by a terrific crash, to find their home tumbled in wreckage about them and the rusty prow of a tramp steamer protruding into the library; or of how a quiet supper was suddenly disrupted when the yardarm of a passing schooner smashed through the dining-room window and swept the table clear.

Both shores of the Bosphorus are indented by frequent bays and harbours, and in general it will be found that an indentation on one shore corresponds to a cape or promontory on the other. Most of the bays are at the mouths of valleys reaching back into the hills on either side, and a great many of the valleys have streams that flow into the Bosphorus. Almost all of these are insignificant; only the Sweet Waters of Europe and the Sweet Waters of Asia have any claim to be called rivers, and these are quite small. Both shores are lined with hills, none of them very high, the most imposing being the Great Çamlıca (267 metres) and Yuşa Tepesi (201 metres), both on the Asian side; nevertheless, especially on the upper Bosphorus, the hills often seem much higher than they are because of the way in which they come down in precipitous cliffs into the sea. In spite of the almost continuous villages and the not infrequent forest fires, both sides are well-wooded, especially with cypresses, umbrella-pines, plane-trees, horse-chestnuts, terebinths and Judas-trees. The red blossoms of the latter in spring, mingled with the mauve flowers of the ubiquitous wisteria, and the red and white candles of the chestnuts, pervaded by the songs of nightingales and blackbirds, give the Bosphorus at that season an even more superlative beauty.

Let these general observations suffice, and let us now explore this most fascinating strait in more detail from the deck of a Bosphorus ferry. But Bosphorus ferries are whimsical boats, flitting back and forth between the continents without apparent reason. And so our description will have to be a somewhat idealized one, which assumes that we sail up the European side of the strait and down the Asian, stopping where we please along the way.

BEŞİKTAŞ

The first village (though now part of the city) on the European shore of the lower Bosphorus is at Beşiktaş, a short distance beyond the

Palace of Dolmabahçe, which we visited on our last stroll. Various explanations have been advanced for the name Beşiktaş, or Cradle Stone, the most probable being that it is a Turkish adaptation of the Greek name, Diplokionion, the Twin Columns, from two lofty columns of Theban granite which stood near the shore. In Byzantine times there was a famous church of St. Mamas here, a port, a royal palace and a hippodrome. These have vanished without a trace, but there are still two or three Ottoman monuments of some interest.

The first of these is the türbe of another great pirate-admiral of the Golden Age, the famous Hayrettin Paşa. This is one of the earliest works of Sinan, dated by an inscription over the door to A.H. 948 (A.D. 1541–2). The structure is octagonal, with two rows of windows. The upper row has recently been filled in with stained glass; and the dome has been rather well-repainted with white arabesques on a rust-coloured ground. Three catafalques occupy the centre of the türbe, and in the little garden outside is a cluster of handsome sarcophagi.

Hayrettin Paşa, better known in the West as Barbarossa, died in 1546 and on the fourth centennial of his death a statue was unveiled to his memory in the square facing his tomb. It is by far the best public statue in the city, a vivid and lively work by the sculptor Zühtü Müridoğlu. On the back are six verses by the poet Yahya Kemal which may be translated thus:

> Whence on the sea's horizon comes that roar?
> Can it be Barbarossa now returning
> From Tunis or Algiers or from the Isles?
> Two hundred vessels ride upon the waves,
> Coming from lands the rising Crescent lights:
> O blessed ships, from what seas are ye come?

Yahya Kemal Beyatlı (1884–1958) might best be described as the G.K. Chesterton of modern Turkish poetry, and he resembled Chesterton in other ways as well: one used to see his enormous bulk ensconced at one of the cafés in Bebek imbibing vast quantities of beer or rakı and holding forth to a group of admirers, among whom the senior author of this guide once or twice had the honour to be included.

Opposite Barbarossa's türbe is a brick and stone mosque, another work of Sinan; this was founded by another High Admiral, Sinan Paşa, brother of the Grand Vezir Rüstem Paşa. Inscriptions on the şadırvan and over the entrance portal give the date A.H. 963 (A.D. 1555–6) as that in which the mosque was finished, two years after the death of its founder. The mosque is interesting architecturally, though not particularly attractive. Its plan is essentially a copy of Üç Şerefeli Cami (1447) at Edirne. Its central dome rests on six arches, one incorporated in the east wall, the others supported by four hexagonal pillars, two on the west, one each to north and south; beyond the latter are side-aisles each with two domed bays. Thus far the plan is almost like that of Üç Şerefeli Cami, but while there the western piers are incorporated in the west wall, here Sinan has added a sort of narthex of five bays, four with domes, the central one cross-vaulted. The proportions are not very good and the interior seems squat and heavy. The same indeed is true of the courtyard, the porticoes of which are not domed but have steeply-sloping penthouse roofs; the cells of the medrese occupy three sides of it. Sinan seems to have been least happy when he was more or less copying an older building; thus the mosque of Kılıç Ali Paşa at Tophane, a miniature copy of Haghia Sophia, and this copy of Üç Şerefeli Cami, also much smaller than the original, are among his least successful works.

There are also two Greek churches in Beşiktaş, both of them dedicated to the Panaghia (Blessed Virgin). Both churches in their present form date to the mid-nineteenth century. There is also an Armenian church, Surp Asvadzadzin (the Immaculate Conception), which is known to have existed on this site since 1655; the present building was erected in 1856 and restored in 1987.

Just to the left of the ferry-landing we see the Naval Museum. In the garden of the museum there are arrayed a number of ancient cannon, many of them captured by the Turks when the Ottoman Navy was the scourge of the Mediterranean. The most important exhibit in the museum itself is the famous chart of North America done in the first half of the sixteenth century by Piri Reis, the great Ottoman admiral, explorer and cartographer. Within the museum there are exhibits from all periods of Turkish naval history, ranging in date from the Ottoman period up to the present century. A separate building houses the museum's incomparable collection of pazar caiques, the beautiful rowing barges that were used by the sultans to travel to their seaside palaces and pavilions along the Bosphorus and Golden Horn.

ÇIRAĞAN PALACE

About 500 metres beyond Beşiktaş the ferry passes the Çırağan Palace Hotel, also known as the Kempinsky. The hotel, which was completed in 1987, is built on the site of Çırağan Sarayı, and its seaside section preserves the original façade of the palace. Çırağan Sarayı was built during the reign of Abdül Aziz and was completed in 1872; the sultan died there on 4 June 1876, five days after he had been deposed. His death was officially declared to be a suicide, but the suspicious circumstances suggested to many of his contemporaries that he had been murdered. His nephew and successor, Murat V, was so mentally disturbed at the time of his accession that he proved unable to rule and was soon after deposed in favour of his brother Abdül Hamit II, who chose to live in Yıldız Sarayı rather than in Dolmabahçe or Çırağan. After the adoption of the Constitution of 1908, Çırağan was restored and used for a time to house the second Turkish Parliament. Then in January 1910 the palace was destroyed by fire, leaving only the blackened façade on the Bosphorus, which was restored when it was built into the new hotel.

YILDIZ PALACE AND PARK

A short way beyond the Çırağan Palace Hotel we come to the entrance of Yıldız Park and the grounds of Yıldız Sarayı. Just beside the entrance to the park stands Mecidiye Camii, built by Sultan Abdül Mecit in 1848; it has a very quaint, but ugly, minaret, in a pseudo-Gothic style. At the north-eastern corner of the gardens, just outside the upper entrance to the park, is Hamidiye Camii, built in 1886 by Sultan Abdül Hamit II.

The gardens here, originally known as those of Çırağan, are first mentioned in Ottoman history in the reign of Murat IV (r. 1623–40), who bestowed them upon his daughter Kaya Sultan and her husband Melek Ahmet Paşa. The gardens of Çırağan became famous during the reign of Ahmet III (1703–30), the Tulip King, who gave them to his son-in-law, the Grand Vezir Nevşehirli Ibrahim Paşa. Ibrahim Paşa hosted the Sultan and his court in the Gardens of Çırağan in a series of parties that began each year on the night of the first full moon in April, a delightful custom that lasted throughout the epoch known in Turkish history as the Lale Devri, the Age of Tulips. The first imperial structure known to have been erected here was a pavilion built for Mihrişah Sultan, mother of Selim III (r. 1789–1807), but this has now vanished. Yıldız Sarayı, the Palace of the Star, first began to take form during the reign of Mahmut II (r. 1808–39), and the buildings that one sees today date from his reign to that of Abdül Hamit II (r. 1876–1909), with most of the structures dating from the latter period.

One can enter Yildiz Park either from the Bosphorus road or from the upper entrance (Dağ Kapısı), which is situated off Barbaros Bulvarı. Either way, one can walk through the park, which is virtually the last extensive bit of greenery left on the European shore of the Bosphorus. A number of kiosks and greenhouses on the palace grounds have been restored by the Turkish Touring and Automobile Club, including Malta Köşkü, Çadır Köşkü, Lale Sera (Pink Conservatory), and Yeşil Sera (Green Conservatory), with the first two now serving as cafés and the latter two as tea-rooms. The setting of the café outside the Malta Köşkü is superb, with a romantic view of the Bosphorus through a frieze of greenery, giving one some idea of how beautiful the shores of these straits were in times past.

The grandest and most interesting structure at Yıldız Sarayı is the Şale, so-called because of its resemblance to a Swiss chalet. This consists of two buildings, the first erected in 1889 and the second in 1898, the latter apparently the work of the Italian architect Raimondo D'Aronco, who brought the Art Nouveau style of architecture to Istanbul under the name of the Stile Floreal. The Şale has some 50 rooms, the largest and grandest being the magnificent Reception

Hall, with its ceiling decorated in gold leaf; other splendid chambers being the Hall of Mother-of-Pearl and the Yellow Parlour. The Şale was used principally as a residence for distinguished guests, one of the most notable being Kaiser Wilhelm II, who in his visit with Abdül Hamit II in 1895 formed an alliance between Germany and the Ottoman Empire. The Şale has been restored in recent years and is now open to the public as a museum.

TÜRBE OF YAHYA EFENDİ

A few yards beyond the entrance to Yıldız Park a steep but short street leads to the very picturesque türbe of Yahya Efendi, a foster-brother of Süleyman the Magnificent, whom his mother nursed as an infant. The little külliye, consisting of a türbe and a medrese built by Sinan presumably shortly before Yahya's death in 1570, is now enveloped by various wooden structures of the nineteenth century, and it is hard to see either or even to ascertain what is left of the medrese; its dershane at least appears to be intact. The türbe communicates by a large grilled opening to a small wooden mosque with a baroque wooden dome. The various buildings themselves are picturesque, but even more so are their surroundings, where topsy-turvy tombstones lie scattered among a lovely copse of trees, through which one catches occasional glimpses of the Bosphorus. The appearance of this place seems not to have changed across the centuries, for Evliya describes it as being "in a deep shaded recess of the hills, luxuriant with plane, cypress, willow, fir, and nut-trees." Evliya goes on to say that "Yahya Efendi is buried on the top of a hill overlooking the sea; the four walls of his türbe are covered with the inscriptions of a hundred thousand divine lovers breathing out their feelings in verse. Even now he converses every Friday night with Hızır Ilyas, taking from him lessons in mysticism." The place is evidently very holy and is always thronged with pious people at their devotions.

ORTAKÖY

The next village on the European shore of the Bosphorus is Ortaköy, the Middle Village; one is not sure between what: it is very far from the middle of the Bosphorus. There was a Byzantine church of St. Phocas here and the village was called after the saint as late as the sixteenth century; the modern Greek church preserves this dedication.

On the main street in Ortaköy there is an ancient hamam which appears to have been wholly overlooked by writers in modern times; it was built by Sinan for a certain Hüsrev Kethüda. This has recently been restored and now houses a café. The interior is curious and unlike any other existing Sinan hamam. From a camekân of the usual form (though confused by a modern gallery), one enters a rather large soğukluk consisting of a central area in two unequal bays each covered by a cradle-vault; at one end are the lavatories, at the other a bathing cubicle. From the central area one enters the hararet which, instead of being the usual large domed cruciform room, consists of four domed areas of almost equal size; the first two communicate with each other by a wide arch and here, instead of the central göbektaşı, there is a raised marble sofa or podium against one wall and with larger domes than those in the sofa-rooms; these serve as bathing cubicles. There is also another cubicle, cradle-vaulted, which is entered from the sofa-room. An arrangement of this general type is seen in a number of the older and smaller hamams, but here, where the area is large enough, the reason for it is not apparent. The bath is double, the women's section being exactly like the men's.

There is also at Ortaköy a very striking mosque on a little promontory at the water's edge; Arseven picturesquely says that to one sailing up the straits from the Marmara "it seems to be placed here like a Maşallah that wards off the evil eye from the Bosphorus"! It was built in 1854, on the site of an earlier mosque, by Sultan Abdül Mecit and its architect was Nikoğos Balyan, who built the Dolmabahçe mosque and palace. But it is a much better building than those; although the style as usual is hopelessly mixed, there is a genuinely baroque verve and movement in the undulating walls of the tympana between the great dome arches.

On the shore road near the mosque there is a Greek church dedicated to St. Phocas. The church was built in 1856, but the parish undoubtedly dates back to the Byzantine period. One block farther along the road and on the same side we see the Etz Ahayim (Tree of Life) Synagogue. The original synagogue here dates back to the

Byzantine era, though the present building was erected only in 1913. Elsewhere in Ortaköy there is an Armenian church dedicated to St. Gregory the Illuminator, dated 1837–8.

THE BOSPHORUS BRIDGE

Just outside Ortaköy we pass under the first Bosphorus bridge, opened on 27 October 1973, the 50th anniversary of the founding of the Turkish Republic. At the time it was the fourth longest suspension bridge in the world, 1,074 metres in length between the great piers (just seven metres longer than the George Washington bridge over the Hudson), with its roadway 64 metres above the water. Surprisingly enough the new bridge, with the graceful curve of its cables and the thin line of carriageway, actually enhances the beauty of the lower Bosphorus.

KURUÇEŞME

Kuruçeşme, the next village on the European shore, was up until recent years disfigured by coal, sand and gravel depots, but these have now been removed and replaced by an attractive park and promenade, part of a programme to restore the shores of the Bosphorus to their former beauty. There are three old churches in the village, two of them Greek and the other Armenian. The Greek churches are St. Demetrios and St. John the Baptist, both of which were first mentioned in 1684. The present church of St. Demetrios dates from 1798, while St. John was rebuilt in 1834. Both of them have sacred springs, that of St. Demetrios dating back to Byzantine times. The Armenian church, Surp Haç (Holy Cross), may date from the Byzantine era, though the present structure is due to a rebuilding in 1834 by Karabet Balyan. The wooden mosque on the shore road in the village was built in the eighteenth century by Tezkireci Osman Efendi, with a handsome çeşme in front.

ARNAVUTKÖY

Arnavutköy, the Albanian Village, has one of the most picturesque harbours anywhere along the Bosphorus; its sea-front is lined with picturesque old wooden houses. The oldest house along the shore is the red yalı, or seafront mansion, of Halet Çambel, the distinguished archaeologist, which was built in the years 1820–30. Along the shore there are several excellent fish restaurants.

There are two Greek churches in the village, which still has a small Greek community. Both churches in their present form date from the late nineteenth century. The one near the shore road, the Taxiarkes, is dedicated to the Archangels Michael and Gabriel; the one in the upper village to Profitis Elias (Prophet Elijah). Both churches have sacred wells. The large mosque on the seafront, Tevfikiye Camii, was commissioned by Mahmut II and built in 1832 in the neoclassical style.

The interior of Arnavutköy is also quite charming and picturesque, particularly if one takes the back streets and lanes and climbs the slopes of the hills and valleys on which they are perched. On the hill above in a superb position are the buildings of Robert College, an American coeducational lycée, founded in 1871 as the American College of Girls. The American College for Girls was the first modern lycée of its kind in Turkey and produced many women who played a leading part in the life of their country, the most famous being the writer Halide Edip Adıvar. In 1971, on the occasion of its centennial, the American College for Girls was amalgamated with the boy's lycée of the old Robert College, a little farther up the Bosphorus, with the new institution taking the latter name and occupying the site in Arnavutköy.

Off the point of Arnavutköy, Akinti Burnu (Cape of the Current) is the deepest part of the Bosphorus, over 100 metres in depth at the centre of the strait. Here the current flows so fast that it is very hard for sailing vessels to round the point. Apparently crabs also found it difficult and leaving the sea walked overland across the point, for Gyllius, after quoting Dionysus Byzantius and Aelian in his support, says: "I myself saw there stones worn down by the long procession of crabs;" and he adds: "And even if I had not seen it, I should not have thought it far from the truth that stones should be worn down by the hard claws of crabs, since we see that ants can dig out furrows and make a path by the continuous attrition of their feet."

Rounding Akinti Burnu, we enter the calm waters of Bebek Bay, one of the most beautiful on the Bosphorus. Lush rolling hills with groves of umbrella pines and cypresses rise up to form a verdant backdrop to the bay, a green frieze of trees between the blues of sea and sky. Just before the village we see on the water's edge the old Egyptian Embassy; then, just past the landing-stage, a little mosque built in 1913 by Kemalettin Bey, a leader of the neoclassical school of Turkish architecture. Like most of his buildings it is a little lifeless and dull, although the setting is quite pretty. The village itself is still attractive, though it is rapidly being ruined by the proliferation of restaurants, cafés and bars. There are still a few old wooden houses of the late Ottoman era in the back streets; the oldest is the Kavafyan Konağı, dated 1751. There is also a Greek church dedicated to St. Haralambos, dating from the mid-nineteenth century; in times past this was a dependence of the Iviron Monastery on Mount Athos in Greece.

BOSPHORUS UNIVERSITY

On the hill between Bebek and Rumeli Hisarı, the next village along the shore, stand the buildings of Boğaziçi Universitesi, or Bosphorus University. This Turkish university was established in 1971, occupying the buildings and grounds of the old Robert College. Robert College, which in its time was the finest institution of higher learning in Turkey, was founded in 1863 by Cyrus Hamlin, an American missionary who had baked bread and washed clothes for Florence Nightingale's hospital in Üsküdar. The College was named after Christopher Robert, an American philanthropist who provided the funds to build and run the institution. During the 108 years of its existence the College had on its staff or itself produced a number of men of some importance. Several of its professors occupied themselves with the antiquities of this city, and some of their works have been much used in the preparation of this guide. The most important of these were the works of Alexander van Milligen (1840–1915); his two great books, *The Walls of Constantinople* and *Byzantine Churches in Constantinople* are still the standard works on their subject. Largely through the munificence of van Milligen, the University has a very important and extensive library of books about the city, including a remarkably complete collection of foreign travellers to the Levant in ancient and rare editions. Graduates of Robert College–Bosphorus

University include two prime ministers of Bulgaria and two prime ministers of Turkey, Bülent Ecevit and Tansu Çiller, the latter being the only woman ever to hold that post.

The site of the University is superb and from its terrace one commands a stunning view of this most beautiful part of the Bosphorus. Just below the terrace is the attractive house which once belonged to Tevfik Fikret (1867–1915), for many years professor of Turkish Literature at Robert College and one of the leading poets of his time. His house, which is now a memorial museum, is called Aşıyan, or the Nest; it is on the left of the graveyard road which leads up to the University. Like most house-museums it is a little dreary, but the man was not. He was an idealist and utopian socialist, convinced that the salvation of Turkey lay in its youth, which he idealized in the person of his son Haluk, to or about whom he wrote a moving series of poems. But the young man had his own ideas about his future, for when he came of age he went off to the USA. and became a Presbyterian minister!

RUMELİ HİSARI

After Bebek Bay the Bosphorus quickly diminishes to its narrowest stretch, about 700 metres in width. It was here that Darius chose to construct his bridge of boats, designed by the Greek engineer Mandrocles of Samos, when in 512 B.C. he led an army of 700,000 men against the Scythians. While his army crossed the Great King watched from a stone throne cut into the cliff about where now stands the north tower of the castle. The throne of Darius and the two commemorative columns which he erected on the site used still to be shown in antiquity.

The village of Rumeli Hisarı is dominated by and takes its name from the fortress of the same name built by Fatih Mehmet in 1452, the year before he conquered the city. It is a splendid late medieval fortification, the object of which was, in cooperation with the older castle on the other side, Anadolu Hisarı, to cut the city off from communication with and possible aid from the Black Sea; hence the castle was originally called *Bogaz-kesen,* a sort of pun which means both "cut-throat" and "cutter of the strait". In this object it was perfectly successful, but after the fall of the city it had no further military function, and the north tower was used as a prison, especially for members of foreign embassies. The castle spans a steep valley with two tall towers on opposite hills and a third at the bottom of the valley at the water's edge, where stands the sea gate protected by a barbican. A curtain wall, defended by three smaller towers, joins the three major ones, forming an irregular figure some 250 metres long by 125 metres broad at its maximum. Fatih himself selected the site, drew the general plan of the castle, and spent much time in supervising the work of the 1,000 skilled and 2,000 unskilled workmen he had collected from the various provinces of his empire. He entrusted each of the three main towers to one of his vezirs: the north tower to Saruca Paşa, the sea tower to Halil Paşa, his Grand Vezir, and the south one to Zaganos Paşa, with the three of them striving with one another to complete the work with speed and efficiency. Over the door to the south tower an Arabic inscription records the completion of the castle in the month of Recep A.H. 856 (July–August 1452); it had been begun just four months previously. The castle was restored in 1953, in connection with the celebration of the 500th anniversary of the Conquest of Constantinople. Unfortunately the restoration demolished the little village of picturesque wooden houses inside the fortifications, but this was probably inevitable. The area inside has been made into a charming park, and the circular cistern on which once stood a small mosque (part of the minaret has been left to mark its position) has been converted into the acting area of a Greek-type theatre: here in summer productions of Shakespeare and other plays are given against the stunning background of the castle walls and towers, the Bosphorus, and the glittering lights of the villages of Asia.

There are three mosques along the shore in Rumeli Hisarı. The first of these that we see is Kayalar Mescidi, built in 1877 by Şeyh Ahmet Niyazi Efendi to replace the mescit of the dervish tekke that had been erected there in the second quarter of the seventeenth century. The second is Hacı Kemalettin Camii, commissioned by Mahmut I in 1743 to replace the original mescit from the time of Fatih. The third is Pertev Ali Paşa Camii, at the foot of the main street in the village; this was erected in the mid-seventeenth century and restored in 1972. There is also an Armenian church dedicated to St. Santuht; the present building was erected in 1856, but the original church may go back to the time of Mehmet the Conqueror.

FATİH MEHMET KÖPRÜSÜ

Fatih Mehmet Köprüsü, the second Bosphorus Bridge, spans the strait just above the two fortresses of Rumeli Hisarı and Anadolu Hisarı, the same place Darius constructed his bridge of boats in 512 B.C. The new bridge opened in 1988, exactly 2,500 years after Darius first spanned these straits between Asia and Europe. The palatial seaside mansion just before the bridge is the Zeki Paşa Yalısı. This is believed to have been built by the French architect Alexandre Vallaury in the last quarter of the nineteenth century.

BALTALİMAN AND EMİRGAN

From Rumeli Hisarı onwards the Bosphorus, even on the European side, becomes more and more rural, a succession of picturesque villages following one another with wider and wider spaces of open country between. At Baltaliman, which comes next, there is a long and fertile valley watered by a perpetual stream and flanked by a long avenue of plane trees. Contiguous is Emirgan, named after that Persian prince, Emirgüne who surrendered the town of Erivan to Murat IV without a battle. Emirgüne later became the Sultan's favourite in drinking and debauchery and was rewarded by the gift of a palace in this village. There are still the remains here of an ancient yalı, parts of it possibly going back to Emirgüne's time, but mostly built later by a Şerif of Mecca, Abdullah Paşa. The Şerifler Yalısı, as it is now called, has recently been restored. The village square is very picturesque, shaded by plane trees beneath which throngs of people are continually imbibing coffee which the excellence of the local water makes particularly delicious. Beside the square stands a baroque mosque, partly of wood, built in 1781–2 by Sultan Abdül Hamit I. It consists of a large almost square room curiously unsymmetrical, and its decor is quite elegant in its baroque way. Just above the village are the famous tulip gardens of Emirgan, well worth a visit in spring.

The Turkish Touring and Automobile Club has now restored a number of old Ottoman kiosks around the Emirgan gardens and converted them into cafés known as Pembe (Pink) Köşk, Sarı (Yellow) Köşk, Beyaz (White) Köşk and the Kir Kahveleri, thus making this one of the most delightful places on the Bosphorus to spend an afternoon or early evening enjoying a drink in beautiful surroundings.

At the northern edge of the village we see the Atlıköşk, the Kiosk of the Horse, which takes its name from the bronze statue of a horse on its front lawn. This is the former residence of the late Sakıp Sabancı. An annexe to the mansion now houses the Sabancı Museum, which has a distinguished collection of Turkish calligraphy and paintings, as well as other objects of Turkish, European and Far-Eastern art.

İSTİNYE

Beyond Emirgan comes the deep indentation of the bay of Istinye which, says Gyllius, "after the Golden Horn must be acknowledged the largest bay and the safest port of the entire Bosphorus, rich as this is in bays and ports." Its Turkish name, Istinye, is a corruption of the Byzantine, Sosthenion, itself a corruption, according to one account, of the ancient Leosthenion, from the name of a companion of Byzas who is said to have settled here; another version says that the Argonauts erected a statue here in thanksgiving *(Sosthenion)* for aid given by a winged genius of the place against their enemy on the opposite shore, King Amycus.

YENİKÖY TO TARABYA

At Yeniköy, the Greek Neapolis (the names have the same meaning, New Town, in both Turkish and Greek), the Bosphorus turns sharply north-west. This is an attractive village with seaside restaurants, a beautiful avenue of plane trees, and handsome yalıs mostly modern and luxurious. There are three churches in the village, two of them Greek and the other Armenian Catholic, all of them dating from the mid-nineteenth century. There is also a synagogue dating from the 1870s; this is thought to have been endowed by Abraham de Camondo, the famous banker and philanthropist.

At Yeniköy begins the long line of summer embassies with their beautiful gardens and parks: first that of Austria, then a little farther on at the small village of Kalender that of Germany; still farther on at Tarabya a succession of them: England, burnt down in 1911; France, burnt in 1923; Italy, rebuilt in 1906; but all still with lovely parks. When towards the beginning of the nineteenth century the seashore came to be preferred to an inland site, the summer embassies moved from the village of Belgrad in the midst of the forest of that name to Tarabya and acquired or were granted land by various sultans. The village retains in a slightly modified form its Greek name Therepeia (cure, healing) given by the Patriarch Atticus (r. 406–25) from its salubrious climate, the older name having been Pharmakeus, the Poisoner, because Medea had there thrown away her poison. The waterfront in Tarabya is lined with excellent but expensive restaurants where well-off Stamboullus come to watch one another eat. The village once had one of the largest Greek communities on the Bosphorus and there are still three Greek churches there, though services are held there only on the feast days of the saints to whom they are dedicated.

BÜYÜKDERE AND THE BELGRAD FOREST

From Tarabya the shore curves almost directly westward and one comes in a short distance to Kireçburnu (Lime Point), anciently known as Kleidai tou Pontou, Keys of the Pontus, because from here one can see directly into the Black Sea. A kilometre or so beyond this, at the end of the westward reach of the Bosphorus, stands the large village of Büyükdere at the north end of a wide bay; here are the summer embassies of Russia and Spain. Its Turkish name means Large Valley, while one of its older Greek names is Kalos Agros, the Beautiful Meadow. It is indeed a very lovely and fertile valley with fine old trees through which a road leads into the Belgrad Forest. In the midst of this forest once stood the village of Belgrad, made famous by the encomiums of Lady Mary Wortley Montague. The village was founded in 1521 by Süleyman the Magnificent after his conquest of the city of Belgrade, when he transported a certain number of the inhabitants of that city and settled them here in order to look after the reservoirs and other waterworks with which the forest abounds. The village has long since disappeared, but its name survives in that of the forest.

The waterworks, aqueducts and reservoirs, which are scattered here and there in the hills between this place and the upper end of the Golden Horn, are very impressive indeed. The aqueducts are almost entirely the work of Süleyman the Magnificent and his great architect Sinan, though some of them doubtless replaced more ancient ones. The first aqueduct one comes to, indeed, not far up the valley of Büyükdere, is later, the work of Mahmut I, finished in 1732, and conveys the water from his reservoir and several others to the taksim in Taksim Square. Mahmut's reservoir, or bend in Turkish, is a very magnificent one, with its great dam of Proconnesian marble.. The two aqueducts of Sinan that are most easily visitable because they are on the main road are also the longest and most impressive. Both are near the village of Burgaz, the ancient Pyrgos. The first is called the Bent Aqueduct *(Eğrikemer)* because it consists of two segments that meet in an obtuse angle; it is 342 metres long. This aqueduct seems to have been built originally by Andronicus I Comnenus (r. 1183–5); it was in ruins when Gyllius saw it, and Sinan must have rebuilt it pretty completely, for all the visible masonry appears to be of his time. Sinan's other aqueduct, Uzunkemer, the Long Aqueduct, is beyond Burgaz; it is 716 metres in length and strides across the valley in a most Roman fashion. These two aqueducts span the valley of the Barbyzes, the stream now called Kağıthane Suyu, which flows into the Golden Horn. This stream and its twin, the Cidaris or Alibey Suyu, together form the once-famous Sweet Waters of Europe, which in the eighteenth century was a favourite resort of Ottoman society. The Alibey Suyu is also spanned by two aqueducts of Sinan; these are much harder to find for the road is quite bad. They are also much smaller but at the same time more picturesque because they are closely hemmed in by high hills. The one across the Alibey Suyu itself is generally called Justinian's (in Turkish, however, Maglova Kemeri); Gyllius saw this too in ruins, but it was entirely rebuilt by Sinan. The other, across a tributary of the Alibey, is appropriately called Güzelce Kemer, the Handsome Aqueduct, for it is indeed very pretty. All these four aqueducts, together with several smaller ones, conduct the water from various reservoirs scattered throughout the district and convey it to the taksim at Eğri Kapı on the Sixth Hill, from where it is distributed throughout Stamboul. Sinan was working on this elaborate system of aqueducts during the years 1554–64.

SARIYER

Returning to the Bosphorus, we now sail on to Sarıyer, a very lively village inhabited largely by fishermen and their families. The Sarıyer fish market, the closest outlet for the Black Sea fisheries, is one of the best and most colourful in the city. It is located right next to the little harbour of the village, where the picturesque local fishing boats unload their catch. There are a number of good restaurants on the quay of the fishing-port itself.

One of the old mansions along the shore highway leading into Sarıyer, the Azaryan Yalısı, now houses the Sadberk Hanım Museum, a unique and rich collection of antiquities and Turkish works of art, including beautiful examples of Ottoman costumes and embroideries.

THE EUROPEAN SHORE OF THE UPPER BOSPHORUS

Those proceeding by road up the Bosphorus from Sarıyer will notice a little roadside shrine on the side of the hill above the Bosphorus just before coming to Rumeli Kavağı. This is the türbe and shrine of a Muslim saint named Telli Baba, who is reputed to have the power of finding suitable husbands for young women who pray there. After their weddings the brides come here in their gowns to fasten talismanic coils of silver wire around Telli Baba's tomb and offer up to him their prayers of thanksgiving. The saint's tomb is housed in an ancient stone building that looks as if it might have been a Greek church, perhaps once the shrine of a Christian saint venerated by the local Greek mariners praying for safe return from voyages on the Black Sea.

Two kilometres beyond Sarıyer we come to Rumeli Kavağı, the last ferry-stop on the European shore of the Bosphorus. Above it are the very scanty remains of a Byzantine castle, later taken over by the

Genoese, by whose name it is usually known. This castle formed a pair with Yoros Kalesi on the Asian hill opposite, the much more considerable remains of which are a dominant feature of the view from most parts of the upper Bosphorus.

At Rumeli Kavağı, not only the ferry but the public motor road comes to an end. Anyone wishing to explore the upper Bosphorus must hire a boat at Sarıyer or Rumeli Kavağı and take to the sea. The excursion is one of extreme delight for the country is wild, rugged and desolate, but very beautiful. Now for the first time on the Bosphorus one finds sandy beaches hidden away in romantic coves; grey herons haunt the cliffs, black cormorants dive into the limpid water, great clouds of sheerwaters, those "lost souls" of the Bosphorus, skim the surface of the sea, torn by frequent schools of dolphins. The scene is still much the same as when Jason and his Argonauts sailed past on their way to Colchis in quest of the Golden Fleece, and these upper reaches are particularly rich in memories of that stirring adventure.

Except for the two Byzantine or Genoese castles above Rumeli and Anadolu Kavağı, the fortifications of the upper Bosphorus all date either from the end of the eighteenth century or from our own time. Thus the batteries below the castles at the two Kavaks were built in 1783 by Toussaint and increased in 1794 by Monnier, two French military engineers employed by Abdül Hamit I and Selim III.

Just beyond Rumeli Kavağı and still accessible by the public road is Altın Kum, Golden Sands, the first of the sandy beaches, with a restaurant under a pleasant grove of acacia trees. But beyond this point we sail along for two or three kilometres below precipitous cliffs, sparsely covered with scrub and uninhabited, nay uninhabitable. At length one reaches a wide but shallow harbour called Büyük Liman, anciently the Harbour of the Ephesians; one sees the ruins of a number of stone buildings, among them a hamam; the beach is sandy and the valley behind is wooded and attractive, a pleasant place to swim.

After another kilometre or so past even more cliffs, one comes to a strangely shaped and craggy point well named, Garipçe (strange or curious), or, anciently, Gyropolis, Town of Vultures. This too has a fortress built in 1773 by the Baron de Tott. Here King Phineus lived and here he was plagued by the Harpies who seized his food and befouled his table until he wasted away to a wraith; at last the Argonauts arrived and the winged sons of Boreas, Zetes and Kalais, taking pity on the ancient king, their brother-in-law, chased away the noxious creatures. In return Phineus, who was a prophet, advised them about the rest of their journey and especially about how to avoid the baleful Symplegades. These, indeed, were clearly visible from his very palace, two great rocks at the mouth of the Bosphorus, one on either side, which were supposed to clash together with great rapidity and violence, thus making it very dangerous if not impossible for ships to enter or leave the strait. Phineus told the Argonauts to let loose a dove which would fly between them; if it was caught, they were to give up their journey, but if it got through safely, they were to wait till the rocks opened once more and then row their hardest. The Symplegades just shaved off the tailfeathers of the dove and slightly damaged the stern-works of the Argo.

The Symplegades, the Clashing Rocks, were also called Cyanean, the Blue Rocks, or in Turkish Öreke Taşı, the Distaff Rock or Midwife's Stool. The European one is a striking feature at the very mouth of the Bosphorus, formerly some 100 metres offshore at Rumeli Feneri, the Rumelian Lighthouse. There is a tiny village here and the remains of a fort built in 1769 by a Greek engineer. The Rock, which is now joined to the shore by a concrete mole, is about 20 metres high and something less than 200 metres long, divided by deep fissures into several parts. On the highest plateau stands what is left of the so-called Pillar of Pompey. "The ascent to this peak," says Gyllius, "is not open except by one approach, and this, extremely narrow, so that one must climb up on all fours." Nowadays there are two approaches, one slightly easier than the other, but both disagreeable enough for one who is terrified of heights. The reward of intrepidity is a fine view of the Black Sea and the Bosphorus, and the base of Pompey's column. It is not really a column base but an ancient altar, decorated with a garlanded ram's head and other reliefs now much worn; it once had a Latin inscription, no longer legible, the transcription and interpretation of which are matters of discussion. Certainly neither altar nor column had anything to do with Pompey, and we do not know who first gave it this misleading name: it was after Gyllius' time evidently, since he does not mention it. He thought the altar was probably a remnant of the shrine to Apollo which Dionysius of Byzantium says the Romans erected on one of the Cyanean Rocks. The column itself, with its Corinthian capital, toppled down in April 1680 and had utterly disappeared by 1800. There is now a simple fish restaurant on the Rock, with its tables set out on the breakwater at the very end of the Bosphorus.

THE ASIAN SHORE OF THE UPPER BOSPHORUS
We now cross the Bosphorus and sail down the Asiatic coast. Curiously enough the Asian shores of the upper Bosphorus are very imperfectly known and seem to have been rarely visited even by the few authors who write about them. The only safe guide is Gyllius, for he alone appears to have explored the region in detail. Even Gyllius' account, however, is not altogether free from difficulties, for he never gives the Turkish names of places in this region, perhaps because in his time they didn't yet have any. Nevertheless, there are four places in his narrative which can be identified with certainty; the Rhebas River, the Promontorium Ancyraeum, the Promontorium Coracium and the Fanum Jovis; and from these the others can be worked out. The Rhebas still retains a version of its ancient name: Riva or Irva Deresi; it is a river that flows into the Black Sea about four kilometres beyond the mouth of the Bosphorus, and just beyond it is the great table-like rocky islet in the sea which he calls Colonean but is now known as Eşek Adası, Donkey Island. Riva is very attractive and picturesque with its Genoese castle at the end of a long sandy beach; it is a fine place to swim and picnic.

The Ancyraean Cape is Yum Burnu, Cape of Good Omen; as its hopeful name might imply, it is just at the mouth of the Bosphorus. In Gyllius' time it was called Cape Psomion; it was here that Jason took aboard a stone anchor for the Argos, hence its ancient name of Ancyraean. The reef or rock which has the best claim to be the Asian Cyanean stands immediately under the southern cliff face of Yum Burnu and is thus described by Gyllius, a description which is perfectly applicable to this day: "The reef is divided into four rocks above water which, however, are joined below; it is separated from the continent by a narrow channel filled with many stones, by which as by a staircase one can cross the channel with dry feet when the sea is calm; but when the sea is rough waves surround the four rocks into which I said the reef is divided. Three of these are low and more or less submerged, but the middle one is higher than the European rock, sloping up to an acute point and roundish right up to its summit; it is splashed by the waves but not submerged and is everywhere precipitous and straight."

The bay to the south of Yum Burnu is now called Kabakoz Limanı, the Harbour of the Wild Walnuts; in Gyllius' time it was known as the Bay of Haghios Sideros (that is, St. Anchor – the half-remembered story of the Argonautic anchor had given rise in the minds of the medieval Greeks to an apocryphal holy man!). On the south this bay is bounded by a point not named by Gyllius but nowadays called Anadolu Feneri Burnu, after the lighthouse (*fener*) on the promontory above. Below the lighthouse a village of the same name clings perilously to the cliff. Just south of this is the bay which Gyllius calls Ampelodes, now Çakal Limanı, the Bay of Jackals, fringed by savage and rocky precipices. The next promontory beyond this, unnamed by Gyllius, is now called Poyraz Burnu. (In Turkish *Poyraz is* the fierce north-east wind which howls down the Bosphorus in winter; its name is a corruption of Boreas, the Greek god of the north wind.) On Poyraz Burnu, just opposite Garipçe and like it strangely shaped, is a fortress built in 1773 by the Baron de Tott, and another small village. The long sandy beach to the south is now known as Poyraz Bay; the Greeks of Gyllius' time called it Dios Sacra, "because, I suppose, there was once an altar here either of Jove or of Neptune, the other Jove." This is one of the most pleasant places on the Bosphorus to swim and spend a leisurely afternoon. This bay is bounded on the south by Fil Burnu, Elephant Point, called in Gyllius' time Coracium, Rooky, "because the Greeks of this age say that ravens are wont to build their nests there." The long stretch of concave coast between here and Anadolu Kavağı is hardly to be described as a bay, so rugged and precipitous is it. It is now called Keçili Liman, Goats' Bay, and we have seen not only goats and sheep but even cows grazing on its rather barren slopes.

We now come to Gyllius' Fane of Jove, by which he means the temple of Zeus Ourious, Zeus of the Favouring Wind, and the Hieron or holy precinct where there were shrines of the Twelve Gods. Keçili Liman is bounded on the south by a cape still known by a version of its ancient name, Yoros or Yeros Burnu, doubtless from Ourious. The temple or temples were founded by Phrixos, evidently on a "stop-over" while the winged ram with the golden fleece was flying him towards Colchis. Another version is that the shrines were founded by Jason on his return journey; but we must refer our readers to Gyllius' lengthy and erudite discussion of the pros and cons: he did like his mythology to make sense! At all events, the Hieron must have been somewhere near the site now occupied by the so-called Genoese Castle. Like the opposite castle above Rumeli Kavağı, this one is not really Genoese but Byzantine, as is shown by various Greek inscriptions still to be found in the walls. About the middle of the fourteenth century both castles were taken over by the Genoese who assumed responsibility for the defence of the northern approaches to Constantinople; they may have repaired and extended the fortifications. Gyllius rather oddly describes this castle as small though it is in fact by far the largest fortress on the Bosphorus, almost twice the area of Rumeli Hisarı; doubtless he was thinking not of the long surrounding walls but only of the citadel itself, probably the only part still inhabited in his day. Evliya tells us that Beyazit I built a mosque there and that Fatih Mehmet restored and garrisoned it.

ANADOLU KAVAĞI TO BEYKOZ

Below the castle to the south is the village of Anadolu Kavağı, the first village of any size on the Asiatic shore and the last stop on this side of the Bosphorus ferry. The fortifications here, like those at Rumeli Kavağı, were built in 1783 by Toussaint and increased in 1794 by Monnier. To the south of the village, above the capes of Macar and Sütlüce, is the hill now known as Yuşa Tepesi, Hill of Joshua, though the Joshua in question seems not to have been Judge of Israel but a local Muslim saint. The hill, except for Çamlıca the highest on the Bosphorus – over 200 metres – was anciently called the Bed of

Hercules, but is better known to Europeans as the Giant's Grave. This is the place of which Byron wrote:

> The wind swept down the Euxine, and the wave
> Broke foaming o'er the blue Symplegades,
> 'Tis a grand sight from off the Giant's Grave
> To watch the progress of those rolling seas
> Between the Bosphorus, as they lash and lave
> Europe and Asia, you being quite at ease:
> There's not a sea the passenger e'er pukes in,
> Turns up more dangerous breakers than the Euxine.

The sight is grand indeed, for one can see almost the entire course of the Bosphorus from the Black Sea to the Marmara. On top of the hill is an enormous "grave" some 12 metres long: it was a very large giant evidently.

Opposite Büyükdere the coast forms a long shallow bay with rather dangerous sandbanks in the sea and a rugged and inhospitable coast-line. At Selvi Burnu, Poplar Point, the coast turns east to the charming valley of the Tokat Deresi. Here Fatih himself built a kiosk and so also later did Süleyman, a place described by Gyllius as a "royal villa shaded by woods of various trees, especially planes"; he goes on to mention the landing stairs, "by which the King, crossing the shallow shore of the sea, disembarks into his gardens." It is from these landing stairs that the place gets its modern name, Hünkâr Iskelesi, the Emperor's Landing Place, which in turn gave its name to the famous treaty that was signed here in 1833 between Russia and the Sublime Porte. The present little palace was only built in the middle of the nineteenth century by the Armenian architect Sarkis Balyan; it is now used as a hospital, but is still shaded by a lovely grove of plane trees.

The large village of Beykoz, Prince's Walnut, is still extremely pretty and rural in spite of several large factories that have been erected in the neighbourhood. Here, Dionysius, Gyllius and Evliya agree, is the one place in the Bosphorus where swordfish are caught, and Evliya gives an entertaining account of the method:

There is a dalyan or structure for fanging the swordfish; it is composed of five or six masts, on the highest of which sits a man who keeps a lookout for the fish that come in from the Black Sea. When he sees them drawing near, he throws a stone into the sea in order to frighten them, wherein he succeeds so well that they all take the direction of the harbour, where they think to find security, but fall into the nets laid for them in the water. The nets being closed, on warning given from the man sitting in the lookout, the fishermen flock round to kill them without their being able to make any resistance with their swords. The fish if boiled with garlic and vineyard herbs is excellent.

There is still a dalyan at Beykoz that is used to catch different sorts of fish, though no longer the swordfish. The modern method of catching a swordfish is to harpoon it from a rowboat while it naps on the surface of the water.

Gyllius is at pains to show that Beykoz was the home of the savage Amycus, king of the no less savage Bebryces. He insisted on boxing with any stranger who landed on his coast and, since he was the son of Poseidon and the best boxer in the world, he always killed his opponent. At last, however, he met his match in one of the Argonauts, Polyduces (Pollox), son of Zeus and Leda, who was even better than he and killed him. The grave of King Amycus was pointed out in antiquity and it is rather strange, as Lechevalier remarks, that Gyllius failed to identify it with the Giant's Grave. On the spot where King Amycus was killed there grew up an *insana laurus,* an insane bay-tree, which resembled Banquo's "insane root which takes the reason prisoner."

Beykoz has a very extraordinary çeşme in the public square. "This fountain," says the *Hadika,* "has not its equal in beauty in all the villages of the Bosphorus." It forms a sort of domed and columned loggia, very pretty indeed, and quite unlike any other Bosphorus fountain; its inscription dates it to A.H. 1159 (A.D. 1746) and the *Hadika* says it was built under the superintendence of one Ishak Aga, inspector of the customs.

BEYKOZ TO KANLİCA

South of Beykoz at Incir Köyü, Figtree Village, is the charming valley of Sultaniye Deresi, where Beyazit II established extensive gardens. A little farther on is Paşabahçe, the Pasha's Garden, so called from the palace and gardens established here by Hezarpare Ahmet Paşa, Grand Vezir under Murat IV; its mosque was built in 1763 by Mustafa III. The village now manufactures glass as Beykoz used to do, and as at Beykoz, various factories have been erected here without, however, entirely destroying its attractiveness. About Çubuklu, the next village to the south, Evliya tells an amusing story: "Beyazit II, having brought his son Selim I from Trebizond to Constantinople, gave him in this place in a fit of anger eight strokes with a cane *(çubuk)*, which eight strokes were prophetic of the years of his reign. At the same time, he said to him, 'Boy, don't be angry, these eight strokes shall fructify during eight years of reign.' Selim stuck the dry cane into the ground, praying to heaven that it might strike root and bear fruit. The Şeyh Kara Şemseddin and Beyazit himself said, 'Amen;' the cane began to take root and even now bears cornels, five of which weigh a drachma."

The village was anciently called Eirenaion, Peaceful, and had a very famous monastery founded in 420 by St. Alexander for his order of Akoimetai, the Unsleeping, who prayed in relays day and night. Now it has gasoline installations, but is still in a very beautiful and fruitful valley.

On the hill above the village is the palace of the Khedive of Egypt with its distinctive tower, a characteristic landmark on this part of the Bosphorus; it was built by Abbas Halim Paşa, the last Khedive (that is, hereditary Viceroy), about 1900, and for a palace of that date has considerable charm. Its western façade overlooking the Bosphorus is semicircular with a handsome marble-columned porch and a semicircular hall within; the trees have grown up too much and spoil the outlook from here, but the upper floor, especially the tower room and a charming loggia on the roof, command some of the finest views on the Bosphorus. The Turkish Touring and Automobile Club has restored the mansion and redecorated it superbly in its original Art Nouveau style; it now serves as a luxury hotel and restaurant.

KANLİCA TO ANADOLU HİSARI

Kanlica has, since the time of Evliya at least, been famous for its yogurt, the best in the Istanbul area, which it is pleasant to eat in one of the little restaurants that are to be found around the very attractive, plane-tree shaded square by the iskele. The village, which is unspoiled by industry, boasts a mosque of some interest. The mosque, on the far side of the square, was founded in A.H. 967, or A.D. 1559–60, as the Arabic inscription over the door tells us, by the vezir Iskender Paşa; it is a minor work of Sinan. Of the very simplest type, it has a wooden porch and roof with a flat ceiling; but both porch and roof are clearly later, indeed modern, reconstructions, for Evliya says that it had a wooden dome inside. The founder's türbe is nearby.

Between Kanlica and Anadolu Hisarı are the remains of the oldest yalı on the Bosphorus, that of the Grand Vezir Köprülü Amcazade Hüseyin Paşa, built about 1698. All that exists of the original house is the wreck of a once very beautiful room built out on piles over the sea. The central area has a wooden dome with spacious bays on three sides of it; a continuous row of low windows in these bays lets in the cool breezes and gives views of the Bosphorus in all directions. But the astonishing thing about it was the exquisite and elaborate moulding and painting of ceiling and walls with arabesques, geometrical designs, floral garlands, in enchanting colours and in gold; especially lovely was a long series of panels above the windows each with a vase of different flowers. Towards the beginning of the twentieth century an attempt to rescue this unique room from ruin was made by the Society of the Friends of Istanbul, who published a sumptuous album of hand-gilded and coloured plates with a preface by Pierre Loti and descriptive text by H. Saladin. Since then, however, the room has been totally neglected and is now in the last stages of decay. It is said that a restoration is planned in the near future; one hopes that it is not already too late to save what is left of this once beautiful and historic yalı.

ANADOLU HİSARI

We come now to the Anatolian Castle opposite the Rumelian one. The castle was built by Beyazit I Yıldırım, the Thunderbolt, probably in 1390 or a few years later. This is the Beyazit whom Marlowe makes introduce himself as the Turkish Emperor:

> Dread Lord of Affrike, Europe and Asia,
> Great King and conquerour of Grecia,
> The Ocean, Terrene, and the cole-blacke sea,
> The high and highest Monarke of the world.
> *Tamburlaine*, 1, 940 seqq.

But a few scenes later we find Tamburlaine entering in triumph and "two Moores drawing Baiazeth in his cage, and his wife following him." Beyazit appears to have committed suicide soon after; and the legend has it that in order to avoid the ignominy of seeing his wife perform menial services for a possible conqueror, as Beyazit had had to do, no subsequent Ottoman sultan ever contracted a legal marriage. This tale is singularly unfounded since several later sultans were in fact legally married, including Fatih Mehmet and Süleyman the Magnificent.

The castle is a small one consisting of a keep and its surrounding wall, together with an outer wall or barbican guarded by three towers; parts of the barbican have been demolished. Gabriel suggests, on the basis both of historical sources and methods of construction, that only the keep and its wall were built by Beyazit, the barbican and towers being added later by Fatih Mehmet at the same time that he was building the fortress opposite. It is a pretty little castle and well deserves the name of Güzelce, the Handsome or Charming One, by which it was originally known. And the village which surrounds it is very attractive; from the quiet and picturesque street that borders the castle along the sea, there is one of the best views of the superb fortifications of Rumeli Hisarı. In this street also is one of the very few surviving namazgahs, or open air mosques; it consists simply of a stone mihrab and a stone mimber standing at one end of a grassy plot of ground surrounded by low walls. Since the namazgah is mentioned in the *Hadika* but not by Evliya, one may take it that it was established some time between 1660 and 1780. Unfortunately it is in a rather dilapidated condition.

THE SWEET WATERS OF ASIA

The village is bathed on the south by one of the two rivers known to Europeans as the Sweet Waters of Asia. This one is called in Turkish Göksu, or Sky Stream; the other, a few hundred metres to the south, is Küçüksu, or Little Stream. Between them, in what was once a lovely meadow, there are a small palace and an elaborate çeşme, the favourite resort on holidays in Ottoman times of the *beau monde*: it is still a resort, though the *monde* is not so *beau* (at least not socially), and beside Küçüksu is a swimming place with an artificially sandy beach.

The Küçüksu Çeşme, one of the most beautiful baroque fountains in Istanbul and a favourite subject for artists in the nineteenth century, was founded by Selim III in 1806. The Sultan's name and the date of foundation of the fountain are given in a long calligraphic chronogram of 32 lines inscribed across all four faces of the çeşme, ending with these lines:

> And our course wishes to be of this water now,
> And to be as tall as a cypress tree, a fragile beauty
>   in the meadow
> Hatif, tell us a date worthy of this soul-caressing fountain
> Küçüksu gave to this continent brilliance and light.

The palace of Küçüksu, a pretty little edifice on the lip of the sea, was erected for Sultan Abdül Mecit in 1856–7 by Nikoğos Balyan on the site of several earlier imperial residences, the first of them apparently dating from 1752. Abdül Mecit at first used Küçüksu only as a pied-à-terre on day-trips from Dolmabahçe, and so the palace did not include bedrooms in its original design. But several chambers were converted into bedrooms later in the nineteenth century, when Küçüksu was used to house visiting dignitaries, a role it continued to serve in the first half-century of the Republic. In recent years the palace has been restored and it is now open as a museum.

Just next to the beach at Küçüksu stands the largest and grandest yali of them all, that of Kıbrıslı Mustafa Emin Paşa. Built originally about 1760 but added to and redecorated later, its façade on the Bosphorus is over 60 metres long, mostly of one storey only but with a central part of two. The rooms are arranged with great symmetry around three, rather than the usual two, great halls: of these the eastern one is perhaps the most beautiful, paved in marble with a marble fountain in the centre under a vaulted ceiling decorated with exquisite mouldings and painted panels of bowls of flowers; to north and south slender wooden columns with Corinthian columns divide the central space from two bays, one giving directly onto the sea, the other providing the entrance from the garden. Four superbly proportioned rooms open from this hall, two overlooking the Bosphorus, two the garden Still farther to the east is an enormous ballroom and a charming greenhouse with a pebble-mosaic pavement and a great marble pool with a curious fountain. The harem occupied the western wing of the house and was the oldest part of it: unfortunately it was demolished in the early 1970s.

KANDİLLİ TO ÇENGELKÖY

We are now in the village of Kandilli, where there are several charming yalıs, of which perhaps the handsomest as well as the best preserved is that of the Counts Ostrorog, built about 1790, distinguished by its rust-red colour. It is named after the Ostrorogs, a noble French-Polish family who moved to Turkey in the late eighteenth century. The last of the line, Count Jean Ostrorog, died in 1975. On the hill above is the palace of Adile Sultan, sister of Sultan Abdül Aziz. The palace was built in 1856 and restored after a fire in the 1980s; it is now a secondary school for girls.

The next ferry stop is the adjacent village of Vaniköy. Above Vaniköy we can see the tower of the Istanbul Rasathane, an astronomical observatory and seismological research centre. The Rasathane has a small but interesting astronomy museum, with a collection of the instruments and manuscripts of the sixteenth-century Turkish astronomer Takiuddin.

The large and imposing building on the shore south of Vaniköy is the Kuleli Officers Training College. The original building here was a barracks erected in 1828 by Mahmut II; Sultan Abdül Aziz replaced this in 1863 with the present *Empire*-style building, whose flanking conical-capped towers are landmarks on the Asian shore of the Bosphorus.

It was more or less on this site, probably, that the Empress Theodora, Justinian's wife, established her famous hospice for fallen women, called Metanoia, or Repentance, of which Procopius writes with such bitter irony: "Theodora also devoted considerable attention to the punishment of women caught in carnal sin. She picked up some five hundred harlots in the forum, who earned a miserable living by selling themselves there for three obols, and sent them to the opposite mainland, where they were locked up in the monastery called Repentance to force them to reform their way of life. Some of them, however, threw themselves from the parapets at night and thus freed themselves from an undesired salvation." The irony consists in the fact that, according to Procopius, Theodora was herself a harlot, and utterly unrepentent.

Çengelköy, the Village of the Hooks, so-called according to Evliya because after the Conquest a store of Byzantine anchor hooks was found here, is an exceptionally pretty village with at least one extremely handsome yalı, that of Sadullah Paşa, dating from the late eighteenth century. The seaside village square is very picturesque, shaded by venerable plane trees and graced by a lovely baroque fountain. There are good restaurants on the square where one can dine while gazing down the Bosphorus towards the skyline of Stamboul.

BEYLERBEY

We now approach the Bosphorus Bridge once again as we come to the village of Beylerbey, known anciently as Stavros, or the Cross. Next to the iskele there is an imperial mosque known popularly as Beylerbey Camii. According to its dedicatory inscription, this was built in 1778 by Abdül Hamit I as part of a very extensive pious foundation, the other buildings of which, however, are not grouped round the mosque, as is the usual practice, but are near Yeni Cami in the old city. The mosque, a work of the architect Mehmet Tahir, is an attractive example of the baroque style, its dome arches arranged in an octagon, vigorously emphasized within and without, its mihrab in a projecting apse, richly decorated with an assortment of tiles of different periods from the sixteenth to the eighteenth century. The mimber and kürsü are unusually elegant and beautiful works, both of them of wood inlaid with ivory. It has two minarets, the second one added later by Mahmut II.

Beyond the village, and almost directly under the Bosphorus Bridge, we now come to the Palace of Beylerbey. The palace and the village were named after a Beylerbey, an Ottoman title that literally means Lord of Lords; this was Mehmet Paşa, Governor of Rumeli in the reign of Murat III (r. 1574–95). Mehmet Paşa built a mansion on this site at that time, and though it eventually vanished, the name Beylerbey lived on. The present Palace of Beylerbey was built for Abdül Aziz in 1861–5 by Sarkis Balyan, brother of Nikoğos Balyan, architect of Dolmabahçe Sarayı. Beylerbey was used mainly as a summer lodge and as a residence for visiting dignitaries, one of the first being the Empress Eugénie of France, later visitors including the Emperor Franz Joseph of Austria, the Shah Nasireddin of Persia, and King Edward VIII and Mrs. Simpson of England. Abdül Hamit II lived here after his return from exile in Salonica, dying in Beylerbey in 1918. In recent years the palace has been splendidly restored and is now open as a museum.

The palace is divided into the usual selamlık and harem. The ground floor of this three-storey building houses the kitchens, with the state rooms and the imperial apartments on the two upper floors, a total of 26 elegantly furnished rooms, with six grand salons. The grandest of these salons are the Yellow Pavilion and the Marble Pavilion, the latter focused on a large pool with an elaborate cascade fountain. Beylerbey is as elaborately furnished and decorated as Dolmabahçe, including Hereke carpets; chandeliers of Bohemian crystal; French clocks; vases from China, Japan, France, and the imperial Ottoman workshops at Yıldız; and some superb murals by painters such as Aivazovski. The Royal Stables have also been restored; these occupy the building to the right of the palace as one looks at it from the sea. From the sea the palace is extremely attractive, with its two little marble pavilions at either end of the marble quay and bordered by lovely gardens.

Beyond Beylerbey we come to Kuzguncuk, another pretty village adorned by a very handsome yalı with a rounded façade on the

Bosphorus. After this we come to Üsküdar, the last (or the first) town on the Asiatic shore of the Bosphorus. From here our ferry sails back to the Galata Bridge, where we complete our journey up and down this most beautiful and historic strait.

23

A Last Stroll

Our tours have now taken us through nearly every part of the city and to most of its historical monuments. But, as we have perhaps learned on our strolls, Istanbul is much more than just an inhabited museum, for the old town has a beauty and fascination that go quite beyond its history and its architecture. One is apt to feel this when seated at a *çayevi* or *meyhane* in a sun-dappled square, or while taking one's ease in a vine-shaded café beside the Bosphorus. Little has been said of the Stamboullus themselves, but the visitor will surely have experienced innumerable examples of their grave friendliness and unfailing hospitality. Much of the pleasure of visiting or living in this city derives from the warm and relaxed company of its residents. *"Hoş geldiniz!"* (Welcome), they say to the stranger who arrives in their city or their home; and when one leaves one is sent off with a *"Güle Güle!"* (Go with Smiles), as if to lessen the inevitable sadness of departure. But how can one not feel sad when leaving this beautiful city.

But before we leave let us take one last stroll through Stamboul, to visit an enchanting place which we have somehow missed on our earlier tours. This is the venerable district of Kum Kapı, which lies at the foot of the Second and Third Hills along the Marmara shore. There are no monuments here of any historic or architectural importance, just a wonderful old Stamboul neighbourhood. The harbour of Kum Kapı, the ancient Kontoscalion, is the last of the Byzantine ports still left on the Marmara coast of the city. It is always filled with picturesque caiques and the quayside is often carpeted with brilliantly-dyed fishing nets spread there to be dried and mended. The fish market there is one of the liveliest and most colourful in the city; the shouts and cries of the fishmongers are liable to be in any of several languages: Turkish, Greek, Armenian and even Laz, raucous and ribald in all four.

From the port a cobbled road leads down under the railway line and through the now almost vanished remnants of the ancient Porta Kontoscalion. In Turkish times this was known as Kum Kapı, the Sand Gate, whose name now survives in that of the surrounding neighbourhood. Up until the beginning of this century one could still see on the tower to the left of this gate the imperial monogram and coat of arms of Andronicus II Palaeologus (r. 1282–1328).

A short distance along we come to the picturesque village square of Kum Kapı. (Another discovery of our strolls is that Istanbul is really a collection of villages, usually clustering around a mosque or a market square such as the one we see here.) The square has an old street fountain in its centre and is surrounded by the stalls and barrows of a fish and fruit and vegetable market, as well as several excellent fish restaurants. (Up until the early 1970s one of these restaurants was called Cansız Balık, the Dead Fish, but its one-eyed Armenian owner was persuaded that the sign frightened away customers and so he has changed its name.) When we have had our fill and more we can sit by the window and watch the infinitely varied procession of local life passing through this most colourful square. At times like this we feel that the old town, for all its faults and flaws, has managed to retain some of the humane qualities of communal life and rich connections with the past that have been lost in most modern cities. In that mood we think of our own strolls through Stamboul and of the dear friends who were our companions here, many of them now departed and some gone forever. We think too of Evliya Çelebi, who has been our companion-guide for so long, and wonder what he might say if he could once again walk through the streets of his beloved town, so changed but so much the same. Knowing him as we do, we imagine that he might repeat the words of his contemporary, the historian Solak Dede, whom Evliya quotes in the *Seyahatname:* "'Oh, my God,' said Solak Dede after finishing his *Description of Constantinople,* 'let this town flourish till the end of time!'"

Appendices

BYZANTINE EMPERORS

Constantine the Great, 324–37
Constantius, 337–61
Julian the Apostate, 361–3
Jovian, 363–4
Valens, 364–78
Theodosius the Great, 379–95
Arcadius, 395–408
Theodosius II, 408–50
Marcian, 450–7
Leo I, 457–74
Leo II, 474
Zeno, 474–91
Anastasius 1, 491–518
Justin I, 518–27
Justinian the Great, 527–65
Justin II, 565–78
Tiberius II, 578–82
Maurice, 582–602
Phocas, 602–10
Heraclius, 610–41
Constantine II, 641
Heracleonas, 641
Constantine III, 641–68
Constantine IV, 668–85
Justinian II, 685–95
Leontius, 695–8
Tiberius III, 698–705
Justinian II (for the second time), 705–11

Phillipicus Bardanes, 711–13
Anastasius II, 713–15
Theodosius III, 715–17
Leo III, 717–41
Constantine V, 741–75
Leo IV, 775–80
Constantine VI, 780–97
Eirene, 797–802
Nicephorus I, 802–11
Stauracius, 811
Michael I, 811–13
Leo V, 813–20
Michael II, 820–9
Theophilus, 829–42
Michael III, 842–67
Basil I, 867–86
Leo VI, 886–912
Alexander, 912–13
Constantine VII Porphyrogenitus, 913–59
Romanus I Lecapenus (co-emperor), 919–44
Romanus II, 959–63
Nicephorus II Phocas, 963–9
John I Tzimisces, 969–76
Basil II, 976–1024
Constantine VIII, 1025–8
Romanus III Argyrus, 1028–34
Michael IV, 1034–41
Michael V, 1041–2
Theodora and Zoe, 1042
Constantine IX, 1042–55
Theodora (for the second time), 1055–6
Michael VI, 1056–7
Isaac I Comnenus, 1057–9
Romanus IV Diogenes, 1067–71
Michael VII Ducas, 1071–8
Nicephorus III Botaniates, 1078–81

Alexius I Comnenus, 1081–1118
John II Comnenus, 1118–43
Manuel I Comnenus, 1143–80
Alexius II Comnenus, 1180–3
Andronicus I Comnenus, 1183–5
Isaac II Angelus, 1185–95
Alexius III Angelus, 1195–1203
Isaac II Angelus (for the second time), 1203–4
Alexius IV Angelus (co-emperor), 1203–4
Alexius V Ducas, 1204

THE LATIN OCCUPATION
Baudouin I, 1204–5
Henri, 1205–16
Pierre de Courtenoi, 1216–19
Robert, 1219–28
Baudouin II, 1228–61

BYZANTINE EMPERORS IN NICAEA
Theodore I Lascaris, 1204–22
John IV Vatatzes, 1222–54
Theodore II Lascaris, 1254–8
John IV Lascaris (co-emperor), 1258–61
Michael VIII Palaeologus (co-emperor), 1258–61

RESTORATION OF BYZANTIUM
Michael VIII Palaeologus, 1261–82
Andronicus II Palaeologus, 1282–1328
Michael IX Palaeologus (co-emperor), 1295–1320
Andronicus III Palaeologus, 1328–41
John V Palaeologus, 1341–76
John VI Cantacuzenus (co-emperor), 1341–54
Andronicus IV Palaeologus, 1376–9
John V Palaeologus (for the second time), 1379–91
John VII Palaeologus, 1390
Manuel II Palaeologus, 1391–1425

John VIII Palaeologus, 1425–48
Constantine XI Dragases, 1449–53

OTTOMAN SULTANS

Osman Gazi (chieftain, not sultan), ca. 1288–1326
Orhan Gazi, 1326–62
Murat I, 1362–89
Beyazit I, 1389–1402
(Interregnum), 1402–13
Mehmet I, 1413–21
Murat II, 1421–44, 1446–51
Mehmet II, 1444–6, 1451–81
Beyazit II, 1481–1512
Selim I, 1512–20
Süleyman I, 1520–66
Selim II, 1566–74
Murat III, 1574–95
Mehmet III, 1595–1603
Ahmet I, 1603–17
Mustafa I, 1617–18
Osman II, 1618–22
Mustafa I (for the second time), 1622–3
Murat IV, 1623–40
Ibrahim, 1640–8
Mehmet IV, 1648–87
Süleyman II, 1687–91
Ahmet II, 1691–5
Mustafa II, 1695–1703
Ahmet III, 1703–30
Mahmut I, 1730–54
Osman III, 1754–7
Mustafa III, 1757–74
Abdül Hamit I, 1774–89
Selim III, 1789–1807
Mustafa IV, 1807–8
Mahmut II, 1808–39

Abdül Mecit I, 1839–61
Abdül Aziz, 1861–76
Murat V, 1876
Abdül Hamit II, 1876–1909
Mehmet V, 1909–18
Mehmet VI, 1918–22
Abdül Mecit (II) (Caliph only), 1922–4

NOTES ON BYZANTINE ARCHITECTURAL FORMS

The earliest buildings to be used as churches in the ancient world were chiefly of two types: the basilica and the centralized building. The basilica, developed in Hellenistic and Roman times for a variety of public purposes, was for several centuries the plan most widely adopted for ordinary churches. It is a long rectangular building divided by two rows of columns into three parts, a wide central nave flanked by an aisle on each side; at the east end of the nave is a semicircular projection or apse. The entrance, at the west and opposite the apse, is generally preceded by a vestibule or narthex, which in turn opens into a large arcaded courtyard or atrium. Dozens of early examples of this plan are to be found in all parts of the Roman Empire, but in Istanbul only one pure basilica has survived, the church of St. John of Studius, built in 449–50, now partly ruined, but whose basilical structure is still clearly visible.

The early basilicas had pitched roofs and flat ceilings. Later, chiefly in the reign of Justinian, an innovation was made by introducing a dome. Two ancient examples in Istanbul survive intact: Haghia Eirene and Haghia Sophia. The nave of the former is covered at the east by a large dome, at the west by a smaller, slightly elliptical domical vault; otherwise it is a very typical basilica. In Haghia Sophia the enormous central dome is supported to east and west by two semidomes of equal diameter and there are other modifications which to a superficial view conceal its essentially basilical plan.

The other type of classical building sometimes used for churches was of a centralized plan, round or polygonal. In Istanbul there remain the very scanty ruins of a few such buildings of a very early period, but the most famous and beautiful is somewhat later in date, the church of SS. Sergius and Bacchus built by Justinian in 527. In form it is an octagon inscribed in a rectangle with a projecting apse and a large central dome. Between the eight piers which support the dome, there are pairs of columns on the ground floor and gallery level, thus making continuous ambulatories except in front of the apse. SS. Sergius and Bacchus closely resembles the contemporary church of St. Vitale at Ravenna.

The 250 years after Justinian (roughly 600 to 850) were a period of decline and confusion, unfavourable to the arts. When architecture began to revive in the ninth century, a new type of church building came into vogue, generally known as the cross-domed church. In this type a central dome is surrounded in the axes of the building by four long barrel vaults resting on four strong corner piers, thus forming an internal cross; on three sides are aisles and galleries, so that the exterior is rectangular. At the east end the wide central apse is flanked by two smaller side apses; thenceforward three apses became habitual, demanded by the developed ritual; and at the west there is the usual narthex. In Istanbul the clearest and grandest example of this type is the church of St. Theodosia (Gül Camii), probably dating from the eleventh century.

Another type, often considered as a mere development of the plan of the cross-domed church, though it may have had an independent origin, has been called by several names, but we shall identify it as the four-column church because its most striking internal feature is the four columns which here take the place of the corner piers of the earlier type as supports for the dome. These churches are all small and tall, more or less square on the exterior, but preserving the cruciform plan within. There are no galleries, except sometimes over the narthex, but the four corners of the cross are occupied by bays domed or with domical vaults on high drums; these, together with the central dome, form a quincunx, by which name this type is sometimes known. The four-column church first appears in Istanbul in the ninth or tenth century and thereafter became almost standard; its small size was suitable to the declining revenues of the shrinking Empire, while its interior form provided ample areas for mosaic and fresco decoration. In Istanbul no less than eight examples survive, of which perhaps the most typical are the two churches which form parts of the complex building of St. Saviour Pantocrator (Zeyrek Camii).

All the Byzantine churches in Istanbul are built of brick, including Haghia Sophia, and they were generally little adorned on the exterior, depending for their effect on the warm brick colours of the walls and the darker areas of windows which were usually plentiful and large. Towards the end of the Empire in the thirteenth and fourteenth centuries, exteriors were sometimes enlivened by polychrome decoration in brick and stone, seen at its best and most elaborate in the façade of the outer narthex of St. Theodore (Kilise Camii) or in that of the palace of Constantine Porphyrogenitus (Tekfur Saray). As if to compensate for the relative austerity of the outside, the interior of the churches blazed with colour and life. The lower parts of the walls up to the springing of the vaults were sheathed in marble, while the vaults, domes and upper walls were covered in gold mosaic. The most magnificent example of marble revetment is that in Haghia Sophia where a dozen different kinds of rare and costly marbles are used, the thin slabs being sawn in two and opened out so as to form intricate designs. The Great Church was of course unique, though there may have been a few others of Justinian's time almost equally lavishly covered with marble. But even the humbler and smaller churches of a later period had their revetment, largely of the common but attractive greyish-white Proconnesian marble quarried from the nearby Marmara Island. Most of the churches have now lost this decoration, but an excellent example survives almost intact at St. Saviour in Chora (Kariye Camii).

The mosaics of the earlier period seem to have consisted chiefly of a gold ground round the edges of which, emphasizing the architectural forms, were wide bands of floral decoration in naturalistic design and colours; at appropriate places there would be a simple cross in outline. Quantities of this simple but effective decoration survive from Justinian's time in the dome and the aisle vaults of Haghia Sophia. It appears that in Haghia Sophia at least there were originally no pictorial mosaics. In the century following Justinian's death, however, picture mosaics became the vogue and an elaborate iconography was worked out which regulated what parts of the Holy Story should be

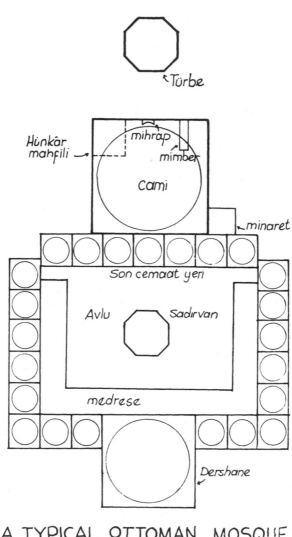

Türbe

Hünkâr mahfili

mihrap

mimber

Cami

minaret

Son cemaat yeri

Avlu

Sadırvan

medrese

Dershane

A TYPICAL OTTOMAN MOSQUE
plan no: 28

represented and where the pictures should be placed in the church building. Then came the iconoclastic age (711 to 843) when all these pictural mosaics were ruthlessly destroyed, so that none survive in Istanbul before the mid-ninth century. From then onward there was a revival of the pictorial art, still in the highly stylized and formal tradition of the earlier period, and all the great churches were again filled with holy pictures. A good idea of the stylistic types in vogue from the ninth to the twelfth centuries can be seen in the examples that have been uncovered in Haghia Sophia.

But in Istanbul the most extensive and splendid mosaics date from the last great flowering of Byzantine culture before the fall. At the beginning of the fourteenth century were executed the long cycles of the life of the Blessed Virgin and of Christ in St. Saviour in Chora, which have been so brilliantly restored in recent years to their pristine splendour by the Byzantine Institute. To this date also belong the glorious frescoes in the side chapel of that church and another series of mosaics, less extensive but hardly less impressive in the side chapel of St. Mary Pammakaristos (Fethiye Camii). The art of these pictures shows a decisive break away from the hieratic formalism of the earlier tradition and breathes the very spirit of the Renaissance as it was beginning to appear at the same date in Italy. In Byzantium it had all too short a life.

GLOSSARY OF TURKISH ARCHITECTURAL TERMS

avlu: courtyard of a mosque

cami: mosque; mescit, from which the European word mosque is derived, means a small mosque

dershane: the lecture hall of a medrese

dar-ül hadis: school for learning sacred tradition

dar-ül kura: school for learning the Kuran

dar-üş şifa: hospital

hamam: Turkish bath

hücre: a cell of a medrese where a student lives

hünkâr mahfili: raised and screened box or loge for the sultan and
his suite

imaret: public kitchen

kervansaray or han: inn or hostel for merchants and travellers

külliye: building complex forming a pious foundation (vakıf) and
often including mosque, türbe, medrese and other buildings

kürsü: preaching chair used on ordinary occasions

kütüphane: library

medrese: a school or college sometimes forming the courtyard of a
mosque

mektep or sibyan mektebi: primary school

mihrab: niche indicating the direction of Mecca (kıble) towards
which all mosques are oriented; from Istanbul this is very
nearly south-east

mimber: tall pulpit to right of mihrab used at the main Friday
prayer

müezzin mahfili: raised platform for chanters

şadırvan: fountain for ritual ablutions

son cemaat yen: porch of a mosque (lit. "place of last assembly")

tabhane: hospice for travelling drevishes

tekke: convent for dervishes

türbe: tomb or mausoleum, often in a mosque garden

Note: the forms *camii, medresesi, türbesi* and similar forms for other
words are used when a noun is modified by a preceding noun; thus
Sultan Ahmet Camii, but Yeni Cami, New Mosque.

The mosques of Istanbul fall into a small number of fairly distinctive types of increasing complexity. The simplest of all, used at all periods for the less costly buildings, is simply an oblong room covered by a tiled pitched roof; often there was an interior wooden dome, but most of these domes have perished in the frequent fires and been replaced by flat ceilings. Second comes the square room covered by a masonry dome resting directly on the walls. This was generally small and simple but could sometimes take on monumental proportions, as at Yavuz Selim Camii, and occasionally, as there, had side rooms used as hostels for travelling dervishes. At a later period in the eighteenth and nineteenth centuries a more elaborate form of this type was adopted for the baroque mosques, usually with a small projecting apse for the mihrab.

The next two types both date from an earlier period and are rare in Istanbul. Third is the two-domed type, essentially a duplication of the second, forming a long room divided by an open arch, each unit being covered by a dome. It is derived from a style common in the Bursa period of Ottoman architecture and hence often known as the "Bursa type" (see the plan of Mahmut Paşa Camii). A modification occurs when the second unit has only a semidome. Mosques of this type always have side chambers. A fourth type, of which only two examples occur in Istanbul, also derives from the earlier Selçuk and Ottoman periods; a rectangular room covered by a multiplicity of domes of equal size supported on pillars; this is often called the great mosque or Ulu Cami type.

The mosques of the classical period – what most people think of as the "typical" Ottoman mosques – are rather more elaborate. They derive from a fusion of a native Turkish tradition with certain elements of the plan of Haghia Sophia. The great imperial mosques have a vast central dome supported on east and west by semidomes of equal diameter. This strongly resembles the plan of Haghia Sophia, but there are significant differences, dictated partly by the native tradition, partly by the requirements of Islamic ritual. In spite of its domes Haghia Sophia is essentially a basilica, clearly divided into a nave and side aisles by a curtain of columns both on ground floor and gallery level. The mosques suppress this division by getting rid of as many of the columns as possible, thus making the interior almost open and visible from all parts. Moreover the galleries, at Haghia Sophia as wide as the aisles, are here reduced to narrow balconies against the side walls. This is the plan of Beyazit Camii and the Süleymaniye. Sometimes this centralization and opening-up is carried even farther by adding two extra semidomes to north and south, as at the Şehzade, Sultan Ahmet and Yeni Cami. A further innovation of the mosques as compared with Haghia Sophia is the provision of a monumental exterior in attractive grey stone with a cascade of descending domes and semidomes balanced by the upward thrust of the two, four or six minarets.

Another type of classical mosque is also derived from a combination of a native with a Byzantine tradition. This consists of a polygon inscribed in a square or rectangular area covered by a dome. Its prototypes are the early Üç Şerefeli Mosque at Edirne and SS. Sergius and Bacchus here; the former has an inscribed hexagon, the latter an octagon. In the classical mosques of this type (both hexagon and octagon being common) there are again no central columns or wide galleries, the dome supports being pushed back as near as possible to the walls, thus giving a wholly centralized effect. Though this was chiefly used by Sinan and other architects for mosques of grand vezirs and high officials, the most magnificent example of this type is the great mosque of Selim II at Edirne, Sinan's masterpiece and the largest and most beautiful of all the classical mosques.

Almost all mosques of whatever type are preceded by a porch of three or five domed bays and generally also by a monumental courtyard with a domed arcade. If there is only one minaret – as in all but imperial mosques – it is practically always on the right-hand side of the entrance.

All imperial mosques and most of the grander ones of vezirs and great lords form the centre of a külliye, or complex of buildings, forming one vakıf, or pious foundation, often endowed with great wealth. The founder generally built his türbe, or mausoleum, in the garden or graveyard behind the mosque; these are simple buildings, square or polygonal, covered by a dome and with a small entrance porch, sometimes beautifully decorated inside with tiles. Of the utilitarian buildings, almost always built round four sides of a central arcaded and domed courtyard, the commonest is the medrese, or college. The students' cells, each with its dome and fireplace, opened off the courtyard with a fountain in the middle, and in the centre of one side is the large domed dershane, or lecture hall. Sometimes the medrese formed three sides of a mosque courtyard, and very occasionally they take unusual shapes like the octagonal one of Rüstem Paşa. These colleges were of different levels, some being mere secondary schools, others of a higher status, and still others for specialized studies such as law, medicine and the hadis, or traditions, of the Prophet.

Primary schools too (sibyan mektebi) were generally included in a külliye, a small building with a single domed classroom often built over a gateway and sometimes including an apartment for the teacher. Tekkes, or convents for dervishes, do not usually differ much in structure from medreses, but the dershane room, which may be in the centre of the courtyard, is used in tekkes for dervish rituals.

The larger imperial foundations included a public kitchen and a hospital. Like medreses these were built round a central courtyard, and the hospitals (dar-üş şifa or timarhane) are almost indistinguishable from them, also having cells for the patients and a large central room like a dershane used as a clinic and examining office. The public kitchens (imaret) instead of cells have vast domed kitchens with very characteristic chimneys, and also large refectories. They provided food for the students and teachers of the medrese, the clergy of the mosque, and the staff and patients of the hospital, as well as for the poor of the neighbourhood. One or two of them still perform the latter service. All these institutions were entirely free of charge and in the great period very efficiently managed.

Fountains are ubiquitous. They are of three kinds: the şadırvan is a large fountain in the middle of a mosque courtyard used for ritual ablutions; the sebil, often at the corner of the outer wall of a mosque precinct, is a monumental domed building with three or more grilled openings in the façade through which cups of water were handed by an attendant to those who asked; the çeşme is also sometimes monumental, often in the middle of a public square, but more frequently it is a simple carved marble slab with a spigot in the centre and a basin below: up until recent years scores of these were still in use to provide much of the population of the city with all the water they received.

Of the secular buildings the most important are the inn or hostel, the Turkish bath and the library. The hostel was usually called han if in a city, kervansaray if on the great trade routes; while tabhane was a hostel originally designed for travelling dervishes. Like so many other buildings it was built round one or more courtyards but was in two or three storeys, the lower one being used for animals and the storage of merchandise (since most travellers were merchants journeying in caravans), the upper ones as guest rooms (see the plan of Valide Hanı). The bath or hamam, a rather elaborate building, is fully described, including a plan, in connection with the Cağaloğlu Hamamı. The library (kütüphane) was often a simple domed room with bookcases in the centre; like the mektep it was sometimes built above the monumental gateway of a mosque enclosure, but it was sometimes independent and more elaborate (see the description of the Atif Efendi library).

Except for Topkapı Sarayı and the unique palace of Ibrahim Paşa, all other palaces until the nineteenth century, however grand, were built almost entirely of wood and have long since perished in the many fires that have ravaged the city. For the seaside mansions (yalı) along the Bosphorus, a few of which still survive, see the description of the Kıbrıslı Yalı.

In Turkish architecture there are no "orders" as these are understood in the West, and how this did infuriate the classically minded travellers in the old days: it was chiefly on this ground that as late as the eighteenth century they kept making such remarks as "the Turks know nothing of architecture," even though they often greatly admired the building they were describing! Nevertheless in the great period there were two recognized types of capital: the stalactite and the lozenge. The stalactite is an elaborate geometrical structure chiefly of triangles and hexagons built up so that it resembles a stalactite formation or a honeycomb. It is directly derived from Selçuk architecture and is used not only for capitals but often for portal canopies, cornices, and even pendentives and squinches. The lozenge capital, apparently introduced by Sinan or anyhow not much used before his time, is a simple structure of juxtaposed lozenges. Neither capital is very satisfactory compared with the Doric, Ionic or Corinthian, because both, especially the lozenge, give a too-smooth, weak transition from the cylinder of the column to the square of the impost. In the baroque period bad imitations of western types of capitals came into vogue, almost always hopelessly weak. And until the baroque period all Turkish arches had been not round like Roman ones but pointed like the Gothic, and sometimes of the ogive or "broken" type that is often so effectively used by Sinan. It should also be noted that the Turkish dome resembles the hemispherical Roman, Byzantine and Syrian type, not the more common western ovoid type invented by Brunelleschi, which is structurally double: even when Turkish domes are double, as in some türbes, each dome is structurally independent of the other.

Of decoration applied to architecture, far and away the most brilliant and striking is the Turkish tiles. It was not until fairly recent years that the full importance and uniqueness of the Turkish wares were recognized: they used often to be called Rhodian ware or else lumped together with Persian pottery. Even though the potters were sometimes Persian – as well as Greek, Armenian and Turkish – the tiles were altogether different from Persian ware. They were manufactured chiefly at Iznik but also sometimes at Kütahya and Istanbul. In Istanbul chiefly three periods of Turkish ceramics are represented. In the early period from the Conquest to the mid-sixteenth century we find extremely plain tiles without design, deep blue or a lighter green or turquoise, usually hexagonal and sometimes overlaid with an unfired pattern in gold. More interesting are the tiles in the *cuerda seca* technique: instead of a painted design covered by a transparent glaze, in these tiles the glazes themselves were coloured and the colours were prevented from running into each other by a hair-like dividing line of permanganate of potash outlining the design (hence the name *cuerda seca*, dry cord); if visible at all this line is deepest purple or black. The predominating colours of these tiles are apple-green and bright yellow with subordinate blues and mauves. They are very beautiful and very rare in Istanbul: see the description of the Şehzade's türbe and of the porch of Çinili Köşk where the most extensive examples occur.

About 1550 this lovely technique gave place to the no less beautiful and more famous Iznik style, where the design is painted on the clay and covered with an absolutely transparent glaze. Here the predominant colours are on the purest, most unblemished white ground, deep blue, light blue, shades of green, and above all the matchless tomato red. This was made with a clay known as Armenian bole, found near Erzurum in eastern Anatolia. It has to be laid on very thick so that it protrudes from the surface of the tile like sealing-wax. The technique of using it successfully is extremety tricky and was only completely mastered towards 1570 and lost again about 1620, so that the absolutely perfect tiles of this type are confined to this half century. In tiles before and after this date the bole tends to be a bit muddy and brownish and lacking in clear outline. But at their best the Turkish tiles between about 1550 and 1650 are quite incomparable, and unique.

After this the tiles, like most other things in the Empire, began to decline. A short revival was made about 1720 when the last of the Iznik potters were settled at Tekfur Saray in Istanbul, but this hardly outlasted the first generation. Thereafter inferior European tiles or even more inferior imitations of them became the vogue. There has been a considerable and praiseworthy revival of the old style in our own day, so that really good modern tiles (now made at Kütahya and Iznik) are sometimes hard to distinguish, at first glance, from the great ones.

SİNAN'S EXTANT WORKS IN ISTANBUL

The following is, as far as we are aware, the first chronological list of Sinan's surviving buildings to be attempted. It is intended to be complete as far as buildings in Istanbul are concerned; but buildings not in the *Tezkeret-ül Ebniye* are excluded unless they form parts of külliyes or other buildings which are in the *Tezkere*, or unless there is other unimpeachable documentary evidence for them; also excluded are a certain number of buildings originally constructed by Sinan, but so completely reconstructed at a later date as to contain little or nothing of his work: such, for example, are Kasım Paşa Camii and Cihangir Camii, and a few others. The list may have minor omissions or inaccuracies, almost inevitable in a pioneer attempt, but we believe it includes all Sinan's surviving buildings of any importance in the city.

The great majority of Sinan's works can be dated accurately by historical inscriptions on the buildings themselves; others may be dated by documents in the Divan archives or by their vakfiyes (charters of foundation). A few dates in the list are conjectural, based either on descriptions by foreign travellers or on the *floruit*, or else the date of death of the founders. In a very few cases we have not been able to suggest a date. For the *Tezkeret-ül Ebniye*, the list of Sinan's works drawn up by his friend Mustafa Sa'i, we have used the text as given in Ahmet Refik's *Mimar Sinan* (Istanbul 1931); the text given in Rıfkı Melül Meriç's *Mimar Sinan Hayatı, Eseri* (Ankara 1965) is a mere conflation of various undated and unidentified manuscripts and is exceedingly misleading. For the relevant Divan archives see Ahmet Refik's *Türk Mimarları* (Istanbul 1936); and for various vakfiyes and other documents see Ibrahim Hakkı Konyalı's *Mimar Koca Sinan* (Istanbul 1948) and the same author's *Koca Mimar Sinan'ın Eserleri* (Istanbul 1950).

HASEKI HÜRREM
  On the Seventh Hill: *Cami, medrese, şifahane, imaret, mektep*; Insc. 945 (1538–9)
DRAĞMAN YUNUS BEY
  Near Fethiye Camii: *Cami, mektep;* Insc. 948 (1541–2)
HAYRETTIN BARBAROS
  Türbe at Beşiktaş; Insc. 948 (1541–2)
  Hamam near Zeyrek Camii; before 1546 when he died
ŞEHZADE MEHMET
  At Şehzadebaşı: *Cami, medrese, türbe, imaret, mektep, tabhane;* Insc. 950–5 (1543–8)
HÜSREV PAŞA
  Türbe at Yeni Bahçe; Insc. 952 (1545–6)
MIHRIMAH SULTAN

At Üsküdar: *Cami, medrese, mektep*; Insc. Zilhicce 954 (Jan.–Feb. 1548)

RÜSTEM PAŞA

Han at Galata; about 1550 (see Gyllius *De Topographic Constantinopoleos,* lib. IV, cap. 11)

Medrese near Mahmut Paşa; Insc. 957 (1550–1)

SÜLEYMANIYE

On Third Hill: *Cami, seven medreses, imaret, şifahane, dar-ül kura, hamam, türbe of Süleyman, türbe of Hürrem, kervansaray, mektep*; Insc. 957–64 (1550–7)

IBRAHIM PAŞA

At Silivri Kapı: *Cami, türbe*; Insc. 958 (1551)

SÜLEYMAN I

Six aqueducts in the Belgrad Forest; 1554–64 (Divan archives)

KARA AHMET PAŞA

At Topkapı: *Cami, medrese, türbe, mektep*; Vakfiye dated 2 Ramazan 962 (21 July 1555)

SINAN PAŞA

At Beşiktaş: *Cami, medrese*; Insc. 962 (1554–5)

HASEKI HÜRREM

Hamam at Haghia Sophia; Insc. 964 (1556–7)

CAFER AĞA

Medrese at Haghia Sophia; Insc. 967 (1559–60)

HACI MEHMET PAŞA

Türbe at Üsküdar; Insc. 967 (1559–60)

ISKENDER PAŞA

Cami at Kanlıca; Insc. 967 (1559–60)

IBRAHIM PAŞA

Medrese at Isa Kapı (a ruin); 1560, see Öz, *Istanbul Camileri,* I, 100

RÜSTEM PAŞA

Türbe at Şehzade Camii; Insc. 968 (1560–1)

Cami at Uzun Çarşı; 969 (1561–2), see Vakfiye

MOLLA ÇELEBI

Cami at Fındıklı; Insc. 969 (1561–2); inscription on hamam now destroyed

FERRUH KETHÜDA
Cami at Balat; Insc. 970 (1562–3)
SELIM I
Medrese at Yeni Bahçe; erected in memory of Selim by Süleyman; 970 (1562–3); inscription on minaret
HÜRREM ÇAVUŞ
Cami at Yeni Bahçe; 970 (1562–3); inscription in *Hadika* now lost
MIHRIMAH SULTAN
At Edirne Kapı; *Cami, medrese, mektep, hamam*; (970–3); Evkaf documents: see Konyalı, *Eserler*, 161–5
YAHYA EFENDI
At Beşiktaş: *Türbe, medrese*; about 1570 when he died
SOKOLLU MEHMET PAŞA
At Kadirga Limanı: *Cami, medrese*; Insc. 979 (1571–2)
At Eyüp: *Türbe, medrese, dar-ül kura*; about 1572
PERTEV PAŞA
Türbe at Eyüp; Insc. 980 (1572–3)
ŞAH HUBAN
At Yeni Bahçe: *Türbe, mektep*; about 980 (1572) when she died
MIMAR SİNAN
Mescit at Yeni Bahçe; 981 (1573–4), see Öz, *Istanbul Camileri*, I, 105
HAGHIA SOPHIA
Two *minarets* and other repairs; 981 (1573), Divan archives
TOPKAPI SARAYI
Kitchens, reconstructions and additions; 982 (1574), Divan archives
SELIM II
Türbe at Haghia Sophia; Insc. 982–5 (1574–7)
ZAL MAHMUT PAŞA
At Eyüp: *Cami*, two *medreses, türbe*; probably about 1575, Zal's *floruit*
SOKOLLU MEHMET PAŞA
Cami at Azap Kapı; Insc. 985 (1577–8)
TOPKAPI SARAYI
Salon of Murat III; 986 (1578), dated tile in room

SEMIZ ALI PAŞA
Türbe in garden of Mihrimah Camii, Edirne Kapı; 988 (1580), date of his death

KILIÇ ALI PAŞA
At Tophane: *Cami, türbe, medrese, hamam*; Insc. 988 (1580–1)

MURAT III
Row of *shops* below Beyazit Camii; 988 (1580), Divan archives

ŞEMSI AHMET PAŞA
At Üsküdar: *Cami, medrese, türbe*; Insc. 991 (1583–4)

ATIK VALIDE (NURBANU)
At Üsküdar: *Cami, medrese, imaret, kervansaray, şifahane, tekke, dar-ül kura, dar-ül hadis, hamam*; Insc. 991 (1583–4)

RAMAZAN EFENDI
Cami at Koca Mustafa Paşa; Insc. 994 (1585–6)

MIMAR SINAN
Türbe and *sebil* at the Süleymaniye; Insc. 996 (1587–8), though probably built earlier

For the following buildings which appear in the *Tezkere* we have not been able to find definite dates: Ahi Çelebi Camii and Bali Paşa Camii (repairs or construction only: probably very early work before he became Chief Architect, since after 1538 he would hardly have undertaken repairs to relatively unimportant buildings); Hüsrev Kethüda Hamamı; Kapı Ağası Hamamı (a ruin with no indication of date); Nişancı Mehmet Bey Medresesi (a complete ruin); Semiz Ali Paşa Medresesi (perhaps between 1561 and 1565 when Ali was Grand Vezir); Siyavuş Paşa Türbesi (built for some children who predeceased him; he was buried there himself when he died in 1601); Şehzadeler Türbesi (a problematical building perhaps not by Sinan though it appears in the *Tezkere*).

In the above list there are about 120 buildings mentioned, practically all of which can safely be attributed to Sinan in whole or in part. Of these 24 are mosques, 27 medreses, 20 türbes, eight hamams, four imarets and three hospitals. This is a phenomenal amount of work for one man to have accomplished even in a career of more than 50 years, and even with the help of an *atellier* including many skilled architects. And one must add to it a large number of buildings which have perished entirely or been totally reconstructed, not to mention many others in various parts of the Ottoman domains, some of them of great grandeur and importance.

Indexes